M000249816

Why Don't You Just Talk to Him?

WHY DON'T YOU JUST TALK TO HIM?

The Politics of Domestic Abuse

Kathleen R. Arnold

Oxford University Press is a department of the University of Oxford. It furthers
the University's objective of excellence in research, scholarship, and education by
publishing worldwide. Oxford is a registered trade mark of Oxford University Press
in the UK and in certain other countries

Published in the United States of America by Oxford University Press
198 Madison Avenue, New York, NY 10016, United States of America

© Oxford University Press 2015

All rights reserved. No part of this publication may be reproduced, stored in a re-
trieval system, or transmitted, in any form or by any means, without the prior
permission in writing of Oxford University Press, or as expressly permitted by law,
by license, or under terms agreed with the appropriate reproduction rights organization. Inquiries concerning reproduction outside the scope of the above should be
sent to the Rights Department, Oxford University Press, at the address above.

You must not circulate this work in any other form
and you must impose this same condition on any acquirer

Library of Congress Cataloging-in-Publication Data
Arnold, Kathleen R., 1966–
 Why don't you just talk to him? : the politics of domestic abuse / Kathleen R.
Arnold.
    p.   cm.
Includes bibliographical references and index.
ISBN 978–0–19–026228–0 (hardcover : alk. paper) 1. Family violence.
2. Marital violence. 3. Victims of family violence. I. Title.
HV6626.A76 2015
362.82'92—dc23
                2015007972

9 8 7 6 5 4 3 2 1

Printed in the United States of America on acid-free paper

To Hannah with all of my love and
in memory of Arthur Devaun Martin

CONTENTS

Why Don't You Just Talk to Him?

Introduction: Why Don't You Just Talk to Him? The Politics of Domestic Abuse

In this book, I want to address the broad relationship of Enlightenment, capitalist, and liberal notions of contract, rationality, mutuality, and egalitarianism to violence. While these broad rubrics have often been synthesized in political norms of citizenship as being peaceful, rationally arrived at, and mutual (for example), I would like to highlight their inextricable relationship to violence. That is, violence is not merely something that creeps in and corrupts this otherwise civilized liberal-democratic tradition but rather something that constitutively informs it: violence is a regular feature of the American politico-economic tradition. A concrete instantiation of this relationship is the issue of domestic violence, which I believe deserves treatment as an issue of mainstream political theory. The issue itself illuminates a number of contradictions in this tradition that ensure that targets[1] of intimate partner violence are positioned as less-than-citizens, and this relegation to (at best) second-class citizenship is something that bears on the status of all Americans.

I was inspired to write this book based on a combination of theoretical interests and personal experience. The first reason is tied to my philosophical interest in the work of Friedrich Nietzsche and Michel Foucault, who have explored how modern power purports to be more humane, noncoercive, and egalitarian than previous Western political arrangements or so-called primitive societies, at the same time that it masks its own violence and hierarchy.[2] And perhaps counterintuitively, while many analyses draw on empirical facts and political issues to challenge overly abstract or idealized theory, I hold that with regard to this particular issue, a broader political theoretical approach will actually constructively challenge significant presuppositions of dominant policy (notably symmetry arguments, discussed later) today, including the mainstream focus on the target of violence. What is particularly interesting is how violence itself (coupled with abuse) is manifest in US society in ways that have been assimilated or denied. I propose that a "realist" approach to political power, broadly drawing on Nietzsche's and Foucault's analyses of power will best link what appears to be private to the political, showing a continuum of violence that doesn't merely link the two spheres but explodes any absolute distinction between the two. A second reason for writing this book is tied to an interest in the practical implications of this denial of violence. I wanted to understand how and why domestic violence is not prevented, and why it is often the targets of abuse who are "punished." The three components of this puzzle are (1) understanding the abuser as an anti-Enlightenment figure who is rational according to most standards, often rewarded by society, and yet increasingly abusive over time; (2) analyzing why policy and grassroots "help" for domestic abuse often ignores the abuser and pathologizes and punishes women; and (3) considering why, nevertheless, conventional discourse often holds that women and mothers experience preferential treatment by these institutions.

Related to this, the same sources suggest that there is some sort of cognizable, unified "system" that helps domestic abuse targets once they—as individuals—get the courage to get help or leave. It has only been after years of personal experience, research, and nonprofit participation in this field that I have realized that there is very little societal or political recognition of these contradictions. Very few mainstream institutions or conventional texts offer a broad political view of abuse, and ironically the most knowledgeable interlocutors—grassroots advocates who use political, legal, and therapeutic models to work with the abused (rather than individual, psychological, and apolitical methods)—work for institutions that are underfunded and by necessity invisible.[3] While they may not conceive of themselves as following the work of Michel Foucault, their approach is squarely Foucaultian in their acknowledgment of power as a relationship, their recognition of inequality in abuse situations, and their orientation toward strategies of resistance rather than pathologization of the victim. Indeed, the word *victim*—to the degree that it would connote purity, helplessness, and an absolute asymmetry—must be replaced by the term *target*. This shift in terminology would necessarily bring the focus back to the abuser and would avoid the overfocus on those who have been abused. Although domestic violence advocates and court advocates often understand abuse better than family lawyers and psychologists, they do not get the social recognition they deserve, and they can even be sued for "practicing law."[4] These advocates and the nearly invisible organizations they work for demonstrate that the power dynamics I discuss are not absolute and that resistance is possible. But it can take years to find this sort of help, and the institutions can help women for only a short period of time, given their budget constraints.

Furthermore, despite the economic losses of partner separation and divorce, not to mention economic abuse (which can affect even the wealthiest women), many of these advocacy-oriented groups can only help individuals who are officially under the poverty line. Nevertheless, they make a difference in challenging conventional paradigms and offering a different model of advocacy that allows the abused to be recognized as agents *during* the process of seeking help and not simply when there has been a clear "success."[5] Their approach is often a mix of legal and more therapeutic remedies focused on a target's strengths (and not her weaknesses or pathologies) and situating her abuse in a broader context of women's subordination, intersecting with class bias, ethnic prejudices, and racist challenges. These institutions and advocates contest the status quo, which includes a range of discourses and institutions that overly focus on the target of abuse as the responsible party, deploying punitive mechanisms that could make any abused individual regret trying to get help. A key difference between advocates and counselors working for these nonprofits and psychologists, family lawyers, and anger management and co-parenting leaders is that the former group often uses a broad-based, contemporary feminist-intersectional approach grounded in undergraduate coursework or their own experience as a target of abuse, in contradistinction to the more dyadic, clinical, and distancing approach of the apparently better trained latter group. To use the language of domestic abuse researchers, the former group recognizes numerous forms of asymmetry (i.e., that abuse is largely unequal) while mainstream approaches often assume symmetry.[6] The latter group often draws on conventional approaches in psychology, therapeutic groups, and family law that often reinforce a depoliticized view of abuse, offering "solutions" that can be damaging to targets while attempting to keep the family unit intact. This may not mean forcing a couple to stay together but rather focusing on mutual provocation and symmetrical injuries and losses, and relying on solutions that force couples to communicate and negotiate. At base, these solutions often compartmentalize abuse, conceptually isolating it, and in effect they hold that the abuser was only provoked to abuse one person—his actions do not affect children, nor do they reflect broader societal and economic systems of inequality and tolerance of violence. In this way, the very premises of conventional notions of domestic abuse ensure a "disaggregated" system of power, turning solutions back on the family unit.[7]

Like the fragmented domestic abuse "system," quite a lot of the literature on abuse focuses on specific aspects of intimate partner abuse, examining one part of the issue. While this micro-level approach can be valuable in exploring clinical, legal, and medical issues, among other things, understanding domestic abuse in a broader context is also necessary. In fact, to the degree that some dominant approaches have accepted the statistics on abuse or accepted dominant policy concepts and paradigms, policy and academic work can merely replicate societal misunderstandings of a more complex issue. More recent interventions have sought to work out the political context and meaning of domestic abuse and the relative inadequacy of shelter, medical, and therapeutic responses.[8] Outside of political science and theory, although there are a far greater number of books on domestic abuse, most of them are clinical, legal, empirical, or oriented to self-help, and thus the subject could be reinvigorated through an exploration of its political theoretical dimensions.[9] In his 2009 text *Coercive Control*, domestic abuse expert Evan Stark remarked that much of the literature on this subject "has been atheoretical to the extreme, beholden to outdated conceptual models"[10] and

> by all accounts, there appears to be little difference between how researchers and helping professionals are approaching coercive control and how they approached domestic violence—documenting individual acts without identifying their political context or consequence, once again depicting the bars without grasping that they are part of a cage or that the resulting harms infect the very core of what makes us a free people.[11]

These statements must be modified given some very interesting texts that do seek to understand this issue more broadly and politically, including lengthy and very thoughtful responses to his work.[12] Nevertheless, these texts are still in the minority and I suspect that this is because they do not support dominant policy and shelter approaches to domestic violence.[13]

A particular difficulty Stark identifies, which is pursued in this book, is the violence-centered definition of domestic abuse that leads to ineffective policies, inadequate shelters, and impunity for abusers. In brief, focusing on isolated incidents of violence not only reduces a more complex understanding of domestic abuse; this focus has also allowed for gender symmetry arguments.[14] Symmetry arguments are based on the idea that men and women are equally violent, and, even if there is unequal violence on the man's part, the woman must have provoked him. In isolation, symmetry arguments can make sense. For example, Linda Mills uses this as a basis for her research and counseling, assuming that abusive couples and families interact violently and coercively but could replace these behaviors with better modes of communication.[15] Considered on its own, this sort of approach[16] is logical and perhaps helps some couples and families experiencing violence. Symmetry assumes a few things: first, that men and women are equally injurious and that women are capable of the sorts of physical and emotional assaults that men are[17]—this is despite years of policies and jurisprudence that have assumed that women are physically smaller and weaker than men, justifying their exclusion from a range of jobs and positions throughout history.[18] Second, the use of restorative justice (Mills's approach) in the case of asymmetrical abuse would paradoxically assume a context of relative political and economic equality in which the manipulation and assaults of one party have the same effect as the coercion and violence of the other party.[19] Third, a restorative justice model is an Enlightenment one that interprets interpersonal violence as something that can be replaced by communication, with the proper education, forgiveness, and counseling. The assumption is also developmental, leading couples from primitive to more civilized behavior, and thus denying that violence and aggression can coexist with rationality, communication, and apparently contractual or consensual relations. Fourth, and most problematic, this sort of model with its attendant issues can often displace other forms of domestic abuse in research, policy, and "extralegal" responses to abuse. The combination of symmetry claims and Mills's restorative justice methods should be one possibility among many others, when analyzing intimate partner abuse. They are more pernicious if and when they are used to discount the possibility of asymmetry and hence would indicate a will-to-truth in their singular pursuit of a neat answer that effectively turns inequality back on abuse targets.

Symmetry arguments have also been based on empirical data that may be problematic. First, they rely on self-reporting in a sphere that is widely acknowledged to be marked by underreporting and unsuccessful attempts at getting help.[20] Second, like counting other "invisible groups" such as the homeless on the street or undocumented immigrants, current empirical accounts could be focusing on a narrow segment of the population—those in shelters, participants in clinical studies, and individuals in batterer intervention programs—and then making wide-ranging, more speculative claims based on this subset of the population.[21] Even broader studies going beyond these institutions would be suspicious given current discourses that portray a myriad of relations as being mutual, egalitarian, and a product of choice.[22] Third, many studies that claim symmetry simply count the number of violent incidents, including accounting for women pushing or hitting back, which then allows for an unequal situation to appear equal.[23] Symmetry arguments justify simple, individualized solutions that focus on education and counseling and, again, deny the radical inequality of domestic abuse. This paradigm is supported by recent trends in family law and counseling for families in which violence occurs. In both spheres, the family is dealt with as a unit, leaving intact familial hierarchies and working outside of individual rights provided for by the Constitution.[24] While I do not want to discount symmetry entirely, I would like to point out as problematic the degree to which these models have dominated policy and end up turning a lot of abuse back on the target.

In contrast, the type of domestic abuse I examine in this text is asymmetrical, what Michael Johnson has called "intimate terrorism" and Evan Stark has conceived of as "coercive control."[25] Again, I do not want to claim that this is the only type of intimate violence. As stated above, many researchers have concluded that women are equally violent in intimate relationships.[26] Instead, I question the ubiquity of symmetry, suggesting that asymmetry may be far more prevalent if broader structures of subordination are taken into account. Exploring this radical inequality, I analyze how Enlightenment understandings of intimacy are often imposed on these unequal situations, effectively obfuscating domination and aiding the abuser. These trends have only become more profound, Kristin Bumiller argues, as they have become bound up with neoliberal approaches to abuse and thus reinforce a depoliticized, individually oriented analysis of abuse, self-help (rather than recognizing societal violence), and depoliticized, egalitarian solutions (e.g., couples therapy, mediation, and dual arrests). In brief, it is far simpler to blame the victim than to prevent abuse or to solve it more broadly.

Informed by personal experience, volunteer work, and related research, my knowledge of this particular subject leads to a distinct vantage point. On the one hand, rather than the privileged perspective of a shelter volunteer or researcher, my approach is from the bottom up, maintaining a focus on the perspective of the abused. On the other hand, I am not seeking to transcend the conventional literature so much as to link together what appears to be a fairly diffuse set of texts and policies—from clinical to legal—in order to provide a different perspective. Taken separately, various research and policy prescriptions are indicative of the state as a site of contestation (i.e., the fact that the state is not unified but made up of institutions and agents that are in conflict). Taken together, a more punitive set of mechanisms becomes apparent, unfairly punishing targets of abuse while ignoring abusers. In this context, it becomes clear why targets do not have formal mechanisms to speak for themselves and how their informal resistance (or micro-resistance) is often ignored or misunderstood.[27] Although I cannot cover every possible facet of this subject, I will discuss a few of the most significant reasons this particular area is inadequately researched as a political problem and how this inadequacy is generated and reinforced by similar assumptions at the policy, enforcement, and shelter levels, not to mention in media coverage.

The first and most important issue is believing that targets of abuse are somehow irrational or incapacitated in their choices. In this view, they blindly get involved with an abuser; stay with abusers, despite the fact that they are absolutely free to leave; and then they eventually get help from a consistent and open network of legal and extra-legal agents (in Foucault's words: agents who work in public institutions but whose jobs are not directly political, such as psychologists, social workers, ministers, nonprofit organization advocates, and so on). This linear story assumes that certain women fall into these sorts of relationships for individual reasons, unrelated to societal pressures, traditional gender roles, and societal acceptance of the link between sex and violence.[28] The linear narrative I have just described is linked to other problematic assumptions:

(1) The target is not responding to real threats or controlling power dynamics; even being a victim of violent assault indicates a "choice" to stay in the relationship; she has somehow been duped by the abuser.
(2) When the target finally gets help, the help is there. The assumption is that there is a clear protocol followed by shelters, the police, and policymakers (not to mention doctors, counselors, school personnel, and therapists) and that help is clear and consistent.[29] Related to these preconceptions is the idea that if particular agents—such as police officers, therapists, or judges—have received special training in this area that they will do their job and treat the target fairly.
(3) Abuse is violence-centered and spectacular—otherwise it doesn't exist. The target can only prove abuse through visible marks that can be easily documented.[30]
(4) Policy, courts, and shelters "prefer" women and are "biased" in favor of mothers; abusers will be punished when they are finally caught.

In this book I challenge these ideas and demonstrate how misleading and damaging they are. Most important, if the narrative doesn't work this way and it turns out that most abusers act with impunity and that, in fact, it is targets who are often "punished," the actions and threats of the abuser are actually real. Borrowing a term from gender-based asylum cases, "state inaction" plays a crucial role in perpetuating intimate abuse on American soil. State inaction, combined with a backlash against single mothers and targets of abuse more generally, would ensure that targets of abuse not get consistent help from extra-legal or legal agents or groups (informal or formal political institutions). In turn, the entrapping power mechanisms that an abuser has set cannot be escaped as easily as many assume.

Numerous studies have also confirmed that women try to escape their circumstances several times and seek help quite often, but the same authors only conceive of them as "agents" when they finally do flee. Paradoxically, this asks the woman to risk everything—her home, source of income, her children, and even her life—before she is recognized by researchers or policymakers as worthy of political recognition.[31] As I note in exploring two important asylum cases, this is an incredible sacrifice demanded of a target, and the lack of social recognition of what she has lost leads to "incomplete mourning" or a traumatic reintegration into society. But the second difficulty, again, is in believing that targets of abuse will be helped and not ignored or even punished for their efforts. What I want to emphasize is that because the narrative above is a wish and not reflective of reality in any way, those who experience abuse are often judged and criticized. Their experiences, choices, and attempts to get help are often ignored. While the power dynamics I describe and analyze in this book are not absolute and there is room for micro-resistance, mass resistance, and policy change, those who set debates, make shelter rules, and propose policy need to understand targets of abuse as actors with valid fears, who are subjected to a range of power tactics that cannot simply be solved through a shelter stay or one-time aid. Indeed, the "system," granted that it's fragmented and a site of contestation, often makes things worse. For these reasons, despite popular claims of gender bias for women and mothers in courts,[32] the issue of domestic abuse shows the opposite: a clear bias against targets of abuse and either indifference to or the rewarding of the abuser.[33]

In turn, violence-centered approaches to domestic abuse ignore the broader context of abuse itself as well as societal supports for committing abuse with impunity. Abuse situations often involve systematic emotional degradation, social isolation, economic control, and attempts to alienate children's and relatives' affection—violence is only one small part of an abuser's tactics. The remedy for each issue is often distinct from others if indeed there are remedies.[34] Thus, responding to each facet of abusive behavior can turn into a full-time job. Additionally, family lawyers, counselors, and the police usually are not broadly trained in this area, if they are trained to recognize domestic abuse or treat it as a legitimate problem at all.[35] Their narrow focus often leads them to misunderstand the situation, often in the direst of circumstances.[36] Furthermore, even in the case of clear violations and abuse, a target cannot possibly prosecute every violation against her—it is far too costly and time-consuming.[37] But abusers are also often very successful because the state refuses to prevent abuse or to help targets. What is more surprising, however, is in its pursuit of gender "neutrality" the state will often punish the target of abuse rather than the abuser. While an abuser can largely act with impunity, even in cases of violent assault, women are punished in the following ways: they can be diagnosed with mental illness for having been abused and this diagnosis in turn can be used to argue that they are incompetent (legally or as guardians of their children)[38]; they can be arrested if they seek help for an assault if a police department has implemented "dual arrest policies"; they can be geographically restricted by the abuser such that they are trapped in a county or state for years, which can harm them socially and economically, not to mention facilitating abuse, harassment, and stalking; and they can lose custody of their children if children witnessed abuse (this is called "failure to protect").[39] Rather than being helped, targets of abuse are often treated as if they are hysterical and unfortunately, because there is little effective help out there, abusers often do better when psychological tests and lie detector tests are administered.[40]

Some examples from my social circle include a friend who was regularly grabbed and choked by her husband and thrown down the stairs by him when she was pregnant. Despite her privilege, she had no marks to prove this abuse and no witnesses, and there are no clear processes by which to get help anyway. She succeeded in divorcing him but continues to be forced to deal with him through joint custody. Another friend was awakened in the middle of the night by her husband and when she reached out to get him to stop shaking her, he became infuriated. She ran into a closet to call 9-1-1 and when the police came, her husband claimed she assaulted him and she was arrested. She never told her family or friends because she felt so ashamed. As he continued these tactics, she managed to move away and divorce him but continues to share custody of their children. Yet another friend was regularly abused by a boyfriend and when she finally got the courage to call 9-1-1, she was crying and the boyfriend was not. He asserted that she had attacked him and she was arrested. While she got away from this particular boyfriend, she became involved with a charming sales representative who eventually got to know her story and police "record." After a year, he began using this story as a threat against her while beginning increasingly violent assaults against her. Like many other abusers, he cycled through "love," withdrawal, and then assault, proposing to her and eventually impregnating her. Although we have lost touch, at the time of our last conversation, he was regularly punching her in the face at the numerous public events they attended (in the car, to chastise her) but he constantly warned her that he could have her arrested again if she told anyone. A student of mine who was from a military family told me a similar story about her family. Her stepfather regularly beat her mother; one time her mother was beaten to the point of not being recognizable. However, because the mother was hysterical, when the military police showed up, they threatened to arrest the mother unless she stopped crying. Another student in my feminist theory class had been given a black eye by her ex-boyfriend. As she waited outside my class, two men walked by her, and one looked at her and laughed. He said to his friend, "That's what they get when they don't shut up."

In all of these cases, the abuser's control and violence were ignored, while the target became an object of abandonment, denigration, or punishment. While many of my friends left when they could, I understand why others seek help more cautiously. While none of them was a victim in the sense of being passive or duped, they all knew better than any shelter volunteer or researcher that the help is not only not out there (not consistently and not to the degree that they really need), but that they could be arrested if they seek it. While there are cities where the police are trained to recognize domestic violence (Portland, Oregon, is a notable example), this is not the norm and it presumes that training can wipe away years of misguided assumptions about domestic abuse, not to mention some police officers' own use or acceptance of violence and control in their personal lives. Training and screening are certainly better than nothing, but overall there is no unified system, and the available resources are inadequate at best and punitive at worst.

For all these reasons, abuse doesn't work like the narrative above; its all-encompassing features range from economic marginalization, alienation of affection (e.g., of children and relatives), social isolation, verbal abuse, and low-level physical assaults, to harassment while one is working and other attempts to disrupt a target or her children's well-being. All of these features are ignored politically and legally.[41] What this conceptual blindness does is to reinforce the assumptions above. I want to emphasize that many of an abuser's tactics are real, and the target's fears are often valid. Indeed, because the abuser actually often acts with impunity and quite a lot of the solutions dealing with this issue entrap women, the target's fears of the abuser are grounded in reality, even if his emotional abuse has affected her self-esteem. In this regard, it is important to note that emotional control and denigration can happen in a number of different settings that are often marked by hierarchy—this does not mean that the target of abuse (e.g., an employee who is treated badly) does not have legitimate fears. If a more expanded definition of abuse is allowed, which then links gender abuse to broader dynamics of social subordination, it cannot be claimed that women are duped even if their perceptions are overly tied to those of the abuser. If state inaction and blaming the victim are actually the norms guiding this fragmented and ineffective system, the fact that women have a hard time leaving is not a result of individual and yet mass delusion. As I argue throughout this book, domestic abuse should be viewed as a political issue rather than a personal issue with political consequences. All of these points suggest how profoundly things need to change.

Part of this project is not only to illuminate specific features of institutions dealing with domestic violence but violence in American political values (particularly notions of intimacy) and norms that are conventionally held to be peaceful, rational, and mutual. In this discussion, I not only critique the limits of liberal, individualized, legally oriented "rights" but also alternatives based on sympathy, caring, or charity. I examine how calls for pity and emotion to induce action cooperate with the worst aspects of the Enlightenment to assimilate and preserve violence. If calls for pity or sympathy are linked to "family values" or maternal feminism, these theories could preserve the family unit at the expense of individual needs or rights.[42] Calls for sympathy, combined with policies and practices that celebrate the family unit, do not merely ignore the plight of women in this situation but (if their theories are put into practice) arguably make their situation worse. Rather than ameliorating the most undemocratic aspects of Enlightenment or rationalized power structures, these varying trends together are inextricably bound to the very norms they purport to correct, and they actually function with today's domestic abuse regime, cooperating with violence by *requiring* violent acts to occur in order to acknowledge abuse rather than focusing on preventing it in the first place.[43]

The broader political difficulty in this discussion is one that has already been identified by theorists like Carole Pateman: the family has been construed as both private (i.e., apolitical) and yet a necessary precondition for the liberal, autonomous citizen to operate in the public sphere and hence, the family has an ambivalent political status.[44] While authors like Hobbes and Locke recognized that the unequal treatment of men and women in the State of Nature and the home led to artificial and unjust inequalities,[45] early feminists like Mary Wollstonecraft and later John Stuart Mill argued that the public-private divide was artificial and if tyranny could happen in the home, supported by public law, democracy had not been fully achieved. In fact, the law allowed for the legal suspension of women's rights.[46] Today these conflicts remain unresolved and overlap with other unresolved issues such as racism and class bias. Yet when domestic abuse occurs, people seem satisfied that there is enough awareness about domestic abuse and institutions to help these women that it is really up to the women to get the help they need.[47] It is a matter of the woman finding the courage to confess what is happening so that people will finally aid her. These sorts of attitudes must be challenged; they are pernicious and particularly dangerous for targets of abuse, who may spend inordinate amounts of time and money seeking remedies that further entrap them in the legal system without ever stopping the cycle. Instead, notions of political agency must go beyond a narrowly legal framework and a rights-based notion of citizenship. To do this, we must not assume that there is an easy and clear break between "public" and "private." In fact, like employment policy, policies that pertain to the private sphere reach far into personal life, despite claims to the contrary. Some obvious examples are the state's approval (or lack thereof) of same-sex civil unions; policy regarding contraception and abortion; and in-depth policies on family arrangements in the case of divorce, separation, child custody, and welfare.

This ambivalence about what constitutes the political is evident in the Enlightenment notions that continue to guide mainstream ideas about intimacy.[48] Even given challenges to the nuclear family, Enlightenment notions still structure conventional views of intimate partnerships, conceiving of intimacy (in whatever form) and roles such as parenthood as being mutual, equal, and contractual. It's important to note that communication serves as both the vehicle and as evidence of mutuality, consent, and equality. Intimate violence, which is purportedly eschewed by rationalization and Enlightenment ideals in general, is conceived of in the same ways: if there is interpersonal violence on one side, the other party must have incited it; if a woman ever hits back, she is not defending herself but rather showing that she is also violent, and hence abuse has its basis in provocation (and therefore, she cannot complain, much less report incidents of violence[49]); and, like issues of rape, if there was consent in entering the relationship, violence after consent (e.g., consent to go on a date, to move in together, or to get married) is permissible. In this way, there is an unacknowledged puzzle or contradiction: while violence is often held to be the opposite of equality, consent, and communicative relations, *intimate* violence is often conceived of in Enlightenment terms despite the inherent paradox. Rather than recognizing this problem, egalitarian language suggests that targets are somehow responsible for what occurs. Notions of a clear and predictable "cycle" of violence bolster these assumptions, suggesting that abuse is systematic, structured, and logical. Instead I contend that it is important to explore how domestic abuse[50] is more like terrorism: it is intermittent and varied, and violence strikes at unexpected moments— not during predictable interactions—and therefore, provocation is not a factor.[51] The situation is not equal and targets should not be made to be responsible for their abusers' actions.

In the past, targets were often urged to leave their abusers, as I discuss in Chapter 2. Nevertheless, even as targets are sometimes still encouraged to leave, today there is a tendency to keep families intact and instead require that the couple communicate. The societal pressure to communicate is inextricably linked to notions of contract, consent, and mutuality, but despite the egalitarian premise of communicative theories, it is the target of abuse who is the focal point of the abuse "system" rather than the perpetrator. Thus, she is often cast as both the provocateur of abuse but also the suitable object for enlightenment,[52] who can then bring the family or couple back together. In this way, she is cause and solution, while the perpetrator is left alone, as walking contradiction: both an Enlightenment and anti-Enlightenment figure. This paradox is only possible if, as I suggest above, contemporary views hold violence as the opposite of liberal or Enlightenment values and yet intimate violence as embodying these norms. In turn the pervasive pressure (from social workers to schools to lawyers) to talk with the partner or former partner is destructive, because there is an assumption that the perpetrator can change through dialogue and that his words are indicative of progress and improvement. It also implies that targets of abuse are responsible for changing their abuser. Linked to this societal refrain of "Why can't you just talk to him?" is the notion that his mere existence shows "interest" in improving the matter. If he is a parent, his presence (rather than actual performance of duties or stability) is viewed as being beneficial to the child, while the mother is expected to perform daily sacrifices that are "natural" and therefore dismissed.[53] In fact, disturbingly, the family law system is marked by asymmetrical gender roles such that men more often "win" in filing for full child custody cases than women, despite rhetoric to the contrary.[54]

For all of these reasons, one obstacle to understanding this issue is overly focusing on the targets of abuse and ignoring or underestimating the importance of the abusers as well as the legal and political context that permits intimate abuse to continue occurring. As I explain in Chapter 3, gender-based asylum claims to the United States are also, rather bizarrely, judged in highly individualistic ways. Indeed, I argue that the key cases have only been successes when the abused individuals have been cast as spectacular and unique. What is bizarre about this, however, is first that human rights norms are only accepted if someone is a member of a persecuted group. Second, what constituted "credible fear" in these cases often happened because of state inaction combined with harms at the private and civil society levels, thus challenging any pretense of an exceptional and unique individual. These cases help to illuminate the social and political costs of focusing on the abused but not the abusers at the same time that they also provide a clear and compelling framework for determining abuse as a group harm occurring in a legal context and with political consequences. Further, the cases bring to the fore the fact that communication is not neutral—that policymakers and courtrooms often structure testimony to fit the dominant policy paradigms and expectations. In turn, these dynamics provide for a fascinating comparison to the treatment of long-term American residents who are abused.

In sum, I want to explore how it is possible that American society is more aware of domestic violence today and yet continues to treat it as if it is a private matter; as if it is equally generated (both parties are to blame, even as the target becomes the center of blame, punishment, and therapy); and as if it's not tied to broader societal trends of control. I will draw on Foucault's concepts of bio-power (which I define in terms of gender and not just race, as is currently the fashion) and disciplinary power, connecting both to a form of "realist" political thought that recognizes that violence and politics are interconnected, even in liberal democracies. It's important that realism acknowledge deep inequalities rather than effacing them. Realism then exposes the degree to which Enlightenment assumptions, including liberal notions of contract and consent, mask violence. Or worse, they facilitate the suspension of rights, broadly conceived. But there is a second aspect to this issue: proceeding with Enlightenment notions based on rationality; mutual understanding and communication; and equality when dealing with power dynamics that are not merely violent but radically unequal and antithetical to these very values.

Conceiving of this anti-Enlightenment model, I suggest that an abuser believes that his target is radically unequal to him, and thus his actions aim at destruction and not misguided passion.[55] It is significant to note that while abuse may occur during a conflict, it often happens when the target is happy or has just accomplished something; it can occur when a mother and children demonstrate their love for each other; and it often happens when a target has been weakened in some way (she is asleep; she is pregnant; or she is sick). Unlike rational models based on the transformative value of knowledge, an abuser can go through therapy or a batterer intervention program (BIP) and yet continue to abuse his target.[56] In fact, because therapy, for example, is based on an egalitarian model, the abuser can speak at length about his feelings of victimization, and the target is often asked to consider how she "provoked" him.[57] These sessions can often do more damage to the targets of abuse, encouraging women to blame themselves and to restrain their own activities even more than the abuser has. And regardless of the treatment, most studies on abuse cycles show escalation of controlling behaviors and violence over time, which is why I suggest it is more of a spiral than a cycle.

Abusers do better in these egalitarian situations because unlike targets of abuse, they feel pleasure and a release when they act cruelly.[58] Thus, their control over someone else actually helps them perform better on psychological testing as compared to the "normal" human subject who is emotionally battered, socially isolated, and often violently assaulted (but in ways that are often hard to prove). Over time, the violence escalates not because the situation empirically gets worse (i.e., not because the relationship is more conflictual) but because, similar to the body's response to certain drugs, both parties become accustomed to the previous level of abuse. The level of control over another person's life defies reason, while any efforts at getting help, self-defense, or flight can lead to even greater efforts at control and violence. Thus, when people urge a target to stand up for herself, fight back, or flee, they do not understand that resisting endangers her even more.

For all of these reasons, the abuser does not fit Enlightenment models at all, and society often supports this aberration, assimilating it and normalizing what is truly pathological.[59] My aim is not to suggest a new paradigm of human nature, but I do want to suggest a model of behavior that is socially constructed but largely untreatable. I have developed this model, which I describe as "monstrous" in Chapter 4, through reading Freud's notion of the "death drive" in *Civilization and Its Discontents* in conjunction with the relatively limited studies on abusers by Lundy Bancroft and Evan Stark, combined with well-known patterns of cycles of abuse. I suggest that abusers are monsters in that they defy common notions of mutuality and consent, not to mention egalitarianism, individual autonomy, and conventional ideas of guilt.[60] But rather than standing outside of society, I suggest that this societal subject is a product of and key actor in a society already riven by these contradictions. These monsters find support in societal currents that celebrate violence against women[61] and which encourage a sort of "tough love" or "Dr. Phil" approach of blaming the victim and ignoring the abuser. An abuser's beliefs are supported and not challenged by blameful and unsympathetic societal discourses about domestic abuse targets.

In particular, Patricia Evans suggests that abusers and their targets occupy "two different realities"—that of the abuser is "power over," which is based on competition and domination. Power over requires a degraded Other.[62] In contrast, a target operates according to "personal power," which is based on "mutuality and co-creation."[63] Drawing on her insights,

I reinterpret her theories as emblematic of broader debates in political and social theory regarding the ethical turn in Enlightenment and liberal analyses versus power politics and realism. Her work also identifies behavior patterns rather than relying on individualized models dependent on the public-private divide. These patterns demonstrate how an abuser is successful through exploiting Enlightenment, justice-oriented ideas and notions for the purpose of domination. By attacking his partner's successes, undermining her work, or attempting to alienate the affections of a child, an *abuser attacks the core of his partner's identity*; he takes what is essentially good or successful and attempts to destroy or destabilize it. In Evans's work, charges of mutual victimization, nagging, or fights are epiphenomenal to this more destructive set of aims. A target unsuccessfully relies on justice-oriented ideas and communication, mistakenly thinking that there is some cause for abuse or a rational plan of action to combat it or deal with it. While Evans recognizes that these patterns are ideal types, the tensions between these two realities are an innovative way of exploring how abuse occurs and why normal modes of egalitarian or Enlightenment-oriented solutions will not work. Very similar to Foucault's observations about modern psychoanalysis and other forms of "pastoral power," Evans observes that "the more the partner shares her hopes and fears with the abuser . . . the more the abuser views her openness as weakness; the more superior he feels; the colder he becomes. . . . The more the partner shares her interests and goals, the more the abuser . . . diverts her from them, and reestablishes his control. . . . The more the partner brings up topics and attempts to engage the abuser in conversation, the more the abuser withholds. . . ."[64] And so on. Evans's work demonstrates how and why communicative behaviors will not work in this context and in fact become sources of information for the abuser to refine his cruelty and denigrating practices.

Her model of an abuser is Nietzschean in the sense that abusers create their reality, including defining the context, perceiving problems, and reacting to the problems they have constructed. Abusers do not act according to the sorts of ethical norms Nietzsche found in the Judeo-Christian model, but more according to the norms of the Greek nobility, defining what is good and bad according to their reality. They do not feel guilt per this model but instead indulge in the pleasure of doing bad for bad's sake.[65] But some crucial differences between a Nietzschean superman and Evans's "reality I" abuser are that abusers need a hostile external stimulus; they often cultivate a sense of victimization, cynically using legal protections meant for targets against them; and they are highly dependent on societal validation and the corresponding blame and lack of sympathy society often shows for women or feminized subjects who are abused. In this context, what is important to note is that shelter workers, therapists, judges, and the myriad of other "helping" agents often perpetuate these dichotomous realities rather than seeking to transcend, overcome, or obliterate them. These opposing dynamics are increasingly prevalent as "Why don't you just leave?" is eclipsed by discourses and policies that are based on the goals of keeping the family together and perhaps replacing politico-legal solutions with counseling or other therapeutic interventions ("Why don't you just talk to him?").[66] At the same time, there is a great deal of prejudice and punishment against mothers who do not leave, even if one discourse has become increasingly dominant. The result is a series of mixed messages and—as I discuss in the following chapters—double binds.[67]

Lundy Bancroft's self-help texts and clinical studies provide further insight into Evans's model, delineating a pattern that abusers often establish. This pattern defies conventional notions of abuse—that abusers are provoked by nagging or overly communicative women, or that abusers are mentally ill, drug addicts, or were abused as children. Even if abusers have alcohol issues or are mentally ill, Bancroft (and others) suggest that these are not causal factors but exacerbate the situation.[68] Instead, Bancroft suggests a more complex reality in which abusers fit the norms of "reality I"—often better than their targets, who are eventually worn down by abuse—and yet operate in "reality II" (applying Evans's terminology to Bancroft's work).[69] Indeed, he exposes how abusers can cynically manipulate the language of the courts, therapy, and other egalitarian solutions to abusive situations to further control and undermine their targets. It is this imbrication of the two "realities" that is particularly fascinating to me in constructing an alternative view of domestic abuse. Bancroft and Evans do not rely on a simplistic cycle of abuse, as is often portrayed in some of the 1960s and 1970s accounts of abuse, which go something like this: the abuser is insecure and acts out; he is then contrite and begs for forgiveness; there is a period of silent withdrawal; and the cycle begins again.[70] Against this Enlightenment or Judeo-Christian model of abuse and then guilt, Evans and Bancroft argue that an abuser feels pleasure and needs more: this is why emotional and physical abuse escalates over time. Targets do not often buy into the rhetoric of their abusers but do mistakenly seek help from therapists, lawyers, and shelters invested in a dyadic/conjoint model, thus perpetuating the cycle by their adherence to Enlightenment notions.[71] Finally, the pattern of abuse that Bancroft and Evans analyze shows how abusers have common patterns divorced from any individual couple's context and how abuse is perhaps cyclical but also terroristic: attacking what is good in a woman or a relationship; changing tactics or complaints; intermittently "loving" the woman and then withdrawing. It is this intermittency that creates a destabilizing spiral that is more complex and weblike than predictable.[72]

I also draw on Evan Stark's work, which links the practical and on-target observations of these two authors to a Foucaultian analysis of current policy. Stark, like the other two authors, has spent years in the field, focusing not only on targets of abuse but also abusers. He has served as an expert witness in domestic violence trials and retaliatory homicide trials of women who killed their abusers, not to mention working in shelters and with policymakers. Stark's work is an interesting intervention in the debate that Evans opens up. First, rather than denying the legal and psychological constructs that focus on the target as victim and provocateur, he takes two key categories of pathologization—PTSD (post-traumatic stress disorder) and BSW (battered woman syndrome)—and problematizes them. He insists that most targets of abuse do not really show symptoms of these two diagnoses and in fact are strategic operators effectively resisting their abusers and the society that refuses to help them. His investigation of coercive control effectively works within parameters set by the current system and then challenges these parameters. In Stark's work, the abused woman exercises micro-resistance and protects herself and her children to the best of her abilities. Any violence or retaliation is a reaction—not in the sense of Nietzschean ressentiment—but more in the sense of a Foucaultian double bind in which we participate in the very mechanisms that may entrap us.[73] Stark's aim, he says, is to investigate these mechanisms as strategic, portraying the target as an autonomous agent in a bad position, and ultimately shifting the focus back to the abuser.[74] While Stark's work is not without issues,[75] his focus on targets' resistance to abuse as strategic and self-preserving helps to construct a broader, more political view of abuse. Coercive control is not merely supported by society but enacted by shelter programs, policies, and therapeutic interventions that continue to blame targets for the abuse they suffer.

I have chosen these three authors as representative of broader politico-theoretical issues, which I analyze throughout this book. Although the work of Evans and Bancroft is not aimed at an academic audience, I connect their insights to more general themes in political theory and feminist theory. Their work challenges academic studies that follow the rules in terms of method and subject, but which are often blinded by various issues: an overly narrow focus on targets, not perpetrators; going along with policymakers' and courts' discursive and normalizing power structures, rather than undermining or truly questioning them; and making targets of abuse Other, rather than truly revolutionizing views of this subject. Importantly, these authors recognize patterns of abuse that show a process independent of any intimate situation or individual provocations. In this way, their analyses are closer to the view that the US government has of domestic abuse in other countries: abuse is tied to status, and broad social, political and economic tolerance of gender inequality, abuse and assault. These two interpretations—one, juxtaposing Enlightenment orientations to anti-Enlightenment behavior, and two, two recent asylum cases that recast domestic abuse as political speech and feminism—help to build a theoretical view of domestic violence in realist terms.

What is interesting, as I discuss in Chapter 3, is that the United States and the international community now recognize domestic abuse as a form of torture,[76] despite the undemocratic approach to long-term residents of the United States who are abuse targets. While I do not want to idealize human rights,[77] this framework at least gives the issue political legitimacy and recognizes its immutable and inescapable gendered characteristics. I draw on this framework to compare how two asylum cases—*The Matter of RA* (a woman fleeing abuse in Guatemala) and *The Matter of LR* (a woman fleeing abuse in Mexico)—based on domestic violence claims have been handled by the US government, analyzing how resistance and flight were interpreted as "feminism" in a positive sense. On the one hand, the legal analyses regarding these cases showed a deep understanding of domestic violence as being rooted in society and in views of women as "property"; these categories are valuable in recasting how and why domestic abuse occurs. On the other hand, these two women were each required to engage in life-and-death struggles with their abusers and to flee from their homes and communities, leaving behind nearly everything, in order to be granted asylum status. Their "political speech" and "feminism" (both designations by the Department of Homeland Security) occurred at the level of mere life reducing the scope of the political to its barest dimensions. These two categories provide an interesting juxtaposition to the communicative, apolitical policies and solutions for abused long-term residents. From a different perspective, the tensions in these two cases are invaluable in structuring not merely how we interpret domestic abuse differently in the cases of long-term residents but also how political acknowledgment is inadvertently premised on "incomplete mourning," requiring an absolute break from the past.[78] The United States's treatment of long-term residents who seek help for abuse has both important similarities to these two cases but one important difference: the asylum cases are interpreted as political and therefore are acknowledged as being politically legitimate issues, while abuse cases in the United States are viewed as being private, because they are conceived of as mutual and a product of choice. We offer a "haven" to these refugees (granted, at great risk and cost for each woman) and yet we often blame and punish long-term residents who seek help within our territory.[79]

Indeed, to the degree that today's domestic abuse system reinforces patterns of abuse, it also perpetuates a process of "incomplete mourning," a term Bonnie Honig has used with regard to immigrants' assimilation and the demand that they cut off all ties to the past.[80] Very loosely referring to this term, I suggest something a bit different: that the current demands of domestic abuse targets to sacrifice nearly everything to get help do not merely depoliticize the context of domestic abuse, but reduce the target to a victim with no past, no political identity, and no ties to the community. Considering domestic abuse in these broader contexts, I believe, will challenge the value of predominant models based on symmetry, conjoint therapy, and the deformalization trend in family law, which together seek to keep the family intact despite evidence of hierarchy and abuse.[81] Recasting these terms as concrete instantiations of (problematic) Enlightenment assumptions, I believe that a realist approach to these power dynamics will uncover how these policies are profoundly undemocratic.

Domestic violence is a complex subject, and I hope to shed new light on how society itself engenders and maintains the violence and abuse it purports to help. Gender roles figure prominently in this system—something that has been ignored in conventional and popular arguments.[82] In this particular case, it is absolutely crucial to challenge this popular mindset— gender does matter and domestic abuse can explode notions of fixed racial or class identity. No one who is subject to asymmetrical abuse can be privileged, but given this observation, intersecting structures of subordination lead to very different impacts on individual targets of abuse (both with regard to how they experience abuse and available solutions). While I only briefly explore intersectionality in the conclusion, I adhere to an intersectional analysis in conjunction with my revised reading of realist power relations. On the one hand, this can mean treating abuse as a unitary category in order to emphasize how it affects a target in numerous ways. On the other hand, recognizing the differential effects on individuals and communities that are already in dire straits illustrates the degree to which change is needed. Hence, as I first treat this subject as if it were a monolithic category, I recognize that it is equally important to explore how poorer women, particularly women of color, are caught in a web of intersecting power dynamics that further subordinates them. It is now well-established that poorer women, for example, have fewer resources in the case of abuse or are treated even more unfairly than wealthier women in the family law and criminal law systems. Alternatively, immigrant women—particularly undocumented immigrants—face numerous obstacles in navigating less than welcoming institutions.[83] Nevertheless, I also examine how nearly all women or feminized subjects who are in this situation are legal subordinates and further that this demonstrates that this issue is pertinent to all women in the United States. Just as Catharine MacKinnon argued that rape law is an index of women's status in society, I argue that domestic violence legislation, decisions, and norms are an index of the status of all American women.[84] This does not mean that all intimate conflict is abuse or that all women are abused, but that the relative impunity of domestic abuse in intimate relationships is indicative of and supported by gendered political inequality more broadly. To the degree that this heteronormative, sexist dimension characterizes policy and shelter approaches to LGBQT intimate relations,[85] traditional gender norms are not only maintained but obviously highly damaging in misunderstanding the basis of intimate abuse outside of the traditional marriage contract and heteronormativity.

Despite more than three decades of advances in awareness, education, and policy about domestic abuse, it seems that things have merely changed but are not necessarily better. Aside from the motivations for writing this book that I have identified, a key puzzle investigated in this book is how someone could be the target of a broad range of controlling and abusive tactics (of which violence is some part) and yet not really be able to get help, short of fleeing.[86] For this reason, my analysis will be largely negative. My conclusions are not that things are hopeless, but for those who are in this situation and suspect that the police, lawyers, and the court (for example) will not *necessarily* help them, they are right. If nothing else changes, targets and nonprofit agencies must adopt a guerrilla-style repertoire of tactics to protect themselves.[87] Alternatively, if radical change were to be implemented, violence must be prevented (or rechanneled) and abusers must be held accountable and not subjected to weak "therapeutic" methods that only empower them to abuse more effectively. The focus must be taken off the targets of abuse and shifted to the actual perpetrators.[88] At minimum, for women in this position, I hope you know that you are not alone; at best, I hope this book effects significant change and that lawyers, judges, social workers, and the police reconsider how they deal with domestic abuse.

CHAPTER 1

The Politics of Abuse and Realism

INTRODUCTION

While domestic abuse has been identified as a problem for centuries, it has only recently become the object of social scientific research. Through the 1970s, domestic abuse was viewed as asymmetrical, and the key question was not whether gender mattered, but whether the woman deserved it. The feminist movement at this time linked asymmetry to broader inequalities in American women's lives, and the emerging shelters at this time were a model of grassroots democracy, being led by the targets and volunteers. But there were few laws penalizing abuse, and the police often refused to intervene. Over the next decade, things began to change. Initially, some of the first significant legislation beginning to criminalize family violence was introduced and some funding was allotted for shelters and other domestic violence programs.[1] Mandatory arrest laws were also gradually introduced, primarily for two reasons. First, the results of the Minnesota Domestic Violence Experiment (MDVE) suggested that mandatory arrest might deter abusers from abusing. Second, there was a rather horrific case of domestic abuse in which Tracey Thurman, a woman living in Torrington, Connecticut, called the police several times because her husband was assaulting her.[2] When the police did not help her, she was severely injured and paralyzed. She sued the city of Torrington and was awarded damages. Both of these events led to an increased push for greater accountability for police to make decisions and enforce the laws.[3] Although even today mandatory arrest is not a policy in every state, it has become an increasingly popular tactic until recently.[4]

By the time of the 1994 passage of VAWA (Violence against Women Act),[5] the problem of domestic abuse had certainly become much more well known as a public issue, and there was more support for targets in the form of shelters and organizations. But from roughly the 1990s on, the issue has been treated in public policy less as a feminist issue and more as a clinical one.[6] This is partly because the shelter system itself has become more professionalized, displacing key sites where feminist theory could become praxis. But changes have also occurred as empirical research began to claim gender symmetry in intimate partner abuse. With these shifts and other changes in welfare, in the economy, and in marriage itself, conventional policy and literature approaches have tended to depoliticize intimate abuse and treat it as a private psychological matter.[7] There are also a number of unresolved issues regarding definitions and profiles of abuse more recently, particularly because while the number of major injuries in domestic assaults has decreased, domestic abuse may have increased.[8] From a broader point of view, the growth of legislation, public awareness, and police liability are all signs of progress in some way, but a new set of unresolved issues has cropped up—notably, the increasing dominance of symmetry arguments even as mandatory arrests and batterer intervention programs become important policy tools. Second, because definitions of violence continue to dominate what counts as abuse, even these progressive moves leave violence intact (which I explain below). And finally, the broader economic, societal, and political roots that allow for intimate control and assault are not being challenged—in fact, one could argue that a new set of problems and contradictions has arisen. For these reasons, despite some of the advances discussed above, quite a lot of common attitudes about domestic abuse are prematurely celebratory.

One of the most significant popular assumptions is that policies and other "help" (like shelters) aid women in clear, consistent, and truly constructive ways. This assumption is tied to a broader conception that society is not the problem, nor is the system that helps targets of abuse; instead, the main problem is the women themselves. For example, on a typical episode of *Law and Order*, detectives discuss how an abused woman must get the "courage" to report her abusive husband. The underlying premise is that women have become so mesmerized by their abuser and his tactics that they don't understand that they are really free. When the abused woman finally calls the police or goes to a woman's shelter, it is presumed, she will get dependable help from qualified professionals. It is also assumed that any legal action abused women take will support their role as victims of a crime and appropriately punish the abuser.[9]

These assumptions can also be found in articles in popular magazines[10] and in scholarly research,[11] in which it is asserted that the crucial problem with abuse is actually the target, who just won't leave or who won't seek help.[12] These presuppositions reduce domestic abuse to a private, individual level, often portraying the victim as a victim of herself—not of the abuser, nor of society.[13] Sometimes a broader context is evoked—implicitly or explicitly—if the target is considered a racial or ethnic Other. The pattern seems to be to critique not only the targets of abuse but also their "culture" or "race." Class bias is also clear in a profound lack of understanding: for example, seeking help may not be possible in poorer neighborhoods, and if it is, seeking help may come with multiple negative economic effects that deter targets from taking action.[14] These dynamics are similar to what Jacqueline Rose has exposed in her review of analyses of female suicide bombing: women are either analyzed in conceptually isolated, narrow psychological terms or as victims of their violent and irrational culture.[15] Either way, the political context of the female suicide bombers is ignored, while they are either portrayed as their own worst enemy or as victims of their inferior, sexist culture. In fact, this approach—viewing an individual in conceptually isolated terms and thus ignoring political, economic, and historical contexts—has been used and criticized since at least the 1800s.[16]

What is interesting is how some mainstream academic studies merely crystallize these societal presuppositions rather than challenging them. For example, Evan Stark and, separately, Kathleen Ferraro et al. have highlighted the absurdity of articles that constantly ask "Why doesn't she just leave?"[17] Both sets of authors point out that the majority of women do seek help and the majority of women do leave, but these efforts are not recognized by common assumptions, policy, or mainstream academic articles.[18] Conversely, the progressive measures discussed above (increasing awareness of domestic abuse as an issue, stronger policies, and more shelters) do not really put targets out of danger—they are law-and-order solutions that can have limited deterrence effects or make things worse.[19] As Evan Stark argues, this is because fundamental mistakes are made in conceiving of what counts as abuse. To Stark, two key cases of the 1990s (the cases of Terry Traficonda and Nicole Brown Simpson) exemplify the sort of abuse that is now prevalent—coercive control; and despite each woman's efforts to seek help, she was murdered. Stark notes that "the danger faced by Terry Traficonda and Nicole Brown Simpson was not taken seriously because neither woman had been severely injured and because the hostage-like components of their abuse had no legal standing."[20] He feels that this is because researchers focus on horrible incidents and downplay others: "Ironically, focusing on incidents of severe violence trivialized the strategies used to entrap Terry, Nicole, and millions of women in similar situations, leaving them unprotected."[21]

A different way to put this is that while these solutions may have been well-intended, they produce a new gendered subject that embodies the contradictions of symmetry arguments, favors therapeutic approaches over criminalization, and reflects a trend toward family values over individual rights. Thus, for example, mandatory arrest not only carries the threat of dual arrest and thereby a criminal record for the target of abuse but, as I argue throughout this book, the target may end up being "punished" far more than the abuser in many other ways, while the abuser will most likely not see any jail time or face serious consequences. Accordingly, the popular assumptions in television shows like *Law and Order* discursively form a "problem" that becomes the basis of policy prescriptions, ensuring that targets are misunderstood and cannot get the help they need. But the issue goes deeper, because the definition of domestic abuse itself is up for grabs. Thus, while "we" tend to blame abused women for being in an abusive relationship, for not leaving; and for not seeking help, public policy, mainstream academic studies, and popular attitudes often define *abuse* such that it's possible to argue that most women are really not abused.

Two trends are predominant: sometimes the notion of domestic violence is dismissed entirely,[22] based on symmetry arguments or presuppositions about mutual provocation; other time, domestic abuse is defined mainly in terms of violence and often spectacular violence, rather than mechanisms of control, which then excludes most targets of long-term abuse.[23] A third trend depoliticizes the other two: there's an emphasis on communicative, contractual solutions to abuse, with the goal of keeping the family intact and neutralizing any broader economic or political claims on society. *Control* is a term I discuss below; in short, it means a range of physical, emotional, and geo-spatial tactics that make up a far more complex, consistent, and far-reaching form of abuse than mere acts of violence.[24] In contrast, these tendencies—dismissing the notion of asymmetrical abuse or defining it only as isolated instances of spectacular violence—presuppose that domestic abuse doesn't happen unless a woman was beaten beyond recognition; she has a clear, documentable story with witnesses and the police take her seriously; and she cannot have tried to defend herself or the violence will be viewed as "mutual." In effect, both trends are linked in dominant views of relationships as being rooted in mutuality, equality, and freedom, thus denying the very possibility of asymmetrical violence and abuse (which I discuss in more depth in the next chapter). Abuse can then be conceived of as what Alan Dershowitz has called the "abuse excuse" (granted, he is using it in a slightly different way): abuse (like rape) cannot happen between two consenting adults who have had intimate relations. But the second tendency is rooted in the same premises, as violence must be extraordinary and the target's story absolutely pure and unassailable. The binary mode of operation—abuse either consists of extraordinary violence, or it occurs in a context of mutuality and equality, such that it doesn't "count"—can also be tied to the view that abuse is a product of mutual provocation or as misguided passion or "morality" (i.e., in the context of traditional or religious gender roles[25]); with both interpretations, abuse is often viewed as nonexistent.[26]

Recent scholarship that seeks to classify types of abuse can replicate one of the main problems in policy: defining abuse as almost entirely centered on violence (as a physical act). This focus in turn diminishes other forms of abuse (verbal abuse, threats, monetary control, social isolation, and so on), which are now generally called "control" in the abuse literature (or, in Evan Stark's words, "coercive control,"[27] as discussed in the previous chapter). For example, while authors like Kathleen Ferraro argue that issues of control are an important addition to the growing body of literature on intimate abuse in the 1990s, she and her co-authors contend that once violence itself is defined, labeled, and appropriately compartmentalized, types of control will map onto the more foundational dynamic of abuse: physical violence. Thus control is epiphenomenal to violence and the chief problem remains—a violence-centered definition of abuse—which is why she and her co-authors can dismiss a "'feminine' slap in the face" as having no effect on a woman at all, in contrast to "a terrorizing pattern of beatings accompanied by humiliating psychological abuse. . . ."[28]

As Ferraro states, "a slap in the face sometime in the last 12 months is likely to have little impact on self-esteem and may not even be witnessed by the children. A systematic pattern of assault and psychological abuse is another story."[29] Significantly, Ferraro dismisses the blow in gendered terms, appealing to a paradigm of violence of which only "masculine" violence counts. Ironically, this elevates men's status: only their violence is a legitimate object of concern. It also assimilates "feminine" violence (i.e., makes acceptable) and ignores how a context must have occurred in which there was such a breakdown in physical boundaries that this "feminine" man hit his female partner. This sort of typology is often replicated in the domestic violence literature rooted in symmetry arguments. This literature merely counts the number of violent acts in a relationship without considering the broader context of abuse, without considering whether targets' "violence" was actually self-defense.[30] Further, despite years (if not centuries) of claims that women are generally smaller and have less muscle mass than men,[31] there is little consideration of the consequences of this allegedly symmetrical violence.[32] In contrast, drawing on control as a predominant interpretation of abuse can help to contextualize what appears to be a single blow, and the damage to children will be more evident.[33]

As this example suggests, the bar for what counts as abuse is incredibly high; it must be "a terrorizing pattern of beatings accompanied by humiliating psychological abuse"[34] in order to be legitimized as violence. Moreover, somehow a line is drawn between partner abuse and the effect on children; miraculously, it is assumed, a woman can be physically abused and the children will have absolutely no awareness of this.[35] These perspectives are only possible if violence is conceptually reduced to this one extraordinary event, and the behavior and lack of boundaries that led to violence are ignored; and if the unit of analysis is individual, such that attachments between parents and children are denied. Somehow, children are magically untouched by these acts only because they are marked by spectacularity and singularity—that is, the slap by some means occurred in a sort of vacuum.[36] In contrast, if violence were considered merely one instance of a more general context of control, which includes economic deprivation, threats, psychological abuse, and attempts to pit family members against one another, a slap in the face might be more meaningful.[37] Accounting for this broader pattern of abuse would also entail going beyond the individual as the unit of analysis. We would need to recognize that the denigration and abuse of the mother, for example, would affect children, and we would not expect women to "take a hit" and suck it up. In fact, the desire for a "systematic" pattern of abuse with spectacular and documentable violence is a will-to-order that often doesn't capture the spiral of abuse, which resembles terrorism more than predictable and systematic violence.

Michael Johnson, who has worked with Ferraro (including on the article cited above), makes a clearer, less gendered case for a typology of violence in his 2008 book, *A Typology of Domestic Violence: Intimate Terrorism, Violent Resistance, and Situational Couple Violence*. In this text, he has argued that situational couple violence often entails a conflict that is relatively mutual, in which violence was used by one party or the other but which overall does not characterize the relationship. Johnson interestingly argues that most empirical studies claiming symmetry reflect studies of couples experiencing this sort of conflict. In contrast, he defines intimate terror as defined by regular assaults and injuries, but importantly rooted in control. His arguments are compelling, because they do not dismiss symmetry claims altogether but rather contextualize them and reduce their analytic power. Accordingly, he also allows for asymmetry (intimate terrorism) rather than holding that situational couple violence and symmetry characterize all intimate conflict. Even despite these excellent points, as an analytic tool, Stark's notion of control is more compelling for two reasons.[38]

First, throughout his 2008 book, Johnson notes that emotional abuse, control, and economic abuse are what entrap women in abusive and damaging relationships—not the violence per se. In fact, he relates a story of a colleague who was subjected to various forms of intimate control and then violence later, only as the relationship was ending. As he argues, this particular story is also an example of intimate terror, but it does not fit a violence-based notion of abuse, nor a symmetrical one. Rather, coercive control was the base and the escalation of violent acts epiphenomenal to this control. As Stark argues, this story is not anomalous but is now the norm as abusers have adjusted their tactics to avoid arrest and incarceration.[39] What is interesting to me is that if this is true, targets' experience of violence does not match up with older law-and-order approaches to domestic abuse or with popular conceptions of either abuse or its solutions. In fact, the nature of violence is not eradicated but assimilated to the current situation, mapping onto a broader political context of control (normative disciplinary power for feminized subjects in intimate relationships).[40]

Accordingly, I interpret domestic abuse in terms of economic, political, and social inequalities and find that (1) it is profoundly asymmetrical when going beyond a mere "calculus of injuries"[41]; (2) it is seamless in that no one event or violent incident characterizes abuse—rather, it constitutes a series of constant attacks and withdrawals economically, spatially, emotionally (and in many other ways), alternating with periods of intense attention and what appears to be "love"; (3) it is punctuated by extreme actions that are very often unprovoked, unpredictable, and which occur during "happy" periods (or, for example, while a target is sleeping or has just experienced a validating event); (4) it appears to be "pre-modern"[42] to the degree that it is tied to the family, passions, and love, but an abuser's tactics are highly controlled and often premeditated (that is, even if his actions appears to be highly emotional and irrational, abuse relies heavily on society's disciplinary mechanisms and the availability of technology to control a target)[43]; (5) against the notion that an abuser can somehow be emotionally and physically abusive to his partner, including instances of economic deprivation and social control, and yet be a "good father," abuse entails both a context of control that often affects the entire family as well as divisive family dynamics that involve pitting family members against each other or threatening to take away the children from the mother.[44] Most important, as I stated in the previous chapter, asymmetrical abuse (which I equate with the term *domestic abuse* in this book) is rooted in the premise of inequality and aims at destroying the core of the target's being. All of these characteristics defy conventional understandings of intimacy and domestic abuse (which I discuss in more depth in Chapter 4). Thus the abused woman is caught in a trap—on the one hand, she knows that she is being treated badly.[45] On the other, she can try to get help and often have her claims dismissed, ridiculed, or turned back on her. Even worse, by turning to authorities, she can be arrested, because of dual-arrest policies that aim at treating intimate violence in gender-neutral terms;[46] she can be the subject of investigation if a child is involved (e.g., she can be blamed for "exposing" a child to an abuser); or she can even be subject to removal proceedings (i.e., deportation).[47] Beyond these consequences, the economic consequences of reporting an abuser or facing an arrest if there are dual-arrest policies can severely impact poorer women.[48] Accordingly, "help" is not something that can be expected, nor is it often sympathetic or charitable.

The conventional perspectives of abuse that I have identified above—that either abuse doesn't exist at all (because it's symmetrical) or that it must be violent, spectacular, individual, and temporally discrete (not to mention documentable)—explain why help is often unhelpful. In reality, the power dynamics of control are far more complex and extensive than the binary mode of operation: symmetry or spectacular, horrific violence. Again, Stark's examples—the cases of Terry Traficonda and Nicole Brown Simpson—are emblematic of this problem in that the situation of both women needed a more complex and contextualized understanding of intimate abuse. In more contemporary times, there continue to be cases in which a lot of people knew an abuser was controlling, stalking, and harming his partner but it wasn't until she was dead that they took these tactics seriously. The case of Michelle Warner, a 31-year-old Houston mother killed by her ex-boyfriend, exemplifies this. When interviewed about Warner's death, her best friend stated, "'He's done other crazy things. Nothing extra-violent; he'd push her up against the wall, that type of thing. He's threatened her.'"[49] When this news had broken, the particular phrase—"'nothing extra-violent'"—stuck with me. There was and is a fundamental way in which violence is assimilated until it goes too far, but at this point the damage is irreparable. The attitude of her best friend crystallized the difficulty Stark has identified.[50]

Added to the definitional problems that reduce or ignore abuse and law-and-order approaches that are not getting to the root of the problem are shelter policies that often replicate the dynamics of abuse and control. Rather than preventing violence or even prosecuting abusers, shelters frequently assimilate violence and a crisis orientation through geo-spatial isolation and secrecy. Significantly, shelters normally protect individuals *after* abuse has occurred and thus, abusive acts *must* happen to gain entrance into a shelter. Shelters also remove decision making from "clients" by establishing strict rules without their input (that is, clients must adhere to shelter rules in order to gain admission and protection). The imposition of these rules without resident feedback is in turn tied to a greater professionalization of shelter workers (that is, it is no longer rooted in the 1970s grassroots ethos of allowing women to speak for themselves but a more hierarchical relationship of professional-client relations).[51] More broadly, shelters have witnessed the growth of disciplinary mechanisms as they are increasingly tied to social service bureaucracies and as targets of abuse are increasingly pathologized. All of these dynamics have a complex history, which I discuss in the following chapters, but the main point is that the majority of shelters do not prevent abuse. In fact, although shelters, domestic abuse advocates, and counselors most likely have good intentions, shelters are not merely like a Band-Aid but can also serve to further undermine women's political agency and status, not to mention allowing abuse to be committed with impunity. Like refugee camps, they symbolize the successful deployment of coercion and violence as well as the further displacement of the targets rather than the perpetrators. But as I discuss in Chapter 3, in contrast to the treatment of refugees, targets of abuse are pathologized and subject to new mechanisms of psychological control.

Thus, help for abuse can lead to new forms of domination and surveillance, while requiring violence to occur to "count." I am interested in why popular views (especially the idea that the help is out there) are prevalent; why some of the mainstream social science literature often merely echoes these conventional views rather than challenging them; and why and how "help" often further traps and controls targets of abuse rather than truly aiding them. In essence, I want to explore the broader meaning of these power dynamics and what they signify about gender roles, women's political status (and correspondingly, feminized subjects[52]), and about violence in our society more broadly. Further, I would like to examine why this sort of violence and domination is tolerated and assimilated rather than rejected.

I believe that the study of domestic violence should be interpreted as political violence rather than merely individual violence, and more broadly, it should be examined as a form of domination and control rather than violence per se. Because this research is oriented toward the status of women, I focus on abuse against women and the degree to which traditional gender roles and heteronormativity structure many of the conventional approaches to understanding abuse in mainstream policy, research, and shelters.[53] To the degree that one can also apply these gender divisions and heteronormativity to LBGQT relationships, I am not excluding these relationships. But nevertheless, I have heeded the warning of authors like Cheshire Calhoun and others that significant damage is done when authors merely extrapolate from one analysis (heterosexual) to another (e.g., lesbian) without understanding the unique specificity of the latter case. In this way, my focus on gendered dynamics also attempts to avoid heteronormativity in simply applying one social problem to the other.[54] To put it differently, I am not interested merely in studying violence but also what this means about women and feminized subjects, including abuse targets in the LGBQT communities whose abuse is subjected to conventional heteronormative symmetry arguments. In this interpretation, I find it far more interesting to see how heterosexual gender norms are often attributed to a wide range of experiences, intimate configurations, and individuals' behaviors without the subjects ever claiming these identities as the causal factors in their own experiences.

CONTEXT: A CULTURE OF VIOLENCE?

Although any generalization about contemporary US politics should be suspect, it is probably not too controversial to argue that Americans are relatively tolerant of violence, and thus the main question is really which forms of violence are viewed as illegitimate and which are viewed as legitimate?[55] Additionally, the relative tolerance of, say, racist and sexist speech and images can be linked to violence against women and racial minorities.[56] However, despite arguments regarding both direct and indirect harms to women given violent and objectifying images of women in music, popular films, and other media representations, various efforts to modify them or hide them (e.g., blocking them from children's view) are often challenged zealously as challenges to free speech.[57]

Kimberlé Crenshaw and Catharine MacKinnon have written about this culture of violence in different but complementary ways. Like Crenshaw, MacKinnon explores facially neutral policies but which nevertheless have selective impacts in their enforcement; both authors examine cultural messages that do not merely assimilate or tolerate violent sexual images but actually celebrate them. I would like to focus on some important insights in her work, without adhering to the entirety of her project. In particular, I am interested in how her views on pornography could help to analyze dynamics in many Hollywood movies, popular music, and media images. In particular, MacKinnon's discussion of "pornography's positive-outcome-rape scenario"[58] links violence, the sexual act, and gender together in ways that can be extended beyond pornography. If in fact the dominant message in her insight is that force, nonconsent, and sex are often linked in jokes, popular music, and films, her rather singular focus on pornography (and the criticism she has received for this) can be challenged.[59] Indeed, MacKinnon's observations connect with observations by other legal and political scholars, such as Carole Pateman, Susan Bordo, and Crenshaw, to elucidate the linkages between sex, gender, and violence—particularly as they also intersect with race, ethnicity, and class.[60] As MacKinnon argues, the connection between sex and violence highlights a major confusion in rape law, such that legal theorists and agents often debate whether an act was sex or violence. She suggests, like these other authors, that this is most often too dichotomous; in fact, they are often united in the popular mind.

This insight is echoed in Crenshaw's investigation of the 2LiveCrew obscenity case in which the Supreme Court implicitly distinguished between art, sexual prurience, and violence.[61] Indeed, she holds that the "case illustrates the ways in which obscenity doctrine asks the wrong question with respect to sexual violence. . . ."[62] While she believes this case was indicative of racism—linking African American men to both violence and sex (which then meant their lyrics were devoid of artistic worth and thus obscene)—she also felt that it served as an excuse to erase African American women as subjects in this discourse. Instead, Crenshaw convincingly argues, figures like George Will used it as an opportunity to racialize violence against women, thus using black women as a proxy for his concern about white women.[63] In this way, the linkages MacKinnon makes are deployed only when sex and violence are connected in the acts performed by racial Others, as Crenshaw argues. Crenshaw's insights not only highlight the specificity of African American women's experiences, combined with tokenism (which she thinks can be more damaging than erasure at times[64]), but also more generally demonstrate how jokes, video games, lyrics, and media images often unproblematically link sex and violence. In turn, she argues that children are affected, learning that "unlike that of men, however, women's sexual value is portrayed as a depletable commodity: By expending it, boys become men and girls become whores."[65]

The connection between media images and intimate violence carried out with impunity is not hypothetical, however: Crenshaw argues that children are significantly affected by familial violence, and she notes that "nearly 40% of all homeless women and kids have fled violence in the home and about 63% of young men between 11 and 20 who are in prison for homicide killed their mother's batterers."[66] Both legal theorists suggest that the judicial and discursive separation between sex and violence is indicative of political and economic inequality, intersecting with race, class, and sexual orientation. To put it more simply, there is often greater tolerance of violence against those who are viewed as unequal and thus deserving of abuse.[67] Violent imagery, the frequent portrayal of sex as violence, and the empirical reality that gender violence often goes unpunished has a disciplinary effect on women. This is true, in terms of geospatial confinement, including isolation in the home and accompaniment in public, as well as dress, and temporal confinement. These sorts of considerations broaden the dimensions of how actual violence is viewed, particularly as these dynamics can affect all women and not just the abused. Furthermore, the sex-violence link also connects rape policy and attitudes about rape with domestic violence, challenging dichotomies like public-private, married-unmarried, and love-hate. In fact, in some respects, this disciplinary effect—which is indicative of a "culture of control"[68]—is perhaps more noteworthy than isolated acts of violence in understanding why there seems to be such great tolerance for gender violence in popular culture and policy.[69]

Despite the affinities between their work, MacKinnon's radical feminism has been consigned to the dustbin of history,[70] while Crenshaw's "Mapping the Margins" article is probably one of the most cited. While there are several forceful critiques of MacKinnon's work,[71] I believe it is valuable to review her insights in the context of intersectional analyses such as Crenshaw's; it's just as important to recognize that both authors have developed a theory of gender violence, why it occurs, and how to analyze it, and that these analyses have important commonalities.

A FOUCAULTIAN INTERPRETATION OF RADICAL FEMINISM: REALISM

I propose that MacKinnon's analysis of the facets of the social construction of sexuality illuminate specific and important features of gender control, violence, and domination that can lead to a realist account of intimate violence. Without discounting the numerous critiques of her work,[72] I will highlight her contribution to an understanding of violence through the law in this chapter. Most important, MacKinnon investigates how gendered asymmetries in intimate partnership violence are linked to a more general context of normative enforcement of traditional gender roles and gender typing, even if this violence is not always in the context of heterosexual relationships. She then argues that intimate abuse and violence are committed with impunity due to the normative influence of gender naturalization on laws and enforcement. Her analysis challenges conventional assumptions about equality before the law and what has historically been conceived of as an inalienable right: the right to bodily integrity. Further, her work exposes (or exposed, in the past)[73] common deficiencies in feminist literature that ignore the significance of the threat of violence with impunity and the meaning that this has for women's political status. In particular, unlike many other feminist theorists, MacKinnon does not cordon violence off to the private sphere; instead, like Kimberlé Crenshaw, she makes important linkages between legal and extralegal institutions; societal and political norms; and the consequences of these political dynamics on women more generally.

Both MacKinnon and the relatively less well-known Colette Guillaumin offer a theory of violence and gender that cannot be ignored. Despite their affiliation with Marxism, I will treat both authors in Foucaultian terms, in order to highlight the specific power dynamics each elucidates, while treating their broader, more universalizing claims as if they were local, genealogical, and contingent. As I discuss in the conclusion to this book, my methodological approach also takes into account the necessity of adopting an intersectional approach to the politics of domestic abuse, an approach that is compatible with the realist theory I discuss below. In effect, I believe that their arguments are more rather than less powerful, once these Enlightenment tendencies are properly contextualized and their universalizing claims reduced.

Neither author argues that violence happens to every woman in their respective Western countries (the United States and France) but rather that the very threat of violence has a disciplinary effect on women.[74] More specifically, to both authors, violence is merely one part of a larger attempt to effect gender domination. To Guillaumin, the threat of violence leads to spatial confinement, and to MacKinnon, the inadequacy of rape law is an "index" of women's political status.[75] Rather than analyzing women's reactions to these dynamics, both authors claim that the threat of violence and spatial confinement have a normative message and disciplinary effect that indicate something about gender hierarchy. Both authors note that women are urged to internalize the notion of the "threat" of rape or assault (as Guillaumin discusses) and confine their movements, sticking to their prescribed gender roles.

Like MacKinnon, Guillaumin argues that marital violence, abuse, and the more public threat of rape all serve to constantly reaffirm women's powerlessness and minority status. Her observation that this leads to spatial confinement in public and spatial isolation in the home broadens what could otherwise be a narrow focus on legalism and rights. Guillaumin calls the web of power dynamics that make women's status inferior (particularly as this intersects with class and race) "sexage," arguing that all women (not just mothers or wives) are expected to give up time (continually and not on the clock, like exploited workers) performing domestic duties and caring for others, unremunerated. Sexage includes bodily obligations such as obligatory performance of the sexual act, constraints on the availability of contraception and access to abortion.[76] Taken together with spatial confinement and the fact that the parameters of child-rearing are politically and socially constrained, women's inequality is evident. Guillaumin essentially ties women's identity as sexual beings and reproducers to economic exploitation, exploitation of the body itself (sexage connotes a form of bodily appropriation that is not true of exploited workers[77]), and geographical immobility.

As Guillaumin argues about 1970s France, "Women . . . are not permitted to go to all neighbourhoods (nor all places), just as night hours are totally forbidden to them, under threat of severe penalty if they infringe such a prohibition."[78] Like connect the dots ["as in children's number drawings"], these social norms "give shape . . . [to] a relationship of appropriation."[79] As indicated above, appropriation is different from worker exploitation, for example, for at least three crucial reasons: there is no beginning and end to "sexage" (the appropriation of women) as there is for the work day; spatially, there is a relationship of confinement that is not true of workers; and third, not only is one's labor exploited but one's body is also "appropriated" in various ways. While the first aspect of sexage is often acknowledged, even by conservative writers and politicians (the performance of free "caring" labor in and outside of the home[80]), the other two are perhaps less obvious. As I interpret Guillaumin's work today, in the context of the United States, I believe that spatial confinement and bodily appropriation take form in the following ways (although the list is not exhaustive): (1) social and legal norms about what a good mother is (expectations that she is the primary caretaker of any children and that she will make work outside of the home secondary to this key role[81]); (2) legal norms in divorce and custody disputes that geographically confine the mother (as the primary caretaker) to a county or state; (3) prohibitions on travel with children in the case of separation or divorce, without the father's permission; and (4) social norms about rape, marital rape, dating violence, and emotional abuse that attempt to socially isolate women. In this way, violence itself is not at the center of women's domination; rather, it is the *threat* of violence, daily acts of material appropriation (e.g., of children, of labor), social expectations of mothers' duties to children, and legal norms that effectively award fathers rights (with a beginning and end, and which have a passive character) and mothers duties.[82] All of this could broadly be categorized as control: a form of cultural or societal control that can be distinguished from the control of intimate abuse, but which also makes it possible.[83] While it cannot be said that the law and society are fully in agreement, it can still be asserted that social norms of motherhood combined with laws in child custody and divorce cases as well as welfare and contraceptive laws can work together to produce a sort of domination that is both legal and extralegal, to borrow Foucault's term from *Discipline and Punish*. To Guillaumin, all women are implicated in this web of expectations, whether they are mothers or not: sisters, aunts, and nuns, for example, are all expected to take charge of the sick, disabled, elderly, and young.[84] In this way, religious institutions and welfare institutions (among others) work with familial expectations to blur the boundary between public and private, effecting a broader material and physical appropriation of "the class of women" than the mere instantiation of marriage would suggest.[85]

Guillaumin's work should not be read as a victimology but rather an analysis of the meaning of attempts at confinement in terms of power, time, and space. Her examination of physical appropriation, in particular, suggests the degree to which gender norms seek to control women's movements and occupation of public space to a significant degree. She goes further to note—as many authors have done before and after—that women's circumstances are then taken to reflect their nature. Individual women can and do act outside of these prescribed roles all the time, but as Judith Butler notes with gender dress codes, they are also often punished for doing so (for changing their performance of gender).[86]

Taken together, the force of Guillaumin and MacKinnon's work indicates that the privacy of the home—where abuse often happens—is frequently thought to mark the distinction between illegitimate violence (in public, by a stranger) and legitimate violence (nonexistent violence: in the home or in public, by one's partner).[87] But, of course, these distinctions are blurred in the law, and de facto, they produce a set of unresolved tensions. The law is crucial in establishing these distinctions, but societal messages are also important in disciplining women. Thus, the very threat of rape or assault by a stranger is translated into a dress code for women, in which women are urged to watch what they wear. Women are also expected to ensure that they are accompanied at night and to limit their public activities.[88] The disciplinary message to girls and women—that they will be blamed for assaults—has its counterpart in intimate partner violence, thus (again) blurring the line between public and private and hence legitimate and illegitimate violence.

Just as women are blamed for going out at night and walking home alone; for wearing a miniskirt or jeans that are deemed "too tight"; or for going to a restaurant or bar alone and being the subject of unwanted attention, harassment, or violent assault, women in the home are also blamed for their partner's control and abuse. But it is no longer a question of occupying public space, dress, or the time of day; instead, women are blamed as the recipients of violence, abuse, threats, insults, and bizarre behavior simply because they "agreed" to cohabitate with this person. Their very occupation of private space constitutes tacit consent to these acts, just as the very occupation of public space constitutes consent to strangers' assaults or date rape. Rather than delineating two separate spheres or classes of women (or feminized subjects), these dynamics of course overlap and are mutually constitutive. In both cases, the law and media will ask how the woman provoked the assault, granted that the criteria are different: in the first case, what the woman was wearing, what street she was walking down, what bar she went to; in the second, how she provoked her partner—cooking food incorrectly, wearing the wrong facial expressions, or stepping out of her boundaries as a partner.[89] Authors in the popular media often seek the cause of the abuser's actions, even when the causes seem incredibly superficial and the acts are terroristic and homicidal.[90] In both cases, as Susan Bordo notes, women do not actually speak or act—instead their bodies, facial expressions, or clothing "speak" for them.[91]

Hence, Guillaumin argues that threats of gender violence committed with impunity lead to attempts at spatial confinement that signify women's diminished political and economic status. Even if these attempts are merely attempts and the threat of violence is just that—a threat—these sites of contestation signify power inequities. MacKinnon's theories are more legally oriented but serve as a complement to Guillaumin's. As MacKinnon argues, the law on assault and abuse is significant in determining women's formal political status. This is different from arguing that this is the actual condition of all women; rather, she is examining the importance of laws that effectively control but do not prohibit violence against women.[92]

MacKinnon's main points about violence and the law include the following:

(1) She notes the specificity of gender in certain relations of violence. For example, statistically far more women are violently and sexually

assaulted than men; among children older than 12, far more girls than boys are assaulted, harassed, and/or inappropriately treated. While these facts do not preclude violence by women and against boys and men, there is a systematic pattern of violence against girls and women that can be identified.[93]

(2) Whether one is attacked or not, the pervasiveness of this violence-with-impunity has a normative and disciplinary effect on all women in the sense that it "forms . . . the material conditions of their epistemological experience"[94]; it should be noted that MacKinnon is not making any claims about the substance of the effects on women in this particular statement; her categories—"material conditions" and "epistemological experience"[95]—are substantively empty, which would leave room for an intersectional analysis of identitarian specificity, even while recognizing these broad power dynamics.

(3) Significantly, for these types of actions (rape, intimate violence), mens rea is taken into account,[96] which means that the perspective and intentions of the perpetrator define whether violence or a criminal act happened or not.[97] If normal criminal law can serve as a sort of analog to these acts, taking mens rea into account for violent (and lesser) crimes should be a shocking reversal of power relations, effectively making targets subordinate and their own stories automatically suspect, while the abuser's intent and actions are elevated and determine whether a crime was committed.

(4) Accordingly, women's perspective and experiences—that is, their rational judgments and communication—are then discounted or pathologized, effectively challenging claims that "communicative action" (as Habermas theorized) is possible at the level of rights in the current context. In fact, Foucault's observations about discursive hierarchies and the therapeutic gaze[98] are far more relevant to this issue; communication and discourse are most often used to entrap and blame targets of violence rather than helping them. (This Habermas-Foucault debate is discussed in Chapter 3.)

What is important in MacKinnon's work is to recognize that gender violence is alleged to be private—thus emotional, irrational, unequal, passionate—and yet also public in its qualities, because it is allegedly contractual, consensual, and linked to broader societal trends of violence and gender inequality. In this way, MacKinnon's work shows the blurred boundaries between private and public. Foucault suggests similar power dynamics in *Discipline and Punish* as well as *The History of Sexuality*, volume 1, in his analyses of legal and extralegal networks of power as well as linkages between the private sphere where sex (broadly conceived) happens and a public policy that is increasingly bio-political in orientation. Foucault acknowledges these tensions as well as broader dynamics of a more general inequality of oppression, even as micro-techniques of power also individualize.[99] Similarly, as MacKinnon argues, these personal relationships are more rooted in power, hierarchy, and proprietary notions of relationships than privacy per se. The point is that there is a "broad axis of stratification" (as Fraser and Nicholson put it[100]) that defines women's status in some way, if not their daily lives.

Furthermore, MacKinnon's work demonstrates the inextricable relationship between systematic violence committed with impunity against women—if only hypothetically: de jure it is regulated, de facto it can happen with impunity. The norms and threats that make both possible are meaningful in terms of discerning normative, discursive and disciplinary power involving women. A similar argument is made by John Stuart Mill in his comparison of slavery to marriage; the laws regarding marriage ensure that de jure, women lose nearly every right: economic rights, the right to bodily integrity, the right to work, and so on. [101] While he notes that de facto, not every woman experiences these losses, this remark only mitigates the important observation that by law, every woman *could have been* deprived of most life-sustaining rights and protections. The only reason many weren't in fact deprived of these rights was due to the charity of their husbands.[102] Even if legislation cannot entirely define any individual's life, it seems clear that in a democracy, no one could possibly be free or a democratic actor if she were also completely rightless, her rights being contingent upon the arbitrary will of another. As Hannah Arendt has called attention to the plight of the stateless and noted that if they survive, it is only due to the charity of political agents—not because they actually have "the right to rights," Mill's arguments suggest a similar conclusion. Women who can be attacked with impunity; economically marginalized by their partners; and stalked, harassed, and deprived of life-sustaining rights cannot be called citizens. In this respect, MacKinnon is correct to argue that laws are the index of the political status of women.[103]

MacKinnon's work highlights what formal rightlessness signifies politically—in this respect, her analysis is not about any individual women at all. It is a commentary on the capriciousness of the law and the potentiality of acting with impunity. MacKinnon's work also brings up another important point: like rape, the difficulty in ascertaining whether something is domestic violence is not because it's in the private sphere per se but because there is a continuum of violence and sex, spanning the public and private, such that it is confusing as to where the line stops. In the same way, broader dynamics of violence, and violence against women in particular, are on a continuum. To put it more simply, the violence and control of domestic abuse are supported by the broader community in its own acceptance of violence against and control of women.

Another aspect of this is not merely the continuum of violence itself but the continuum of violence against women, such that dynamics of rape both resemble and overlap with aspects of domestic abuse.[104] These in turn can be related not simply to the acts themselves but also the gendering of public space by which warnings about rape and call boxes do not merely signal help but serve as a warning to women to curtail their public activities at all times or they could be held responsible for any attacks.[105] Whether women choose to internalize these norms and confine their own movements or not, such signifiers as public discourse, posters, and call boxes are similar to color warnings in airports, serving as a constant reminder that danger is possible. These disciplinary messages encourage us to think that we must be suspicious of others and withdraw ourselves. Similarly, the warnings regarding rape and sexual assault urge women to retreat to the private sphere and to view the possibility of assault as always possible. Paradoxically, neighborhoods without call boxes or rapid police response can feel like sites of abandonment, even though both abandonment and overpolicing signal a type of confinement.

Considering rape laws, marital rape laws, and domestic abuse policy together, the status of women is certainly in question. As MacKinnon states with regard to rape—but I will broaden this statement a bit— violence and abuse against women are "regulated but not prohibited."[106] Furthermore, this violence is not merely a mistake or somehow marginalized but a crucial element of public discourse, legal debates, and popular discussions (for example, see Katie Roiphie's book on date rape or Alan Dershowitz's pronouncements on rape, date rape, and domestic violence).[107] Discursively, women are viewed as having deserved their assaults;[108] (more rarely) as innocent victims who need protection; and as perpetrators of violence themselves in localities that use dual-arrest policies.[109] In contrast to mainstream views and academic currents, domestic violence must be viewed as having a political basis and important political consequences. As I discuss in Chapter 3, in discussing two important refugee cases, "political" does not merely signify outward deployments of power but also "state inaction," which allows private actors to think they can act without accountability and to abuse with impunity.

In sum, MacKinnon's and Guillaumin's work calls attention to the following points regarding domestic violence:

- Intimate partner violence is epiphenomenal to broader mechanisms of abuse, which are rooted in domination and control.
- Abuse is linked to other societal dynamics—including political and economic—that blur the boundaries between private and public spheres.
- Abuse committed with impunity is a marker of inequality; it is an important epistemological condition of a certain gendered reality, even if it is not an ontological condition.
- Alternatively, even if a woman doesn't experience violence, there are disciplinary effects on women. For example, there is the threat of violence as we witness neighbors' and friends' assaults. There are also news stories about attacks and potential attacks.
- Public policy will often blame the target of violence or ignore the crime that was committed in the cases of rape, marital rape, and domestic abuse.

All these observations demonstrate how Mackinnon's attention to violence does not hyperbolize women's condition or victim status but rather points to a serious political problem that cannot be construed in any other way (i.e., violence and control do not act as a proxy for something else) and which is largely ignored, trivialized, or marginalized by other authors today insofar as they dismiss her work. Together, facets of the political nature of abuse could be broadly categorized as creating a culture of control.

Drawing on MacKinnon's analysis of attempts at domination through weak rape laws; norms regarding sexual and intimate violence; and domestic violence, Butler's work on gender performativity produces an interesting hermeneutic lens. Rather than interpreting these laws as representing some sort of material fact, we can ask (via Butler's work in *Gender Trouble*) which subjects and power relations these policies (and the policymakers who formulated them) attempt to construct. What sort of discursive figure is established through these laws and political norms? How are broader gender norms pathologized in these attempts at establishing and reinscribing gender hierarchies?

Like other "minority" texts,[110] Butler's *Gender Trouble* radically overturned major conceptions in philosophy (including existentialism and Foucaultian approaches to power) and feminist theory. Among other important ideas, she argued that what has been taken to be a material fact—the human body—is in fact imbued with social meaning. In this way, the body itself is not a blank slate and therefore, even the alleged materialism of gender (as opposed to other forms of identity) can be challenged. Drawing on and yet going beyond existentialist and Freudian insights, Butler argues that femininity and masculinity are established through acts and repeated performances. Hence, we perform femininity: accusations that women are not feminine enough, are tomboys, and so on prove that femininity is a set of practices and norms—not a material or natural "thing." Rather than undermining the possibility of agency or feminism, Butler's work opens a space for the possibility of gender transgressions, including micro-resistance and, perhaps, mass resistance to oppressive masculine norms. The good news is that if these "material" facts can be shown to be performative (not biologically determined or material), then they can be subtly altered, openly challenged, and/or hyperbolized (as in drag). As a general observation, her work thus shows that while there may have been gender hierarchies throughout history, claims that gender inequality is rooted in some sort of material reality that defies categorization must be challenged. That is, it refutes claims like de Beauvoir's that the body itself is a tabula rasa and thus has universal meaning; this observation in turn leads to a call for differentiating among societies and adopting a more poststructural and intersectional approach to issues of gender inequality and domestic violence.

Thus, for example, a claim that domestic violence is a sort of ahistorical, universal category because it has existed since the dawn of time effectively obfuscates the specificity of gender hierarchies and abuse in their more localized and historicized contexts.[111] If we take Butler's work seriously, the historical continuities are less interesting than their more local historically and geographically specific manifestations. This is particularly true as abusers can control and harass their targets using technology in ways that weren't true in the past.

The value of Butler's work extends beyond historicization, though. Her insights point to how research on intimate partner abuse could reinscribe gender roles and their meaning rather than challenging them. For example, Andrea Westlund has analyzed how targets are pathologized by psychologists and psychiatrists—abuse targets have diagnoses in the DSM (the *Diagnostic and Statistical Manual of Mental Disorder*),[112] but abusers do not. Westlund links these diagnoses to a broader cultural discrediting of feminine practices and norms (e.g., being self-sacrificing, putting others first, not having an individualistic orientation).[113] Alternatively, some authors argue that abusers and abuse targets are relying on and performing gender roles through abusive relations, as if this were the sole cause of abuse or as if there were a rational basis of abuse that could be explained, interpreted, and even predicted through traditional gender roles. But what if the state, contemporary counseling, welfare, and family law actually create these gendered subjects through the deployment of their power relations? Although not about intimate abuse at all, Butler's work illuminates how domestic violence policies and assumptions *produce* these gender roles (rather than the reverse), granted at the extreme. Further, her work suggests how intimate control is gendered through action—surveillance, threats, withholding—which in turn could lead to hypermasculine and hyperfeminine ideals that guide policymaking on abuse, modern psychology, police interventions, and shelter rules for targets of abuse. Two asylum cases I explore in Chapter 3 demonstrate the degree to which gendered meaning is almost completely imputed by the state. In this way, women who flee domestic abuse from other countries (and other women claimants who want protection from civil society actors) are forced into portraying their claims as "feminist," but as Julietta Hua has argued, this often implicitly requires their designation as "failed feminists."[114] These cases beautifully illustrate how gendered meaning is imposed on more complex dynamics of abuse and violence, but this gendering is a trap. Thus, while MacKinnon's work demonstrates how legal practices and norms shift the blame to the victim and not the perpetrator, Butler's work makes these observations more profound. These observations, in turn, do not reflect some common reality or ontology per se but do reveal norms—particularly norms of violence—that serve as disciplinary mechanisms for women. The issue of domestic abuse, considered with Guillaumin's concept of "sexage," also uncovers a facet of bio-political significance in the contemporary United States as the body itself becomes the site of political meaning. Bio-political gendered norms thus structure understandings of violence, particularly who is allowed to wield violence and act in self-defense and who is not.

VIOLENCE AS POLITICAL VIOLENCE—REALISM?

Men's control of the production and use of tools and weapons is confirmed as the necessary condition of their power, based upon violence (the male monopoly of weapons) and upon the underequipment of women (the male monopoly of tools). –Paola Tabet, quoted in Guillaumin, 164

How are you going to be nonviolent in Mississippi, as violent as you were in Korea? How can you justify being nonviolent in Mississippi and Alabama, when your churches are being bombed, and your little girls are being murdered, and at the same time you are going to get violent with Hitler, and Tojo, and somebody else you don't even know?

If violence is wrong in America, violence is wrong abroad. If it is wrong to be violent defending black women and black children and black babies and black men, then it is wrong for America to draft us and make us violent abroad in defense of her. And if it is right for America to draft us, and teach us how to be violent in defense of her, then it is right for you and me to do whatever is necessary to defend our own people right here in this country. –Malcolm X[115]

The worst curse that was laid upon woman was that she should be excluded from these warlike forays. For it is not in giving life but in risking life that man is raised above the animal; that is why superiority has been accorded in humanity not to the sex that brings forth but to that which kills. –Simone de Beauvoir, 64

The violence which governed the ordering of the colonial world, which tirelessly punctuated the destruction of the indigenous social fabric, and demolished unchecked the systems of reference of the country's economy, lifestyles, and modes of dress, this same violence will be vindicated and appropriated when, taking history into their own hands, the colonized swarm into the forbidden cities. To blow the colonial world to smithereens is henceforth a clear image within the grasp and imagination of every colonized subject. –Frantz Fanon, 5–6

These quotes all indicate that violence itself structures political inclusion and exclusion and that the denial of the right to bodily integrity on the one hand and to self-defense on the other are not merely forms of rightlessness or exploitation but a more thorough relation of domination (a relation of bodily appropriation, as indicated by Guillaumin's term *sexage*). The quoted authors do not see the Enlightenment as a higher developmental plane to which we could all move, once violence were to be replaced by knowledge, therapy, and communication. Rather, Enlightenment values serve as obfuscating mechanisms of universality and peace even as they provide the instruments for violence with impunity, a culture of control, and discourses of victim-blaming. The quotes above indicate a realism that understands but does not glorify violence and its political importance in the Enlightenment context. In this way, violence is not merely the measure of political inclusion, but violence as self-defense and self-definition are the only ways that the target of abuse can go from being a spectator to an actor.[116]

As the first quote suggests, these power dynamics signify the concentration and legitimation of power in the hands of one party as exercised over another.[117] In turn, this power imbalance illustrates how abuse, control, and violence are linked to societal power relations and thus are political in nature even if they occur in "private." The revision of Weber's famous observation about the modern state having the monopoly on violence brings attention to the crucial and yet often-denied link between political power and various forms of gender inequality. The division of who gets to legitimately wield violence and who is denied the right to resistance or self-defense shapes the contours of inclusion and exclusion. In fact, the realism of the "wretched of the earth" illuminates how domestic abuse is a political matter in which some violence is legitimated and the violence of self-defense is not.[118]

A realist reading of domestic abuse would accept that violence and inequality are not abnormal aspects of intimate or societal relations in the contemporary United States. Policymakers or counselors would not argue, for example, that egalitarian, mutual forms of interaction such as consent, a (marriage) contract, or communication preclude the possibility of violence. Accepting that asymmetrical violence does occur would not then condone it, but would at least acknowledge that it is not an anomaly. My aim is not to glorify violence or to elevate the right of self-defense to a lofty status but to piece together a vision of realism from the position of the margins, the wretched of the earth, and the second sex. Passions would not be denied or gendered but, like violence, viewed as part of the variable, fluctuating human condition.

Likewise, a realist reading would not focus on singular, isolated acts of violence in order to define violence away or deny it. A realist in the tradition of Machiavelli or Foucault does not find intrinsic meaning in history or history's progress but certainly advocates viewing power relations in broader contexts, including contexts of hierarchy or class stratification. That is, realism does not merely entail acknowledging violence but also entrenched inequalities and how emotional coercion, psychological manipulation and denigration, and economic abuse are all "war by other means."

Recent discussions about the resurgence of "political realism" are relevant to this issue, in that violence, passions, and discursive subordination are all key parts of abuse and policies regarding abuse. The renewed interest in realism comes at a time when political theory and philosophy are being criticized for their tendency to elevate ethics and education over and above politics. This ethical turn effectively depoliticizes the exercise of analysis itself, accepting that ethical solutions and education should rightly displace politics. These concerns are directly relevant to analyses of domestic abuse that first mistake consent, intimacy, and rationality (or communication) as eradicating coercion or displacing violence. As discussed in the previous chapter, there is a failure to recognize that one party may be operating in Enlightenment terms while the other party's actions and communication aim at destruction of the core of the target's identity and being. For example, abused women may legitimately feel afraid and marginalized (their emotions are thus rational), while abusers often feel satisfaction after coercive, emotionally denigrating or violent acts (thus evading the typical model of criminal actions and guilt).[119] The second issue, which maps onto the critique of the "ethical turn" in political theory, is the sorts of solutions that are egalitarian, mutual, and communicative for abuse situations. The ethical turn in philosophy is mirrored in solutions to abuse: counseling and mediation, co-parenting classes, and batterer intervention programs that replace the political and displace democracy.[120] This turn indicates a shift—albeit not an absolute one—from "Why don't you just leave him?" to "Why don't you just talk to him?" While this shift seems to place a burden on the abuser to investigate his own actions and change, as I argue throughout this book, these methods continue to rely on disciplinary power and panopticism against domestic abuse targets in more insidious ways, at times reinforcing their status as controllable, dependent, infantile, and pathological.

As I discuss in Chapter 4, a primary issue is that moralism often actually justifies violence and control—the two work together all too well. This is evident in a society that tolerates and even encourages the intimate control of women, including by violence and spatial immobility. But domestic violence solutions also rely on security and order, paradoxically reinforcing the linkage between morality and violence. This is exemplified in asking a woman who has already been isolated from her family and friends (including her own children at times), economically marginalized (even if wealthy), and treated as a subhuman to be shuttled into a system that is similarly isolated, where she also gives up her autonomy. Essentially, stability and order justify control and are the opposite of dialogue, mutuality, and creative tension. The law-and-order version of realism seems like liberal doublespeak: we are a representative democracy guided by the rule of law, but US laws also permit a politics of order in cases of emergency, in which elite leaders and agents can operate outside of the guidelines of democracy. The term *justice*, in this context, seems like a straw man: no single notion of justice guides our polity and instead, we turn to the mechanisms of liberal representation—rights—as evidence of political legitimacy. The sort of realism that would evade these issues would not pretend that certain terms—whether they are *justice, ethics, order* or *stability*—are inherently neutral or even democratic.

The danger of conflating ethics and politics—or easily linking the two, without acknowledging how they may potentially conflict—is the use of "apolitical or extrapolitical models of how ideal theory could be enacted in the world."[121] Take, for example, the use of education to replace democratic agency: "here, educative models, in which public reason through debate and discussion is thought to lead to the dissemination and transformation of political values, take the place of politics."[122] Alternatively, normative political theory may seek the best policy or moral framework for political elites, evading the messier process of conflict, dialogue, and compromise. In the latter case, the appeal to power elites assumes that they operate more freely than the demos. Both sorts of interventions presuppose that one set of norms can be found that represent a sort of universal morals or ethics, which must be taught or imposed but not questioned, reformed, altered, or rejected by the demos.

Rather, a Machiavellian realist approach would entail a more fragmented and yet constructive politics, with an active and creative demos. Morality in and of itself would not be eschewed unless it directly conflicted with this vision of democratic realism—for example, if it justified gender control, abuse, and violence and violation with impunity. But neither would it seek to operate on the basis of any human nature, nor would it seek to educate people or tame their instincts. Rather, it would guarantee the bodily integrity of all, without seeking consensus or appealing to rationality. In this way, passions and reason would commingle, and such an approach would enact power politics on behalf of equality and democratic action. It would not offer therapeutic or educational programs as the primary tools to reform abusers or seek to blame targets; in fact, it would recognize that these are depoliticizing moves that do not solve the underlying political issues. Further, realism would eschew any "absolute ends" for a consideration of the means, celebrating not merely goals, rights, and institutions but democratic "tumult" in Machiavelli's words.[123] If this involved the demos, targets of violence would determine their own political meaning and how, why, and when they need help. Abusers would not be asked to be reasonable or be sent to batterer intervention programs as an ultimate solution, but rather would be prevented from engaging in controlling and violent behaviors altogether. No moral or educational crusade would need to be involved—rather, the law would prevent the systematic and yet terroristic behavior of one group over another on the basis of citizenship as both protective (rights) and more importantly, as a positive, active notion of political status.

Rather than focus on *The Prince*, for example, the sort of realist perspective I am theorizing draws on Machiavelli's work in the *Discourses*, particularly his focus on tumult during the Roman Empire and how the "disunion of the Senate and people" created "extraordinary results."[124] Instead of providing a historical argument for the national security or law-and-order politics of some realist arguments today, his analysis of the Roman Empire celebrates the seizure of power by the demos and the provision of mechanisms for the people to vent their emotions.[125] By allowing for these tumults, the people were more active as a whole and each group became the "most assured guardians of Roman liberty."[126]

Similarly, the civic religion of the Roman Empire was far more politically effective in keeping a lively and engaged citizenry than the values of the Catholic Church of Machiavelli's time:[127]

> For, as our Religion shows the truth and the true way (of life), it causes us to esteem less the honors of the world: while the Gentiles (Pagans) esteeming them greatly, and having placed the highest good in them, were more ferocious in their actions. . . . the ancient Religion did not beatify men except those full of worldly glory, such as were the captains of armies and princes of Republics. Our Religion has glorified more humble and contemplative men rather than men of action. It also places the highest good in humility, lowliness, and contempt of human things: the other places it in the greatness of soul, the strength of body, all the other things which make men very brave.[128]

In contrast, Machiavelli finds that Catholicism encourages its adherents to "think more of enduring their beatings than in avenging them."[129] Thus, whereas in *The Prince* he urges the Church to retreat from the temporal realm, in the *Discourses* he also critiques Christian values from a theological standpoint. As Machiavelli argues, however, this is in part because the wielder of morality is hypocritical: preaching selflessness, love over material well-being, and the notion that the meek shall inherit the earth.[130] At the same time the Church was selling indulgences; engaging in torture (as he indicates about King Ferdinand of Spain, he went too far to be called a great leader[131]); and effectively dividing territories with no program for unity (as he accused Pope Julius of doing), because the Church was exercising an authority that it shouldn't. It was preventing unity of the patria by unwise, selfish crusades in the name of Christianity. However, as Nietzsche later would, Machiavelli also critiques the very foundations of Christian morality, which he argued were founded on passivity; a deep hatred of the material world in favor of a future in heaven; and a desire for consensus and uniformity. Instead, paganism was a better spiritual orientation for politics, because it celebrated life on earth, commingling the spiritual and earthly; it was premised on action and affirmation—not passivity and withdrawal; and it involved multiple gods and truths rather than a single God or moral code.

Drawing on this source of passionate, realist politics, an insightful realist perspective would not divorce itself from any ethics whatsoever (in particular, a democratic ethos), but rather would develop a distinctly political logic.[132] As authors like Sheldon Wolin and Mary Dietz have noted, against Straussian arguments, Machiavelli did not totally reject morality but rather wanted to replace the moral systems of his time that undermined any possibility of politics—that fragmented and divided to no positive or constructive end.[133] Paganism provided a better context for the flourishing of a politics in which institutions were constantly challenged; tumults were welcome as conflicts that brought about necessary change; and in the example of the Roman Empire, the people were actively involved in *creating* political spaces.

To take a step back, politics itself was not equivalent to order, stability, or security but rather designated the power dynamics of a celebratory, participatory, and active demos that were at times in harmony and at other times in conflict. In terms of my project, this approach does not deny inequalities but views them as temporary rather than as biological essences; conflict is not evil in and of itself; and violence may not be desirable but is certainly part of human interaction. A realist approach would not assume that a woman who has been subjected to a range of traumatic practices can then simply negotiate with her abuser on equal terms. A realist perspective celebrates the tumult of finding solutions outside of the Enlightenment dyad and the liberal contract; it provides for an unequal and coercive set of conditions and proceeds from this perspective. Machiavelli's politics in the *Discourses* is oriented toward full civic participation, celebrating those who work for their liberty, shunning hereditary wealth, and promoting a lively, engaged, changing polity. This perspective challenges law-and-order solutions, hierarchical shelter rules, and family-oriented law and therapy—tumult would suggest that "creative tension" (as Martin Luther King famously put it[134]) must come from the demos (in this case, the targets).

Some contemporary interpretations of power politics (realism) miss these dynamics of Machiavelli's thought, often ignoring Machiavelli's "morality" only to justify a "pure" politics of order, security, and emergency. I discuss these limitations because they are relevant to the law-and-order approaches to domestic violence (e.g., mandatory and dual arrests) and batterer intervention programs in lieu of criminal sentencing.

Realism is not helpful if it maintains the status quo minus any democratic orientation whatsoever. William Galston reviews and seemingly advocates such a political realism, with its attendant binaries of peace-violence, emotions-rationality, order-justice, and so on, which do not seem to truly deviate from current power arrangements but merely remove their ethical bases (with an orientation toward justice) and democratic bases (dialogue, debate, or even citizen action).[135] Galston's review of this new realism does this in at least two important ways: first, by grouping together most of the literature without distinguishing between authors such as Jeremy Waldron and Bernard Williams and the realism of authors such as Chantal Mouffe or Bonnie Honig.[136] In doing this, he misses a chance to distinguish between dialogue, democratic instability, and healthy tensions on the one hand and negative conflict and violence on the other. Further, he engages in static binaries that make what counts as political or even "real" a negative and narrow determination. Second, despite Galston's claim that he is merely reviewing the literature, he operates according to the base assumption that order must replace justice to define the political. Instead I believe that this ignores a variety of very interesting concepts of the political and also replaces one absolute, static universal with another, as if it is neutral and somehow doesn't require the same sorts of deliberation and mutuality that justice would.

In this sort of interpretation, the worst-case scenario sets the tone, justifying authority in times of emergency; claiming that a superpower may get more done than a human rights organization; or defending the alleged necessity of torture, mass indefinite detention, and military trials with secret evidence. Similarly, blunt approaches to domestic abuse do not actually tackle deeper roots of the problems of gender control—in fact, they increase poverty and retaliatory assaults, and they congeal coercive dynamics in the family and community. That is, the eradication of morality from politics does not increase the power of the demos but in fact brings the demos to a level of spectator, witness, or object of power. The political centered on the emergency thus justifies the concentration of power in a few hands, a lack of transparency or checks and balances, and the willing suspension of the law in the name of security. Even beyond these observations, these sorts of arguments reinforce the centrality of the nation-state even as it has become an outdated political term in many ways because it is a system that is either anarchic or guided by a superpower.[137] Rather than investigating the degree to which "crisis" is manufactured by the very power arrangements being maintained, it is taken as a self-evident given.

More broadly, this form of contemporary revision of realism, of which Galston's text is symptomatic,[138] first defines realism as if there were a "real." That is, the real is taken for granted as a static, obvious object to be uncovered and analyzed. This depoliticizes power relations and authority by ignoring their socially constructed, local, and historically specific nature. Second, related to claims about the "real," the political is narrowed to a specific and special realm rather than serving an architectonic role. The realism of these authors appears to be an elite activity, that is, related to the opposition between elite groups (analytic theorists versus realists) that claim to represent the real, but end in reinforcing the status quo such that liberal democracy is not questioned, a preference for institutional analysis is still at the heart of these analyses, and grassroots dynamics and solidarity are ignored.

Conventional realist theorists hold the notion that violence is inevitable but also often claim that human rights and peace projects are not similarly inevitable. Human rights are posited as fanciful, utopian ideas that have never been implemented successfully. This makes violence almost godlike—it cannot really be controlled if it is inevitable—and it becomes its own goal and cause because all a government can do is to stabilize it, while human rights are viewed as unnatural and so ideal or abstract that they cannot be implemented. Finally, realist theories are often interpreted in masculine terms in which the feminine is not merely rejected but is viewed as the antithesis of these approaches to understanding power and politics.

The realism I propose has similar premises—designating the political as its own unique area of study, accepting violence as part of life, and seeking to avoid idealist theory—but also deviates from the ideas above. Starting with the base of Machiavelli's *Discourses* and Nietzsche's will to power, authors such as Weber, de Beauvoir, Fanon, and Malcolm X do not see the eradication of violence in modern life but rather the importance of acknowledging the asymmetry of who holds the monopoly on violence and who does not. Against Weber's famous linkage between the modern state and violence, Freud, de Beauvoir, Fanon, and Malcolm X believe that those who get to wield violence in everyday life and those who are allowed to defend themselves with impunity, are autonomous political subjects. In contrast, those subject to violence with impunity are denied the "tools of transcendence" (referred to in De Beauvoir's quote) which dehumanizes them. Symmetry arguments and empirical research asserting symmetry, dual arrests, and calling women who defend themselves "violent" or "violent resisters" (rather than labeling their actions as self-defense) are evidence of this. Refusing to reject these terms, each of these authors believes that "equality" will only be achieved when the victims or witnesses can become actors, with the full power of violence and the right to resistance. All three link this violence to a broader politico-economic context that allows some to beat, torture, and kill and others to be their targets.

In this alternative form of realism—the realism of the margins and subaltern—human rights, civil disobedience, and other civil society groups do not necessarily have to be conceived as the antithesis of violence. Instead, they promote debate and enact "realist" engagements with daily conflicts, passions, and violence that conceive of the human or civil as products of conflict. This is a realism that does not construct utopian projects outside of power or violence but which directly engages violence and seeks other methods to redress its consequences.[139] This sort of realism is evident in Karuna Mantena's exploration of Gandhi's program of nonviolence. She explores Gandhi's civil disobedience as a direct engagement with domination, negative conflict, and violence rather than as a denial of it. In her reading, it is not a utopian escape requiring political withdrawal, but rather a significantly "realist" encounter with individuals and groups that often wield violence, coercion, and inhumanity in the name of absolute ethics.[140] Mike Davis has noted a similar solution with Central American refugees fleeing civil war violence: evangelical religions have dealt far more effectively than other more formal and distant religious institutions with their trauma, unprocessed emotions, and continued political marginalization in the United States.[141] Davis's analysis recognizes the need to deal directly with emotions, passions, and violence. Religious communication then does not replace emotions or passions but instead is bound up with them. These evangelical efforts in turn could foster a grassroots political integration process in the face of the American state's designation of these individuals as nonpersons and/or criminals before they were given legal status. Similarly, approaches to understanding domestic abuse would necessarily link asymmetrical power dynamics to concrete instantiations of violence to fully appreciate this political problem. Against the easy dichotomies between peace or violence, rationality or emotions, order or justice, I believe that numerous power processes and hierarchies are established with domestic abuse (both in terms of actual abuse and abuse policy) that escape these easy divisions. Emotions and passions would not be feminized and thus pathologized but viewed as a crucial part of the political. Targets of abuse would not be *forced* into mediation, co-parenting classes, or couples counseling, not to mention some experimental "forgiveness programs"[142] (which are part of restorative justice approaches) but rather would be given a chance to act, leave, and protect themselves and their children without punishment.

In the case of domestic abuse, realism is both helpful and not helpful in several ways. From one perspective, realist theory is already in operation when policymakers, judges, and the public argue that boys will be boys. Male violence, abuse, and passions in the home are not actually denied but assimilated by public policy, family court judges, and society more broadly. For example, a man's (allegedly) out-of-control passions are interpreted as a sign of love or even interest in a child or a woman, and his violence is an extension of the family relation: it is not worth investigating or preventing—that would be an invasion of privacy or an attempt to "legislate morality." This sort of interpretation of intimate abuse and violence allows for passions and violence, not to mention asymmetry. Nevertheless, this realist interpretation of power is not applied to targets of violence. Instead, their passions seemingly evoke control and violence (that is, power silences emotions, passions, and moral concerns). What is evident is that control and normative power help to legitimate violence and discount or criminalize self-defense.

As Foucault points out, knowledge-power thus effects a greater context of control in which violence is a part but not the central mechanism. Recognizing a culture of control does not diminish the importance of violence but rather connects media images, discursive threats and denigration, and claims of equality in the midst of trauma to violence. Foucault notes about modern power that "wars are no longer waged in the name of a sovereign who must be defended; they are waged on behalf of the existence of everyone; entire populations are mobilized for the purpose of wholesale slaughter in the name of life necessity: massacres have become vital."[143] Similarly, I suggest that many of the policies treating domestic abuse and normative assumptions in the popular media are linked in bio-political and disciplinary modes of neoliberal governmentality. Despite MacKinnon's critique of poststructuralism,[144] I find that her theories help to identify the biologically and culturally reductive subjectivities produced by bio-political policies and assumptions, and thus her work is a subset of this realism. But to the degree that her account is lopsided—investigating the victims and not the abusers—a realist account doesn't seek to avoid a full account of violence, which necessarily begins with the abusers themselves.

CONCLUSIONS

I have identified as least a few obstacles to understanding domestic abuse as a political issue, both in terms of its exercise but also in how it is treated as the law. First, the focus has been on targets, evidencing that abusers' passions, control, and violent acts are denied or assimilated by societal norms, the laws, and the "help" targets can get. This imbalance, of course, not only reflects gender inequality but produces and enacts it. Second, the conventional focus on race and class (for example) are further excuses to retain attention on targets and to pathologize certain groups, drawing attention away from broader norms about gender inequality, control, and acceptable forms of intimate violence. Thus, I want to emphasize the degree of denial that violence is a crucial part of contemporary US politics, at least in political theories. The welfare-warfare distinction sets the context for claims that make violence anomalous and only attributable to the poor, racial or ethnic others, "white trash," and the uneducated. But these efforts at conceptual isolation also have other effects. In practice, those deemed as irrational and violent have historically been denied the tools of aggression and self-defense;[145] their violence and violent resistance to oppression is often viewed as traitorous, terroristic, and illegitimate.

On the other hand, violence wielded by powerful groups despite their lack of political legitimacy is considered justifiable or at least tolerable. Vigilantes and wife-beaters, for example, may not be considered model citizens but their actions are viewed as being rooted in God-given, inalienable rights.[146] In particular, gender violence is tolerated in the public and private spheres; it is assimilated into military culture; and it is a support for the neoliberal move to the feminization of labor.

A third obstacle to seeing intimate partner violence as political is refusing to see how bio-power and disciplinary power function together in this instance. Claiming that bio-power and disciplinary power are distinct and even mutually exclusive is related to other dichotomies in political theory (e.g., the welfare-warfare split, and ethics versus realism in analytic theory). In looking at Foucault's theories as a whole and how bio-power and disciplinary power work together, his analyses may be the basis of a more "realist" perspective in the context of modern power relations. Only then can we view not just the targets but the hidden actors (abusers) and those who are behind the "gaze" (extralegal and legal agents who support and assimilate violence).

All of these points could be more broadly summarized as widening the scope of what counts for the political (as Foucault did, for example, with prisoners, "madness" and psychology), rather than narrowing it as recent proponents of realism seem to advocate. Ironically, viewing power not merely as negative—including conflict-ridden, violent, and irrational—but also positive—including dialogical, affirmative, and constructive—will allow for an adequately political view of an issue that directly affects a significant number of women and which is often supported by the media and enabled by policies and aid. In the next chapter, I discuss some of these ideas in more concrete terms, providing context for the debates that follow in this book. This investigation will help to make the case that this issue is not only political but also says something about American women's status today and the status of feminized subjects. In the following chapter, I discuss gender-based asylum claims that help to synthesize the notion of the political and its relation to domestic abuse.

CHAPTER 2

The Context of the Problem

INTRODUCTION

As I have discussed in the Introduction and Chapter 1, mainstream policy responses and conventional scholarship on intimate partner abuse today are not merely limited, but often reveal a misunderstanding of the unequal and gendered nature of domestic abuse. In this chapter, I review and analyze these tensions in terms of historical limitations in family law that block attempts to help asymmetrical abuse; broad changes in welfare law and how these changes have affected family law; transformations and divisions in shelters as representative of changes in extra-juridical help for targets of abuse; and conventional approaches to therapy that add to these contradictions and tensions. Despite the fact that this issue is relatively new and the web of formal and informal political actors making up this system is disaggregated and sometimes in tension, I trace some overarching trends in these different but often mutually reinforcing areas.

Very broadly, the discussion of domestic abuse is not new in Western European and American modern texts. Like other trends in the private sphere and civil society, authors like Wollstonecraft and John Stuart Mill questioned how democratic polities could challenge tyranny in the political sphere but tolerate it in the home.[1] Authors like Mill and turn of the twentieth century reformers linked abuse to economic inequality and sometimes alcoholism.[2] Up through the 1960s, these discussions were radical in certain respects, tying abuse to broader issues of women's inequality and incomplete democracy. More conventional debates did not make these broad linkages but always conceived of abuse as asymmetrical.[3] While at times these texts perhaps overfocused on the poor and immigrants, they did not interpret abuse as equal (i.e., symmetrical) in any way: they did not assume that women could simply resist physical attacks, nor did they hold that women could easily flee their families and communities, and most important, they understood how political and economic inequality were tied to intimate abuse.

Various changes in family law in the nineteenth and early twentieth centuries, as I discuss below, reflected reformers' efforts to protect women, if not give them active political rights.[4] However, these laws also often interpreted rights as a zero-sum game—women's gains could be construed as their husbands' losses.[5] Additionally, women's advances were (and often still are) interpreted as leading to the potential breakup of the nuclear family.[6] Family law in the United States has attempted to address all these needs with the consequence that today, intimate relations are far more varied in their legal status, but courts seek to keep these "families" intact, even if the parents live apart or were never married. Adjudication is "deformalized," which means (1) that the family is dealt with as a unit and individual rights cannot be protected; (2) any conflicts are dealt with on a case-by-case basis, often treating information or disputes as if they were new (in contrast to criminal law which accounts for past history); (3) legal precedent is taken into account less in family law (again, in contrast to criminal law); (4) extra-legal opinions and actors are an important part of this deformalized system, often wielding a great deal of unrecognized political power while also insinuating themselves into private matters in an invasive way.[7] While these approaches make family law extraconstitutional and preserve family hierarchies, changes in other areas—research, welfare policy, and shelters—not to mention the greater influence of neoliberalism since the 1980s contribute to a legal situation that now asserts equality and symmetry in abuse situations while continuing to treat familial disputes in hierarchical, sexist ways. That is, discourses of individual rights and autonomy obfuscate the degree to which legal agents make decisions based on families as a unit, drawing on traditional gender roles and leaving family hierarchies intact. The result is to blame targets for their abuse while forcing them to negotiate with their abuser and to submit to egalitarian solutions.

How we arrived at this situation is far more complicated than just these trends in family law, however, and again, involve changes in the welfare system. These changes include the protection (granted, a problematic sort of protection) of women's rights in the 1970s and early '80s to keeping the family intact from the 1990s on. At the same time, the shelter system went from a grassroots, women-led model to a more impersonal, hierarchical model from the 1990s on.[8] These recent developments have entailed communicative interventions, from legal mediation to counseling for targets.

Like the divisions between the 1970s grassroots approach to intimate abuse and more recent, clinical policy interventions, counseling for domestic abuse has been divided between the conjoint model, which seeks to keep the family together, and a more individualized, feminist approach that counsels women apart from their partners and seeks policy solutions that do not force women to negotiate with their abusers. But regardless of the approach, most counseling and domestic abuse programs target women and not abusers. In this way, ironically, women are both problem and solution while their abusers often stand outside this system entirely. This redoubling process then deploys and maintains two different realities:[9] targets of abuse are subject to Enlightenment, communicative, rationally based interventions while abusers and their violent acts are assimilated to these norms but also remain outside as anti-Enlightenment figures (these issues are discussed in more depth in the next two chapters). The result is that very broadly, the grassroots, women-led movement that viewed abuse as inherently asymmetrical and tied to political and economic inequality has largely been eclipsed by a return to the family (granted, families that are now nontraditional) while also asserting women's equality and therefore symmetry in abusive and violent situations.[10]

Today, changes in welfare, family law, and policies that adhere to symmetrical models of abuse work together with conjoint therapy. In fact, discourses of feminist autonomy could be cynically redeployed to mask power relations based on older, more traditional adjudication and counseling processes that make individual rights claims almost impossible in any formal sense. These latter trends are perhaps neoliberal, as Kristin Bumiller argues, in that they seek a neat, low-cost solution to family disputes while also leaving intact major gender divisions and hierarchies.[11]

Other dynamics of subordination followed a similar trajectory—particularly the civil rights era of the 1960s and 1970s that identified the multiple systems of subordination in race, ethnicity, immigration status, and class bias (among other things) but which became politically neutralized during the 1990s amidst discourses of equality and individual responsibility. Neoliberal rhetoric cultivated discourses that simultaneously proclaimed the end of inequality and turned any lingering issues into personal or cultural backwardness or a culture of dependency.[12] While these trends are not absolute, they are dominant—particularly in an era of government bankruptcy and economic polarization. They neatly retain hierarchies while blaming those who assert their rights against abuse, exploitation, and discrimination. I will first discuss family law; then changes in welfare and shelters; and then analyze trends in psychology regarding domestic abuse.

LIBERAL RIGHTS AND FAMILY LAW

In *On the Jewish Question*, Marx brilliantly examines the development of political rights and universal suffrage as positive, in terms of marking the progress of critical consciousness and the hope of universality, but also incredibly limited in a few important ways. Despite the egalitarian premises of citizenship and the presupposition of a universal connection between citizens, political rights as actually practiced were limited and their premise of equality did not characterize daily life. Further, their conception was not truly universal but based on an overly individualized, property-based notion of rights as commodities, which were used in competition with others. He analyzes how political equality and citizenship promise—albeit abstractly—the transcendence of older divisions in society, allowing for both autonomy and social solidarity, but with no practical manifestations of this egalitarian inclusion in daily life. Furthermore, even these abstract rights are already deficient because universality can only be defined negatively against particularism. That is, the deficiency lies in the fact that universality is not truly transcendent of old divisions, which would entail a negation of the negation, but instead is only defined by what it is not. For instance, religious toleration is granted in response to religious prejudice, but this retains rather than eradicates the importance of religion as a political category. But everyday life is not even based on this problematically defined universalism. Civil society becomes the sphere of lived daily life in which rights are conflated with possessions, producing a radical individualism that is essentially egoism. In turn, asserting rights claims in a context of instrumentally deploying egotistical and competitive power dynamics leads to the notion that one person's gain is another's loss. To the degree that rights are meaningful they deny or ignore social divisions, exploitation, and inequality, perpetuating class hierarchy and the status quo. More recent interventions on rights note that identitarian challenges to inequality refuse to see complex social interactions and subject positions that defy classification under any one identity.[13] This static sort of thinking simply adds identities or harms together; often subscribes to a view of power operating as a nested hierarchy; and continues to conceive of the state as a monolith.[14] Returning to Marx's essay helps us to keep a focus on how power and identity are configured and often taken as natural or given.

Using Marx's critique as a framework, Frances Olson's older essay[15] on the family and market highlights these issues, particularly as they pertain to the history of family law and women's rights. As Marx's complex analysis indicates, there is a balance between purportedly universal rights and individual autonomy, the promise of equality and inclusion versus lived daily reality, and the problem that rights often mask broader structural inequalities. Olson innovatively recasts these issues by comparing societal and legal notions of the family to conceptions of the market. Importantly, each sphere is the purported opposite of the other: market relations are based on individualized notions of agency and competition while the family is conceived of as a group and a site of love and sympathy.

As Olson remarks, historically the market has been viewed as an arena of greed and self-interest but also individual achievement and autonomy. In contrast, the family is understood as hierarchical and emotional— attachments are emphasized over individual rights—but it is also conceived of as a bastion of selflessness and a haven from competition. In the American legal tradition, the family model has been cast as "altruistic" (thus with an acceptance of family hierarchies and inequalities) because altruism has been thought to be more effective than individualized rights at keeping a family intact.[16] Family law has been influenced by dominant conceptions of each sphere (individual rights versus conceiving of the family as an undifferentiated whole), experimenting with individual rights in the context of the family, with contradictory and therefore ineffective results. Granting individual rights at a time when women had no political or economic power outside of the family or attempting to introduce individual rights in a group context often led to increased interpersonal conflict and maintained structural inequalities. As Olson rightly noted, individualism and equality were pitted against paternalistic benevolence and inequality. Since that time, family law has attempted to take into account this antagonism between individual rights and the family as a hierarchical unit. However, in the midst of the continuing inequality of women as a class, particularly with intersecting levels of subordination, this was a contradictory effort at best. As Olson describes, governmental views of the family went from a hierarchical, group (family unit) notion of power to more individual remedies in the 1800s. However, as reformers learned, individual rights did bring gains but also reinforced structural subordination. Eventually a revised family model was adopted, which sought to transcend the problems of the previous two stages but which is marked by many of the older, unresolved issues.

In liberal democracies such as the United States, the early views of the family roughly followed Sir William Blackstone's legal formulation that marriage made man and woman one: their contractual relationship led to the suspension of individual rights and natural law.[17] Reformers in the 1800s accepted some of the basic familial configurations while attempting to ensure that women gained a "separate legal status," including expanding the possibility of child custody to mothers (if it was in the "best interest of the child"), allowing women to file for separation, to testify in courts, and to have limited property rights.[18] But in the context of major inequalities, while these individualized efforts were indicative of progress, they also reinforced structural inequalities such that men's power over property, the family, and child custody was not significantly challenged. In fact, Olson notes that individual rights inserted in the context of these hierarchical, group-based power relations could divide people and make the more powerful party less sympathetic to the weaker party.[19] For example, if men still retained major economic power and greater property ownership, allowing women some control over their personal property merely consolidated inequality, but now with the appearance of greater political legitimacy.[20] In the area of child custody, if mothers were recognized as having some guardianship rights over children in the event of the husband's death, for example, this did not change the father's ultimate decision-making power over the children either in the family, in the case of divorce, or after his death.[21] In fact, in the context of major political and economic inequities, the introduction of individual rights could make things worse. For example, if uncontested divorce were introduced, thus allowing the premise of greater equality for each party to leave a relationship, this could allow a stronger legal basis for men to abandon families than in the past.[22] In the same case, men's unequal earning power is even more to their advantage after the parties separate or divorce, so the appearance of legal equality merely masks the growth of economic inequality. And less easy to quantify, Olson argues, is that although men's social standing is not significantly altered after divorce, women's social status often diminishes in several respects.[23]

Nevertheless these changes did allow for some opening to the "erosion" of "intrafamily tort immunity,"[24] significantly changing perceptions: instead of the view that a husband had a moral duty and right to chastise his wife, this chastisement was now viewed as assault and battery.[25] While this adjustment in perception has not led to wholesale change, Olson's legal history demonstrates how family law changed, beginning in the late 1800s, to try to improve women's lives, even as men and women remained politically, economically, and socially unequal. Despite the fact that family hierarchy has been maintained, these shifts gradually helped to make assault less "socially legitimate," and this has certainly aided some individual women.[26] Drawing on Marx's juxtaposition of the hypothetical universality of political rights to profound particularisms and hierarchy in the civil sphere, Olson remarks that individualizing rights in the midst of a hierarchical, family-oriented legal context can blind judges and the police to the connections between various forms of subordination and the reluctance of wives and intimate partners to report abuse. On the other hand, Olson suggests that the intimacy presupposed in the familial model could hypothetically lead to lowered burdens of proof, thus permitting a wife "to obtain injunctive relief against a battering husband without making the showing normally required for such relief."[27] Thus the burden of proof could be lowered in cases of "interspousal violence."[28]

In the late 1800s, family law began experimenting with individual rights for family members as a result of the "legalization movement."[29] Because individual rights were introduced in a context of profound inequality, these rights merely reinforced wives' inequality and removed the incentive for the more powerful party—husbands—to act charitably. As a new tactic to avoid these pitfalls, the "deformalization" movement began in the early 1900s. As Olson notes, deformalization was and is a legal effort to give a family legal status (against "delegalization," which views it as entirely private[30]) but also to place the interests of the family unit above individual interests and rights. As discussed above, this shift would then involve not only legal interlocutors but also—to use Foucault's language and to interpret Olson's insight in a Foucaultian manner— "extralegal authorities" that would nevertheless wield a great deal of interpretive and normative power in seeking to keep the family intact. Deformalization also means not treating the family in formal legal terms, but allowing some wiggle room (in Olson's words "ad hoc adjustments" [31]) in how power dynamics and inequalities are treated. Essentially, deformalization would seemingly resolve some of the issues of the past, without threatening the family unit. From a more cynical perspective (my own), it would explode basic constitutional protections and individual rights, allowing for a parallel legal system that would entrench status quo gender roles and structures of subordination. Essentially, it is a solution that seeks to have it both ways: discursively asserting consent, contract, and thus a pretense of equality, at the same time that individual rights are trumped by family hierarchy, and traditional gender roles are inevitably perpetuated.

As Marx may have predicted, this movement has had great costs, even as it sought to resolve issues of the past. Importantly, today courts and legislators accordingly push consensual models of conflict resolution rather than asserting or protecting individual rights. Thus "it may force the weaker party to accept a resolution that gives her far less than she would be entitled to in a formal adjudication."[32] Even more significantly, "women who try to deal with battering husbands through the family court system may well find themselves the victims of continued battering"[33] as the family unit and the father's primacy go unchallenged. While Olson notes that these solutions merely perpetuate the status quo (which is marked by "domination" and "hierarchy"[34]), I would like to go one step further and argue that contemporary solutions to family conflict and intimate abuse, such as mediation, co-parenting classes, and counseling can make what is coercive and radically unequal appear to be equal. In the next chapter, I will analyze these dynamics in terms of Habermasian communicative theory and Foucault's notion of disciplinary power. The egalitarian solutions that are often mandated by courts today make unequal abuse, harassment, economic deprivation, and violence the responsibility of both parties, thus assimilating violence and abuse rather than solving them.

As Olson rightly contends, "deformalization violates notions of the rule of law and may result in ad hoc readjustments that are themselves oppressive."[35] The combination of circumstances she has analyzed demonstrates how significant injustices can occur, even when the parties involved are citizens or have legal status. The configuration of the law and its procedures suspends the autonomy of the citizen and the rule of law, as Olson remarks. In this way, solutions that seemingly meet Habermas's criteria for communicative action are rooted in and produce hierarchy and coercion. Olson further argues, as Foucault would, that "the welfare of family members may come to depend upon the uncontrolled discretion of state agencies, with the result that the state may directly dominate family life."[36] Even with greater federal devolution of welfare responsibilities and a withdrawal of the state in significant ways, one can appreciate the continued role of teachers, counselors, the police, guardians ad litem, and many others in fostering these arbitrary and unjust power dynamics.[37]

It is only in this broader legal context that the current inequalities in adjudicating intimate abuse and violence—even among the unmarried—can be understood. The preference for deformalization and keeping the family unit intact are evident today, even as the family unit has changed and many couples never marry in the first place. The analysis that follows will necessarily be overly broad, given that different localities vary in how they approach intimate violence. First, as I discuss in Chapter 4, despite the breakdown of traditional marriage and greater varieties of intimate partnership, the state can enforce notions of contract, consent, and familial solidarity even more harshly (including as a punitive mechanism) than in the past. Rather than replacing the man with the state, as was suggested by Piven and Cloward in the 1960s and 1970s, the state appears to encourage intimate solidarity, even in the context of poverty, high degrees of conflict, and abuse, in order to abjure its own responsibility in adjudicating individual rights, correcting structural subordination, or providing a social safety net.[38] This could be true even when the "family" was never intact in the first place, thus coercively instituting intimacy where there was none. Family unity is then elevated above individual rights to bodily integrity. Similarly, in the absence of individual rights, it is evident how perpetrators' violence is both assimilated and ignored, how their silence can be power, and how mothers in this situation are subjected to "maternal ideology" (that is, as part of a family unit with no separate identity) and can be punished far more harshly than abusers. While Olson's history is dated in certain respects, her theoretical analysis is highly relevant to the dynamics I investigate throughout this book. In sum, the state may be fragmented but can overall seek to achieve older forms of coverture based on the family/hierarchical and altruistic model through new means.[39]

Changes in child custody have mirrored the changes outlined above, moving from the father's exclusive custody to the mother's (when the "tender years doctrine" held that children fared better with the mother than the father[40]) and increasingly today to joint custody to remedy perceived mistakes of the past. Joint custody can be awarded not merely to reflect extant relations with a child but to reward a father for paying child support (although the two are not supposed to be linked[41]) and secondly, to promote and reward fatherhood and father's rights.[42] As Lundy Bancroft argues, the promotion of father's rights began to occur as early as the 1970s and by "the 1980s fathers were winning at least joint custody in a majority of the custody battles they undertook and winning sole custody more often than mothers, a situation that remains today."[43] Interestingly, Bancroft finds that "the fathers who are taking advantage of this imbalance are largely abusive ones; researchers have found that abusers are twice as likely as non-abusive men to seek [sole] custody."[44]

The concern for fathers' rights is more of an "ought" than an "is": the state promotes fatherhood in part to reinstate traditional gender roles, even in new intimate configurations, and perhaps more important, to ensure that the mother and child do not end up on welfare rolls.[45] Given the greater prevalence of joint custody and the sensitivity to father's rights, the alleged preference for mothers in court (which today still headlines any Google search) is no longer empirically true if it ever was, in any unqualified sense. Conversely, once paternity is established and the father is in good standing with the court (is paying child support and has regular visitation with a child), it is much more difficult to use instances of violence, neglect, or harassment to limit visitations.[46] This is, in part, because the family unit is held above any individual right but also because the men's/father's rights movement has reasserted a powerful influence over social and legal thinking.[47] As Bancroft notes, once these processes are set in motion, judges tend to compartmentalize abuse, holding that the husband's abuse of the wife, for example, will not lead to abuse of a child; abusing the mother near or in front of a child is not enough to change visitation; and other forms of control (short of violence) do not constitute child abuse.[48] Bancroft argues that this indicates a perverse hierarchy of values: "for some reason even a man who is physically violent to his partner is not considered a bad role model by most family courts, whereas a drug dealer would be, even though abusers do at least as much damage in society, including causing a similar number of deaths annually."[49]

Given the shortcomings of this system—which could be said to allow for arbitrary state power and reinforcing the value of the traditional nuclear family at the expense of individual rights—Olson notes that there may be some individual gains (mediation is cheaper than going to court and it is possible for women to gain something in mediation). But she also hints that the more negative aspects of this system can further be reinforced by "oppressive" community courts and a conservative locale. While the Violence against Women Act itself remains in contention and key parts have been invalidated,[50] the few programs that have been sponsored through VAWA funding have not led to greater abuse prevention or even higher incarceration rates for abusers.[51] Olson's predictions are borne out in Keith Guzik's 2007 examination of mandatory prosecution in domestic abuse cases in the Midwest.[52] Under VAWA, these policies have been implemented in many locales to treat domestic violence like any other crime[53] and to recognize the difficulty a target of abuse may have in charging her partner with abuse. But Guzik argues that conservative juries mitigate the radical potentiality of these policies.[54] He finds that even in cases in which the abuser confessed and the burden of proof was actually met, juries do not convict, for several reasons: (1) first, there's the "many-headed hydra" argument, in which it is argued that if a particular instance of intimate abuse is prosecuted, this will open the floodgates to thousands of new cases in an already overburdened court system; [55] (2) a man's right to "put his hands on his wife" will then be challenged, invoking the fear that any actions in the home could be construed as abuse[56]; and (3) despite the fact that these policies are supposed to prosecute abuse as if it were an individual crime, the victim's fear in pressing charges is cast as "lack of cooperation," which can weaken a case.[57] In a conservative locale, in which intimate violence is tolerated,[58] juries are primed to dismiss cases, particularly when attorneys make these arguments. Guzik also argues that mandatory arrests of abusers could "allow batterers to avoid internalizing blame and confronting their accountability for violence. The state's increase in governance over batterers might come at the cost of actually charging them."[59] In effect, even given ostensibly well-intended statutes, Guzick's account shows that the societal context shapes legal enforcement. Tolerance for intimate violence and a disproportionate focus on targets of abuse further complicate any easy solutions.

In sum, family law is legal and yet has extralegal characteristics in treating the family as a unit and thus undermining individual rights; in reinforcing traditional gender roles, even in the context of the increasing prevalence of nontraditional partnerships; and more broadly, as a result of these two underlying principles, in largely operating extraconstitutionally. When coercive mechanisms and violent assault occur, this framework is clearly not operating according to individual notions of responsibility and culpability. Coercion, extortion, and assault are thus reframed as conflict, seduction, and provocation.[60] Past histories are usually not reviewed by judges and court personnel will often grant a no-contact order, knowing that it will be violated.[61] These different factors can lead to a situation in which a target must constantly reexpose herself to harassment and violence to get state protection, because these decrees are not effective or long-lasting. Nevertheless, if a target has children, her flight either is highly illegal (she can be accused of kidnapping) or can lead to geographical restriction by a judge. Regardless, targets have to seek court permission to leave a county or state or face severe consequences.

Further, the degree to which courts then focus on the mother with far more scrutiny than the father, having higher expectations of the mother's duties and sacrifices than the father's, mirrors legal responses to rape.[62] In both cases, stranger assault is held to constitute a crime while even superficial knowledge of the perpetrator or "consent" to interact with him is held to mitigate any determination of injury. In cases of rape, coercion, and assault, the state of mind of the perpetrator is central to determining whether injury occurred, and counterclaims against his target have legal efficacy (even if we do not formally take mens rea into account in the United States).[63] Corroboration, documentation, and official reports are often required as proof because the target's word is insufficient to establish the truth of any harm. Nevertheless, a key difference between domestic abuse and rape (if and when they do not overlap[64]) is the repeated effects of coercion, abuse, and violence over time.

Domestic abuse is not something every woman in the United States will experience in her lifetime. If she does, however, her chances of getting help through the law (or the ability to charge her abuser in court) are minimal. Evan Stark argues that because ". . . assaults against partners are treated as a second-class misdemeanor. . . . the chance that a perpetrator will go to jail in any given incident is just slightly better than the chance of winning a lottery."[65] A target of violence may escape her situation, but it may be despite the law or only marginally because of it. Nor will it be because society overall is sympathetic to abused women[66]—in fact, once she has the "courage" to "admit" she is being abused, she will be subject to a myriad of reactions ranging from incredulity to ridicule and occasionally to constructive advice, kind words ("you don't deserve it"), or aid. Her abuser will most likely remain free whether or not she chooses to press charges; but the word *chooses* is disingenuous. There is little choice in this matter for the reasons discussed in the previous chapter: (1) with a violence-centered definition of abuse, most abuse does not "count" as domestic violence; (2) even if the abuse is considered actionable, a woman can also be charged for resisting her attacker (and thus blamed for the initial attack[67]); and (3) a woman is almost always blamed—regardless of the level of abuse, according to policy definitions—for not having simply left and not having the courage to get help.

But the help doesn't "count" unless the woman is "successful"—this poses a serious problem in creating the documentation to prove abuse. A target's "success" is dependent on whether the police actually believe her and not only give her a case number, but take her report accurately (as she recounts the events and not as they interpret them), which in turn validates her story as documentary evidence from an authority.[68] However, the truth is, even if police officers have received some training, it doesn't guarantee that they can (or want to) implement it in practice.[69] Similarly, most therapists are not equipped to deal with domestic violence and do not even know that counseling a couple in an abusive situation is considered highly damaging and dangerous.[70] That is, most conventional therapists do more harm than good and actually produce documentary evidence that helps the abuser.[71] These agents end up not helping targets who are often desperate and afraid not only for their own well-being but for that of their children.[72] Ironically, each attempt to get help allows time to pass, and the spectacular event that could have been prosecuted is increasingly less "fresh" to a prosecutorial agent. As time passes and it appears that the target didn't seek help (because it wasn't successful, because she was blamed, or because the agent refused to take a report), it appears that there is no danger. Then the cycle can begin again. Given that these low-level agents cannot help, it should not be surprising that it is close to impossible to prosecute domestic violence successfully. Consequently, most abuse occurs with impunity.

WELFARE, SHELTERS, AND DOMESTIC ABUSE

One of the reasons that policies and other forms of help for domestic abuse are often fragmented and ineffective is that this issue has only been acknowledged as a legitimate one fairly recently. Domestic abuse was recognized roughly at the beginning of the 1970s and only gained a literature in the 1990s, according to Kathleen Ferraro and Michael Johnson.[73] Perhaps another way to put it is that while there were numerous accounts of intimate partner abuse in the early modern and modern period[74] the topic did not take form as an independent, scholarly body of research in the social sciences until the 1990s. As noted above, while in the past, abuse was legal and sometimes accepted, it was also widely criticized. A key difference between past writings and more contemporary accounts, however, was that through the 1970s, abuse was viewed as rooted in political inequality and was therefore interpreted as asymmetrical.[75] In this way, critiques of domestic violence before the 1990s treated women who were abused as political subjects, deserving of rights, while from the 1990s, there has perhaps been an increasingly depoliticizing tendency to treat these women as "clients" or objects of study, pathological subjects, and even antifeminists.[76] These trends are not absolute but can indicate a change from a broader political and feminist perspective to a narrower view, leading to a body of work that maintains a critical distance from its subject, thus depoliticizing the issue.[77]

The shelter movement of the 1970s reflected this earlier political and feminist perspective: as Evan Stark recounts, shelters sprang up in the 1970s and were truly grassroots, allowing targets of abuse to identify what they needed and to speak for themselves.[78] However, Stark notes that by the 1990s, shelters were no longer run by abuse targets but were more professional and psychologically oriented. Targets of abuse were treated as clients who must submit to rules and programming by staff.[79] By this point, numerous political and economic changes had occurred such that a backlash against feminism and single mothers had led to a conservative (often religious) co-optation of domestic abuse policy and shelter help.[80] Homeless shelters make a similar distinction: they either approach homelessness as an individual, psychological issue or (more infrequently) as a political issue, tied to a shortage of low-income housing and tenants who do not know their rights. In the first case, exemplified in shelters in Washington, DC, the homeless are treated as if they are victims of themselves; less often, in some cities like Boston, shelters treat the issue as if it were political and legal, providing legal advocacy for the homeless so that they won't be illegally barred from their housing again.

The second model treats shelter residents as citizens whose voices matter, even if this system, like the domestic violence shelter system, is still imperfect.[81]

Thus, similar to and overlapping with policy interpretations of domestic abuse, quite a lot of research in the 1980s and 1990s focused on the individual pathology of the homeless rather than viewing homelessness as a structural issue and investigating why homelessness suddenly exploded from the mid-1960s on. In my work on homelessness, I have argued that the constant focus on the (alleged) mental state of the homeless ignores how widespread homelessness is and how many others are considered at risk of homelessness.[82] Domestic abuse is similar in that the consequences rather than causes are investigated, but in this particular case, the causes are embodied in the figure of the abuser, who is largely ignored. Other factors that more broadly affect the homeless—lack of transportation, poor educational opportunities, a difficult job market at low-tier levels— certainly affect targets of abuse as well. But a second commonality between the two groups is how they are treated in shelters—not simply as displaced but irrational, lacking in basic life skills, and needing paternalistic guidance.[83]

A comparison of the homeless shelter systems in Boston and Washington, DC, demonstrates how public policy and shelters, as institutions of policy enforcement, produce a particular type of political subject. The dominant discursive orientation of the shelter systems in Boston (which was legally oriented in the late 1980s and early 1990s) and in Washington, DC, (which was oriented to mental health in the same time period) had significant consequences on changing the actual problem. In short, the Boston system assumed that the homeless were poor and might not be aware of their legal rights. It was held that once they knew their rights, they would not become homeless again. Other services were also provided but not in a paternalistic or blaming way.[84] In contrast, the broad spectrum of DC shelters didn't hire housing advocates or legal advocates; instead, they wanted individuals with mental health experience and degrees to take care of a population they assumed to be mentally ill and relatively incompetent, if not also lazy. This approach depoliticizes homelessness and marginalization, ignoring broader trends in economics, welfare policy, housing, and so on. It works in that it diverts attention from much more important causes of displacement, but ends in perpetuating homelessness. I became convinced through my research that the increasing popularity of the individual, pathologized model in shelters and research indicated that perhaps society didn't really want to solve homelessness. Rather, it wanted to criminalize and punish poverty.[85]

The domestic abuse system (or network of powers) has important parallels with the homeless shelter system in the focus on the abused and not the abuser; the absolute refusal to prevent abuse before it happens; and the paternalistic attitude toward targets of abuse, combined with blame and individual pathologization. The refusal to recognize that violence is endemic to our society—even in our most egalitarian and contractual relationships—and that it is merely assimilated and rationalized (not erased) is ignored, just as recessions, unemployment, and lack of affordable housing are ignored when considering homelessness. The connections between abuse and politico-economic inequality are also dismissed or used to create a multilayered discourse of blame and pathology.[86]

The 1990s marked a turning point in the laws regarding the poor, racial minorities, women, and immigrants. Americans were affected in many ways by welfare changes that introduced time limits; the endorsement of low-tier, low-paid jobs; and the promotion of two-parent, heterosexual marriage. All these changes were oriented less toward ethics and more toward reducing the welfare rolls, according to Anna Marie Smith.[87] The same welfare changes allowed for federal devolution of an already extraconstitutional and undemocratic immigration policy to be implemented at the state and local levels, which ensured that foreigners had even fewer rights than previously and thus, foreign abuse victims particularly vulnerable.[88] Welfare changes also transformed policy approaches to the family, shifting from a sort of acceptance of single motherhood (the replacement of the man with the state) to a conservative affirmation of traditional gender roles and heteronormativity. The result of this is not necessarily to succeed in increasing the numbers of married couples but to reward fathers for not taking off when children are born out of wedlock. The new paradigm for fathers in welfare and family law places them in the categories of deadbeat dads versus "the payers."[89] The "payer," through paying child support, is accorded full visitation rights with his child(ren), including the right to geographically restrict the mother and children to a county or specific area. The mother, who in popular opinion "wins" in this sort of situation, is not accorded the same rights but instead the duties of being a primary caretaker and yet the necessity of earning a living. These roles—the breadwinner who has rights and the primary caretaker who has duties[90]—reinforce gendered divisions, forcing the couple into a mutually antagonistic relationship, according to Smith. In the case of domestic violence, these roles create a dangerous situation, effectively allowing the father to control the family from a distance, as long as he is paying. Other changes in the same time period show how a conservative backlash against feminism and normative assertions of equality and individual responsibility have been institutionalized in areas of domestic abuse, family law, and the shelter system.

Smith's research on welfare law is important in understanding not simply how the state effectively targets racial minorities and single parents but also in understanding why and how these changes reinforce legal and counseling efforts to keep the family intact more broadly (i.e., beyond the purview of welfare). The 1996 scaling back of welfare and consequent push for all fathers to pay child support were not particularly moral, Smith argues.[91] The impetus for these measures had more to do with federal and state budgetary concerns—particularly reducing welfare rolls—than any ethical concerns. Nevertheless, the effect has been to reward men who pay child support and don't take off and thus the new subject—the payer—is constructed dialectically against the figure of the deadbeat dad, who leaves or cannot pay support. This payment effectively constitutes their primary duty toward their children and thus, they are awarded full rights as fathers.[92] These rights are, in effect, the rights to have information about and spend time with children, but there are no positive duties that they must exercise. Women, in contrast, bear a disproportionate financial burden and have all of the duties of a primary caregiver, as constructed by legal agreements.[93] As Smith shows, the deadbeat dad figure then permeates public decisions and, she implies, could open up a gray area for arbitrary power because any man who isn't a deadbeat dad has 50% rights without doing 50% of the work to raise a child.[94] At its worst, this can mean that the man who doesn't leave and pays a minimum of child support is then entitled to joint custody rights, even if he has never really taken care of the child and even if there is a history of abuse. Smith's research explains not only changes in welfare, particularly for poor African Americans, but also punitive mechanisms in family law that particularly target single mothers.[95]

However, I would like to problematize fixed notions of class and "privilege." Instead, I hold that domestic abuse, in fact, explodes conventional categories such as race and class, requiring a truly intersectional approach (a subject I revisit in the conclusion to this book). Going beyond Smith's original focus, but noting its value, I believe that the gray area established by traditional gender roles—even in late modern intimate relationships that are often not officially sanctioned by the state—is central to policymakers' and bureaucrats' interpretation of a couple's relationship and allows for a significant amount of arbitrary power. Because the man has fulfilled his minimal duties by not abandoning the child and paying child support, societal sympathy is on his side. The figure of the deadbeat dad sets up an either-or situation in which a man's mere presence is evidence of his "interest" in the child. But beyond that, he can wield considerable power over both the child and mother because of his alleged responsibility as a father. This power may not only be at odds with the daily needs of parenting but can allow him to deploy arbitrary power over mothers and children through what is essentially legal stalking (if he mentions the child in texts and voicemails, some lawyers argue that it is legally permissible to bombard a woman's phone with threats and negative comments); legal criminal trespass (if he is picking up or delivering the child and decides to invade the mother's home); legal economic marginalization (placing high economic burdens on the woman through a mediated settlement and hiding his income and assets—most parties do not go before a judge as Smith seems to think); and legal threats to take away the child (if he mentions legal action in the same set of statements).[96] He can also get away with violent acts if there are no witnesses (except for the child); if he leaves no marks; and if he constantly blames the target for his own behavior. To be prosecuted for violence, he would have to be a stranger; there would have to be witnesses (other than the child); and legal agents would actually have to believe the woman's reports of abuse.[97] As I have argued above, discursive power dynamics are such that reports by targets of abuse are instead minimized, ignored, or pathologized.

Smith rightly emphasizes the differences between poorer women, especially women of color, and wealthy, single, white women who are not forced to name the "payer" to the state, have economic autonomy, and are not accused of child abuse without proof (as welfare recipients are). But although not all women are on welfare, most single mothers are not wealthy[98] and so something is lost with this distinction.[99] Very few women can buy their way out of the gender roles the state effectively places them in upon divorce or a child custody suit. Indeed, as I have indicated, any woman involved in a custody suit can face a significant period of restricted movement, various forms of verbal and emotional abuse by the payer, constant physical violence or threats of violence, and the unequal burden of child-rearing duties in exchange for limited support. She is on the lower end of the gender hierarchy as her needs are placed below the child's as well as those of any father who proves that he is not a deadbeat by doing the bare minimum required. The policing of welfare recipients only makes this inequality more profound, but it doesn't take away from the basic fact that *all* women in this situation are politically subordinated to a significant degree.[100] This is not to argue that women are then equal in their disadvantage through abuse but to demonstrate how abuse is a pervasive and multilayered issue with multiple consequences.

Going beyond Smith's focus on welfare, I also think it is important to consider how employers add to women's difficulties, often "testing" single mothers (and mothers more generally) to see whether they are still good employees but often subjecting them to greater scrutiny and higher standards than their single nonparent or male counterparts.[101] Added to this is the increasingly predominant practice of confining the mother to the county—something any noncustodial parent can attempt to do in court. This geo-spatial restriction can compound abusive power dynamics, effectively trapping someone for years. In sum, domestic abuse often entails the relegation of the mother's rights to secondary status behind the father's and "the best interests of the child" regardless of economic class; substantial income losses for *all* single mothers; and the pervasiveness of abuse (broadly conceived) amongst all classes—thus reinforcing a broader trend of policing the poor while overlooking the same dynamics at other income levels.[102]

Smith also suggests how the constant use of the phrase "the best interests of the child" also seems to be completely cynical; a way more to obscure the decreasing rights of both the mother and child. But going beyond these observations, I suggest that these broad changes in welfare, custody, and views of the family affect all women who are caught up in these multiple and overlapping systems, even if the effects are differential.[103] Despite a logically narrow focus, Smith's work provides invaluable insight into at least two more general shifts in power relations: (1) a conservative backlash against single mothers, which is even more punitive when intersecting gender with class and race; (2) changes in family law and custody arrangements that mirror changes in welfare provisions since 1996.[104] Regarding this second point, these changes have effectively promoted heterosexual, two-parent marriages and punished single mothers as well as parents in the LGBQT community. Many of the current programs purporting to help poor, single-headed households with children or families with a history of domestic abuse reinforce these gender divides, effectively uniting people who were never married. They reinforce a preference for the male "breadwinner" and consign women to accepting duties as a primary caretaker while also urging them to accept low-tier, low-paid service jobs.[105] Motherhood is not elevated in this conservative backlash and in fact poor mothers and domestic abuse targets face the constant threat of having their children taken away.[106]

These difficulties have confirmed my feeling that formal rights are not enough; that conceiving of political agency in this way is not only limited but often further entraps targets of abuse in the system. A better perspective is a societal one in which we understand, first, how violence is assimilated into daily life and second, how women's secondary political and economic status has a great impact on the relative ineffectiveness of the abuse system. Solutions to this issue cannot be individualized if significant improvement is truly desired in this area. In this particular case, a new network of relations must be conceived of that does not lead to this sort of triangulation in which the child is essentially a football.

All of these responses suggest how misguided notions of neutrality, equality, and mutuality are in a situation like this. In fact, it seems that these rubrics are implemented to trump the rights of primary caretakers (most often women) and to allow children to be continuously exposed to dangerous situations in order to promote fathers' rights.[107] These responses are not only unhelpful, but often make things worse. To the degree that they are paradigmatic of societal responses to domestic abuse more generally, policy regarding abuse is first highly political (in the colloquial sense of being biased and oriented toward public opinion). It is also unempirical and disturbingly antigay (the elevation of heterosexual men and fathers). It is furthermore pro-marriage, biologically deterministic (the biological parent is elevated above adoptive parents), and antimother (in terms of making women the primary caretakers, with extensive duties, contrasted with fathers who are endowed with rights). Recent trends in psychology reaffirm the focus on the family as a unit and the privileging of fatherhood in an attempt to keep fathers in the picture. The cost, again, is that domestic abuse occurs with impunity, and psychology often becomes complicit in aiding abusers, whether indirectly or directly, as I explore below.

PSYCHOAFFECTIVE MATRIX AND VICTIM STATUS (RESSENTIMENT)

Given various power relations that depoliticize this issue and often turn blame back on targets of domestic abuse, it is unsurprising that couples counseling and individual therapy are viewed as important methods of handling domestic violence.[108] There are two dominant approaches to counseling in cases of abuse: the more popular approach is the conjoint model of therapy, which treats the family as a unit and seeks to preserve it.[109] This approach is supported by changes to welfare in 1996 and the subsequent psychological studies released during George W. Bush's presidency that uphold the importance of the biological father, regardless of his actual role in the family.[110]

The conjoint model holds that because of the cycle of violence, therapists must accept the fact that women will inevitably stay with or return to the abuser.[111] Improving family relations is then the goal but with the following caveats: because abusers have been found to be largely unresponsive to therapy and the few batterer intervention programs that exist are ineffective, women are treated as both the problem (the provocateur of abuse) but also the solution.[112] Given these presuppositions, there are several consequences: (1) the woman is viewed as the center of all family problems and the cause of abuse (e.g., she talks too much; she is too focused on parenting and thus overly demanding on her husband; pregnancy exacerbates these qualities, including her irritability); (2) nevertheless, because women are more verbal and provide the emotional link among family members, they are better victim-patients, and thus they become the locus of treatment rather than their abuser-husbands; (3) in every sort of scenario in this approach, it is assumed that there are rational reasons for the violence and both causes and treatments can be found[113]; (4) because women are viewed as the cause of abuse but also ideal patients, they are also used to screen for child abuse and held accountable if children are abused.[114] All these assumptions are based on a contractual and egalitarian model of the family at the same time that they leave intact family hierarchies, including asymmetrical acts of abuse and control.[115] This model is further supported by the family law system, changes in welfare that now seek to revalue fatherhood-payers, and perhaps neoliberal approaches to social problems that trim budgets by blaming the victim.[116]

As an alternative to conjoint therapy, a second approach is often practiced by more progressive groups and is at odds with family-values trends and the revaluing of fatherhood and men's rights. It holds that individual counseling is less traumatic for abuse victims, that abuse is largely asymmetrical, and that when society or the state forces couples to negotiate in school meetings, in custodial mediation, or with regard to finances, it is unjust and unhealthy for the target. Further they hold, with Lundy Bancroft, that an abuser who abuses his partner in front of his children is damaging the children. This approach validates the experiences of targets of abuse—even if the abuse is indirect (as in Stark's theory of "tangential spouse abuse" discussed below) or is "only" emotional and financial.[117]

The second approach is more Foucaultian and it accounts for broad structures of subordination, as well as supporting the idea that abuse is asymmetrical. These therapists and legal advocates treat the target of abuse as an individual and are convinced that couples counseling will further traumatize her. Importantly, they will meet with targets whether they are in the abusive relationship or in the process of leaving and do not demand proof of abuse to help someone. They recognize that current legal structures and dominant policy models do not understand the degree to which abuse is asymmetrical and provide strategies not only for dealing with abusers but also with ineffective lawyers, school personnel, and doctors who are often in the position of judging these situations but profoundly misunderstand what is going on.

I will discuss each approach but also challenge the degree to which counselors and therapists have any awareness of an approach at all, aside from a loose understanding of conjoint therapy which simply fits with the egalitarian, relational, and communication-based, rationality-oriented structure of conventional therapy.[118] While Akhil Gupta has investigated this aspect of disciplinary power and bio-power—pervasive ineptitude by bureaucratic agents in an already disaggregated model—the fact is that whether intentional or not, the conjoint model has a normative effect on targets of abuse.[119] To put it differently, counseling often falls back on discursive and normative paradigms of symmetry in abusive relationships but this is largely because of a lack of awareness of other approaches. Because this paradigm is already supported in public policy, family law, welfare changes, and the media, it appears to be "common sense." In contrast, the more individual model—supported by and sometimes based on the work of Patricia Evans, Lundy Bancroft, and Evan Stark—essentially challenges the very basis of Enlightenment assumptions in counseling and thus is not merely unsupported by dominant policy and shelter norms but is perhaps threatening to core ideas in conventional therapy.[120] This approach is "realist" in that it acknowledges violence and profound asymmetries and thus the limitations of Enlightenment models. At its best, it resolves the Habermas-Foucault debate (discussed in the next chapter) not by choosing one theoretical model over another but by situating communicative action in a Foucaultian analytic of power.

The truth is that both approaches are used in counseling and by shelters—sometimes by the same office or therapist—and while there are differences, they both see the woman as the bearer of all responsibility for her abuse but also for getting help. When therapists or lawyers use both approaches, they give mixed messages to women: it is up to you to get help, it is up to you to care for your child and not expose her or him to abuse, but it is also up to you to maintain the essence of some sort of family or visitation schedule. Both approaches can advocate on behalf of the family unit but the second one—the individual model—has far more radical implications in its recognition of broad forms of structural subordination. The second approach, when it is used by anonymous, grass-roots feminist organizations, has a broader view of abuse that recognizes multiple structures of subordination and questions the normative and disciplinary effects (not to mention retraumatizing) of egalitarian solutions like mediation, couples counseling, co-parenting, and so on. The second approach takes the effects of abuse seriously and seeks to avoid triggers that could further harm a target. Ironically, this approach doesn't treat individuals as absolute victims but rather as agents who can and must draw on their strengths to move beyond their current situation.

Linda Mills claims that this is the dominant approach in counseling and shelters, effectively breaking up families and promoting "feminism" at the cost of family unity and community solidarity.[121] But she should not be threatened by this model, because it is largely underground and is a blend of the 1970s-style, consciousness-raising, political approach to women's issues with more contemporary sensitivities to the LGBQT communities, single mothers, and different modes of political effectiveness. As stated above, it does not fit comfortably with changes in welfare, family law, heteronormativity, and the backlash against feminism. Contrary to Mills's claims, Bumiller indicates that the family model can "coercively" enforce family cohesion[122] even when the target is not interested in getting help as a family. In this way, the conjoint approach creates a self-fulfilling prophecy that makes the cycle of violence theory true. That is, if conjoint therapy is premised on the idea that abused wives always return to their husbands, the Enlightenment-oriented (dyadic, consensual, symmetrical) and family-based assumptions ensure that the target is offered little alternative but to remain. Bumiller also suggests that the conjoint model allows for the state to sort of give up on solving the problem of domestic abuse as a broad political or social issue. Instead, accepting the cycle of violence, the link between extralegal authorities and the states is to manage and control victims as patients.

While Bumiller only hints at this, the danger of increased medical intervention when there are no corresponding changes in family law, welfare, police enforcement, or shelter policies is that simply recognizing and exposing abuse may actually exacerbate the denigration and violence rather than solving it. An excellent clinical article on domestic abuse exposes these problems while also encouraging medical personnel to learn how to predict abuse.[123] Throughout this article, the authors examine how empirical studies regarding abuse screening and predictions of future injury are inconclusive. Instead, they conclude that the best person to predict the abuse is the target, who can communicate this through her speech, testimony, and confidences with the doctor or nurse. Nevertheless, the authors also continue to advocate for advanced screening mechanisms to help predict violence and abuse, but never state to what end. The increase in screening could in fact be merely an invasion of privacy or a trigger for traumatic memories, given the absence of any legal mechanisms to prevent or adjudicate abuse. Given the fact that most targets know when they and their children are in danger far better than anyone else, it is puzzling that this article seems to advocate screening and professional expertise over and above trusting targets and really implementing change. In a similar vein, abuse is also often labeled an "epidemic" or a "disease" which does not merely depoliticize and medicalize the issue, but which takes the entire focus off the abuser.[124]

The abuse itself—economic control, social isolation, alienation of children's affections, and physical assault—is never actually questioned or challenged in any of these spheres. Rather, even in the more Foucaultian counseling methods, the target is still the responsible party (in terms of changing the situation). The irony is that she becomes pathologized, while the abuser does not. Some authors, like Andrea Westlund, recognize that the domestic abuse system may actually aid abusers: "The extensive web of impersonal disciplinary practices created by modern institutions leaves spaces for batterers to exercise personal and corporal forms of power over their partners and children."[125] Indeed, a woman may be diagnosed as having a personality disorder if she admits she is being subjected to abuse, control, or deprivation whereas the abuser will not. Westlund identifies the degree to which abused women are pathologized, while abusers are ignored: "battered women's 'abnormalities' have been described and redescribed within the psychiatric literature of the twentieth century, characterized as everything from hysteria to masochistic or self-defeating personality disorder (SDPD) to codependency. . . ."[126] As she suggests, this pathology is merely an extension of female norms,[127] which she notes are in effect pathologized, as well as serving as the antithesis of "universal" (privileged male) norms. Accordingly, female-typed behaviors are reinforced and yet serve to undermine targets' cases against abusers and/or entrap them in some other way. For example, "self-defeating personality disorder (SDPD)"[128] involves "'sacrificing one's own interests and putting other people first' that are 'virtually a role requirement for women in our [culture].'"[129] "Sprock, Blashfield, and Smith note that 'it is particularly disturbing that personality disorder behaviors seen as characteristic of women appear to be . . . close enough to society's stereotype of women that normal women who adopt traditional roles may be receiving personality disorder diagnoses."[130] Significantly, there is no corresponding category in the *Diagnostic and Statistical Manual of Mental Disorders* category for male traits and, particularly, for control and abuse.[131] This reversal—the pathologization of targets but not their abusers—seems especially indicative of inherent gender biases in the domestic abuse system that cannot simply be reformed. In essence, women are blamed for being abused; for reporting it; and for defending themselves or seeking help. Their pathologization is not just blame, however—it can legitimate protective legal measures that invite more surveillance and control, including state supervision of a mother's relationship with her children; the removal of a woman's decision-making rights by a court because the abuse has rendered her irrational; and therapy and medication for her issues while the abuser is ignored. Thus, crucially Westlund acknowledges that "'helping professions' participate in precisely this kind of disciplining."[132] When she notes that many women do seek help, she suggests that it is not the women who are pathological but rather the domestic abuse system.[133] Westlund acknowledges how this reversal in focus—stigmatizing targets of abuse and making them the focus of hierarchical, paternalistic therapeutic interventions—is often mirrored in the judicial system.[134]

Accepting the bizarre focus on targets of abuse (rather than focusing on abusers), two key strategies to protect targets of domestic have been claiming that a target suffers from either battered woman syndrome (BWS) or post-traumatic stress disorder (PTSD).[135] Both defenses have been used to explain why targets of abuse (1) do not seek help; (2) are "uncooperative" when asked to press charges;[136] (3) might wait a long time to report abuse; and (4) expose children to abuse.[137] Nevertheless, all these assumptions are faulty: the first point is absolutely unproven and if institutional apathy, inefficiency, and even disdain for women seeking help are accounted for, one would see that targets do often seek help but the help is not out there. Second, it is perverse to use the term *uncooperative* when institutional mechanisms focus on the target and not the abuser, with much higher costs for the former than the latter and thus, targets are being blamed for not pressing charges in a system that is highly unjust. This injustice is compounded when many communities do not feel like the police act as community officers but instead act with brutality themselves or do not respond to calls.[138] A further risk is that the target will be arrested along with her abuser. With regard to time and exposure of children to abuse, while these may be valid claims, the social work and justice systems cannot blame mothers and threaten their custody and then think targets of abuse will turn to the same system.[139] The judicial tolerance of this charge of "exposure" to abuse (i.e., asking if the perpetrator is a good father, thus compartmentalizing abuse) flies in the face of this particular charge and highlights how the "best interests" of the child seem more like a disciplinary measure aimed at the abused.[140] To put it differently, gendered differences are absolutely clear when a man's abuse of the mother is not recognized as having any effect on children when considering custody and visitation, but conversely, abused mothers are often charged with exposure to abuse—thus, punishing the mother but not the actual perpetrator.[141]

Evan Stark's theory of coercive control, which he has successfully used in courts as an expert witness, seeks to expand the notion of trauma, but in such a way that the focus eventually goes where it rightly should: on the perpetrator.[142] Stark argues that BWS and PTSD require specific symptoms that most abused women do not actually have.[143] In fact, it is not injury per se that constitutes control or the hostage-like effect of domestic abuse but the successful implementation of a myriad of tactics of control by the abuser combined with state inaction when targets do seek help. Stark's theory seeks to make sense of a broader context of control, emotional alienation (particularly pitting family members against one another), economic deprivation, and low-level assault that characterize an abused woman's life. Over a period of time, according to Stark, two things occur. First, a hostage-like feeling of extreme isolation occurs, not only because of the abuser but also because of the blaming attitudes of most psychologists, lawyers, police, and judges. The blame, misunderstanding of this issue, and lack of help, combined with broader structures of subordination that continue to make women unequal to men, all serve to ensure a target's radical isolation from society and ensure that her abuser is threatening her very existence. Second, there is a breaking point in this context, in which the woman feels like her life is in jeopardy—the breaking point is not necessarily a violent incident but reflects the accumulation of institutional inaction, societal blaming, and interpersonal denigration over time. Citing Charles Patrick Ewing's work on this subject, Stark notes that "most battered women eventually 'experience a turning point when the violence of abuse done to them comes to be felt as a basic threat, whether to their physical or social self or both.'"[144] This turning point challenges conventional ideas of a cycle of abuse in which the woman returns repeatedly until one day she doesn't (as indicated in Waits's more conventional treatment of this particular facet of abuse[145]). This cycle has been used against women to remove children from mothers but has not been used against men,[146] and thus Stark's challenge to this is important.

While one could argue that Stark is still bringing focus on the target, at times claiming that a woman put up with abuse or didn't report it, his Foucaultian approach is twofold. First, he seems to want to work within conventional approaches to this issue only to challenge their very bases. Thus, he begins with a heavy focus on the target to expand current views of pathology and "learned helplessness."[147] He then explicitly states that this approach has successfully led to reframing the woman's actions in response to the abuser's, thus critically shifting the focus back to the main actor who has been all but ignored at nearly every level. When and if this refocusing occurs, the unique character of an abuser is evident. This includes considering how his behavior defies certain Enlightenment presuppositions of equality, mutuality, or guilt. Nevertheless, Stark notes, abusers are often masters at using Enlightenment discourse to justify and reframe their actions. At its best, Stark's notion of coercive control puts the target's actions in a broader societal context and indirectly explains why abusers are empowered to abuse. As he argues, broader, unresolved issues of structural subordination that continue to make women second-class citizens form the politico-economic context in which abusers feel they can act with impunity. Conversely, traditional notions of femininity, which continue to have a great deal of influence on workplace arrangements, familial divisions of labor, and judicial decisions, blur the lines between excessive control and force and "normal" gender differentiation.

Interestingly, Stark's work as an expert witness has also affirmed his belief that if a target is viewed as a victim, she often loses the case.[148] But if her tactics within the abusive relationship are reinterpreted as micro-resistance, she is not only viewed as independent and "empowered" but also treated better by judges and juries.[149] Thus, against what seems to be a variety of social and legal institutions seeking to put women back into their place (as weak, apathetic), it is only when targets of abuse are framed as fully independent political agents, capable of rational decision making, who react to abusers strategically and not hysterically, that they are then treated as subjects worthy of justice.[150] Stark's analysis of this strategic reframing thus challenges the worth of identifying oneself as a victim.

The term *victim* has been discussed in very new and interesting ways in the past decade and a half. On the one hand, if a target of abuse were viewed as a true victim of a crime, worthy of not merely protection but also in telling her story and defining what she needed, the "victim" label would indicate the proper allocation of responsibility. More succinctly, the label would imply that the situation is not at all equal (i.e., that intimate abuse is not symmetrical).[151] But, on the other hand, as Stark notes, given the current context of gender subordination, the label invites dismissal or ridicule—not respect and genuine sympathy.

In *States of Injury* Wendy Brown indicates the irony of recognizing that the state and liberal rights have deep and inherent problems but turning to rights and the state as "the solution" to the very same problems.[152] Unsurprisingly, operating at this level reproduces the status quo rather than challenging it, effectively depoliticizing what appears to be democratic power. Drawing on Brown's work on ressentiment (which I discuss below), Paul Apostolidis compares workers' reactions to abuse in a meatpacking plant.[153] This abuse includes economic exploitation but also swearing and physical attacks, not to mention physically intensive and dangerous labor conditions. Apostolidis finds the workers use two general strategies in response: a legalistic approach that at times embraces a victimized identity and that looks to the state to rectify various injustices, and a broader, less state-centered approach that involves educational efforts, attempts not only to democratize the workplace but also to democratize interpersonal relations in their grassroots groups. This latter approach, which could be characterized as a grassroots one is more efficacious and democratic to Apostolidis.

Similar to these exploited immigrants, domestic violence victims are not merely politically unequal in a formal sense but also sworn at, denigrated, attacked, and humiliated on a daily basis. In conditions that attack physical well-being itself, it is understandable that targets would want to reach out to the state, whether they are domestic abuse targets or abused immigrants. Nevertheless, Apostolidis shows that these efforts are often stunted or rejected while the sources of group solidarity are often weak. In contrast, he argues that the grassroots movement, with a long-term vision of the political issues and their solutions, was more far-reaching, did not require state approval, and fostered lasting social bonds (even though there were also animosities). Referring to Brown's work, Apostolidis classified the first group as drawing on ressentiment, which Brown argues is inherent in liberalism. This is not an emotional evaluation as much as it is a critique of how liberalism produces these outcomes, which confer a victim status to a group without actually doing anything to improve its circumstances. Indeed, extralegal and legal institutions can draw on the language of victimization and underprivilege to foster blame and claim pathologization as part of a conservative backlash.

Citing Nietzsche, Brown reminds the reader that ressentiment is the moralizing revenge of the powerless, "the triumph of the weak as weak."[154] Both Apostolidis's and Brown's work are interesting in conceiving of the limits of liberalism. In asserting liberal rights, a wronged group is essentially forced to adopt the position of victim but this claim also often leads to a backlash of blame and individual pathologization. To be clear, the focus of this critique is on liberalism itself and not targets of abuse. Highlighting an "individuating" notion of power that is "reactive" rather than active, Brown and Apostolidis expose the multiple discourses of blame and loss that position abuse targets as victims and as undeserving of state help. Morality is invoked to depoliticize and shame targets, while making state power stronger in the area of control but impotent in a democratic (active, creative, positive) sense. Both Bumiller's and Mills's notions of a "feminism" that either promotes the notion of "sexual violence" (Bumiller) or the breakup of families and communities on behalf of domestic violence targets (Mills) highlight a binary mode of operation that makes discourse static and polarized. This binary mode of operation exposes the limits of liberalism and seeking state help, including the incredibly narrow view of what counts as "feminism."

As Bumiller rightly suggests, what results is not constructive help for targets of abuse, but the expansion of state power at certain levels with the concomitant abandonment of these "victims" at others. This increase in state power depoliticizes (or de-democratizes) the political terrain, effectively emphasizing the state as punisher and protector. As Brown points out, this power is not neutral but distinctively masculinized: "The prerogative of the state, whether expressed as the armed force of the police or as vacillating criteria for obtaining welfare benefits, is often all that stands between women and rape, women and starvation, women and dependence upon brutal mates—in short, women and unattenuated male prerogative."[155] As Stark, Bumiller, and Brown have all indicated, the authorities that constitute the "state" (including extralegal authorities linked to state efforts to police and provide welfare) cynically use the language of gender equality in their deployments of power.[156] Nevertheless, this "bears all the familiar elements of male dominance. Through its police and military, the state monopolizes the institutionalized *physical* power of society. Through its welfare function, the state wields *economic* power over indigent women, arbitrarily sets the terms of their economic survival, and keeps them dangling and submissive by providing neither dependable, adequate income level nor quality public day care."[157]

Linked to my discussion in the next chapter, what occurs then is a lack of state recognition of women as a "group" except as potential victims. Interestingly, if women were recognized as a visible social group with "immutable" characteristics, they would at the very least receive the heightened scrutiny that racial minorities receive (granted, the effects of this recognition are largely symbolic).[158] But further, in varying contexts involving women who need help, the state has increasingly sought to define feminism. This appropriation of the term *feminism* then neutralizes and homogenizes what in fact has been fragmented and far more radical than the socially accepted, discursively formed feminism that liberal representative democracy has conceived of.[159] As I discuss in the next chapter, feminism is then reduced to self-defense (literally: resisting an abuser's attacks) and thus fits a broader tendency to narrow feminism to "women's interests," all the while repudiating the idea that women are subordinated in any substantial way.[160] The term *neoliberalism* is appropriate when considering how many public functions have been taken over by the business sector and the increasing blurring of the lines between private and public. Moral and political questions are then subsumed to economic calculations, explaining (again) why victims become the target of any intervention and not the perpetrators or broader structures of societal violence.[161]

Given the varying but related changes I analyze above, the "victim" label confers pathology, requiring a medical and therapeutic treatment or law-and-order intervention, but no broad-based political solutions. This classification—as victim and cause—signals what Bonnie Honig has discussed as "incomplete mourning."[162] This occurs when individuals are asked to make a clean break with their pasts—perhaps never seeing family or friends again; giving up their language, traditions, and foods; and wholly adopting a new set of practices, a new community, and a new place to live. This sort of demand entails a denial of individuals' fate and normative rejection of accounting for or witnessing what has been lost. It is hard to recognize that abusive situations are markers of dashed dreams and very real threats and losses and harder still to politicize these losses. Like demands made of immigrants and refugees, conventional power relations often require wholesale repudiation of the past and a clean break. Domestic abuse victims are encouraged either to stay (and change) or to flee at the expense of all relationships and material possessions. Conventional shelters merely consolidate these tendencies, requiring that targets give up even personal decision making as a condition for them to remain.[163] Gradual or partial change, mixed tactics, and mourning are not part of these strategies. It is in this sense—of recognizing incomplete mourning—that I think Linda Mills and quite distinctly, Carissa Showden, express concern about judging women who choose to stay and work things out. Granted that these authors are very different, but both recognize that targets of abuse are not merely victims: they also have very real attachments and identities that cannot be so easily abandoned.[164] Granting respect to these authentic losses and threats that abused women face would ironically expand the boundaries of their identity from victims to that of women—their other identities and rootedness would not be so easily subsumed by their status as victims if their agency, capacities, and attachments were honored in formal and informal political arrangements.

SOLUTIONS/CONCLUSION

It should be evident that targets of abuse face very real threats and are in fact even more endangered when they seek state help. As I have explained above, there are numerous mechanisms of power today that obscure this inequality and which force a target to continually negotiate with her abuser. This is especially true if they share custody of a child. "Talking" can mean making concessions, standing up to him, threatening to leave, attending mediation sessions, or getting counseling, for example. Regardless, communication is often conceived of as the answer to mitigating abuse. This is because, at base, people tend to think the abuser has a reason for his actions, his withdrawal, his threats, and how he treats his child(ren).[165] Related to the refrain "Why don't you just talk to him?" is a related question: even in cases of prolonged abuse and murder of a target, the media and political agents ask why the abuser did this. Even when the complaints of an abuser and his claims of victimization are utterly imaginary and he perverts the "facts," doctors, school personnel, psychologists, and lawyers think there must be some grain of truth in the matter. Despite these presumptions of rationality and mutuality, the burden of communication is almost completely on the target of abuse. This inequality in communication (which I discuss in the next chapter) leaves open a gray area for misunderstanding the abuser's actions and motives, essentially construing them in liberal, egalitarian terms.

Abusers' acts are normalized and translated into terms like "interest"[166] or even caring, while the emotions of their targets can lead to their arrest (even in the context of violent assault), their pathologization, and in the worst case, the loss of their legal autonomy. Like many other discourses, it is not that targets of abuse are hysterical and abusers are emotionless and controlled but rather that men's emotions in this context are viewed as justifiable but misguided passion, or as frustration at the male crisis in power.[167] Their emotions are thus translated into rational speech. This is due in part to the fact that in welfare law and family law men's roles in a family—especially when children are involved—are still conceived of differently from women's, and thus a man's "involvement" or "interest" leaves more room for positive rights, while women's roles as wives and mothers are conceived of as duties. It is also partly due to the gendered hierarchies in conventional approaches to therapy. Thus, as I have explored, women can be accused of hysteria without showing any emotion; their rationality and motherhood are in question because the standards are not the same; and they are put in a double bind when they try to report danger. If they report abuse, they can be further accused of not properly documenting their cases or for exposing a child to abusive situations, for example. In this context, communication is highly unequal but communicative mechanisms assimilate this inequality into the language of mutuality. The result is that somehow abusers not only go unpunished but are often rewarded as husbands and fathers, while targets of abuse are placed in double binds that indicate a sort of rightlessness unaccounted for in conventional liberal theory.

As I have discussed, psychological research, family law articles, and media articles most often focus on the target—how she chose this relationship, how she was duped into staying, and how she could leave if she just got the strength. However, the few texts on abusers show that abuse cycles are almost completely unrelated to the individual characteristics of the target.[168] This is not to say that abuse is entirely impersonal but that abuse has its own logic as well as social supports. As discussed in the introduction, against theories of mutual provocation or the idea that abuse occurs during a fight, abusers often act when targets are happy, enjoying themselves, or have an important work deadline. Attacks also frequently occur when targets are sick, asleep, or physically vulnerable in some way. Sudden changes in mood are a crucial part of the cycle and the more unreasonable the "reasons" are for control and domination,[169] the better in terms of keeping their targets walking on eggshells. Against material arguments (which are based on rationality), abusers will often engage in lengthy court battles even though it is costly to them and not just their targets or their children. And quite a lot of their tactics are built on "soft power"—economic abuse, social isolation, alienation of children's affections—rather than hard power, including overt violence and aggression. Added to this is the dual behavior pattern that allows abusers to hold jobs, charm friends and family, and often contribute to the community, while also controlling and assaulting their partners and children. It is particularly difficult to fathom that an abuser has a cycle unrelated to his target—at least, difficult in the United States, where it is often argued that we are a democracy with an adequate judicial system, and where partnerships (whether formal or not) are mutual, contractual in some ways, and egalitarian. But the cycle of abuse has its own logic that cannot easily be mapped on to conventionally accepted notions of relationships, association, and political interactions. This is because it is the system itself that is the problem. First, there are very few people on the ground (at the enforcement or charity level) who are trained in domestic abuse issues specifically. Psychologists, lawyers, and the police constantly treat the situation as if it is egalitarian, mutually provoked (or provoked by the woman), and they often turn on the person who is most harmed or emotional: the target. This is because "rationality" counts more than discourse, in a way. Quite honestly, even some of those who are trained in domestic abuse do not necessarily implement their training.[170] Second, laws and enforcement do not merely treat the situation as egalitarian but can lead to serious punishments for women who try to get help, as I discussed in the previous chapters.

In this context, vigilante actions are understandable, if not self-defeating. While the state should not be appealed to as the ultimate bearer of authority or protector of well-being, we cannot just give up on the state either, for at least three simple reasons. First, even if one can conceive of state powers as aligning themselves with corporate power and privilege, the state should not be conceived as some god-like entity separate from the demos that created it. Second, if the state is in fact a fragmented, shifting, and contingent set of power dynamics—which I think the treatment of domestic abuse shows—power is not absolute in any sense. It is in these sites and areas of undecidability that resistance can and does occur. Third, given current conditions, women who flee with children or refuse children's visitation will more often than not be harshly punished, while exploited immigrants face even harsher penalties for attempting to escape abuse, including the possibility of detention and removal. For both immigrants and domestic abuse targets, *working outside of the law is incredibly dangerous.* Evan Stark and Lundy Bancroft have each suggested ways in which the "state" (from lawyers to guardians at litem to judges) should change, recognizing the specificity of domestic abuse as something akin to a stranger crime but with multiple entrapping facets that make the level of betrayal (and therefore injury) even more significant. Legal changes at every level must occur, but they should be merely instrumental to fighting or correcting asymmetries caused by control and abuse. They should not constitute the political or enact agency on behalf others. As I suggest in the next chapter, I clearly draw on Foucault's analytics of power but hold that Habermas's theories regarding the importance of civil society—particularly a civil society that is independent of the state—are absolutely crucial in forming solutions to these undemocratic power dynamics.

But I should note that some resistance is already occurring, in multiple ways, even as the powers I have described in this book have a dominating effect. Different strategies—from those of Anonymous (the "vigilante" hacker group) to those of grassroots groups with a feminist-intersectional approach to court advocates—are also part of the political context and provide important challenges to liberalism and its static notion of democratic participation. And while women who are targets of abuse can't necessarily judge the specific harms done to them at this moment, there are a myriad of other tactics that one can use to enact one's political agency.[171]

In the chapters that follow, I will make the case that domestic violence is largely tolerated and accepted by our society, even if micro-resistance and grassroots challenges are certainly present. I believe that targets of abuse should be treated as citizens capable of saying no; capable of testifying on their own behalf; and capable of claiming harms without the need for corroboration. I believe that perpetrators should be held responsible for their actions as a stranger would. But nothing at all will change if discourses about abuse and understandings of it as a unique and entrapping dynamic of subordination are ignored or if abuse is actually tolerated or celebrated. In the next chapter I examine the treatment of long-term residents who are abuse targets in comparison with two key refugee cases based on domestic violence claims. What is interesting is that the government takes a far more enlightened approach to domestic violence in these cases—one that would aid long-term residents if applied to them. Even so, the approach taken in the two cases (*The Matter of RA, The Matter of LR*) is also incredibly problematic in several respects, demonstrating how citizenship itself—the meaning of political speech and feminism—is reduced to mere life. In this way, the subject of domestic violence explodes conventional categories of political theory, pushing us to reformulate terms of political inclusion and exclusion.

CHAPTER 3

Domestic Abuse and the Limits of Communication (Foucault, Habermas, and Beyond)

INTRODUCTION

In the previous chapter I analyzed the various historical trajectories and discourses that have led to a context in which there has been a sort of return to the family and communication-based, egalitarian-centered techniques that depoliticize intimate abuse and trump individual rights and protections. In this chapter, I connect these ideas to two paradigmatic asylum cases.[1] Although immigration procedures and law are different from family law and the domestic violence system, these two cases actually crystallize many of the issues I have identified thus far. I examine these two gender-based asylum cases in two different respects. First, I analyze these cases in terms of how a unique political subjectivity is produced through discourses directly related to the two cases: *The Matter of RA* and *The Matter of LR*. This political subjectivity is discursively shaped through an understanding of domestic violence and how and why women are the targets of abuse in their home countries. What is interesting is how each woman was eventually classified by the US government as part of a social group (based on the immutability of gender and ethnicity, and recognition of intimate partnership as irrevocable) and a nexus was established between the domestic abuse each suffered and their state's respective inaction when they sought help. In defining these categories, the Department of Homeland Security interpreted their attempts to seek help and to flee as "feminism" and their opposition to patriarchal norms in each region as "political speech." These two categories (feminism, political speech) position each woman as a feminist only in dialectical opposition to other women in similar situations and situated in the allegedly unique patriarchy of the regions they are from. In this way, it is an identity of spectacularity that perhaps chastens other women, but which also stops the refugee floodgates from opening.[2] These two cases also indicate how the United States shores up its identity as a "haven for abused women"[3] by accepting these two women from their home countries—RA (Rody Alvarado) is from Guatemala and LR is from Mexico—in ways that are comparable to other gender-based asylum claims of the time but also very different in terms of their political, economic, and geographical proximity to the United States.[4] The cases serve to mask the United States's own history of gender inequality and continued unresolved issues in approaches to intimate partner abuse.

They also point to a dual system in which the domestic abuse in other countries is viewed as political,[5] whereas in the United States, the same problem is interpreted as personal and private. Importantly, arguments for both asylum cases demonstrate an acknowledgment that abuse has its own logic independent of the target's personality or actions (that is, independent of individual responsibility or provocation). Abuse is part of intimate partnership and built into status inequality rather than being personal. Thus, documents related to both cases conceive that domestic abuse is unprovoked and a product of societal mores about women's status, including their identification as "property." Significantly, abuse is interpreted by the US government as being related to social, economic, and political inequality. These cases also rested on state inaction when each woman tried to get help. While this argument—that state inaction linked to traditional gender roles and marriage laws led to political inequality and the possibility of political persecution—has been groundbreaking in allowing some women to seek asylum in the United States, the argument is also circular: the United States could not grant asylum to these women unless circumstances in their home countries were vastly different than in ours, but they are only different because the government's interpretation of their cases requires and discursively produces their extraordinariness. In turn, while no explicit comparison has been made to the plight of abused women in the United States, each category of asylum is dialectically opposed to the purported freedoms of intimate relations in a North American democracy.

The cases also bring attention to key categories of liberalism: what counts as political speech; the right of resistance; how feminism is defined; and the interpretation of violence as political violence. In turn, I believe that exploring the cases in terms of Michel Foucault's work as well as Habermas's illuminates difficulties in how citizenship, political exclusion, and violence are treated. These difficulties problematize the very categories of liberal techniques purported to solve issues of intimate abuse: rationality, mutuality, communication, and the citizens' rights. As I have discussed in the previous chapters and particularly the last, there has been a shift from encouraging targets to flee to encouraging them to stay, to keep the family unit intact, and to communicate to solve the issue of domestic abuse. While this shift is not absolute and targets receive mixed messages, there is a greater emphasis on communication, for example in requiring communication with the abuser related to paternity, counseling, legal mediation, and co-parenting courses.

While neither Foucault nor Habermas writes extensively on gender,[6] these solutions are forms of communication in Habermas's theories as well as Foucault's. For Habermas, rationality, equality, and speech help lead one from ignorance and a position of strategic action or even dominance to examining one's own claims and those of others, to reach some sort of consensus. In contrast, Foucault's notion of bio-power is open to interpreting bio-power as the politicization of gendered biological determinism and identifying violence even in the most rational of arrangements.[7] Rather than focus on liberal categories of identity or group membership per se, I draw on both authors (and others) to analyze the power relations of domestic abuse that produce certain subjectivities, shape power processes, and often determine outcomes. That is, I believe that viewing the issue of domestic abuse from the position of the abused and not that of the state, the literature, or the abuser explodes these taken-for-granted spheres and problematizes Enlightenment understandings of communication as a solution.

Although contemporary theory has perhaps expanded beyond the work of Habermas and Foucault, these two theorists remain important today in understanding discourse and power relations. Both theorists work within an Enlightenment framework but from a critical standpoint, interrogating commonly held assumptions of technological or civilizational progress and faith in capitalist markets, for example. However, the subject of domestic abuse challenges the limits of both theories in ways that common political problems do not. This is because, as I have argued, domestic abuse policy and enforcement often focus on the target of abuse but not the perpetrator, thus ignoring or assimilating the sort of power conceived of as primitive or premodern. Policies and nonprofit help in this area nonetheless often rely on solutions that are egalitarian or consensual in nature and this communication-based, egalitarian set of solutions paradoxically deepens inequality, often perpetuates abuse, and legally entraps the target but not the abuser. Finally, misleading discursive conventions are established—for example, the myth that the court system prefers women and mothers (statistics show the opposite—abusers "win" in most ways[8]); that it is really up to targets of abuse to leave abusers or stand up to them (thus, it is assumed that there are no economic or legal costs involved and that the target of abuse operates in a vacuum[9]); and that targets can become domestic abuse "survivors" (a subject I return to in the conclusion). The discourse on being a "survivor," in particular, indicates that abuse is violent, spectacular, and temporally isolated, and that the current system can adequately identify and help targets to end this violence once and for all—which is misleading at best.[10] These dynamics show not merely a split between popular discourse, policies, and mainstream enforcement (which includes courts, the police, and the shelter system) and the reality of domestic abuse, but indicate how abuse often happens with impunity. In contrast, the target of abuse faces very real economic and job losses: she can lose her children, be geographically confined, or be diagnosed with a mental illness for being in an abusive relationship.[11] There are no corresponding losses or punishments for the abuser, at least in any statistically significant way. Again, the asylum cases I explore below further illuminate these difficulties.

I will develop these arguments further below, but in brief, Habermas's presuppositions about mutuality, equality, consent, and rationality are exemplified and validated by domestic abuse and family policies that require legal mediation, negotiated custodial orders, couples counseling, and anger management and parenting classes for couples with a history of intimate abuse.[12] In this sense, communication is held to not only displace violent words and actions but also, from a developmental point of view, is alleged to bring the couple from a more "archaic" power dynamic to a more modern one.[13] From a Habermasian perspective, these policies would embody the notion that communication takes precedence as a key democratic mechanism. The question I address in this chapter is whether the speech-as-self-defense of the "tortured" can be political speech? Despite his pedigree in critical theory, Habermas often works within established power dynamics (including liberalism), without considering how issues of citizenship and sovereignty are in question when a subject is systematically assaulted and abused.[14]

Foucault's theories anticipate the critique of domestic abuse solutions, all of which have been argued to deepen the already unequal relationship and empower the abuser, and which, I would add, assimilate rather than eradicate violence, domination, and abuse.[15] Foucault's work also helps to predict how the speaking subject, who is most often the target of abuse and not the perpetrator, can become increasingly entrapped in the system that purports to help her. But he also often holds that modern power—disciplinary power and bio-power—operate apart from sovereignty. His later work complicates these assumptions and his notion of "governmentality" hints at the imbrications of the two sorts of power. This later work is important in understanding how the state's deployment of power outside of the rule of law can end up shaping discourse, producing feminist subjectivities, and defining victimhood, even as the state also often portrays intimate abuse as "private."

Perhaps the most important consideration in the work of both authors is their relationship to violence. While arriving at very different conclusions, each author assumes that coercion and violence are either "outside" of communicative relations in a democracy like the United States (Habermas) or secondary to a more knowledge-based, discursive set of relationships (Foucault).[16] To clarify, Habermas analyzes violence as an incursion on the lifeworld rather than as a common feature of contemporary civilization.[17] Foucault's work, if taken as a whole, is more nuanced. While authors like Anna Marie Smith, Zygmunt Bauman, Michael Hardt and Antonio Negri and Paul Apostolidis argue that bio-power has superseded disciplinary power[18]—and thus, more violent power dynamics have displaced older disciplinary techniques—I hold that disciplinary power and bio-power must be analyzed together to understand how Foucault's work does not dismiss violence but actually predicts its more technological, scientific, and technical-bureaucratic applications.[19] In turn, the consideration of both powers together helps to understand dynamics of domestic violence more broadly than simply examining one type.[20] The RA and LR cases crystallize the most important of the communication-violence linkages: self-defense and flight are interpreted as speech, and gender is only proved through victimization, being treated as property, and through political abandonment. Women are not a cognizable political group otherwise. These cases demonstrate the interpretation of political speech as the lowest level of speech (what Arendt would call "mere life" and Giorgio Agamben, "bare life").

In the context of domestic violence, the subject of speech is particularly complex; the violator isn't urged to speak to the degree that the target is. The compulsion to speak—to name one's abuse, to identify oneself to get help—falls on the target. In contrast, the abuser becomes mute through having his actions assimilated by the law or entirely ignored.

Thus, in the context of abuse, there is an imbalance that would violate Habermas's grounding principles of communicative action and, more broadly, his ideal constitutional democracy. Most important, he sees speech as occurring in the context of nonviolence—to Habermas, speech can be evaluated on a spectrum, from strategic speech (opportunistic, goal oriented, and/or not aimed at mutual understanding) to the sort of communicative action that occurs in the lifeworld, aiming at mutual understanding and a respectful examination of truth-claims. The problem is that even given this range, speech is not often that pure—in the home, on the street, and in politics, violence and inequality often undergird even the most "civilized" of political contexts. With the problem of domestic abuse, if a target of abuse speaks—to her abuser, a therapist, a police officer, or a judge—this speech is not the communication of an autonomous individual with full rights but someone who is often treated badly with impunity. The target-speaker may or may not be helped momentarily by the police (but only temporarily, even in the best circumstances), but her problems could be made worse by a therapist or judge. If all of this could be classified as speech, it is the speech of self-defense, of the lowest level of existence ("mere life") and not as a truly political agent, as Arendt has theorized.[21]

What further complicates matters is that this speech of self-defense then (often) obscures the perpetrator's actions. That is, as the law and shelter system are often conceived, speech helps to identify and normalize the actions of the (silent) abuser. As the target increasingly identifies herself as abused, she risks being classified as mentally ill[22] (and even declared incompetent);[23] losing her job;[24] and being charged with exposing her child to abuse (which can be grounds for removal to foster care).[25] Paradoxically, the one who is most powerful is the silent and yet violent one. As the target increasingly implicates herself in a web of blame, help, pathologization, and occasional sympathy, it is *her* speech that sets the context for his (empowered) erasure. Nevertheless, what complicates even Foucault's account of normalization, which in this case bridges bio-power and disciplinary power, is that the documentation that is supposed to prove abuse is not straightforwardly interpreted as it is supposed to be. That is, even for women with some privilege (e.g., economic or white skin privilege), a police officer will often refuse to help, might write the facts incorrectly, or might even arrest the target if *she* is more emotional than the abuser.[26] Even if meticulous documentation is taken, it is idealistic to think anyone actually reads it.

Documentation paradoxically ensures a target may get help but can also put her in an incredibly risky situation, only augmenting the unequal power dynamics. These sorts of dynamics then challenge the meticulous attention to detail Foucault observes in disciplinary institutions. If disciplinary power and bio-power occur in these instances, it is despite bureaucratic inefficiency, imperfect documentation, and an inability to act impartially.[27] From a more contemporary view of Foucault's disciplinary power, it is important to note the fascinating parallel between immigration law and domestic violence policy in that they are largely extraconstitutional and yet also highly bureaucratized. What results is a bizarre mix of formal requirements for someone who has been denigrated, economically marginalized, or assaulted, and yet this law is premised on the absence of constitutional principles and judicial review.[28]

At this point, Foucault's theories seem to be the winner of the Habermas versus Foucault standoff, but there is an important element of Habermas's work that we should keep in mind. As welfare law, family law, and shelters have changed, this social space that provided a context for the sort of civil society Habermas envisioned when he wrote *The Theory of Communicative Action* has disappeared. At this more revolutionary time, shelters embodied Habermas's conception of civil society, which involved self-definition, solidarity, and debate based on ethical and mutual grounds, albeit probably still in a Foucaultian context. Today, because the domestic violence "revolution" has now been co-opted by conservatives and the religious right, not to mention having been professionalized and made clinical, targets' speech has become part of a Foucaultian nightmare. In this context, Habermas's theory is certainly complicated—speech is not speech, help is not help, and perversely, violence is power. Nevertheless, this is not to give up on Habermas's ideals—not because they are possible in the way he conceives of them, nor because there is really an "outside" to power, but rather because in the best circumstances, speech still matters and is really the only way a "target" may truly change her situation.[29] To put it differently, when abused women are treated as legitimate speakers worthy of civil protections and political action, their speech and their self-defense will take on a more democratic meaning than is currently the case. This transformation will not change abusers per se or the societal tendency to blame victims but rather will stop empowering and legitimating them.

Beyond the issue of communication, the debate between Foucault and Habermas revolves around their conception of power. Foucault's radical critique of rationality and the Enlightenment, not to mention attention to the margins, can indicate a sort of realism that Habermas will not admit. If we are to find our way out of the circular mess of intimate abuse, it will not be through a blind faith in reason, communication, or the law, when it is these very things that allow abuse to be committed with impunity and which all essentially punish the victim. But the brief period in which the abused were allowed to speak for themselves and define their own circumstances—from shelter stays to plans of action—demonstrates a need for civil society that Habermas develops much more than Foucault. However, as I hint at in the title of this chapter, my discussion goes beyond the Habermas-Foucault debate to conceive of a fuller critique of violent norms and practices maintained and reproduced through Enlightenment ideas.

In the case of asymmetrical abuse, communication is not futile but being forced to communicate with one's abuser is. This issue highlights the problematic assumptions of liberalism and critical theory: we have not eradicated violence or gender inequality but have assimilated these issues into discourses that ironically focus on the target and not the perpetrator of abuse, domination, and assaults. That is, the law does not turn a blind eye to these forms of violence but instead rigorously goes after the target and not the perpetrator. Furthermore, what is taken to be rational communication does not actually supersede premodern issues such as emotion, intellectual inflexibility, or authoritarian tendencies. In the case of abuse, policies and street-level help in fact highlight and pathologize the emotions of abuse targets while interpreting men's frustrations, men's alleged victimization, and so on, as rational, legitimate, and democratic. If communication, rational deliberation, and mutuality are still valuable, they should only occur in noncoercive circumstances and in truly egalitarian situations. That is, if Habermas's ideal communicative action is to be realized, an entirely different political context will have to be achieved— one that is not outside of power but which recognizes that emotional denigration, economic control, social isolation, and assault are mechanisms of control to be resisted every day.[30] The need for daily action, agency, and resistance challenges more linear approaches that conceive of a social problem, its identification, and then its transcendence. The cases of RA and LR synthesize these issues in ways that examinations of the more fragmented system treating domestic abuse targets for US residents do not.

GENDER-BASED DOMESTIC ABUSE ASYLUM CASES: RA AND LR

> The novelty of modern biopolitics lies in the fact that the biological given is as such immediately political, and the political is as such immediately the biological given. –Giorgio Agamben[31]

In the 1990s, while some very important gender-based asylum cases were filed in the United States, *In the Matter of RA* was considered one of the most important (RA has chosen to identify herself as Rodi Alvarado).[32] Guatemalan teenager Rodi Alvarado married Francisco Osorio at age 16 (he was 21 years old and a former military member). Osorio viewed Alvarado as property and held that his right to abuse her was because marriage essentially sealed this property-like status. His abuse entailed severe and regular physical and sexual assault, emotional tactics (threats, derogatory remarks, waking her up in the middle of the night, manipulating their children), and it even occurred in public.[33] His physical abuse of her was shocking, entailing regular sexual assaults, beatings, attempts to abort their child (through kicking her stomach), and using her head as a battering ram. Despite this systematic pattern of abuse, it is hard to prove. As Alvarado's lawyer Karen Musalo has argued, most women are not as "lucky" as Alvarado in that Osorio has made explicit statements about abusing his wife and why. But for most targets of abuse, Musalo notes, "Persecutors are hardly likely to provide their victims with affidavits attesting to their acts of persecution."[34] Alvarado's testimony has been undisputed, as were her attempts to get help—she contacted the police at least three times and tried to get help from a court at least once.[35] She ran away, attempted suicide, and eventually fled the country without her children. Once she reached the United States, her asylum case did not hinge on the validity of her documentation but the immigration service's requirement that someone fleeing persecution show "social group membership and political opinion" in order to prove that the abuse was political.[36]

The problem in applying for asylum in the United States is that one must have a well-founded fear of persecution and the United States largely defines this in terms of formal political groupings and official national actors and institutions.[37] There are three issues in the context of an abuse case such as Alvarado's. One is that the wielder of violence is a private actor, even when acting in public. His identity was characterized as private by virtue of his marital status, which as Carole Pateman has discussed in the context of Britain and the United States, requires state involvement to recognize and validate the marriage and yet, bizarrely, entails state withdrawal from the "private sphere" in these matters.[38] Guatemalan law makes the wife subordinate to the husband in numerous ways upon marriage, just as the laws of coverture in the United States suspended women's rights upon marriage in the past.[39] Thus, a state-sanctioned contract perversely leads to the suspension of political status and rights, but these losses are cast as private and thus are denied as having any formal political consequences. In turn, "These de jure denials of equality are compounded by discrimination in the administration of justice and application of the law."[40] Alvarado's abuse was clearly "harm" and even "torture,"[41] but the systematic emotional denigration, social isolation, and violent assaults she suffered were private. The state's role in her case was through its inaction: "Courts have long held that threats to life or freedom, or other egregious physical and psychological harms, inflicted by the government or by persons the government is unable or unwilling to control, constitute persecution."[42] However, state inaction can be harder to prove than state action; it requires documenting the lack of documentation.

Second, Alvarado's counsel had to prove she was part of a persecuted group, and this required proving "social visibility." Her counsel's argument broadly rested on "nationality, gender, and marital status"[43] but these designations were difficult to piece together to fit the group visibility rule. The LR case, which I discuss below, was entered as Alvarado's case was being reheard in 2009, in the context of this new focus (as of 2004) on "social groups" and their "visibility" when judging asylum applications.[44] Prior to this case, it was often held that abused women were not part of a persecuted group, as were, for example, an ethnic minority like Somali Bantus.[45] This contrast is important because the basis of Somali Bantus' persecution is not just de jure but also de facto, as they suffer abuses in the hands of both formal and informal political actors. Their social grouping thus rests on both formal and informal criteria, designations that could also be extended to asylum applicants filing gender-based claims.[46]

To prove she was part of a visible social group, Alvarado had to show that her identity as an abused woman was "immutable"[47] and thus gender and marital status both had to be classified as irrevocably unalterable in Guatemala.[48] A "nexus" also had to be established, connecting persecution to social or cultural factors. Significantly, abuse had to have happened *because* of the victim's status rather than provocation or a mutual fight to be classified as "credible fear."[49] Alvarado testified that this was the case, because "It was clear . . . that her husband's animus was not personal to her as an *individual*, but directed towards her as his *wife*; when directly questioned on this point, she testified that her husband would batter any woman to whom he was married."[50] To prove that her abuse was a reflection of group status and not a choice or based in provocation, there are two literatures cited as evidence in her case briefs[51]: one on domestic abuse and the other on why and how it occurs in Guatemala. Interestingly, the sources on domestic abuse in Alvarado's application treat domestic violence as perhaps varied geographically but also united in its characteristics in many ways. For instance, Musalo cites a human rights article on domestic abuse:

> Wife beating is, therefore, not an individual, isolated or aberrant act, . . . but a social license, a duty or sign of masculinity, deeply ingrained in culture, widely practiced, denied and completely or largely immune from sanction. *It is inflicted on women in the position of wives* for their actual or suspected failure to properly carry out their role, for their failure to produce, serve, or be properly subservient.[52]

What is interesting about this statement is that it connects women's inequality, traditional gender roles, and abuse in a broad sense (that is, this could happen for example in the United States) while also indicating that the specificity of culture and other factors can influence a more local analysis. The same author, Rhonda Copelon, also argues that "violence against wives is a function of the belief . . . that men are superior and that the women they live with are their possessions or chattels that they can treat as they wish and as they consider appropriate."[53] And again, Copelon (quoted in Musalo) establishes the connection between gender inequality and violence: "Domestic violence is not gender-neutral. . . . Severe, repeated domestic [abuse] is overwhelmingly initiated by *men and inflicted upon women.*"[54] Similarly, authors Dorothy Q. Thomas and Michele E. Beasley argue that "domestic violence has been revealed [to be] gender specific. . . . Of all spousal violence crimes, ninety-one percent were victimizations of *women by their husbands or ex-husbands.*"[55] None of these quotes single out any territorial locus for "traditional" or "primitive" cultures per se, but describe why and how political, economic, and discursive gender inequality can be linked to a political—and not personal—motive and support for intimate partner control and abuse. A nexus between these various forms of women's political, economic, and social subordination can then be linked to domestic abuse.

This nexus in turn establishes how a private actor can have considerable political support, and therefore the case justifies the classification of "political persecution." The example Musalo gives is of a Jewish store owner who is attacked by his or her competitors who are not directly connected to the Nazis. Nevertheless, they wouldn't have attacked this individual unless "they knew that the authorities would allow them to act with impunity" and this impunity was based on the target's marginalized status.[56] Similarly, female gender roles then are not merely constructed on traditional and nontraditional gender positions or identities but also through this "epistemological condition" of being a woman,[57] which entails the possibility of being attacked by an intimate other with impunity.

Another crucial part of Alvarado's argument was based on "political opinion." This involved not merely the emotional disposition of the abuser, in his view that a wife is property, but also Alvarado's belief that she didn't deserve the abuse. Her attempts to get help, to flee, or to just stop the blows were reinterpreted by the US government as political speech and feminism. Musalo's brief included expert testimony that Alvarado's emotional disposition was anomalous for Guatemalan women; Alvarado's belief that she had the right to live and to escape were indications that she didn't deserve her abuse.[58] These attempts to ward off blows, stop sexual assaults, and flee constitute political opinion because, "A woman's deeply held opinion that her husband does not have the right to violate her physical and psychological integrity is one of the most fundamental expressions of feminism, because freedom from domestic violence is a necessary condition for the attainment of all other societal equalities."[59] But as most domestic violence experts recognize, regardless of country, flight does not constitute freedom: this is usually when death is most likely (that is, murder by the abuser).[60] As a counterpart to this interpretation of Alvarado's fight for her life—which some would argue is at the level of bare life and self-defense and not political speech—her husband Osorio's abuse was also conceived of in terms of power. Her "resistance" to his assaults led to greater escalation on his part.[61] Musalo's incredibly perceptive statement on this could be said about nearly any domestic violence situation that gets to this level: "because domestic violence is quintessentially about issues of power and subordination in intimate relationships, domestic violence is necessarily motivated by status (i.e., social group) as well as by resistance (i.e., insubordination). Osorio's rage at Ms. Alvarado's resistance is consonant with an understanding of domestic violence as purposeful behavior intended to exert power, to eradicate resistance, and to perpetuate subordination."[62]

In sum, this case allowed for a (precarious[63]) group-based argument founded on the woman's country of origin combined with societal values that denigrate and dehumanize women and the absence of any help for victims of abuse. That is, there is now some room for "group" status based on their absolute victimization. Second, government "persecution" in this case (and LR's) has been recast as government inaction; RA was abused and then was denied any form of legal protection. But the abused woman must document these attempts and her lack of success; in this regard, Alvarado had an allegedly stronger case than LR. Arguably, the burdens of documentation are higher in cases like these because gender-based asylum is already removed from what is conceived of as "political." What should also be added is the fact that both cases were resolved by the authority of US immigration judges to grant discretion, which as I note below, means that this case will not necessarily set a precedent.[64]

The *Matter of LR* occurred during roughly the same time period and the abuse she suffered was similar (although it also included a documented murder attempt when her abuser tried to burn her alive).[65] From age 19, when she was in a teacher training program and the school's athletic coach raped her at gunpoint, LR experienced horrific systematic abuse: "For the next two decades he kept her in virtual captivity, using physical force, beatings, and threats of death to her and her family members, to prevent her from leaving him."[66] He regularly raped her, subjected her to emotional abuse, and when she had three children—each a result of rape—he abused them, too. Every time she attempted to escape (including flight to another town and one attempt to come to the United States in 1991), he found her and his violence escalated. An attempt to murder her in a fire was retaliation for one such attempt. When she tried to get police help, they not only refused to help her but told her "common-law husband" about her attempt to report him. When her abuser used their children as hostages, a judge said he would only help her if she had sex with him. She refused and was deemed a bad mother by the judge.[67] She fled again to the United States in 2004, with the children; at this point, she understandably had severe physical and mental issues as a result of the prolonged abuse.

Because of these issues, which were later diagnosed as post-traumatic stress disorder (PTSD), she didn't file her asylum application in a timely fashion—the deadline is one year and she waited to file after entering 19 months before.[68] Her first application was judged "credible" but because she didn't meet the deadline, her claim was denied. When the Department of Homeland Security subsequently became involved, they expressed concern that she didn't try to seek help enough in Mexico and therefore could not properly document state inaction.[69] LR and her lawyers then introduced expert testimony asserting that she had PTSD, which suggested that she experienced "intense psychological distress" when she was confronted with psychological triggers dealing directly with the abuse.[70] In this way, she could function on an everyday level, caring for her children, but found it paralyzing to try to get help. This diagnosis was accepted by the judge (the judge "noted that one symptom associated with PTSD is avoidance of situations that trigger traumatic memories"[71]). However, the judge argued that because she could care for her children and function in daily life, this was "evidence" that she was not disabled entirely and thus could have met the deadline. Thus, the judge both accepted and rejected the diagnosis.

As the issues of "social group" and "nexus" became increasingly important in the post-9/11 era, the *Matter of RA* was influential in creating higher standards for refugee relief but also for opening a new avenue for gender-based asylum petitions in the case of domestic violence. Broadly, LR could be said to be a member of a social group based on gender and the "inability to leave an abusive domestic relationship."[72] But the Department of Homeland Security claimed that LR's social group was not "cognizable." Further, the judge at this time not only concurred with DHS on this but added that her "persecution was not on account of a protected ground. The judge acknowledged that Ms. L.R.'s abuser viewed her as property, but found that *he beat her simply because he was a violent man*, not because of her gender or status in the relationship."[73] This interpretation seems to be completely arbitrary given the nature of the abuse she suffered, which was all significantly gendered (as a woman and mother): including multiple rapes, the inability to go to the police based on gender (subordinate political status), and perhaps a "partnership/marital status" that subordinated her based on this "relationship."[74] Third, using the children as hostages is particularly gendered in terms of the attachments, including "traumatic bonding," that a primary caretaker forms with her children.[75] When she appealed to the Board of Immigration Appeals, DHS argued that her case was too weak (on the basis of group membership).

However, when the Obama administration came in, the DHS position changed to one of greater openness to domestic violence claims. DHS then filed a brief in April 2009[76] that essentially outlined how this case could be filed in order to meet current standards. They suggested two social groups that LR might belong to in order to meet the criteria of "shared immutable or fundamental characteristics, social visibility, and particularity": "'Mexican women in domestic relationships who are unable to leave,' and 'Mexican women who are viewed as property by virtue of their positions within a domestic relationship.'"[77] The DHS brief also stated the requirements for a successful application. An abused woman must show that in her country: "(1) the society and legal norms tolerate and accept violence against women; (2) the government is unable or unwilling to protect; and (3) there is no place within the home country that the woman could move to in order to escape her persecutor."[78] Following these guidelines the counsel for LR and her children finally succeeded on August 4, 2010 (in San Francisco[79]), in getting a grant of asylum based on discretion, with no reason stated. These last two factors are important to note because "Neither the DHS brief nor the judge's decision in LR are binding on immigration judges, the BIA, or federal judges" but they can still have an impact on asylum officers (the first level of the process of establishing credible fear), DHS lawyers, and immigration judges.[80] As Daniel Kanstroom has emphasized in his work on plenary power and the bizarre aspects of immigration law since the late 1880s, *discretion* and *mercy* are both legal terms that indicate the legal use of authority but an authority outside regular law. They do not create a binding rule or precedent per se (that is, they can be used as a precedent but given the absence of constitutional review and given recent changes at the BIA, even these grants of authority are arbitrary).[81] Nevertheless, the impact of both cases has already been felt—according to the latest data compiled[82]—and is certainly an advance for would-be refugees.[83]

However in these two cases of RA (Rody Alvarado) and LR, a unique political identity was formed that singles out both women's feminism as exceptional and inimitable but which simultaneously casts the United States as "A Haven for Abused Women,"[84] effectively disavowing the significant gender inequities in domestic assault, marital rape, and intimate abuse that occur in the United States.[85]

ANALYSIS OF THESE CASES AND SHORING UP OF US SUPERIORITY

These two cases produce a static version of feminist identity based on the requirements of group identity, irreversible gender roles, and state inaction in cases of domestic violence and rape. This identity is notably formed by the asylum system and jurisprudential discourse, rather than being defined by the women themselves. These designations of feminism, group identity, and political speech are not particularly political in any active sense, including not being defined by the individuals involved. Instead these categories rest on assumptions that the culture is to blame and these particular women are in a unique situation based on formal indifference and abandonment because neither Guatemala nor Mexico protects its female citizens.[86] But these two women are also cast as exceptional in their assertion of the right to live and to flee—their "feminism" and "political speech" not only mark them as unique but place them in dialectical opposition to the majority of their fellow countrywomen. In this way, Alvarado and LR's feminism and political speech are only feminist and political by virtue of their exceptional quality—in a sense rejecting all that is Latina, as construed by the US government—which ensures that their successes are legally self-terminating. This sort of feminism is part of a broader narrative of feminism in asylum interviews and hearings and

often involves denigrating one's own country or region as traditional, patriarchal, and backwards[87]—frozen in the past.[88] In this context, feminism entails rejection of one's community but this allows asylum officers
and immigration judges to also cast women's resistance to traditional
norms as "failed feminism,"[89] because their origins signal their complicity
to their own subjection. In this way, the United States government's sympathetic readings of both Alvarado's case and the case of LR as embodying
feminism and political speech should be read in their unique specificity
and the fact that political speech and feminism entail a dialectical rejection of their families, communities, and home states. But again, these de-
terminations produce an undecidable status in that these women can also
be cast as "failed feminists."[90] Their initial "complicity" in abuse is evidence of this failure and the success of their refugee applications is the
ultimate measure of feminism *and* failed feminism.

Despite these difficulties and deficiencies, the United States government treated each of these women as legal subjects capable of representing their experiences accurately, something the "system" does not do for
long-term US residents who experience abuse. In the language of the domestic abuse literature, documents and decisions related to each case recognized that the abuse each woman suffered was "asymmetrical," thus
acknowledging that the abuse was unequal on every level. As I have discussed in previous chapters, although there is no unified system addressing domestic violence in the United States, the general tendency of shelters, counseling, policing, and the legal system today is to assume
"symmetry" in domestic violence situations occurring on US soil. While
there are challenges to the assumption of symmetry,[91] asymmetry arguments are indicative of the second key difference between the two asylum
cases and mainstream approaches to the abuse of long-term US residents:
domestic abuse is portrayed as having a political basis in Guatemala and
Mexico, whereas in the United States, if women are abused, their abuse is
portrayed as private, as a choice, and as based in mutual provocation.
Thus, the crucial differences in distinguishing a refugee case from an apolitical, individual case (i.e., a case occurring in the United States) are the
political and societal contexts of dealing with this issue and not the facets
of intimate abuse.

Like Guatemala and Mexico, marriage laws in the United States historically led to the loss of women's rights. Even today, the impunity with
which marital rape can occur is evidence of this legacy.[92] However, the
United States distances itself from this shared culture of patriarchy and
legal subordination by accepting these two asylum cases and portraying
them as feminism and political speech. Thus feminism and political speech

are not merely a rejection of the (alleged) cultures of Guatemala and Mexico but also serve as conceptual markers that distinguish the United States as civilized and modern in contrast to more traditional cultures.

Further, although a key difference in immigration law in general—which is based on the plenary power doctrine—and the discretionary authority used in these cases would appear to be vastly different from the treatment of US residents, this arbitrary quality certainly characterizes domestic abuse treatment ranging from the terms of family law to police enforcement to more informal modes of governance in shelters and other nonprofit help. Unlike would-be refugees, many women abused on US soil have some sort of political status, but once they are abused, they are often disenfranchised in numerous ways, even if only de facto. In turn, undocumented women who are abused on US soil can hope for a U visa, but they often have difficulties with the required affirmation of the police that the victim fully cooperated with them. All of these cases are characterized by formal and informal modes of discretion and mercy, including punitive mechanisms that can go much farther in punishing targets of abuse than abusers themselves.

What is particularly interesting is that the same behaviors that LR and RA engaged in—from protecting themselves from blows to hiding to fleeing—are often criminalized in the United States. Essentially, while self-defense and flight are interpreted as political speech and feminism in these cases, the same tactics are absolutely criminalized for long-term residents. But it is worth exploring in further depth the meaning of the political speech of the two asylum cases, since they are also a part of US policy toward the abused, even if this policy is in direct contrast to how long-term residents who are targets of abuse are treated.

ABUSE AND SPEECH

Several facets of these two cases should be compared to US dynamics of the treatment of the abused. It is important to note, again, that while laws of coverture are no longer valid in the United States, there are still unresolved issues (most significantly, the issue of marital rape) and legacies of this legal subordination (in pay, amassed wealth, political power, and the continuation of sexist norms in more informal ways) that link the United States to Guatemala and Mexico. The broader point is that there are important similarities between these cases and US cases of abuse—from the interpersonal dynamics to state inaction—even if these asylum cases are supposed to somehow prove (even if tacitly) that the United States is superior. Rather, the key differences in distinguishing a refugee case from an apolitical individual case are the interpretations of what counts as political and feminism, and thus the meaning of speech itself. To put it differently, in juxtaposing these two cases to the more general treatment of abuse victims who are long-term US residents, the tendency to pathologize the US victims of abuse seems directly proportional to the degree that abuse is viewed as mutual and even contractual (a woman chose to be with this type of partner and could always walk out, no problem), rather than political, economic, or societal.

In both cases, one of the most obvious observations is that neither system is set up to prevent abuse but rather to shelter the victim *after* absolutely egregious violence has occurred.

The definitions of abuse—as persecution and torture in human rights terms and as extreme bodily harm in the United States—are also important in that they treat assaults as isolated and spectacular. The lack of acknowledgment that LR's post-traumatic stress disorder could affect her ability to meet the asylum deadline is some indication of a broader tendency to refuse to recognize the effects of emotional abuse on a person during and after the abuse.[93] Related to this observation is the fact that there are difficulties in getting documentation to prove one's case. Both refugees and domestic abuse victims residing in the United States must produce documentation to show "danger," but getting the correct documentation, particularly to demonstrate systematic patterns, is absolutely difficult if not impossible if the targets are being subjected to deprivation, isolation, economic abuse, assault, and a myriad of other forms of control. It is also difficult for those who do not have easy access to medical care or psychologists, not to mention if the police have a hostile relationship with a group or view them as subordinate, but it is similarly difficult for those who are viewed as privileged to get documentation. There is no "danger" if there is no documentation, and this perception increases over time. Every failed attempt to get help is then translated as the absence of danger; over time, in the absence of documentation or help, new attempts to get help fail based on this old evidence. But notably, state inaction in other countries—if it can be proved—is part of the foundation of a refugee claim, while state inaction in the United States is not even recognized, because the laws do not actually enforce these claims.

While our country has more Foucaultian dynamics (it's a fragmented state, with the possibility of resistance and micro-resistance) and some Habermasian dynamics (important civil society actors that are often underfunded but which give support to the abused), it is not a haven for the abused by any means.[94] Rather, it is marked by an inconsistent and often contradictory set of power dynamics that a seasoned target can navigate and perhaps use or escape—a set of possibilities that may not be true in Guatemala or parts of Mexico. In all cases, there is a perverse logic: abuse hasn't really occurred if there is no documentation, but if someone seeks help, they risk further brutalization from their abuser and the justice system. Documentation proves danger but the nature of this danger is such that it is almost impossible to secure the proper amount of documentation. The arbitrary quality of systems purported to "help" victims is almost never admitted. Most notably, it is hard to prove that one called the police and didn't receive help. Further, similar to the sending countries, domestic abuse in the United States is committed with near-impunity, and the system either ignores the target, helps her as a "protected" (i.e. incompetent) victim, or more often, punishes her.

If these things are true, the adoption of the categories that the Department of Homeland Security introduced in these two cases would be a marked improvement over the current system. Indeed, one could argue that the analysis of "persecution" and "credible fear" based on state inaction could apply to this country also, granted that the dynamics are less absolute. Moreover, although I question the degree to which liberal rights are a solution (rather than a limited, entrapping mechanism to neutralize political difference), the recognition of women in the United States as a visible and cognizable social group is worth considering. As I discuss in the conclusion, because gender does not receive any special protection or scrutiny at the judicial level (e.g., in comparison to race) and the 1990s post–affirmative action discourse of women's triumphs and equality are believed, a similar dynamic occurs here as occurs in Guatemala and Mexico.

However, there are two obstacles to recognizing women as a social group with immutable characteristics in the United States. First is the continued reference to Enlightenment or liberal notions of consent, contract, and liberal democracy within relationships (even among unmarried partnerships). The reasoning is fairly simple: because we are free, when we are abused it is our choice. If divorce is legal and granted easily here in comparison to Guatemala, gender cannot be recognized as a key category of violence, subordination, or inequality. It is not immutable or unalterable, as it is in those countries. The second is the continued use of gender-neutral laws in family law, welfare, and even domestic violence solutions that efface inequality and the impossibility of consent or mutuality (even after the target has escaped abuse). While it is true that marriage no longer dominates intimate partnerships and laws are increasingly facially neutral, women are by no means equal today. But perhaps a further obfuscating factor is ignorance about how notions of contract continue to guide conventions regarding intimacy and family; how motherhood can lead to economic biases and wage decreases;[95] and most important, how domestic abuse is both proof of continued inequalities (even if inequality is more fragmented) and a tool of this subordination. In this context, the "nexus" argument—the idea that individuals and groups act more aggressively toward those who are not protected by the law—is also pertinent to understanding how domestic abuse is supported and assimilated in the United States rather than being prevented or punished.

Further, it is important to note that like immigration law, which is guided by an extraconstitutional regime founded on the plenary powers doctrine,[96] this arbitrary quality certainly characterizes domestic abuse treatment as well—from the law to enforcement to shelters and other nonprofit help. While power dynamics are more complex in this case (including the observation that women start off as citizens but, once they are abused, are certainly less than citizens), discretion and mercy are key here, as are punitive mechanisms that go much farther in punishing targets of abuse than abusers themselves. This indicates the crucial difference in the treatment of these two cases as compared to how US targets of abuse are treated: while self-defense and flight are interpreted as political speech and feminism in these cases, the same tactics are absolutely criminalized for long-term residents (and this criminalization is deepened when accounting for race, class, and other forms of bias). But it is worth exploring the meaning of the political speech of the two asylum cases first, since this interpretation is also problematic.

The political speech and feminism of Alvarado's case in particular could also be viewed as self-defense and engaging in a life-or-death struggle (even if this engagement is self-protective and not aggressive). In Hobbes and Locke, this struggle occurs in the state of nature, and civil society is supposed to prevent this sort of occurrence. Hobbes, Locke, and John Stuart Mill (among others) have all recognized,[97] however, that even "inalienable" rights do not pertain to women and especially married women. While Mill does not adhere to natural rights theory and is well-known for arguing that love, family values, and the protection of the home all serve the interests of men, like Locke, he calls into question the degree to which democracy has been achieved if these struggles are still possible. Giorgio Agamben would go further and call this "speech" nonspeech and noncommunication; rather than political speech, this is the speech of bare life.

In Alvarado's case, her speech was arguably not merely self-defense but a source of resistance, but in LR's case, it has been absolutely debilitating, at least as far as the system is concerned. Indeed, LR's inability to "speak" in a timely fashion almost led to her case's dismissal. In both cases, these women may have succeeded in their applications but their speech (as life struggle and as escaping torture) was not without consequence.[98] Interestingly, speech in these cases is not only self-defense but also *is* documentation (or there is no speech, according to legal institutions). But if quite a lot of asylum applicants do not speak in a masculinized (e.g., non-emotional) manner, if even their non-Western body language is viewed as suspicious, or if emotional trauma (whether PTSD or not) means that targets need more time, patience, and openness than the average bureaucratic agent has, then speech-as-documentation is often set up to fail.[99] To the degree that all domestic violence targets who are US residents speak on their own behalf and are often blamed and pathologized, speech can be entrapment. Groups that have already been portrayed as criminal are even more vulnerable to this entrapment. In this context, speech is paradoxically the only way to start a paper trail, but it can be portrayed as the speech of the bad mother, the duped wife or partner, and the woman who was a victim of herself in contrast to the singular and heroic efforts of the martyr-refugee.

A second crucial difference between the speech as self-defense or flight in asylum cases versus cases of US residents is that the latter group can be arrested after a domestic violence assault; in custodial situations, women are now frequently confined to the county by their abusers and the courts. These sorts of policies absolutely preclude flight and exacerbate economic marginalization, not to mention replicating the geo-spatial isolation of intimate partner abuse. In this context, self-defense or retaliation can be cast as mutuality or provocation. Nevertheless, self-defense and retaliatory violence seem logical given the absence of help for abuse targets. The result is that abused women are punished far more than individuals who commit the same "crimes" outside of the context of intimate abuse. The recent Facebook juxtaposition of the George Zimmerman case and the twenty-year sentence of Marissa Alexander (which is currently suspended, pending a new trial), who fired a warning shot at her abusive husband, are not hyperbole but actually demonstrate an empirical trend of disproportionate treatment and sentencing in self-defense situations.[100]

But in the case of would-be refugees, speech-as-flight is also a bit more paradoxical than it appears, because these women must first risk statelessness as a precondition for attempting to gain rights. In this way, they become "unidentifiable beggars" who may be granted asylum, but only as a matter of charity, not right.[101] Similarly, for US residents, even in cases where flight is permitted—for example, in shelter stays in anonymous locations—help is really based on displacement and homelessness. It is a reaction to abuse that ironically replicates the social isolation and displacement of abuse in the home. As I discuss below, this entails "incomplete mourning"[102] as a target is asked to break all ties with the past.

On the one hand, if policymakers used the same approach to abused long-term residents as they did in these two cases, there would be a marked improvement. On the other hand, Agamben's warnings about the conflation of bare life with political life are also important: what counts as political speech and feminism diminishes the meaning of the political, reducing it to biological matters, and treating targets of abuse (whether refugees or long-term residents) as a group to be saved or punished. In this way, the United States' "abuse" of abuse victims mirrors the impersonal aspects of domestic abusers in "backwards" countries.

ARENDT, FANON, AGAMBEN—AND BACK TO FOUCAULT AND HABERMAS AGAIN

In *The Origins of Totalitarianism*, Hannah Arendt famously argues that because the stateless are deprived of even "the right to rights" they also suddenly lack speech and humanity. It is not, of course, that they are biological beings who do not need to eat and drink or who suddenly do not speak, but rather that they have been dehumanized because the alleged distinction between "man" (i.e., man in the state of nature or the individual subject of human rights) and "citizen" does not really exist. The loss of citizenship reduces the individual to a subhuman, whom she variously describes as an outlaw (rather than a criminal), an unidentifiable beggar, or a beast. Rather than taking this literally (as some authors recently have), Arendt is not reinscribing some sort of Aristotelian hierarchy in her political thought, but attempting to show the absolute degree of rightlessness that occurs with statelessness. The most basic rights of man, including those of residence and occupation of public space, are not available to this individual.[103] The loss of citizenship entails a situation in which even the most basic rights cannot be enforced, either in the country in which the individual was residing or in any other country.[104] These individuals are outlaws by virtue of their status rather than any crime[105]—something that Foucault develops in his notion of biopower.[106] As Arendt notes, "Innocence, in the sense of complete lack of responsibility, was the mark of their rightlessness as it was the seal of their loss of political status."[107]

They are expelled not merely from the club of nations and citizenship but from the human community altogether.[108] Like other vulnerable groups and even other power arrangements, mass death is not always the consequence of statelessness—people can live, be fed, and be housed but not because of their rights to these things. Rather, these things are granted through discretion (at the legal level) or charity. The alienation of inalienable rights then removes the preconditions for any political exist-ence, thus ensuring that their speech is meaningless. If speech is what makes us political in some way, if it ensures rationality, consent, contract, and political legitimacy, the speech of those cast outside citizenship is simply in orbit: "their freedom of opinion is a fool's freedom, for nothing they think matters anyhow. . . . They are deprived, not of the right to free-dom, but of the right to action; not of the right to think whatever they please, but of the right to opinion."[109] Speech is not merely literal but con-notes the ability to decide what to eat, where to reside, and when and how to occupy public space. Political speech suggests autonomy, equality, and political status; the ability not merely to have rights (as protective sorts of political status have involved) but also to act on these rights. Arendt has been criticized for some of her presuppositions concerning the private and public spheres, her idealization of the United States despite her damn-ing critique of the nation-state, and her views on feminist thought more generally,[110] but her connection between political status and speech is an important one.

In Arendt, speech is not transcendent, universal, or particularly consen-sual; nor does it necessarily replace violence and coercion. But to the degree that it both performs and is indicative of rights, it is politically meaningful and irreplaceable. In particular, the ability to speak for oneself and to tes-tify about one's experiences shapes the political world. Nevertheless, she finds that survivors' accounts of the horrors of death camps are always suspect and even in the worst, most undisputed cases, there is a suspicion toward the speaker, a desire to blame the victim, and a disbelief that man can be wolf to man.[111] Agamben's work in *Remnants of Auschwitz* explores Arendt's insights in greater depth. What I believe he wants to ask, as do Arendt and Foucault in a different context, is how communication and "ethics" are transformed when one is in a situation that has undercut the possibility of even "mere life" or bare, biological life? Is the communication of the desperate and the tortured really speech? Are ethics even possible when one party is half-dead? Even if the speech of the desperate—the cries for help on a 911 call, for example—could be assimilated to rational, lib-eral norms, any appearance of ethics would merely consolidate this radical inequality. In this context, the "help" of the Enlightenment figure who comes to offer comfort to victims would really be viewed as "an atrocious jest in the face of those who were beyond not only the possibility of persuasion, but even of all human help."[112] This figure has "moved into a zone of the human where not only help but also dignity and self-respect have become useless."[113] If this is true—if there exist political spaces that not only strip individuals of rights and protections but which also simultaneously dehumanize them—the categories of rationality, communication, and ethics "make no sense, [and] then they are not genuine ethical concepts, for no ethics can claim to exclude a part of humanity. . . ."[114]

Agamben specifically targets Karl Otto-Appel's theories in this section of *Remnants*,[115] noting that his struggles to define communicative action arose from a

> European country that more than any other had reasons to have a guilty conscience with respect to Auschwitz, and it soon spread throughout academic circles. According to this curious doctrine, a speaking being cannot in any way avoid communication. Insofar as, unlike animals, they are gifted with language, human beings find themselves, so to speak, concerned to agree on the criteria of meaning and the validity of their actions. Whoever declares himself not wanting to communicate contradicts himself, for he has already communicated his will not to communicate.[116]

However, because speech is a condition that we are born into, it only takes on special meaning when it "bears witness to something to which it is impossible to bear witness, [and only then] can a speaking being experience something like a necessity to speak."[117] To Habermas and his predecessors, the only hope for problems such as these is to set a new course and distinguish among types of communication. But the problem that Arendt has highlighted and which Agamben addresses in more depth is the focus on the exception—the radically excluded who have not merely lost the right to vote but the right to exist, whose "bare life" in essence becomes their political life. Speech and ethics cannot transcend this political undecidability or loss of legitimacy.[118] It is in this sort of context that Frantz Fanon argues that violence—retaliatory violence—will transform the individual from a mute victim to a political actor.

In *On Violence*, Arendt partly responds to Fanon's work in arguing very simply that violence can never be a long-term political project. She critiques Sartre's "glorification of violence"[119] while noting that Fanon's work is more nuanced with respect to this subject.[120] The meaning of the political thus presupposes a cessation of hostilities replaced by governance, the rule of law, and political speech. Nevertheless, like Foucault, she recognizes the possibility that technology, instrumental rationality, and mass murder can be inextricably linked in politics—things that Habermas wants to compartmentalize. That is, Habermas doesn't deny these linkages but argues that instrumental rationality does not have to have the purely negative implications that critical theorists such as Weber and Adorno have found. Foucault, in contrast to Arendt, implies that a certain sort of rationality (disciplinary norms and mechanisms and discursive forms of bio-power) characterizes modern power, but that often torture and physical deprivation are still at the base of these power modalities. In that way, discourse does not supersede violent power relations but serves as a mask, a justification, of a denial, by making equal what is not. Unsurprisingly, Arendt and Foucault, however, recognize that "war" is often the guarantee of politics, not its opposite, as seems to be the case in Habermas. In this way, Arendt's theories, as well as Foucault's, could be recognized as realist in ways that are not true of Habermas's.[121] This is particularly true of Habermas's notion of communication as replacing coercion and violence, rather than making them possible.

In Enlightenment-based theories, Arendt notes, violence is held to "interrupt" historical progress.[122] Other theories, she finds, do not distinguish among "terms such as power, strength, force, authority and violence."[123] Importantly, Arendt concludes that violence is merely instrumental and can never constitute power, which is the ability to "act in concert"[124]: "power is indeed of the essence of all government, but violence is not. Violence is by nature instrumental; like all means, it always stands in need of guidance and justification through the end it pursues."[125] The problem is one she herself recognizes: in the context of colonial oppression, violence and not politics (as she defines them) rules and Hobbes's man in nature—isolated, asocial, competitive, self-interested—is said to be the basis of this paradigm. In order to criticize colonialism, she sets it apart from politics, arguing that it allows the nation to conquer the state (particularly as race becomes more prevalent in these considerations) and for any sort of democratic or representative government to lose the essence of popular sovereignty. Instead, government begins catering to individual, capitalistic needs based on self-interest and greed, essentially killing the political. Nevertheless, while she identifies the impossible situation the colonized are in, she does not address the need for rebellion. More broadly, she only notes the distortion of Fanon's work but not his main premises.

While echoing the warnings of this time period that instrumental reason, liberal government, and technological advances can be harnessed to kill more efficiently, Fanon's work is more explicit than Arendt's regarding the colonial situation. Importantly, he traces an opposite trajectory from rationality and liberal discourse to violence, including attempts by the colonized to engage in Enlightenment-oriented, liberal processes—from voting, to forming political parties, to cooperating with European powers, to accepting technical aid and development workers, to appealing to the UN, and so on. When all these efforts were exhausted, Fanon argues that violence alone would transform the individual from spectator (tortured, colonized, oppressed) to a political actor. Arendt has ruled out this possibility by arguing that violence is hierarchically arranged such that it is a mere instrument of politics but does not constitute speech. Foucault's work would entail a more nuanced account, granted that he is conceiving of power in liberal democracies that are not marked by overt conflict or absolute power. But given this difference, he has recognized how violent acts— various forms of criminality or delinquency—are normalized, formed into discursive subjects, and serve as both disciplinary models as well as bio-political ones. As Fanon argues, this discursive or ideological layer is not possible in a context of overt violence where torture is the norm, where the police barracks constitute a wall between those who belong and those who are cast outside, and where racism is the base for all relations (reversing but not repudiating Marxist terminology). The violence and domination of domestic abuse are closer to the colonial context Fanon describes than mere workplace discipline or the more therapeutic forms of bio-power. In the context of gender domination, it has been up to Foucault's interpreters to analyze feminist micro-resistance, but this micro-resistance does not usually entail self-defense, flight, or retaliatory violence as the basis of liberating and agentic action.

Fanon's work exposes unresolved issues from the Habermas-Foucault debate. As Fanon argues, violence can be discursively cordoned off to former colonies; the UN can whitewash French death squads and ignore the exploitation and rape of former colonies; political parties are co-opted by former colonial powers, and the only option is violence. However, the anticolonial violence advocated by Fanon is not some sort of crude, unprogrammatic violence—at least, not over time.[126] Enlightenment teachings, experience, and liberal representation and discourse all educate the rebels that violence is the only option. This is realpolitik, but not from a Cold Warrior standpoint—it is the realpolitik of those who have exhausted every effort and are finally responding to the context set by the (human rights) abuser. Like Foucault, Fanon's work has been distorted through a reference to "pocket-size absolutes"—if Foucault is the discipline or genealogy man, exposing issues but solving none, Fanon is the unapologetic advocate of violence despite his stage theory of both violence and consciousness. More accurately, if both are read as realists, they do not advocate conflict or wish it away but are not surprised by it—they do not assume that liberal modes of political representation or discourse, including at the UN, will *replace* violence.

Nor is their thinking all-or-nothing. Like Marx, they appreciate half-measures and some liberal solutions to exploitation and domination, but they also see a broader picture. Half-measures do not often change more foundational issues but serve to divert attention from them or cooperate with the powers that dissenters sought to challenge. Unlike the other two, however, Foucault theorizes resistance within domination. At best, his work has allowed theorists and activists to see that even in a situation of absolute domination and even death, individuals can and do act. In the context of this chapter, my discussion of violence is not a celebration of retaliatory violence in the face of near absolute powerlessness but a note that the background context of communication whitewashes a set of liberal rules, discourses, and discursive subjects that are the product of violence and which can only deny this or assimilate it by targeting the targets. This assimilation is not merely exploiting those who are most disposed to communication and therapy—and yet who are politically and economically vulnerable—but also as part of a greater backlash against women's gains and feminism, the programs of feminism (awareness of rape culture, date rape, birth control, support for gender studies and so on), female poverty, the rise of single-headed households, and the feminization of labor since the 1990s.

Considering the Habermas-Foucault debate in a bit more depth, what seems to be at issue in this debate is how each theory comes to represent the problems it seeks to challenge. Habermasian theory appears to reinstate overly broad universalizing tendencies, uncritically advancing reason, communication, and rationality. At best, his framework would omit women through a gender neutral theory, at worst, it would blindly adhere to these categories without recognizing their inherent biases that cannot merely be wished away or reformed.[127] Foucault's theory, on the other hand, appears to mirror the fragmentation, nihilism, and technical reason of the contemporary era. His radical critique of modern power seemingly leads to nothing and in this way is not only absent of any grounding in ethics, justice, or democracy, but also participates in the worst aspects of late modernity.

But from the point of view of the subaltern, the margins, and targets of abuse, Habermas merely reforms issues from the Enlightenment and liberal democracy—partly by denying they exist at all—while Foucault's work is more revolutionary, at least as critique. Rather than being ethics- or justice-free, Foucault's work does not have to lead us nowhere but certainly complicates any easy solutions to difficult political problems. Where Habermas wants us to see progress and have faith in certain forms of communication, Foucault sees genealogy; socially constructed, local truths; and more minute power relations. To Foucault, the worst aspects of communication and human action can be bound up with democracy, producing uneven, inconsistent, power relations. Foucault's actors are never entirely powerless but have intersectional identities and are simultaneously powerful in certain respects and more unequal in others. This is because the focus remains on power as an active relationship, while identities like "victim" or "abused" are merely products of these relations. Foucault's middle period is particularly important in terms of this critique, while his late period perhaps offers a more Socratic or Nietzschean perspective of ethics. Like Nietzsche and the existentialists, Foucault does not give up on issues like human rights or prison reform but contextualizes these efforts inside power. Nor does his analytics of power preclude broad-based analyses of inequality. In fact, it seems cheap and dichotomous to portray his theories this way.

Habermas and Foucault both account for the historical specificity of modern power and particularly the effects of capitalism and bureaucracy. Inherent in Habermas's theory is an account that recognizes progress and development, while Foucault's historicity is flat, mirroring the existentialist notion that history has no meaning per se. While Habermas separates capitalism and governance into competing spheres, Foucault conceives of them in a complex, shifting, and yet overlapping manner. Today, Habermas's theory of communicative action can seem outdated as many of the presuppositions and operations of bureaucracy and capitalism have taken on very different modes of operation since the 1990s: in a neoliberal economy, the dichotomy between private and public has blurred; bureaucracy in the United States has shifted to a more violent and punitive model—perhaps giving up on its educational and enlightening aims, suggesting new modalities of "discipline"—evident in the wars on terror and drugs, but also in shifts in the welfare state and domestic abuse policy (granted, perhaps, as unintended consequences); and the firmly entrenched breakup of the nuclear family that can no longer be captured by the welfare state. To reiterate this last point, we can no longer theorize a simple replacement of the "man/husband" with the "state," as welfare itself has receded and a more punitive and fragmented model has replaced it. While Foucault never developed a theory of gender, his notions of power not only make these fragmentations and shifts unsurprising but also allow us to see how gender can cynically be exploited in the feminization of labor, which therefore also simultaneously brings about the feminization of poverty. In the context of domestic violence, it's not necessary to manipulate or rework Foucault's theories in order to understand how social conservatives and professionals have co-opted this "revolution," turning domestic abuse charges back on their targets.[128] With the greater prevalence of single motherhood, fragmented state institutions and extralegal help can doubly or triply discipline and punish women—but not for any Enlightenment reasons. Disciplinary power now cooperates with bio-power in ways that were only hinted at in the end of *History of Sexuality* volume 1, and which have been under-theorized by contemporary authors who interpret bio-power fairly literally, as race.[129]

Both authors recognize the increasing importance of knowledge, technology, and communication or discourse, but Habermas also conceptually separates these areas of life, while Foucault assumes that they are less readily distinguishable and that individuals acting in these spheres have complex, intersectional identities. Habermas's identification of such roles as consumer, worker, citizen, and client[130] may have been helpful from the 1960s–1980s, which says something about changes in the welfare state and postwar power, but to the degree that these roles limit his conceptualization of civil society today, they are also static and dated. To put it differently, Habermas's focus on civil society as a check on colonization and/or democratic institutions is further limited by the distinction between "universal" and "particular." As Nancy Fraser elucidates, the feminist movement is both progressive and backwards in Habermas's analysis—it is universal in its claims and formation but can retreat into particular identities that threaten an inclusive, broad-based democracy.[131] Despite the pocket-sized absolutes attributed to Foucault and admitting that his theories certainly do not advocate any broad-based democracy, this does not preclude ethical orientations, justice, or democracy. Rather, Foucault's work simply contextualizes late modern power to suggest that most power struggles and the "truths" they are rooted in are "immanent" (as Hardt and Negri frequently note),[132] local, historically specific, and based on flexible, changing individual identities. This does not erase the subject or actor but, as in Judith Butler's work, allows for an entirely new terrain of action and account of micro-resistance once identity and even the body are contextualized as formed by power relations.[133]

While in the Habermasian perspective, the system dealing with intimate abuse is almost thoroughly corrupt, the actors are almost entirely powerless, and there is little to no civil society (in terms of actually preventing abuse or helping targets), from a Foucaultian view, there is more liberatory potential even as the disciplinary and bio-political aspects of state and civil society power must be recognized. In Foucault's analysis, domestic abuse targets are not absolute victims *until* they get help: they can be recognized as actors with legitimate fears who do resist, albeit in very small ways, even while being abused, harassed, stalked, and emotionally denigrated.[134] As political agents, their voices should be heard rather than the voice of others speaking for them. In this way, the Habermasian project of communicative action could and should be important, but in a Foucaultian context: the battle is never over, resistance will always be important, and radical change is needed because the discourses about this particular subject, both pro and con, inadequately portray the lived daily life and experiences of the people most affected.[135]

CONCLUSION

The pervasiveness of domestic abuse and the very real losses that can occur make it understandable why any target would attempt to get help. In the face of myriad abuses that are often nonstop, if pieced together, the desire for help or a rescuer cannot be labeled "ressentiment," no matter how much this term has been reconceived.[136] But the discourse of female privilege and yet blaming of victims, combined with state punishment of those who seek help, will revictimize the victim, more often than not. The cases of RA and LR are both illustrative of these dynamics but also serve as a sort of proxy; if the United States shelters these women, we must be better than their countries of origin. But, as James Scott has suggested in his early work on corruption, the linkages between these countries cannot be denied—they are historical, legal, and international.[137] Thus, rather than indicating absolute differences, US acceptance of RA's and LR's asylum claims could be reinterpreted as acknowledging a shared legacy of legal subordination that authorizes some to act aggressively and subordinates others.

Scott's impulse—to see both connections between countries and yet how each should also be considered on its own terms (as Foucault would urge us to see the political as local and historically and geographically specific)—should be a corrective to the feminist identity formed by these court cases. It promotes views of feminism and political speech that uphold traditional and patriarchal notions of Central American women who reside in the United States and who become bound up in negative discourses of "mañana syndrome,"[138] hyper-reproduction, and anchor babies,[139] all of which form a view of Latina women and mothers on the one hand as usurpers, invaders, and baby machines, and on the other hand as being too traditional, submissive, and family-oriented. Rody

Alvarado and LR are only feminists to the degree that they reject these paradigms, but because these discourses are formed by the US government and media, these women can also be cast as "failed feminists." Both cases highlight a truly intersectional subject,[140] pieced together through considerations of femininity, a sending country's patriarchy and tolerance of violence against women, and the always-already gendered violence of these two cases.

Conversely, the disaggregated system that today provides help for targets of domestic abuse would be much improved if the United States followed the standards and assumptions of these two asylum cases in treating the asymmetrical abuse of long-term residents. This would involve the recognition of women as a visible social group; the immutability of gender identity; the asymmetry of intimate violence in a country with deep and entrenched gender inequality; and the nexus between formal inequality, state inaction, and violence against women.[141] It would also require seeing how women's resistance to domestic abuse is precisely that: resistance (it is defensive and not offensive). In these ways, symmetry arguments, which merely count violent acts but decontextualize acts of violence and broader mechanisms of asymmetrical control, would be radically undermined.

To end with a mixed message, if the United States were to apply similar standards from these cases to cases of domestic abuse occurring on American soil, the political context of abuse and radical inequality produced by control and violence would finally be explicit. Only then would this "system" actually help targets of abuse. But on the other hand, these two asylum cases do not even approximately reflect the courage and single-handed achievements of these two women—the political identity produced by the cases reflects solely on the United States's unresolved issues with gender violence and the current war on immigration.

Foucault's notions of power are not just crucial in engaging in a negative critique but in (perhaps ironically) recuperating the speech and political autonomy of the abused. And even more ironically, this is where his analysis necessarily intersects with Habermas's. The most effective groups at this moment promote a mix of Foucaultian and Habermasian ideals. They allow domestic abuse targets to speak for themselves, to ask for and determine what they need, and even to refuse clinical labels. These groups mix legal advocacy and therapy, thus conceiving of domestic abuse as a problem of unequal power and broader societal and political tendencies, not to mention economic ones, rather than as individual failure or pathology. In this way, they recognize the importance of societal interconnections and advocacy as political advocacy—projects that Habermas focuses on much more than Foucault. These groups also acknowledge that prosecuting any case as domestic abuse is risky and advocate alternative tactics mixed with cautious and limited use of the justice system. They recognize economic abuse and have financial workshops to help counter these abuses; they are suspicious of domestic abuse judges and do not hesitate to file complaints against them; and they are realistic about the limitations of calling the police (even in stations and precincts with a designated officer trained in abuse). They know that egalitarian solutions—mediation, counseling, and various "interventions" involving the abuser—are highly damaging to someone traumatized by abuse. Finally, they do not assume anyone is "privileged" and accept the stories of anyone without requiring documentation. The contours of conventional speech, then, are radically undermined and new performative possibilities—granted, at the grassroots level—are enacted. But these organizations are not the norm and are (in Chicago, at least) woefully underfunded and often in danger of extinction.[142] And unfortunately, they can only help targets for a limited amount of time.

Nonetheless, these organizations are important in their recognition that targets need help—not as victims or objects of charity but because democracy creates a web of power, obligations, and duties that mutually implicate us. Solidarity and not ressentiment characterize these relationships; speech can then have greater meaning.[143] But Habermas's ideal civil society cannot be achieved without Foucault's revised "hermeneutics of suspicion." Foucault's analyses account for the Freudian observation that a significant component of society does not aim at libido or Eros, but instead at disintegration, destruction, and cruelty. Once this has been admitted, the instruments of democracy—rationality, communication, and bureaucratic-therapeutic interventions—will be reduced in their importance, and targets of abuse will be able to, as my daughter would say, "tell their truth." In the next chapter, I explore how Enlightenment understandings of intimacy—particularly notions of contract and consent—paradoxically endanger targets of abuse, and I suggest that abusers are "monsters" in Enlightenment terms. In arguing this, I turn to Freud and contemporary thinker Samuel Moyn to continue the theoretical discussion in another vein.

CHAPTER 4
The Enlightenment and Violence

INTRODUCTION

In the previous chapter, I investigated two gender-based asylum cases to help crystallize many of the issues regarding domestic abuse occurring in the United States. These cases demonstrated how the legal system often creates its own logic, asking targets to shape their experiences and testimony to fit categories created by US asylum adjudicators and immigration judges. As I argued in Chapter 3, Foucault's and Habermas's analyses of discourse and communication are highly relevant to these cases, but upon investigation, one sees that both skirt the issue of violence. Better put, Hannah Arendt and Frantz Fanon more explicitly link the use of Enlightenment reason and liberal political practices to contemporary forms of violence. While Arendt analyzes these connections in striking and significant ways, only Fanon admits that violence itself sets the context in which targets are asked to speak. In this chapter, I continue this discussion by connecting these ideas to Freud's notion of the death drive and Samuel Moyn's more recent critical investigation of sympathy. In brief, Moyn explores the cruel and even violent underpinnings of political appeals to and uses of sympathy, exposing what Freud also finds: the use of Enlightenment reason to assault, destroy, or denigrate others.

Broadly, I investigate how Enlightenment reasoning and practices function in relation to the problem of domestic abuse. I would first like to explain what I mean by "Enlightenment": I am using this term as a historically and geographically specific notion that serves as an umbrella concept. This notion includes the following: liberal, rights-based notions of citizenship that favor overt, formal means of political activity (e.g., voting) and contractual understandings of intimacy that define relationships from marriage and dating to work conditions to citizenship. The term *Enlighten-ment* also connotes an emphasis on such values as mutuality, equality, freedom from coercion, rationality, and consent. Freedom from coercion further suggests civilizational superiority and the relative disdain toward emotions and untamed violence (evidenced in the framing of the asylum cases of the previous chapter). Thus, it entails a hierarchical, developmental project that presupposes that education and assimilation will eradicate violence, coercion, and destruction. I use this term in a double sense: first as a way to identify a broad issue, but second as a contingent, historically and geographically specific set of understandings.[1] Issues related to Enlightenment understandings pervade domestic abuse—from abuse itself to conventional understandings of abuse that are predominant in shelters, mainstream advocacy, and contemporary policy.

Linking my insights from the introduction to the arguments advanced in Chapter 3, it is evident that Patricia Evans's work on verbal abuse poses a crucial problem of the Enlightenment, which in turn challenges many of the core assumptions Habermas has introduced in his theories on communicative action. As Evans explains, a key part of abusive relations is that the abuser is convinced that his target is inferior to him and communication only deepens these unequal feelings.[2] Second, an abuser's aims are oriented toward chaos and destruction rather than healthy goals that aim to uplift individuals or to preserve intimate groupings. This relationship is profoundly asymmetrical, with no necessarily logical cycle or objective, except "power over."[3] In contrast, contemporary domestic abuse intervention programs, therapies, and law-and-order solutions reflect the ethos of the Enlightenment in important respects: a dyadic relationship based on mutuality, consensus, and symmetry. Solutions seek to keep the family intact and rest on the idea of a neat, predictable cycle that professionals must be able to identify so that they can enlighten individuals and interrupt it, saving the individuals from themselves. But as I have also explored, the laws carry within them various issues complicating the Enlightenment norms: there is no possibility of mutuality or individual provocation in a sphere of the law that preserves the family as a group and which is inherently biased toward the male father figure; laws disproportionately hold women responsible for abuse, punishing them in far more profound ways than the abuser; and communicative therapies can lead to invasive and paternalistic involvement in a family's life.[4] This is not even a civil society based on Habermas's notion of instrumental reason, which would at least conceive of individuals working autonomously in some way. Rather, in these solutions one finds developmentally archaic notions of family and love; paternalistic notions of women as the guardians of morality and deserving targets of chastisement; and legal remnants of coverture. The asylum cases do not merely remind us of these links to the past of coverture but force us to face a reality of unresolved contradictions from the past embedded in new (or neo-) forms.

Evans further argues that "reality I" beliefs (in the radical inequality and inferiority of a target) and practices (aiming at destabilization and destruction) are not merely supported by society but rewarded.[5] She links masculinized, aggressive societal beliefs to intimate abuse, exposing what appear to be irresolvable tensions and undecidable statuses. In truth she finds that abusers are rewarded for their behavior and have a mirror in societal trends that celebrate violence, aggression, and war. As I interpret her ideas, abusers twist the Enlightenment to their own ends and these observations are borne out in examples of abusers' behavior given by authors and advocates: turning a target's family members against her;[6] using laws meant to protect targets against them, for example, by calling the police to have a target arrested after assaulting her; and effectively using the law to threaten women, for example, threatening to take a woman to court repeatedly as an abusive tactic.[7] What further complicates matters is that very often rights are tied to societal sympathy.

For example, when same-sex marriage is discussed, quite a lot of arguments against granting these marriages are related to perceptions of societal sympathy or lack thereof. Conventional wisdom holds that laws should only be passed and rights granted when society approves. Women's role in the military was also diminished in the past because of Supreme Court justices' fears of societal sympathy: specifically, justices argued that the public would not support wars if they knew women were fighting on the front lines.[8] And workers' rights have often been linked to societal support, as I have discussed elsewhere.[9] Thus, the role of societal sympathy is important to explore but should also make evident why we cannot wait for consensus or a shift in public opinion to grant rights. This particular contention goes against quite a lot of the social science and political theory on trying to consolidate solidarity or trying to educate people to support rights or a specific issue. Instead, I hold that only when we are *first* politically equal will social sympathy follow. This argument is not particularly new but is something we need to be reminded of as societal sympathy is now used to scale back rights.[10] While authors like Joan Scott and Hannah Arendt have reminded us that we are equal in our differences, de Tocqueville reminds us that true sympathy (i.e., respect) is only possible when political equality has been established first. As de Tocqueville has argued, "The same man who is full of humanity toward his fellows when they are also his equals becomes insensible to their sorrows when there is no more equality" . . . "but as people become more like one another, they show themselves reciprocally more compassionate, and the law of nations becomes more gentle."[11] In fact, as I discuss in the conclusion, rights should be a precondition of democratic liberty rather than being the substance of what is conceived of as the political or democracy.

With a renewed interest since the 1990s in keeping families intact (even families that were never together) and with increasing hostility toward feminism[12] leading to a revaluation of fatherhood, psychodynamic and educational programs have become more predominant concurrent with law-and-order solutions that often lead to dual arrest. Both trends are depoliticizing, fostering Enlightenment norms—communication, mediation, negotiation, classes, and program compliance—without political change or consequence. Essentially communicative solutions seek to neutralize or eradicate the political. Further, in this context, abuse advocates and bureaucratic agents inadvertently exploit the divergence between "reality I" (abuse) and "reality II" (Enlightenment norms that aim at preserving life and fostering bonds). These realities clearly correspond to Sigmund Freud's analysis of the war between Eros (which would be reality II) and Thanatos (reality I), allowing further insight into the one group that is often ignored: abusers.

As I suggested in the previous chapter, as they have historically developed, Enlightenment assumptions have been linked to the privileging of speech but not to the exclusion of violence, even if one is supposed to preclude the other.[13] Violence has not been eradicated but mostly cordoned off into the private sphere or portrayed as acts of "war" (in the purview of international relations and sovereign matters even if wielded domestically). Violence has also been viewed as acceptable for those who are deemed unenlightened in some way—the difference between illegitimate violence and legitimate violence is that the latter would somehow teach a lesson, chastise, or put back in place. Further, coercion and violence are not absent in the public sphere—police brutality[14] and torture[15] of criminal suspects are evidence of this. Even more significant, this violence is not neutral—it is gendered, racialized, and class-biased, among other things. Accordingly, interrogating Enlightenment understandings of intimacy and violence will contribute to a realist approach to the issue of domestic violence, one that accounts for inequalities and violence as crucial mechanisms of modern power.

Following up on my discussion of the Enlightenment in the introduction, here I investigate how Enlightenment notions seemingly operate parallel to a different reality, one which is more controlling, manipulative, and coercive.[16] First, I suggest that from an Enlightenment perspective, the abuser is a "monster." Drawing on Freud's notion of a death drive,[17] I reframe an abuser's actions as aiming at the destruction of a target's core identity. From this perspective, operating according to liberal norms of consent and mutuality in the face of an asymmetrical and more violent orientation will ignore or assimilate the more destructive aims of the abuser. To put it differently, using "soft power" in the face of "hard power" or the presuppositions of "welfare" as a challenge to "warfare" cannot work. To the degree that these distinctions are perpetuated, liberal processes and solutions will mask violence and assimilate it. This is true in terms of the predominance of symmetry theories applied to asymmetrical situations: if he was violent, she must have provoked him; if he threatened her, she must have said something also; if he terrorizes her, she must acquiesce; and so on.

However, second, I suggest that these notions do not merely operate as parallel realities but that Enlightenment notions—particularly manifest in appeals to sympathy, care, and protection—contain the very cruelty and abuse that they purport to heal. In this way, I take cues from the profile of the abuser I construct below to investigate how broad axes of stratification can operate in contemporary US society in highly destructive ways. Sympathy, care, and a politics of victimization all require abuse to occur in the first place; they ask a target to uproot herself entirely to get help or to stay with the abuser to continue the cycle she will inevitably be blamed for. As I state below, in this context victimhood is rightlessness. Ironically, these power dynamics—which are indicative of power based on inequality, violence, and coercion—are whitewashed through turning to ethical reasoning, education, and even "justice." Returning to Foucault, I suggest (as I did in the previous chapters) that disciplinary power and biopower are not antithetical powers but work together today—in this particular instance—to foster destructive and uprooting impulses. This realist reading of contemporary theory should recast abuse as a crucial function of modern liberalism. These difficulties, in turn, should lead to a modification of expectations about communicative discourses and civil society. As I suggested in the previous chapter, communication in and of itself is made less possible as various forces that are often labeled "conservative" (but which are widely endorsed by both political parties) have shrunk public space, resorted to an individual/self-help model accompanied by law-and-order power mechanisms (and nothing in between), and predominant nongovernmental actors have either gone underground or support these changes.

ABUSERS AS MONSTERS

In *Civilization and Its Discontents*, Sigmund Freud states that he wanted to believe that sadism and masochism were a part of Eros, or love broadly conceived. Nevertheless, in discussing the process of discovering the death drive (or, Thanatos), he admits "I can no longer understand how we can have overlooked the ubiquity of non-erotic aggressivity and destructiveness and can have failed to give it its due place in our interpretation of life."[18] It is confusing because love and cruelty are often "alloyed"[19] but "it is in sadism, where the death instinct twists the erotic aim in its own sense and yet at the same time fully satisfies the erotic urge, that we succeed in obtaining the clearest insight into its nature and its relation to Eros."[20] Significantly, the aggressive instinct provides the ego with "satisfaction," but if it is untamed, it is "the greatest impediment to civilization."[21] Freud's observations about human cruelty and violence are borne out by the evidence of domestic abuse researchers. Domestic violence is not tied to love as traditionally conceived[22] and researchers who have worked with abusers find that most feel a sense of pleasure once they know they have caused their target to suffer.[23]

Following Freud's analysis of these two separate but often intertwined drives, as well as his critique of civilization more broadly, I propose that in Enlightenment terms abusers are "monsters." This label can be interpreted in two ways: first, as a severe criticism of the abuser as someone who is outside of humanity, which is not my aim; second, as an individual whose behavior patterns in no way fit the sort of Enlightenment and dominant religious notions of relationships that hold so much sway in contemporary American life. Nevertheless, an abuser can use Enlightenment reasoning and liberal political practices to harm his target and, as I have argued throughout this book, society both assimilates an abuser's behavior and even rewards it. Putting together a model of abuse based on the work of authors who have clinical experience with abusers, one of the most important foundations of abuse is that the abuser believes his target is unequal to him.[24] Based on this belief, an abuser will view her actions or speech as challenges, put-downs, or provocations. As the abuse dynamics escalate, even a target's silence or "making a face" is interpreted negatively by the abuser. This is, again, because it is her very being that is at issue—not what she says or does. As I stated in the introduction, an *abuser attacks the core of his partner's identity*.[25]

As Freud's investigation of the death drive indicates, abuse aims at destruction: not only are a target's accomplishments viewed in a negative light, but the abuser often tries to undermine employment successes[26] or social popularity. He will sabotage relationships without a higher goal in mind—just to exercise power for power's sake. Any efforts to communicate with the abuser are distorted or used as information against the target for future retaliation. Against Enlightenment beliefs, the abuser does not feel guilt after an abusive action like others may—instead he feels a release.[27] Like a person who's taken a drug over time, the abuser gradually needs to increase the intensity of his behavior to feel this pleasure.[28] For these reasons, abuse escalates—because of adaptation to the situation and a greater need for stimulus—not because the couple became more conflictual or external tensions affected the family unit. Further, as numerous studies confirm, most long-term abusers are not receptive to therapy (i.e., they cannot truly get better even if they can feign normal behavior for a while).[29] Having children, consulting family members, and or seeing a therapist does not help the abuser become more moral or learn to consult his conscience[30]—in fact, each effort simply presents a new avenue for enacting abuse by manipulating the target and others.[31]

What is interesting is that there is a gendered component to this that does not eradicate emotions but dichotomizes them. While feminine emotions have historically been viewed as irrational, hysterical, and therefore frivolous, masculine emotions are linked to rationality and are therefore cast as having social utility. For example, with marital violence or rape, it is often argued that men were overtaken by passions. While this could indicate a sort of helplessness or loss of control, it also assumes that passions are in a temporal cycle in which rationality and independence will prevail. Unfortunately, society frequently interprets acts of violence or boundary violations committed by an abuser in the same way: incidents of excessive interaction to the point of criminal trespass, stalking, or violence are often viewed as love gone wrong. What they don't realize is that abusers do not have the capacity to love[32] as Freud would define it: as libidinal bonding and in performing constructive and healthy actions toward others. Indeed over the long term, love (Eros) and violence (Thanatos) cannot co-exist. The pleasure that abusers feel in controlling and harming their targets—the love of doing bad for bad's sake explored by authors from Nietzsche to Freud—is crucial to my argument in this chapter.

In older cycle-of-violence arguments, it was commonly held that the abuser felt remorse and would beg forgiveness. This Enlightenment-oriented notion of guilt and remorse—assumed but not proved—is particularly damaging in misunderstanding the true intent and nature of an abuser. For example, Evans notes that "Susan Haraki, M.F.C.C., a former counselor with Battered Women's Alternatives in Concord, California, has pointed out, in some cases the abuser's denial is so deep that he can minimize the physical damage to almost nothing."[33] Indeed, numerous homicide reports in the media often quote the abuser blaming his partner for his actions: asserting that she was the abuser or had otherwise crossed a personal line.[34]

Second, it is often held in contemporary therapy and conventional wisdom that the abuser was simply a victim of his passions and once he became "rational," he was able to understand what he did and apologize. While this assumption is part of the justification for symmetry arguments and conjoint therapy, it mistakes how the person who committed the abuse may feel the opposite: he will finally feel satisfied. And, as happens with drug habituation, the abuse gets worse because both abuser and target adapt to the previous level of abuse and thus it must increase in intensity and scope for the abuser to feel pleasure but also to get the target to act appropriately (to cry, to beg for mercy, and so on; to submit). [35]

Third, as Lundy Bancroft points out, most abusers show total control when and if the police come; when the abuser's own interest is on the line, the abuse often conveniently ends.[36] Thus, the passions that overtook him conveniently disappear the minute he could be caught. Another way to see this is that abusers and bullies often triangulate people, pitting them against each other or alienating the affections of one party to hurt the other. An Enlightenment understanding of this would superficially argue that an abuser's ability to get along with others—even if it's at the expense of the target—demonstrates that it is the target who is the problem (she is too sensitive; she is making it up; or if he is abusive, why isn't he abusing everyone?[37]). From a Freudian point of view, the abuser's triangulation is aiming at destruction and isolation, not building bonds.

Fourth, despite societal recognition that there is a spiraling cycle of abuse, therapists, lawyers, and society at large tend to view his latent periods as "improvement." "See, he's being nicer"; "See, things are getting better"; "He's stepping up." Or a therapist could argue that if one can predict the abuser's behavior, this will somehow mitigate the damage or allow one to avoid the abuser at these times.[38] It's just not that simple, and the target knows this, even if her efforts to get sympathy or help are not validated in any deep or meaningful way.[39] Freud developed the notion of the death drive as a warning to society that "civilization" was not enough to achieve peace, stability, or happiness. In fact, we could use the tools of civilization to "exterminat[e] one another to the last man."[40] Important to Freud's analysis is the argument that destructive impulses are not *pathological* drives or instincts, and therefore they are not anomalous. And yet we constantly seek to deny them. The surprise that is registered each time a partner kills his target is evidence of this denial.

In Freud's reading, civilization is more of an "ought" than an "is." As a society denies its own destructive impulses or nihilism, repressive mechanisms entail a huge amount of will or effort, even if this will is perverse, meaningless, or uprooting. *For these reasons, I want to suggest that an abuser does not emerge out of nowhere; an abuser's behavior is generated by and mirrors societal forms of violence and can play to societal norms.* In this system, targets of abuse are often blamed and held responsible for "living with abuse." Until we admit that interpersonal violence is not only validated at the societal level but that aggressive instincts have nothing to do with guilt, compensation, mutuality, or equality, we will continue to maintain abuse, empower abusers, and punish targets.[41] For all these reasons, abusers are "monsters"—anti-Enlightenment figures who proceed according to inequality, denigration, and violence—and yet societal dynamics that assume that education, talk therapy, and legal mediation will displace and end violence encourage and support these monsters. In turn, these monsters are both anti-Enlightenment and yet a direct product of the Enlightenment, as I discuss below.

THE ENLIGHTENMENT AS PARALLEL REALITY

In this section, I examine the theoretical roots of Enlightenment notions in relation to violence, as they historically emerged in politically and geographically specific forms. I pursue this line of inquiry to analyze how Enlightenment notions of intimacy and abuse effectively preclude recognizing abuse, much less preventing it or solving it. Tracing the relationship of liberal political thought to violence also highlights how unresolved tensions in liberalism remain with us today and often blur the lines between public and private.

In the liberal tradition, notions of arbitrary violence were bound up with ideas about absolute power. However, authors like John Locke never sought to eradicate violence from the polity but rather to ensure that violence was used wisely (for the purposes of enlightenment, education, and correction), systematically, and moderately (that is, not to the point of death or serious injury). As I have argued elsewhere, this blurred the connection between the legitimate use of violence in the international sphere and power wielded domestically.[42] Thus, as more contemporary authors have noted, the "welfare" and "warfare" states have overlapped in ways that haven't often been recognized.[43] Nevertheless, the assumption that the two are distinct has been implicitly and explicitly endorsed over time, with the consolidation of the nation-state. Welfare is thus conceived of as operating inside the bounds of the nation-state and warfare is deployed for foreign others in the more anarchical international sphere. The result has been to view state violence practiced on citizens as so anomalous (small numbers, mistake) or extraordinary (as wartime necessity as in the Japanese internment or Nazism, but never to be repeated again) that they don't reflect on liberal democracy.[44] That is, warfare may be violent and destructive but it is practiced abroad and against strangers, while welfare is open, egalitarian, and democratic.[45]

Nineteenth-century thinkers like John Stuart Mill and Alexis de Tocqueville viewed society in a more complex way than Locke; nevertheless, they did not reject violence per se. Mill in particular indicates that primitive societies need despotic rule and this suggests the "enlightened" use of violence for "barbarians" but not for citizens of a liberal polity.[46] In fact, he is quite adamant that protective and paternal policies (largely exercised "on behalf of" the poor and/or in the family) in *democracies* must end.[47] Like Mill, Tocqueville recognizes a normative violence—the tyranny of the majority—which "struck at the soul," but he questions whether a democratic society such as the United States would even be able to fight wars. While in Toqueville the distinction—between democracy and civil society on the one hand, and territorial sovereignty, borders, and the powers of war on the other— is still loose, the questions he raises in this regard anticipate later divisions between welfare and warfare. By the early twentieth century, nation-states emerged into a form we find recognizable today, with features such as a heightened awareness of borders; notions of territorial integrity; and the beginning of the distinction between domestic laws and the powers of the state as sovereign war-maker. Again, this entails the alleged dichotomy between domestic laws and political inclusion and the powers of the sovereign state to deal with foreigners, make treaties, and wage war. These notions were also bound up with the predominant hierarchy between civilized and barbarian: the use of violence on colonial subjects (i.e., barbarians) in order to either assimilate them or at least, pacify them.[48] Today, a dominant strand of contemporary liberal theory continues to make the distinction between the extra-juridical exercise of sovereignty abroad and the domestic exercise of power.[49] The latter entails following the rule of law, treating citizens equally, and holds democratic values as the highest in contrast to the necessary violence and inequality of foreign relations. As political power increasingly became based on abstract notions of justice, which rested on rationality and the rule of law, liberal capitalism purported to disavow irrationality, violence, and arbitrary power. The concept of a social contract symbolizes this rationality as well as implying mutuality between the government and the governed.

Hence, although many of these authors who could be identified roughly as "liberal" did not reject violence per se (including Locke, Wollstonecraft, Friedrich Engels, and Mill), they were nevertheless also highly sympathetic to the plight of women and argued that their undemocratic treatment in the private sphere was not merely misfortune but a sign that democracy had not been fully achieved. As Carole Pateman has famously explored,[50] the emergence of modern liberal thought led to the increased characterization of marriage as a "contract,"[51] implying that this was a partnership of two equals who were sufficiently rational to be capable of consent. However, as de Beauvoir aptly put it, marriage then "made a civic corpse of the married woman"[52]; paradoxically, agreement to this particular contract led to the *suspension* of both inalienable rights[53] and civil rights (granted that women only had protective, "secondary" rights rather than the active rights of a full citizen[54]). Although Locke's provisions for the Poor Laws and his contribution to the Constitution of the Carolinas both explicitly and implicitly advocate the use of systematic violence on the poor, his defense of women's inalienable rights to the means of preservation suggests an opposite political ethos. Sections 83–86 of *The Second Treatise* can be read as an impassioned defense of women's inalienable rights to property as a means of self-preservation, bodily integrity (he argues that no one should have the right to physically harm a woman or take away her life), and child custody. Further, Locke argues that if marriage is truly a contract, there should be an exit (i.e., either party should be able to terminate the contract).[55] Furthermore, while Locke's notion of citizenship is relatively weak for all members of a polity, he defends women's right to protection by the law as well as their right to religious belief. In contrast and from the point of view of a radical Protestant, Locke's advocacy of violence, internment, deportation, and indentured servitude for the poor could be justified on at least two bases: (1) they have violated their duty as God's tools to follow a calling and use the earth industriously; (2) the violence of poor laws is impersonal, systematic, egalitarian, and enlightened, in that it is applied equally, predictably, and for the purposes of improvement, to instill a work ethic in the otherwise lazy individual. In contrast, even women's inalienable rights have been suspended, but to Locke there is no rational justification for this suspension. He believes that if all individuals have a soul and we alone are responsible for our souls, women must be made equal in his relatively depoliticized society.[56]

Although she draws from the more radical political tradition of Rousseau, Mary Wollstonecraft exposes the same sorts of deficiencies that Locke does: the very bases of democracy were denied women from birth:

implicit or natural rights to autonomy, rationality, and the free development of the intellect; and the right to earn and keep a wage. As Wollstonecraft notes, even during childhood, girls in her day were denied the tools
to become physically autonomous and intelligent, thus rendering them
artificially weak. Against criticisms of Wollstonecraft as a sort of product
of her times (i.e., as not sufficiently radical),[57] I find her writings to be
more progressive than is commonly thought. Wollstonecraft calls for a
"revolution in manners"[58] and calls for radical reform in nearly every insti-
tution of society. She believes that women should be allowed to occupy
any position in society and that when this is achieved, democracy will
have truly been established. As Pateman has analyzed so well, Wollstonecraft investigates how dynamics that operate largely in the private sphere
have significant political effects. Wollstonecraft purposefully uses the political language of the time, appealing to notions of tyranny: she argues
that "the divine right of husbands like the divine right of kings may be
contested"[59]; men must stop behaving like "tyrannical kings"[60]; and she
claims that society must fight the arbitrary power that men wield over
women.[61] A crucial part of this analysis is to show how the norms encouraging women to be chaste, innocent, and pure also set them up as objects
of pity and thus as victims. Protective laws, based on this mindset, only
infantilize women and consolidate their position as subcitizens.

Although Mill explicitly rejects theories of contract, as well as the
notion of a state of nature,[62] his arguments nicely synthesize the concerns
of Locke and Wollstonecraft. Like Wollstonecraft, he argues that social
norms and customs bolstered by institutional exclusion are largely responsible for naturalizing and justifying the exclusion of women. Women
are forced into roles of weakness and morality, while being denied any
tools to defend themselves. Like the emergence of racism in pre– and
post–Civil War America, discourses that claimed women's inferiority actually proliferated with the advent of democracy.[63] This was both a necessary outcome of democracy—in that the gendered division of labor could
be proclaimed a matter of state interest in the past, but only with the
advent of an allegedly egalitarian, rational system based on consent would
a whole host of exclusions now have to be justified—and yet left a significant puzzle to be solved. How could a country reject "might equals right
doctrines" and "the rule of force"[64] and yet accept that men could legally
take children away from their mothers; deny women all rights to property
and wages; and most significantly, legally permit marital rape, physical
chastisement, and even death?[65] What Mill illuminates is not a simple
matter of the division between the private sphere and civil society or government, but the legal and institutional underpinnings of the violation of

bodily integrity—to the point of death—in areas of life that are for men private, public, and political, but which are for women of this time period entirely private in that their activity in civil society and government is denied or effaced. He notes that these inequalities are portrayed as being natural, traditional, and consensual based on the claim that women never protest. As he discusses, however, women do protest, suffrage movements do exist, and women have even attempted to vote, but these efforts are obfuscated by their lack of formal acknowledgment, even at the level of discourse.[66] For all these reasons, Mill argues that the tyranny that authors like Locke tried to challenge still existed for at least half of the population in the mid-nineteenth century; the fact that "love" or affection may have mitigated these relations did not change the fact that women were denied political liberty.[67] In fact, Locke, Wollstonecraft, Mill, Engels, de Beauvoir, and many others find the intimate basis of this hierarchy all the more disturbing for the way it somehow justifies not only inequality but the radical suspension of even the most basic of rights: the right to self-preservation. If Wollstonecraft and de Beauvoir have criticized women for complicity with this system (and they have in turn been criticized for being sexist on this basis), both have been careful to argue that this complicity is not the consent of an autonomous, unencumbered individual but rather the sign of "choice" in the midst of threats, bribes, and intimidation (words all of these authors use).[68]

All these authors, in one way or another, also address the "might equals right" doctrine, but Locke unfortunately upholds it in matters of marital disagreement: he argues that the man should have the final word "because he is abler and stronger."[69] Locke's reversion to the equation of physical strength with moral and therefore political right poses an enormous problem for the rest of his claims, which can be considered alongside his first and second treatises to the Constitution of the Carolinas. It is this tension, as well as the tensions he has introduced in his notion of prerogative power, that lead to a much less coherent notion of politics than most would suppose. The legacy of this contradiction is still with us today, even if it has taken on different, more fragmented forms. All of these writers argue that women—unlike the idle poor or barbarians and primitives— should not be subjected to arbitrary treatment, and yet they provide for spaces of arbitrariness and violence with regard to other groups, which could arguably be applied to women. In these instances, the language of contract and consent creates a social "fact" that obfuscates these tensions and contradictions; in fact, as Pateman has shown, the marital contract does not eradicate violence or rape but in fact justifies it. Accordingly, the legacy of liberal notions of political inclusion is not one that has rejected violence at all but which has had an inextricable relationship with it, even if an uncomfortable one.[70]

Although de Beauvoir's critique of Engels's economic "monism" is true,[71] Engels's analysis of the marriage contract is still excellent. Unlike the authors above, he does not believe true love exists under modern, liberal, capitalist conditions; in fact, the contract signals hierarchy, a sexual double standard that only limits women's freedom and ensures mutual alienation. In both the work contract and the marriage contract, Engels argues, these agreements lead to the suspension of rights.[72] And in both cases, Engels notes that the state is not concerned about *how* this "free" agreement was reached but only that it was.[73] Nevertheless, the context of inequality in which contracts are only free to the degree that the worker or woman is "freed" from all property, rights, or status is to Engels economic at base and only secondarily legal (or the inequality of the contract is epiphenomenal to economic inequality).[74] He quotes Henry Maine's now-famous theory that modern society has passed from "status to contract," arguing that this contract makes individuals "free" who are in fact not free. To Engels, a contract requires that both parties can "dispose freely of their persons, actions, and possessions and meet each other on the footing of equal rights."[75] Engels holds that contractual language is not a mistake but rather a cynical deployment of egalitarian language to mask the continuation of inequality; what results is not only gender subordination but also profound alienation. Despite Engels's incisive critique of contract (which I have only summarized briefly), his singular focus on economic equality as a solution for gender inequality and the path to true love ignores the specificity of gender, as de Beauvoir,[76] Pateman, and MacKinnon have shown. However, the connection he draws between workers and women is an important one; in both cases, these contracts lead to the suspension of rights rather than signaling equality, rationality, consent, and autonomy. Further, both signal a sort of conceptual ambivalence: on the one hand, the language of contract is invoked, thus discursively portraying both relations as a political matter; on the other hand, once the contract is entered into, both spheres (economic and the *oikos*) are portrayed as apolitical or private. In both instances, it is then easier to understand why exploitative employers and abusive partners consider their employees and targets "property" rather than human (as discussed in terms of the asylum cases in Chapter 3). Interestingly today, despite the prevalence of divorce, single parenthood, and unmarried cohabitation, intimate partnerships are still significantly conceived of in contractual terms (indicated in my discussion of welfare and conjoint therapy in Chapter 2). These notions are important to investigate, because they help to clarify not merely why reality I/Thanatos and reality II/Eros are at odds but also how they can function together to foster the very problem—domestic abuse—that is supposed to be solved.

Although Wendy Brown has persuasively argued that the direct applicability of the social contract no longer holds today, she also notes that there are important remnants of contract theory that are at work in our society.[77] Brown holds that social contract theory held sway when there were more formal contracts in place (e.g., when the marriage contract characterized the majority of intimate relations) and when consent to a democratic system was even a question. Since at least the 1980s, she contends, there are remnants of the contract but quite a lot of power dynamics also rest on self-evidence and the naturalization of their own political origins. With the end of the Cold War and the consolidation of the neoliberal project, an actual contract is no longer the conceptual basis of much of our relationships. While Brown is right that more formalized (and yet, highly theoretical[78]) notions of the social contract have been abandoned, she is also right to suggest that a looser notion of contract still holds, which I believe is undergirded by more rigid notions from the past of what this contract means.[79] For example, Brown argues that Pateman's focus on the marriage contract is challenged by the fact that it no longer characterizes the majority of the population's intimate life. With higher divorce rates, the relative acceptance of LGBQT partnerships, and greater rates of nonmarital cohabitation, we can no longer apply this notion literally to love relationships. The return to the family in family law and welfare law, not to mention dominant counseling methods, all seek to coercively enforce this heteronormative model, even as each of these areas—the law, the welfare state, and psychology—are conceived of as egalitarian and mutual.

In this context, ideas of the contract are still important in denigrating as morally unacceptable relationships and arrangements like gay partnerships, single motherhood, and nonmarital cohabitation.[80] Essentially, the notion of a legitimate contract upheld by the state is contrasted with these more informal, "sinful" or "unnatural" arrangements. Furthermore, in terms of partner abuse, the notion of contract and all that it implies— mutuality, choice, equality, and peace (i.e., the agreement was made in a nonviolent context)—is absolutely pervasive in understanding the lack of sympathy Americans feel in quite a lot of situations. Somehow, even in the worst cases of abuse, exploitation, or violence, Americans can convince themselves that because the person "agreed" to an intimate relationship or to a job, that she or he agreed to everything that happened after that.

It is significant to note that more contemporary forms of intimate partnership that fall outside of traditional, heterosexual, monogamous marriage do not remain undefined or simply on the margins. Rather, again, the less formal relations—while also being defined by these understandings—also serve as the negative referent against which the more legitimized, formal relations are judged. This is true not only for conservative analysts who condemn "illegals" for "stealing jobs" (and so on); who condemn single mothers, unmarried partners, or gay and lesbian couples for destroying family values, but also society at large. This discursive denigration of the more informal relations does not alter the contractual language or Enlightenment presuppositions but adds another conceptual layer to these problems. These assumptions are not merely neutral organizing principles, but they also discipline subjects in various ways, whether they are in a formal contract or not. They efface the hierarchy built into these relationships; they obfuscate broader societal influences that pressure some individuals to consent to unequal relations and assume a heavier burden; and they obscure a legal and economic structure that is not merely inadequate but arguably dangerous for the targets of abuse. Again, a return to the family and notions of symmetry in abuse function together with these dynamics to coercively force communication, to mediate between unequals, and to use therapeutic means to blame targets for provoking abuse.

Intimate relationships are thus conceived of as rational (above passions, violence, and the irrational, for example, and transcending the particularity of private memberships or beliefs); mutual, consensual, and grounded in contract (as a reaction to monarchy, absolute power, and claims of divine right); and based on notions of individual autonomy (which includes not only political rights and protections but which also assumes economic independence). There is, further, an assumption that these categories are neutral (e.g., not racialized, class-biased, or gendered). Correspondingly, Enlightenment norms[81] construct intimate relationships in such a way that a system of mutuality is presupposed; there is a presumed equality; and it is assumed that there is liberty to exit a situation in some way. More specifically, perceptions include: (1) the notion that the partnership was entered into on absolutely equal terms; (2) that the relationship itself was and is also conducted on absolutely equal terms; and (3) that any inequality can be explained by a sort of gendered division of labor, which can be linked to separate-but-equal arguments. All of these assumptions help to justify the current popularity of symmetry arguments as well as mutual, communicative, egalitarian solutions. In terms of analyzing domestic abuse, these dynamics and presuppositions allow us to understand how intimate partner abuse is conventionally understood and why "help" is inadequate.

For these reasons, whether emotional or physical, it is assumed, first, that domestic abuse must be provoked, that it "takes two to tango" and so on.[82] These "malevolent mores" (Patricia Evans's term, which is a nice counterpart to de Tocqueville's notion of democratic mores) can be linked to the greater prevalence of symmetry arguments as well as the return to the family in welfare and family law.

Second, Enlightenment assumptions lead to the dichotomous view of abuse as practically nonexistent or spectacular (injuries must be severe and visible to others). Contradictorily, abuse is also often recognized only if it is consistent, systematic and predictable—criteria that are nearly impossible to meet in the majority of cases.

Third, it is often thought that abuse is personal and private and therefore society is a sort of outside neutral force that may or may not come to the target's aid; society is conceived of as being indifferent and disinterested. Society may help or it may not, but it is not directly implicated in intimate partner abuse. I have disputed this in the section where I argue that abusers are monsters created by society.

Fourth, in cases of emotional abuse (i.e., personal terror), the target of abuse is assumed to be perfectly capable of withstanding threats, including economic threats or the withdrawal of financial support, or threats to take away children. That is, threats are not considered particularly abusive or actionable. Rather, there is a preference for systematic, consistent, bodily injury when determining whether abuse occurred. To put it differently, the link between emotional abuse and domestic violence is denied as targets are urged to just ignore the emotional denigration or turn one's phone off when the demeaning texts begin to appear. This is particularly interesting given the incredible influence of Freud's thought, which is evident in the popular media; we seem to recognize that even the most minor thing can work on an individual's psyche, and yet we ignore how constant daily abuse, combined with threats and physical deprivation, punctuated by acts of violence, could affect a target's perception of reality. To put it differently, it seems irrational for a target to ignore the emotional abuse that often precedes physical assaults or attempts at other material injuries.[83]

Related to this, fifth, common perceptions of abuse are event-specific and temporally discrete. For example, if violence occurred in the past and now the abuser is "merely" threatening and stalking the target, the common perception by judges and psychologists is that the person has changed or is no longer a threat. To put it differently, violent acts are interpreted as if they do not occur in a broader context of emotional abuse or lower-level physical abuse. To a judge, for example, if a perpetrator has not struck his target in four months, there is no "fresh" evidence that he is currently violent.[84]

Sixth, if the abuser acts better briefly or publicly renounces violence, it is assumed he is getting better; if the target proceeds as if these are merely part of his cycles, she is the one who is viewed as being unreasonable. This point is also crucial because what is assumed is that he can improve his behavior without any intervention at all; it is important to note, because we do not often think violent criminals simply change one day, all on their own. This perception is only possible given the other presuppositions I have just outlined: intimate violence is somehow different from all other forms of violence. It is somehow acceptable and can be magically stopped, by sheer will, when we recognize that other forms of violence necessitate far more care and intervention. But even in batterer intervention programs, Lundy Bancroft has found that abusers who have been ordered to enter these programs can be great at making public declarations about how they have changed and reject violence. Nevertheless, many continue to abuse their partners, and those who are the most vocal about their recent self-transformation are often the most immune to change.[85]

Finally, there is a sort of societal compartmentalization by which any form of abuse that is enacted in front of a child magically doesn't affect the child. In this way, the media, judges, and social workers can argue that someone is a "good father" even if he has performed a number of actions that would otherwise be viewed as absolutely criminal and threatening in another context.[86] At the same time, mothers are increasingly blamed and even lose custody of their children. This "places blame upon the mother, the primary target of the violence, for the actions of the abuser. The mother is accused of exposing her children to violence when the exposure is caused by its perpetrator."[87] It is this last point that is perhaps most disturbing in terms of "rights talk": somehow, the abuse of a mother is assimilated such that her rights as a human being are completely divorced from those of the child she takes care of.[88] In fact, abusers are often rewarded for being in their child's life, despite violating norms of decent behavior.

The perversity of this situation highlights the degree to which these perceptions are damaging if political equality and democracy are in fact our goals—even in the realm of family law, which is historically convoluted, contradictory, and like the family itself, hierarchical. Indeed, resorting to formal and economic solutions to abuse is both legitimated by these power dynamics and practically ineffective.[89] These solutions have a disciplinary and yet destructive effect in legitimizing a skewed analysis of intimacy at the formal level, asserting mutuality, equality, and nonviolence where there is coercion, manipulation, and dehumanization.

Intimate partner violence then defies many Enlightenment presuppositions in several ways. First, if there is some degree of mutuality in the relationship, it is asked why the abused person doesn't just leave. Second, why doesn't the person seek help?[90] Third, when and if the person doesn't appear to do the first two things, it can be argued that there was no real danger—if there were, this circular method of reasoning goes, she would have left, right? According to this argument, many women do not leave right away even though they think their partners are making them unhappy and are dangerous. Equal, rational, and documentable communication is a crucial element of these assumptions, particularly in the case of intimate partner abuse. The ability to speak, to have access to the correct authorities at the right moment, and to be able to gather proper documentation all undergird the broader rubrics of contract, consent, and equality. Just as important, it is thought, a woman who has been abused could easily get help if she just communicated what she needed. The following example from a New York working group on domestic violence shows how the system structures "failure to protect," ignoring a target's efforts to get help and blaming the mother while rewarding the abuser:

> After five years in Alcoholic Anonymous, Nola's boyfriend, the father of her two children, began drinking again. The more he drank, the more violent he became. He flew into jealous rages and accused her of sleeping with other men. He would repeatedly shove her, hit her, and once threw her downstairs. Nola, too terrified to leave him, tried to protect her children by taking them away before his violent outbursts. She took the children to her mother's or sister's house when he began to drink. Nola sought family counseling and repeatedly called the police, but he was never arrested. ACS [child protection services] filed a neglect petition based solely on the history of domestic violence. The children were removed without any assessment of the actions she had taken to protect her children.[91]

In this situation the working group notes that the father-abuser is almost always allowed unsupervised visitation and even the possibility of getting sole custody.[92] In effect, societal sympathy does not lead to justice or even the eradication of violence. Rather it supports and maintains a set of Enlightenment norms that uphold notions of consensus and mutuality *while also* placing the entire burden on the abused woman.

Giorgio Agamben's controversial examination of Musselmänner in *Remnants of Auschwitz* clearly demonstrates the limitations of these norms.[93]

I do not mean to equate victims of the Holocaust with abuse victims but rather to suggest that there are limitations to premising any help abused women get on communication, as I established in the previous chapter. Targets of violence cannot always speak for themselves[94]; they are often unable to produce documentary evidence of harm (evident in the example above); and conventionally acknowledged forms of solidarity and resistance are also nearly impossible, given the circumstances. Secondly, the "help" one seeks may not be helpful but isolating or punitive. The majority of therapists are not trained to treat the situation as asymmetrical, and one can only get documentation from medical, law enforcement or legal personnel if they truly understand the situation—most often, they do not. Furthermore, there is plenty of evidence that (1) women do try to get help; (2) women do leave abusive partners; and (3) women do speak about abuse to numerous interlocutors.[95] The problem is that help is structured in ways that reproduces the very conditions it is supposed to eradicate; women who leave abusive partners can still be tied to their exes in significant ways (e.g., child custody, shared property, or geo-spatial confinement); and, significantly, when women speak, they often become the focal point of judgments and rhetoric on abuse, allowing the abusers to be ignored. These barriers to political acknowledgment and inclusion expose the limitations not of the individuals themselves but the complex bundle of political norms that link political inclusion to Enlightenment norms of rationality, autonomy, and individuality, not to mention capitalist notions of property ownership that dominate US notions of rights.

What is more, violence is not eradicated in this system but actively cultivated and managed. Because help for abuse and societal norms regarding abuse are not preventive in any significant way, they merely help victims after egregious force has been used.[96] That is, the requirement that violence be systematic, provable, and documented correctly indirectly *encourages* violence that can later be formalized, assimilated, and discursively used by abuse advocates to describe and manage a situation but not to actually eradicate it. To be clear, violence is not ignored by this system but *must* occur. In this way, the system mirrors the abuses it purports to eliminate.

Significantly, interpreting interpersonal crises as isolated events is a convenient way to ignore broader and more pervasive forms of coercion and arbitrary power. The way that abuse is individually conceived and the threshold one is supposed to reach to be considered a legitimate abuse target has the same effects. Further, despite demands for documentation of systematic abuse, which presuppose societal acceptance of a more contextualized narrative of intimate partner abuse, a person is only designated "abused" by virtue of isolated events. This not only effaces the specific dynamics of partner abuse but also the broader political context that links private violence to societal norms. The tendency to wait until abuse and rightlessness are absolutely at a crisis point then creates a vicious cycle that only reinforces the logic of this limited, individualized, Band-Aid system. Through its crisis orientation, time is compressed, and analyses classifying domestic abuse are accordingly compressed, as are solutions.[97] Solutions are then limited and low-level (as shelter, work, and medicine—but not the prevention of violence), and these seem like the logical answer. As a result, individuals' barest biological needs are perhaps satisfied but the politico-economic context in which the violations occurred is usually left intact.

The worst aspects of this system can be summarized as being too oriented to Enlightenment norms of consent, contract, mutuality, discourse, and rationality. That is, again, individuals hoping to flee abuse are expected to rationally and consistently prove, through documentary evidence, their situation. This presupposes not only that people have the means to speak and communicate in one way, but also that they are somehow politically equal—they can exercise political agency enough to consult the proper authorities; they know what to document and which forms of documentation are acceptable; and they have the means to convey this consistently over time. These expectations can be viewed as "contractual" in that some sort of mutuality is assumed in the ability to communicate how one is abused; there is an assumption of political equality that allows an individual's voice to be heard; and there are broader notions of contract that assume that anyone in an abusive situation could simply walk away.[98]

Against more recent dismissals of radical feminism,[99] I have suggested in this book that Catharine MacKinnon's work as well as Colette Guillaumin's provide a realist framework for analyzing how violence is rationalized (in the Weberian sense) rather than eradicated by the law and some dominant societal norms.[100] Again, in their (separate) treatment of rape, both authors note that it is not just the act of violence itself that characterizes the life of women in a given society but the very threat of this violence as well as its cultural and legal acceptance. This threat disciplines the lives of nearly all women, determining their use of public space, the ability to act autonomously, and the degree to which they are isolated from others. Finding a continuum of violence and political subordination as an inextricable feature of liberal capitalism and not an anomaly or exception helps one understand how violence is merely "controlled but not prohibited" as MacKinnon would say.[101] Similarly, partner violence occurs in a broader context that defies limited, crisis-oriented, individualized, egalitarian, and emotionally neutralized modes of analysis. Radical feminism demonstrates how a narrow, legally oriented, rights-based framework simply manages and controls the problem it purports to solve. If democratic agency, the possibility of solidarity and acting in concert, and politics as a site of contestation (rather than homogeneity and consensus) are really to be implemented, we must develop a different view of domestic abuse.

HELP: PITY AS VIOLENCE

For all of these reasons, "help" is often completely misguided. As I have noted, abuse is often treated as individual and personal; nevertheless, a crucial component in maintaining this conceptual narrowness is how pity for victims is often enacted at the societal level. I have noted that abusers' passions are often assimilated and recast as socially useful while the emotions of targets are often portrayed as irrational and self-destructive. I have also contended that there is a tendency to confer political rights only when societal sympathy is on the side of the group in question. In particular, recent appeals to evoke pity for targets of abuse (including using a care theory framework) are presented as correctives to a more liberal, rational discourse and set of institutions that frame liberal rights. Highlighting the humanity of victims is alleged to further transgress, or at least transcend, conventional liberal, rational politics. However, I find both conceptual categories—pity and humanity—impoverished and argue that they only buttress the traditional framework, disciplining violence but not eradicating it.

In particular, appeals to the pity of different interlocutors assessing abuse cases do not soften or ameliorate the worst tendencies of a narrow, rationalized, legally oriented, rights-based framework.[102] I assert this despite contentions that these emotions correct or even democratize the worst aspects of the Enlightenment on the one hand or that emotions can successfully be eradicated from political processes and relationships on the other. Rather, I believe that claims based on pity, empathy, and humanity are actually a crucial part of the Enlightenment framework, often deepening racial, gender, and citizen-immigrant divides as one set of emotions is validated while the other is hyperbolized and pathologized.

First, rather than truly posing an alternative to Enlightenment norms, theories based on pity or care are inextricably tied to spectacular acts of violence. In particular, to qualify as being abused, a target must prove that she has been the victim of overt, systematic violence.[103] While this may seem logical, it means that being officially considered abused demands two things: (1) constant, overt, "provable" abuse—often to the point of death and yet (2) the ability to produce sufficient documentation of this abuse even despite the political, economic, and physical barriers to doing so (and a corresponding inability to contact the correct authorities at the correct time). These two demands are largely incompatible.[104] As I analyzed in Chapter 2, to the degree that care theory is validated through current forms of family law that put the family unit above individual rights and conjoint therapies that assume symmetry in abuse, an internal logic is developed such that only extraordinary acts of violence are considered noteworthy. For this reason, I argue that together, these norms preserve and systematize violence rather than truly eradicating them.

Where a rationally oriented, rights-based set of norms and institutions has failed, emotions are supposed to move us from apathy to democratic action. These dynamics have important similarities with human rights theory but also overlap with them, as discussed in Chapter 3, which analyzed gender-based human rights claims. [105] Although Sam Moyn explores human rights rather than domestic violence, his analyses of human rights theory and appeals to pity are particularly relevant to my discussion. Moyn's project is to demonstrate at least two things relevant to my own project: that democratic revolutions and the eventual, very recent turn to human rights have often been complicit with the very behaviors and power relations they purport to challenge. Second, the appeal to emotions in particular—on behalf of the oppressed and, more recently, human rights victims—has developed into a depoliticized, individualizing set of power relations that often deny their roots in inequality, coercive practices, and violence.

A crucial observation that synthesizes Moyn's concerns is that appeals to pity (again, assimilated into academia via care theory[106]) emerged from the Enlightenment rather than being conceived as an absolute challenge to it. Sentimentalism and romanticism were conceived of as buttressing new conceptions of political inclusion and rights rather than attempting to undermine these new frameworks. For example, Adam Smith's notion of "fellow-feeling" has been interpreted as a complement to his economic writings and not a challenge or contradiction.[107] And Rousseau's concept of pity undergirded new theories of natural rights and social contract rather than undermining them.[108] Moyn also notes that literary and artistic humanism "strengthened and secularized emotive appeals to dignified and suffering humanity,"[109] which is evidence of historical continuity, not rupture. Nevertheless, part of his point is that these earlier notions of humanity and pity were not bound up in legal formality or rights; in fact, again, they were often used to deprive people of rights and to kill more efficiently. Against the more positive interpretations of the Enlightenment celebration of humanity and humanism, Moyn reminds readers of Arendt's analyses connecting sympathy and murder in *On Revolution*. Challenging Lynn Hunt's relatively whitewashed account of the French Revolution, Moyn urges us to consider Arendt's disquieting contention that "'pity, taken as the spring of virtue, has proved to possess a greater capacity for cruelty than cruelty itself.'"[110]

To put it differently, attempting to depoliticize political rights—to make them conceptually and morally pure and to fully eradicate violence— denies the fraught, uneven, and often "unsympathetic" usages of sympathy, particularly based on humanity.[111] This denial, perhaps paradoxically, leads to a "massively disproportionate" focus on "spectacular wrongs."[112] To Moyn, writers like Hunt are then forced to focus on issues like torture, events at Abu Ghraib, and conditions at Guantánamo and ignore more systematic, seemingly banal forms of abuses, inequalities, deterritorialization, and oppression.[113] Similarly, with regard to domestic abuse, horrific cases are often advanced in the media and on television at the expense of more widespread, seemingly low-level violence and abuse.[114] As Evan Stark points out, this leads to fundamental and pernicious misunderstandings of the nature of contemporary forms of domestic abuse in the United States.[115]

Appeals to sympathy then have serious consequences for attempts to democratize politics.[116] First, while efforts to politicize affective relations are supposed to correct the cold rationality of bureaucratized, individualized systems, their effect is to moralize what should be properly political. Caring and affective relations, including appeals to pity, efface their own inequalities. Those who promote caring and affective relations promote connections to others, concern for the group over the individual, and hold that love and positive emotions will bring stability and peace.[117] However, the older critiques of these theories still hold: they celebrate what has formerly been denigrated (emotions, which as Rousseau held, were women's creation), leaving intact a "separate spheres" mentality;[118] they ignore the *unheimliche* nature of the home in which family relations are highly unstable, unequal, and a poor model for democratic politics;[119] and importantly, as I discuss later, they deny their own acceptance of not only Enlightenment values but also violence and coercion. In terms of the former criticism, the relation of the Enlightenment to care theory is really two sides of the same coin, the latter merely attempting to correct the worst aspects of the former but simultaneously buttressing the importance of the paradigm it is purportedly correcting.

Political, social, and feminist theories based on affective ties could be subject to similar criticisms. They presuppose a simplistic and linear thought process in which appeals to the worst cases of abuse are supposed to arouse the sympathy of otherwise indifferent and morally neutral spectators (whether they are bureaucrats or denizens of wealthy countries who are expected to donate time and money to foreign causes). Outraged emotion is supposed to then lead to concrete, linear action that is easily tracked and observable. The same outcome should occur, if the information is (1) conveyed correctly; (2) communicated dramatically enough to appeal to emotions in the right way; and (3) well-timed, as the crisis may soon be over. All individuals are viewed as having the same emotional reaction to human suffering; having an ability to convert these emotions readily into acceptable, rational forms of aid; and doing what they can for these foreign, distant others that they would otherwise have no linkage to except through their generous commitment of aid. This sort of process is assumed, even while it is criticized, in Rawlsian and post-Rawlsian analyses of rights.

These sorts of interpretations ignore the deeper politico-economic context of what appears to be a deracinated, isolated instance of human suffering; in fact, "we" may be far more responsible for intimate gender violence than is commonly portrayed. First, as MacKinnon demonstrates, violence and subordination undergird liberal, "morally neutral," rights-based modes of political belonging.[120] The appeal to pity, humanity, and charity is thus a will-to-purity, attempting to depoliticize and efface the network of power relations that make "us" far more directly responsible for human suffering than is admitted and allowing "us" to deny our society's own instances of systematic violence.

Second, there are highly problematic and wishful epistemological assumptions behind this reasoning: that sufficient discourse (communication, narrative) will adequately capture the issue at hand[121]; that, consequently, individuals who are exposed to this discourse will have the proper emotions; and these emotions will then be rationally and clearly translated into a calculus of action (if feasible) or reasoned inaction (if not, or there are competing issues).[122] Stephen White's recent work on dearth and depth is illustrative of these epistemological issues, even if it is not aimed at domestic abuse issues in particular.[123] In a talk he gave at Northwestern in the fall of 2010,[124] he provided the example of a middle-class, presumably white student who goes on a service learning vacation and is suddenly exposed to the lives of battered women.[125] White assumes that this student is a sort of blank slate who has never encountered violence or marginalization until this point. He argues that once this high school student is exposed to the outside violence of abused women, the student will become sympathetic to this group, aiding them when she or he can. While White's aim is to explore a mode by which a relatively privileged subject becomes politicized and develops a sort of democratic awareness, the educational process is squarely an Enlightenment one: the innocent subject is exposed to the violence of the other, and she or he will have the proper response to the victims' situations and will then proceed from the experiential phase to a higher communicative phase that will then become the proper political response. However, the hierarchical notions built into this theory are effaced through the denial of violence, instability, and primitive emotions in the figure of the pure, innocent, helping student.

But emotions are not so easily predictable or assimilable. In fact, this student—who may have witnessed violence in his or her home; listened to it in music; and witnessed it over and over on TV and in movies—could learn how abusive men actually largely get away with systematic and prolonged violence.[126] Indeed she or he could understand how, in reality, the system that purports to "help" these victims actually makes them more rightless, while the perpetrators have increased power.[127] This student may have a myriad of reactions that will not be particularly helpful or charitable toward these targets of abuse. The issue is twofold: (1) this model assumes a linear trajectory from raw, unprocessed emotions to a more enlightened set of thought processes that lead to democratic, ethical behavior, but there is no evidence that exposure to abuse makes us more democratic or moral; (2) the model also assumes that the privileged student has been protected from violence, abuse, and misogyny up until this point and only experiences it after traveling to another neighborhood or taking an "alternative spring break."

Current mainstream analyses of human rights (particularly Rawlsian, post-Rawlsian, and Habermasian work[128]), including even Amartya Sen's relatively more sophisticated work, similarly presuppose a morally and politically neutral subject who is just waiting to be educated.[129] These analyses are relevant to the public's understanding of intimate partner abuse—in both cases, there is a victim whose story must sway the public to help. The target is an individual who has cast herself outside of the citizen body and must appeal to society to re-enter. A second important presumption is that violence is not part of life throughout society—it is elsewhere. Violence is then contained in poor neighborhoods, racially Other households, and in primitive, backward countries. The morally neutral high school student is then exposed to this purely foreign example of violence and is able to "help" this victim (who is ultimately the victim of herself). The purity of the self, of course, comes at the expense of the victimization of the other.[130] The morally neutral subject can then experience emotions if they are then readily converted into a sort of liberal, rights-oriented action. Emotions are the necessary catalyst for an educational epiphany. The assumption is that most reasonable individuals will have the same reaction.

Emotions in this context are disciplined and assimilated, not dismissed as the feminist literature has often argued.[131] To put it differently, theorists of racism, postcolonialism, imperialism, and feminism are not wrong to discern the following splits: primitive-civilized; irrational-rational; dependence-independence; particular-neutral/universal and so on. Nor are they wrong to argue that the first part of these binaries has been used to discursively marginalize political and economic Others. But I would like to complicate this account by arguing that these binaries are not absolutes—that emotion and particularity (among other things) have their place in the modern/Enlightened/civilized world *if* they are assimilated, stabilized, and neutralized. Hence, the denigrated half of these pairs is not abandoned or cast aside but actively used, further hierarchized, and discursively tamed.

This is why, I believe, a politics of victimization merely cooperates with the systematic, rationalized relations of exclusion and marginality. These are depoliticizing moves that focus on the humanity of the subject as mere life. Hence, while I agree with Wendy Brown's critiques of a legally oriented, rights-based reaction to violence and abuse (in turn, based on her revised reading of Nietzsche's concept of ressentiment, discussed in Chapter 2)[132] it is not because I see certain targets of abuse as self-pitying victims (to the degree that ressentiment implies self-pity). Rather, the appeal to pity entails the equation of humanity with victimization and not political agency. Following purely legal, individual, rights-based remedies in the face of massive, if not also fragmented, structural inequalities and oppressions often further entraps a person in the same system he or she is trying to escape. Victimhood is rightlessness.

But the danger is not only in removing the political identity and agency of the alleged victim[133] but also in shoring up the denial of the particularity, violence, coercion, and inequality of the allegedly neutral subject who is there to "help." Nietzsche's analysis of these sorts of denials in *On the Genealogy of Morals* is highly relevant to my argument: the denial of violence and coercion—the animal in us—comes from an inability to ruminate on our own actions; a fear of ourselves such that we need to whitewash our norms and accepted behaviors and those of others we admire. However, these attempts at mastery and control of the moral world are not energyless; in fact, it takes a huge amount of "will" to conceive of them and to try to bring about this sort of universality, pseudo-consensus, and purity. This will, in turn, is absolutely violent and inegalitarian, despite claims to the contrary. In this sort of mindset, politics as passion and heroism is traded for a morally neutral, hypocritical, intellectually stagnant framework. To bring the discussion back to the faulty epistemology described above, there is considerable danger in thinking that we are not connected to others through violence and passion and that the only acceptable framework for domestic abuse help is one of the morally neutral, superior, civilized group in relation to a group of absolute victims whose political status has been ineradicably erased.

The faulty epistemology not only denies the violence, misogyny, and racism (among other things) of "our" own families, communities, and nation but also presumes that we will then act on our emotions in the correct way. Indeed, as many authors have noted, providing greater information on human rights abuses in hopes of gaining sympathy can lead not only to compassion fatigue but hostile indifference or opportunistic interventions, cynically using the language of protection to wage even more violence.[134] Issues of domestic abuse face the same obstacles. In effect, the more analytical, rights-based analyses of domestic abuse ignore the limits and dangers of both emotions and rationality.[135] They presuppose a pure and neutral learning environment and thought process with predictable, rational outcomes. What I want to suggest is not simply the inadequacy of care, or claims of affective ties, or pity but the hidden violence and subordination involved in these processes. The moment that an individual is designated as a human being rather than a citizen, and therefore as a victim, is a moment of profound rightlessness. Their alleged elevation in domestic abuse discourse is only at the moment they are pure victims and can prove absolute harm without provocation. The "rights" are thus conceived of in absolutely negative terms: they signal defeat and the stripping of political status.[136]

This is important in understanding the complex power matrices that form abusive relationships—not as outside Enlightenment norms but actually accepted, maintained, and importantly, *fostered* by these same norms. In fact, if the two concepts are taken together and understood in a context of violence, abuse, and inefficiency (in terms of wasting lives, wasting resources, and ruining relationships), an even more disturbing picture may emerge. And if this is true, my observations of abuse, violence, and abandonment may not just characterize the lives of domestic abuse targets but also the lives of other (second-class) citizens or long-term residents.

When abuse, exploitation, or violence occur, assumptions about mutuality, consent, and egalitarianism are not challenged but serve to discipline the targets of abuse in multiple ways. Societal pressures are such that we are supposed to seek formal legal means of redress but when we do, we are often more screwed than when we started.[137] A different way to put this is that crucial elements of violence are not dealt with and what these power matrices amount to is really disciplined violence or rationalized irrationality. For example, because certain directives are applied to both parties, the target can come under equal scrutiny, or the terms of the directive or action could focus more on the target than the perpetrator.[138] Something may be achieved, there is an internalization of norms, and docility is realized in many respects, but these all occur in a context of bodily injury, overt abuse, and the threat of death. One set of dynamics does not preclude the other.

In this context, I have proposed that abuse is more of a spiral than a cycle (accounting for escalation and movement rather than a neat circle that can easily be tracked) and that a combination of disciplinary tactics and bio-political elements can be discerned in these power mechanisms. Essentially, acts of violence do not explode Enlightenment categories but rather Enlightenment categories serve to neutralize violence such that they are portrayed as random acts between two consenting adults. In fact, a key feature of violence is its meaninglessness. However, violence is often understood in a mutual context in which one party provokes and the other party acts violently. Violent acts are also interpreted as isolated and so verbal threats can be distinguished from overt acts of violence. And this logic goes, that of course, all targets could leave. However, I believe that abuse should be viewed as absolutely inefficient, inconsistent, and unprovoked; and the key element of abuse is surprise. This spiral, or escalating cycle, is often characterized by certain patterns: abusers are often intensely "loving," and then they withdraw (an information-gathering period, according to abuse specialist Lundy Bancroft), and then they have an abusive period. But this abuse spiral is terroristic; it is designed to keep the target off-center, and therefore it is not predictable. Despite all these features, all of which challenge Enlightenment and contractual understandings of relationships, there is a disciplinary effect and a sort of internalization of norms that occurs. The terroristic features of abuse ensure that targets are constantly afraid; that to survive they must constantly anticipate the next attack; and that they can never relax. This sort of feeling is also evoked in panoptical structures—violence and abuse are wielded sporadically but the crucial emotion is terror—so the person constantly walks on eggshells, afraid of punishment. The next attack necessarily targets something considered good or rational—to show the victim that even mere bodily gestures or what is considered "good" by others in society is inherently bad when the victim performs the same action. This might be a perversion of normalization, but it rests on the same model—the key is to convince this person (in an abuse situation) that even her thoughts, gestures, and the tone of her voice can all be used against her.[139]

Most important—whatever is being threatened—whether the threat relates to physical harm, job loss, the withdrawal of intimacy, or taking a child away from the primary caretaker—the psychological consequences of abuse are related to the threat of this very real deprivation. Something irreplaceable and necessary for life is being threatened. Thus, even though courts and some analyses isolate the event of violence, arguing that the abuser "lost it" or was momentarily out of control, targets know that abuse is seamless. In reality, even during peaceful periods, the abuser is simply gathering his resources. Again, abusers also terrorize their targets when things are good—when the target has achieved something or when a worker has done a good job. This can be related to disciplinary power in that there is a recognition of achievement or success but like a terrorist act, the crucial element for the abuser is to seize this as an opportunity to show the target that even her accomplishments are somehow suspect or even (secretly) dangerous. A second important part of this is to ensure that the target is caught off guard; attacking someone for doing the right thing, accomplishing something, or for simply being happy makes no sense. The goal, as is the goal in disciplinary power, is to normalize the target, but unlike the goal in disciplinary power, the larger aim is destructive. In this way, the disciplinary relationships defining abuse solutions under neoliberal conditions, often maintain and perpetuate abuse, just as modern expectations of "love" do the same. In effect, a target of abuse could lead a life that is characterized by legal harassment or neutralized terrorism. This individual could receive daily texts accusing her of being a bad mother; of violating her custody agreement; and of acting inappropriately in various ways without any evidence of the claims and without recourse against these harassing messages. Even if there is no evidence for these claims, they are legal in the sense that the "payer"/father is allowed to contact the primary caretaker regarding their child. And, as discussed in previous chapters, abusive fathers are still rewarded for staying in a child's life, even as he abuses the primary caretaker. Similarly, in the workplace, Enlightenment understandings do not prevent violence or punish it but rather assimilate it to its norms. In these ways, the systematicity, normative power, and legally oriented aspects of disciplinary power are combined with bio-power—which in this case involves the suspension of the law for individuals based on their feminized "biological status" rather than any criminal act.

Accordingly, the "help" that is offered is often ineffective, because targets are often blamed for the terroristic tactics of their abusers. If the purpose of the family law system is to foster the best interests of the child, what it translates into is a legal context in which a child can be exposed to violent acts; emotionally manipulated; and constantly subject to her father's denigration of her primary caretaker.[140] In effect, these dynamics treat violence only after it has occurred, essentially permitting all forms of abuse. It also shifts the focus (again) to the target rather than the abuser. Not to simplify things, but how can this be in a child's best interests if we are to believe that this is not really a cynical attempt to reinforce gender roles and keep women off of welfare by forcing them to deal with interested fathers? Nevertheless, gender, class, and racial hierarchies are reinforced and given more power with overt acts of violence.

In effect, Foucault's work shows how disciplinary power and bio-power function together when considering domestic abuse. If bio-power represents the "biological"—including those designated as being tied to their bodies, their hormones, and/or their skin color—disciplinary power tames and assimilates the hitherto "unassimilable." In this way, it is a sick system, but it is a system. The terroristic nature of abuse, combined with the profile of an abuser (whose actions are precisely anti-Enlightenment), further illuminate how abusers' violence is assimilated into society rather than challenged.

CONCLUSIONS

As I have explored in this chapter, violence is interwoven into our societal norms and understandings. Hence, even the most rationalized power systems can assimilate violence and efficiency, and productivity can exist alongside abuse, attacks, and physical degradation. If these observations are true, domestic violence cannot and should not be viewed as merely "intimate" or private but rather yet another instantiation of a rather systematic acceptance and reproduction of violence against (mainly) women.[141] Rather than being shocked or even moved to empathy, the general public tends to focus on the target of violence, asking what she did to provoke the abuse. What was her part in it? Why didn't she leave? Or, why doesn't she just talk to her partner and make him understand that he is hurting her? The presuppositions in these questions are (1) that both parties are "rational," reasonable, and can change; (2) that the abuser is capable of feeling remorse; (3) that intervention as it is currently practiced actually helps women, and thus the entire burden for changing abusive power dynamics is placed on the target; and (4) that liberal, rights are adequate for dealing with these sorts of issues. As I have indicated, there has been a shift from "Why doesn't she just leave?" to "Why doesn't she just talk to him?" that makes these observations about the limitations of rationality and speech even more relevant today.[142]

Connecting these arguments to those in Chapter 3, we can consider the "speech" of refugees in juxtaposition to the individual-pathological speech of the never-quite-victim. As I have argued, premising political inclusion on speech should not lead us to question targets' multiple truths but rather the dichotomous, often unsympathetic system that *produces* this speech. In turn, the binary mode of operation in this dichotomy between pure-political-exceptional refugee and pathological-apolitical-banal abuse target exposes the limits of sympathy as the basis for political solidarities or rights.

I have used Bonnie Honig's notion of "incomplete mourning" as a way to characterize the uprooting, destabilizing aspects of abuse and policies dealing with abuse. As I have argued, it signifies the traumatic break that targets are expected to make in order to get help—either by negotiating with someone who has hurt them or through leaving and potentially losing all other relationships, including economic ones. It is important to note that if targets do not quite internalize their abuser's criticism and abuse, incomplete mourning should stand in for post-traumatic stress disorder (PTSD) and battered woman syndrome (BWS). It is a broader concept that does not individuate and depoliticize but rather captures a greater range of relationships and valid feelings of loss and displacement. In sum, the juxtaposition exposes significant deficiencies in the treatment of abuse targets in the United States.

The most important notion that needs to be dismantled is that abusers fit into the Enlightenment framework of intimate partnership; the second most significant assumption that must be challenged is that the general public and any "help" available are also capable of sympathy, consistency, and pure rationality. In fact, society itself may reflect a far crueler, less empathetic value system than is commonly thought. If these two things are true, liberal rights will often end up trapping abused women rather than helping them. A different conception of power itself, along with a transformed notion of political agency, is needed. These problems thus not only highlight the inadequacy of understanding domestic abuse but the urgency of discarding liberal, rights-based politics. Throughout this book,

I have attempted to identify a problem that has been depoliticized in order to show that it merits attention as a political problem. This particular issue further exposes the fragmentation of the state and the impotency or even entrapping mechanisms of Enlightenment-based, liberal notions of rights and legality. For these reasons, the goal has been to refocus our understanding of these sites of power in order to redirect attention to more democratic solutions. In the next chapter, I will discuss some of these solutions at the political-philosophical level. Following up on notions analyzed in this chapter, I argue that a poststructural, intersectional analysis of this problem is necessary in order to focus on the power relations that activate and produce these dynamics, rather than continuing the unfair focus on targets. I conclude by suggesting that in the future a shared script, influenced by Foucault and Habermas, would signal a radical change in communicative relations. This is a future I hope to experience.

CHAPTER 5
Conclusion

INTRODUCTION/DISCUSSION

In this book, I have tried to show how domestic abuse should be taken seriously by those interested in politics and issues of democracy. Most important, this is because domestic abuse is a problem that is supported by and which exposes tensions between violent orientations and Enlightenment notions. Indeed, as I have argued throughout this book, the distinctions that are often made between violent acts, threats, and other forms of coercion on the one hand and contractual notions of interaction, communicative and educational therapies, and solutions, on the other are not merely two spheres of action. Instead, the latter is often conceived of as eradicating the former. A realist perspective instead recognizes that violence is not just one of the most crucial elements of state sovereignty but acknowledges that at the individual level, those who can legitimately act as aggressors or defend themselves during violent attacks are autonomous political actors. In contrast, when subjects of violence are denied both possibilities, they are therefore denied the tools of transcendence (as de Beauvoir has argued) or even human status (as Fanon rightly contends). Being denied the ability to even defend oneself is not merely rightlessness in a calculus of commodity-like powers; it also takes away the preconditions for democratic liberty and action. The facets of abuse, which are often supported or ignored by the state, thus permit a set of controlling power dynamics that are not merely isolated instances of coercion or violence but rather amount to a relation of bodily appropriation or sexage. Enlightenment values are not simply equal to violence but serve to either obfuscate relations of violence, coercion, and hierarchy or to facilitate them through victim-blaming and "tough love" exercised on targets. It is damaging to refuse to see this as a political problem that affects a significant number of people and has a myriad of consequences that are not limited to or contained by individual lives or the private sphere. Indeed, parallel to economic exploitation, the desire to discursively contain these power dynamics to the private sphere is a refusal to see a more interesting but also troubling blurring of boundaries that make both issues—domestic abuse and economic exploitation—far more complex than many interlocutors would like.

At the level of individual analysis, there are also similarities between economic relations that entail physical appropriation and a target's willingness to enter an intimate relationship, which then turns into a hostage-like situation (as Evan Stark has theorized) with mechanisms of power that control and entrap a target on numerous levels.[1] Against symmetry theories and the Enlightenment notions of intimacy that undergird notions of symmetry, I have suggested that similar to exploited laborers, these abuse targets have valid fears and are reacting to very real threats. These threats and mechanisms of control can range from the emotional—pitting family members against a target[2]—to physical (preventing a target from going to work or physically threatening her if the police arrive)—to economic (e.g., an abuser hiding or withholding income and making the target solely financially responsible for their children but simultaneously doing everything he can to harass her while she is working).[3] In fact, there is very little to suggest that abuse is all in their heads or they have been brainwashed by the abuser.[4] As noted above, like other forms of appropriation in the contemporary United States, abuse situations may occur not because of the explicit legal inferiority of women and feminized subjects but through a complex set of subordinating practices and circumstances that are both facilitated and obfuscated by policies and theories of symmetry, consent, and equality.[5] This becomes clearer after adopting the analysis used by the Department of Homeland Security in *The Matter of RA* and *The Matter of LR* and applying it to the United States.

First, the United States system could clearly be charged with state inaction or even punishment of the target. These failures and punishment significantly contribute to the hostage-like situation that characterizes abuse, thus directly implicating the state in why and how it is not easy to leave. State inaction occurs on numerous levels because the state itself is disaggregated. Although disaggregation is not bad in and of itself, a lack of uniform, fair, and democratic response in this particular case makes any policy and enforcement highly arbitrary. More broadly, uneven, punitive policies say far more about the state and what feminized identities it produces than about experiences of domestic abuse. Second, as in the asylum cases, there is the problem of social group visibility. From a legal stand-point, despite the difficulties in defining race, invidious racial classifications and racist policies are subjected to heightened judicial scrutiny. In comparison, women are not viewed as a legitimate social grouping in any positive sense (even if there has been recent attention to women as an electoral base).[6] In fact, the asylum cases show an opposite trajectory by which individuals only become "women" *through* self-defense and flight; that is, through being pure and unassailable victims. In this way, their "feminism" entails heroic acts of courage and sacrifice that are then retroactively called "feminism" and "political speech" if they successfully navigated their way out of the relationship and the country.

If this incredibly problematic set of definitions were applied to long-term US residents, the commonalities with the asylum cases would be evident. Women only become a group in these cases through successful labeling as a victim group, because they were abandoned by state and local enforcement, and cast out of their own communities. For these reasons, recognition of women as a visible social group entails incredible risks, losses, and bureaucratic maneuvers (to successfully document all this despite the circumstances) that make this social group entirely negative. This is evident in the double binds that emerge from this set of circumstances: inclusion in this group means that targets are pure victims and pathological; privileged and yet deeply flawed; feminists and yet failed feminists. In this way, merely expanding analyses of targets to be more intersectional (for example) or extrapolating from current policy solutions to add services for the poor or disadvantaged will not solve the root of the problem(s) or "empower" anyone. In today's system, being heard or beating the odds and getting one's day in court will not bring a target from victimhood to survivor status but perhaps result in new diagnoses of pathologies, the risks of losing her children or job, and being monitored by an unsympathetic and judgmental court system or counselors. Alternatively, many other targets of abuse are abandoned by the state or police and yet also overpoliced and subject to heightened scrutiny.

This binary mode of operation is perhaps evident in critical discussions of who counts as the ideal victim and who does not. What is evident when putting these various accounts together is that each category is mutually constitutive and entrapping in its own way. The ideal victim does not have the qualities of an active citizen but is docile, by all accounts, and "neutral" in a sort of Aristotelian sense of being middle-class, of indeterminate race, and perhaps married rather than being single. To the degree that this group even exists anymore or has access to the legal system, what is evident is that Foucault's docile individual has taken on a new form: the target who does not show emotion despite what she is being subjected to, who does not inconvenience advocates or lawyers with crying children, and who does not lose her job, despite the circumstances.[7] Women who admit they resisted violent attacks or acted to protect their children, who follow up with advocates or lawyers without being asked to, or who complicate simplistic narratives of abuse may be ignored by the state and have their cases dropped by lawyers and advocacy groups.[8] I wrote "perhaps" because this narrative has been produced in the court system and in academic writings, but it is not the whole picture. There is a whole host of women who never get this far—who never enter the system because the system is not a whole and is not consistent, and attempts to document abuse do not necessarily lead to documentation.[9]

Adopting the flawed but clearly better refugee criteria to interpret domestic abuse in the case of long-term US residents would still be an improvement over the current state of things. This is because the gendered nature of intimate abuse would become clearer and thus so would its political dimensions. In relation to the refugee framework, I have demonstrated a clear nexus between abusive behavior, societal approbation of this abuse, and state inaction or even punishment of the target. In fact, the relative freedom that targets have in the United States (as compared to these sending countries) is arguably mitigated by this punishment. For long-term US residents who are abused, their abusers will most likely go unpunished (unless they kill their targets) and thus there is a total failure of rights, democracy, or justice. Given how this loose system is constructed, all one can hope for is to get away. The definitions and political perspective that the US government has extended to these refugees would be a vast improvement over current treatment of long-term abuse claimants, but this would also highlight the deficiencies of these terms at the same time. Both the refugee system and policies for long-term US residents conceive of abuse as documentable, isolated acts that will end once the target has fled.

However, long term residents who do manage to get away are often still tied to the abuser (through a custody agreement, property, or other ties) and so the control can continue by other means.[10] This is particularly true if children are involved, as the state is often indifferent to abuse and will continue to allow the abuser visitation.[11] Economic abuse and harassment can often continue, even after the target and children have moved away (and if the court is involved, a protective order is only a short-term solution).[12] While authors like Anna Marie Smith have tracked the state's trend in increasingly removing children from a home, particularly in the case of poor African American families, there is quite a lot of evidence that the state is *also* highly tolerant of child abuse and sexual abuse.[13] And, as I have noted, if the rights of the mother are balanced against those of the child—ignoring the abuser altogether—the child is removed from the mother and not the father for "failure to protect."[14] These contradictory tendencies are evidence of state disaggregation but also a more homogenous response: ignoring the abuser completely and focusing on the mother, while using the child as an emotional football. Given all of these factors, the discourse on being a domestic abuse "survivor" seems like a distraction at best and at worst, it gives false hope to targets that they can successfully leave.[15] The term *survivor* is evidence of the Enlightenment will-to-truth that views abuse as an isolated event that can be neatly and cleanly solved without any remaining issues and without entailing significant losses.[16]

I have purposefully invoked exploited workers because at the moment there seems to be some understanding of economic polarization[17] and the nature of low-tier work today, including some societal sympathy for those who are in dire straits, who are not really consenting to dangerous work conditions in an informed manner, and who then find that their work is exploitative on numerous levels.[18] In ways I explored in the last chapter, this sympathy is not often extended to abuse targets, even though the exploitation is far more intensive and thorough in domestic abuse[19] and the threats—often to injure a target or harm her children—can be carried out with impunity, as long as the abuser does not go too far.[20] In fact, domestic abuse is a form of bodily appropriation that goes beyond any system of exploitation[21] or instance of political rightlessness.[22] It is akin to more contemporary forms of labor exploitation—such as in free-trade zones and the US agricultural guest-worker program—where the body itself becomes a site of social inscription. Indeed, this is not a hypothetical comparison, as the feminization of labor, neoliberal work conditions, and the withdrawal of the state all combine with the promotion of the family model in welfare, family law, and therapy to produce this hostage-like situation. Very often, one exploitative situation can reinforce the other, leaving targets trapped, despite their best efforts to resist or get away.[23]

Some current debates have acknowledged these sorts of circumstances, which are simultaneously disaggregated but also often totalizing (i.e., far-reaching and punitive), claiming that micro-resistance (e.g., waiters who spit in customers' food, or maquila workers who comply with dress codes but attempt to thwart sexual harassment) is a political act;[24] that is, that the disenfranchised can exercise micro-resistance, which is a sort of de facto democratic power or act of citizenship.[25] The asylum cases serve as an ideal type to correct this sort of claim. When we consider what has been framed as "political speech" or "feminism," it is evident that while these classifications were expedient, they also provided a vision of democratic action that is at the level of mere life: micro-resistance should not be mistaken for positive political agency. The ability to resist *is* important in viewing targets as political actors who are strategically reacting to oppressive circumstances. Awareness of micro-resistance demonstrates how a target is not gullible or pathological but a strategic actor. The asylum cases help to develop this perspective, because the analytical framework views them as targets of abuse and not the provocateurs; as political agents and not pathologized individuals who need a protective status; and as individuals who have fled despite the state's indifference or encouragement of abuse. Further, the Department of Homeland Security and the immigration judges' interpretation of flight-as-speech and resistance-as-feminism in the asylum cases can be juxtaposed with attempts by long-term residents at self-defense (a target can be arrested for resisting), flight (with children, this can be viewed as kidnapping), and speech and communication, which can simultaneously entrap the target and ironically liberate the abuser (she is pathological while he is rational). For all of these reasons, while micro-resistance[26] may be political, it certainly does not amount to liberty or democratic agency.

A correlate of these observations is that even rights (any right to rights) cannot *constitute* the political—rights themselves should not be up for debate nor mistaken for the substance of democracy. Since at least Karl Marx's time, authors have written about the limitations of civil rights in liberal representative democracy. To put Marx's ideas in Foucaultian terms, liberal rights have often been treated as commodities rather than relationships. In particular, Marx argued that through these rights, we often see in others the limitations of our own rights. In this spirit, Sheldon Wolin has further elaborated that rights are often asserted against one another, in competition and as a zero-sum game[27] rather than as a relationship (Foucault) or to work in concert with one another (Arendt, Wolin, David Held). Given these critiques, advocating a rights-based solution to the puzzles I have explored would be insufficient. Rather, rights should be fundamental in some way (as indicated in having the "right to rights") and *instruments* of the political. They are a precondition of democratic action and should never constitute the substance of citizenship, for if they are, they can then be taken away.

The confusion of rights as the political or as democratic agency is captured in Evan Stark's term "competitive victimization,"[28] which he has noted has occurred because policy has framed different, opposing constituencies—abused mothers and neglected or abused children. In this competition (which ignores the abuser entirely), public policymakers, the police, and shelters have decided to protect child welfare over and above (or against) abused mothers, thus pitting the mother's interests against the child's (and ironically, deepening the process of alienation of affections that abusers often engage in). Similarly, given the current predominance of symmetry theories, Susan Bordo's broader observations about attempts at neutrality in the midst of continuing historic gender inequalities show that egalitarian treatment usually privileges the stronger, more politically powerful party.[29] More broadly, I have argued that the solution to domestic abuse is not to turn to the very state and power mechanisms that have uprooted targets of abuse, even if formal institutions cannot be ignored. This particular issue demonstrates the degree to which political power must be constituted and enacted by the demos and especially those who are directly affected. Like Tocqueville's earlier analysis of how Americans tend to mistake equality (or equality of conditions) for political liberty,[30] I am arguing that basic rights are merely a precondition for democracy but not democracy itself. The right to self-defense, to flee abuse, or to care for one's children without threats or sabotage are merely processes basic to life and preconditions for acting. Today, committing this intellectual fallacy—viewing flight, self-defense, and resistance as informal citizenship—means that rights themselves are up for grabs. They can be removed through public debate or granted with the whims of societal sympathy. Alternatively, what I have suggested in this book is that violence—who is allowed to wield it, who is permitted to act in self-defense—structures political inclusion just as much as seemingly dialogical, communicative modes of political participation. Thus from an analytical point of view, a focus on rights does not fully capture the foundations and mechanisms of political inclusion.

Moving beyond rights-as-the political, the asylum cases also provide the analytical structure of how domestic abuse can be interpreted as a political issue, including identifying the nexuses between state and society, political and private. Moreover, these cases are evidence that even one of the most antidemocratic institutions of the government—notably an agency that is extraconstitutional and has often favored national security over democratic guarantees, the Department of Homeland Security—is capable of viewing abuse as a political issue and providing a clear legal framework for evaluating this abuse as asymmetrical and sexist. But even as the categories they devised are far more helpful in seeing domestic abuse as a political issue, they would still not be preventative in any way if they were applied to US residents and in fact *require* violence to occur to get the state to help. However, the asylum cases do provide a broader notion of what constitutes injury and violence and how the state's actions or inaction are crucial in determining the possibility for a target.

The asylum cases also expose how the private-public divide is a legal construct that justifies inaction or even punishment of a target of abuse. In important respects, domestic violence is not a purely private matter and this divide is an obstacle to moving beyond therapeutic or other individualized solutions. In the asylum cases, consent and Enlightenment views of intimacy do not challenge a view of the partner as "property"— that is, as radically unequal. In fact, as I argued in the previous chapter, consent and contract have often ensured and masked subordination. For all of these reasons, the asylum cases crystallize and make explicit how the *political* contours of intimacy are entrapping, and they illuminate how the death drive links the public and private. Despite their limitations, the asylum cases point the way to a realist interpretation of abuse, which will give a more accurate picture of abuse itself, including accounting for violence and asymmetry, and also point to more constructive solutions.

A crucial part of this realism is drawing on feminist accounts of the legal treatment of intimate gendered assault, but reducing these claims to a more genealogical, contingent, and local set of power dynamics. This realist hermeneutics would extend the acknowledgment of violence and destructive aims from formal political institutions and practices (the state monopoly on violence) to civil society and private actors,[31] recognizing that guarantees of bodily integrity for some are grounded in the right to self-defense and the ability to wield violence with impunity. In contrast, some groups have been denied these "rights," making them targets of coercion and violence. As I have argued, Catharine MacKinnon's work on the legal facets of gendered abuse and violence is a significant part of this realist account, but her analysis is most effective in the arena in which she was trained: the law. MacKinnon's work is important first in her connection of gender to sexuality, which offers a unique perspective on sexism, as opposed to class bias or a power-for-power's-sake argument.[32] But rather than arguing that this connection between gender and sexuality is universal and trumps other identities in importance, an intersectional analysis can reduce (but not dismiss) her claims. The interactive effects of such categories as race, ethnicity, immigrant status, and class may lead to highly differentiated power dynamics, outcomes, and solutions. What this means to me is not that her entire theory should be rejected but that her theoretical claims should be moderated to show that in the particular cases in which women are reduced to sexuality, certain notable power dynamics are at work. What's more, she connects this triad (women-sexuality-sexism) to policies on sexual harassment, rape laws, and gendered abuse and assaults to show how and why violence, harassment, and denigration are committed systematically and often with impunity. A crucial link she makes is the one between sex and violence, and thus she argues that conventional debates about whether rape is sex or violence are too dichotomous. The reason there is such great confusion between the two is that they are inextricably linked—something that Crenshaw also argues but has not been taken to task for as MacKinnon has.[33] These observations help to identify societal linkages of sex and violence (e.g., see Crenshaw's analysis of rap music) that are further connected to the legal confusion between the two categories.

In turn, by dismissing MacKinnon's work as a whole, feminist theorists (or social theorists who challenge the "feminist" label[34]) often fail to theorize the legal aspects of violence and abuse against women. When her claims are reduced and viewed as local, contingent, historically specific "truths," her work can be put in dialogue with the research of other feminist legal theorists who are not labeled radical feminists and who have theorized how the law itself permits gendered violence with impunity. This particular aspect of her argument has notably remained unchallenged and very few contemporary feminist theorists have undertaken such a thoroughgoing analysis of how and why abuse is legally permitted. In particular, when her work is put in dialogue with Guillaumin's and Crenshaw's, the broader connections between the law and its disciplinary effects are made explicit, including the societally accepted melding of love and violence.

An intersectional approach to domestic abuse is necessary not as a hypothetical, democratic approach to this issue but because the social problem itself demands a more fluid theory. It is important to understand (1) how an individual can hold a number of subject positions (for example, positions of privilege and oppression); (2) that Enlightenment notions can coexist with destructive aims, complicating the power relations that construct subjectivities; and (3) that gender itself is often discursively mobilized to chastise abused women. A focus should be on power relations and not identity per se, which should help to refocus attention on those who are being aggressive and bullying, as well as the institutions that ignore, assimilate, or even reward them. The overfocus on victims has had class-biased and racial overtones that lead to the conventional conclusion that abuse is the purview of the marginalized: racial and economic "minorities" and the poor. But even this overfocus does not lead to generous help or a sympathetic court system. There is currently a wide gap between forward-thinking, intersectional analyses of the domestic abuse system and the actual deployment of intersectional understandings of abuse in nonprofits, therapists' offices, or courts.[35] Instead, class and race often become the focus of biologically deterministic claims that hold that if abuse and violence are "natural," any policy, aid, or enforcement must be punitive and controlling.[36] Formal and informal institutions aim at neutralizing this population, accepting on some level that abuse and violence are inevitable. Changes in the welfare system and therapy also influence this discourse, attempting to create or keep a family unit together while denying abuse. Hence, ironically, there are more services for the poor and racial minorities, but they are often ineffective. These services can also perpetuate race, gender, and class biases, among other things, and these agencies and organizations might operate inadequately, because they compartmentalize abuse, conceptually extricating it from economic marginalization, housing issues, inadequate employment, and so on.[37] At the same time, these services are further marred by their purported neutrality, which ultimately rests—as Kimberlé Crenshaw has famously argued—on the model of a figure who has far more resources than average and only needs help in one particular area. I have argued that abuse itself cannot be compartmentalized in this way: abuse is not merely physical but often entails economic deprivation, control, and efforts to undermine a woman's success on the job.[38]

While there are quite a lot of arguments that claim that the feminist movement has actually undermined domestic violence approaches and solutions,[39] it seems clear that there is no singular group or set of ideas that makes up "the feminist movement," and thus, generalized claims that this movement has had deleterious effects create a straw man.[40] Indeed, a discourse of feminine subordination and traditional gender roles often justifies blaming targets of abuse as well as depoliticizing this issue. What is more, I believe that today gender is often imputed on situations that cannot be reduced to gender alone. For example, when I have revealed to political theorists that I have been a target of abuse, the reaction has most often been, "But you're a feminist; how you could you let yourself fall into a situation like this?" The implication is that I have chosen to fill a subordinate, traditional role in my intimate relationship despite my academic teaching and research. This sort of assertion—that we targets are "failed feminists"—ignores the legal complexities of relationships and custody and the long-term effects of economic abuse. One cannot become a feminist and suddenly get out of a situation like this. But this is only clear if we stop looking at the targets for answers and understand how late modern power dynamics do not silence or say "no" to targets but rather produce gendered subjectivities.[41] That is, again, the complex dynamics of abuse are evident if and when we understand the subjectivities and power dynamics that nonprofits and the state *produce*—the gendered dichotomies, the deserving and undeserving narratives, and racialized and class-biased typologies, among others. I believe that a realist, poststructuralist, intersectional feminist approach must be part of realist antiabuse efforts.[42]

A truly intersectional approach should not merely devise an approach to complex identities but complex power relations, defying a fixed subject position for any one person.[43] Reflecting on the methods of some anonymous antiabuse groups I have mentioned in this book, will allow us to see that power is a relationship and not a commodity; that even amidst oppressive power mechanisms, resistance can be asserted[44]; and that terms like *victim* and *oppressed* unjustly place "essence before existence."[45] For example, one of the most powerful exercises I was given by an anonymous group was to identify the weaknesses of my abuser and to identify my strengths. This sort of exercise helped me to celebrate my strengths *while being abused* and to see my ex-boyfriend as a flawed human being, who is not omnipotent, even if he has succeeded in using the law to abuse and harass my daughter and me. This exercise also enacts intersectionality (identifying not merely weaknesses or bad choices but strengths and ingenuity) and defies notions of "empowerment," because it may turn out that we targets already exercise power (even if that power is delegitimized or ignored de jure). For these reasons, intersectionality in analyzing this issue is necessary, but it is not about merging identities—rather, it is about identifying power positions, tactics, and strategic interaction.

In this regard, to the degree that domestic abuse is conceived of as the sort of difference that problematizes homogenous notions of equality, Jacques Derrida's term *differánce* is more helpful than static, universalized identity positions.[46] *Differánce* is a radical, irreducible term that allows not only for intragroup heterogeneity but also for a shifting and contested *individual* identity.[47] This perspective challenges biological determinism and looser claims about human nature (not just in conservative arguments but theories on the Left, including difference, care, and maternal theory), not to mention the male bias inherent in calls for strict equality, gender neutrality, and difference/separate spheres arguments. To authors like Joan Scott and Chantal Mouffe, equality and justice, not to mention protest and solidarity, do not have to rest on group uniformity or even a stable individual identity (particularly as "women"[48]). As Mouffe argues, and as Judith Butler suggests in *Gender Trouble*, the heart of politics can be issue-driven without presupposing any material basis for political identity as women.[49] These perspectives would allow us to recognize that anyone who is a target cannot be labeled "privileged" and conversely that certain social conditions or problems—like domestic violence—often explode analytically static categories of class and race. In this way, the realist politics I advocate is more agonistic, as well grass-roots oriented, and thus less static than the realism of the Cold War generation or some of the recent revivals of realism.

In applying a truly intersectional approach, for example, I challenge the notion of "privilege" among domestic abuse targets. This is not to claim that abuse is the great equalizer or that a rich woman, say, is somehow worse off than a poor woman, but rather to recognize that there is already an overfocus on targets and not abusers and when we make distinctions among the targets, focusing on the privileges of some and the absolute victimization of others, we are missing the agents, power mechanisms, and loci of abuse. For example, in the groundbreaking New York case *Nicholson v. Williams*,[50] which paved the way to criminalizing mothers for being assaulted by their partners, Evan Stark remarks,

> A major lesson from *Nicholson* is that the peculiar biases to which child protection is predisposed by its mission, programmatic structure and peculiar role in our society allow and may even compel its most progressive personnel to engage in morally and constitutionally indefensible practices *with respect to mothers in general* and *in particular to the class of primarily disadvantaged and/or minority women* who were the plaintiffs in *Nicholson*.

Stark's point is that this case sets a dangerous precedent for all abused mothers, with even more unjust and incredibly unfair burdens and punishments for those who are disadvantaged.[51] Stark blames the institutions that were complicit in punishing the victims in this class-action lawsuit, because they were proceeding according to faulty institutional logic. To argue that there is any privilege in being abused—particularly in a system that allows for abuse with relative impunity—is not only empirically untenable but incredibly perverse. In hypothesizing this, one could argue that there is a sort of Protestant ethic of domestic violence: while the poor and racial Others are somehow naturally subject to abuse, anyone who is wealthier or well-educated (for example) somehow should have known better. Their privilege magically ensures that they can escape abuse or easily get help and, by the same logic, if they continue to suffer abuse it is entirely their fault or choice. As we argue these things, the focus comes away from the state, the inadequate shelter systems, and the judgmental, tough-love therapists. To put this issue in Foucaultian terms, the discourse of blame, or Protestant ethic of abuse, serves as a disciplinary mechanism in the context of bio-power, blaming poorer women in one way and so-called privileged women in another. Both Crenshaw and Butler indicate that these conceptual categories are socially constructed and say more about social norms, a particular locality's power dynamics, and the subjects produced than about any individual per se. Truly intersectional work—as in Crenshaw's texts and Ange-Marie Hancock's[52]—acknowledges the varying sites of power, privilege, and inferiority that any one individual can experience, thus complicating any essential claims about a group's status. Significantly, both authors conceive of a methodological approach that recognizes different subject-positions for an individual, which could involve a person's privilege in one context and subordination in another.

If this more flexible approach to identity were used, Foucault's notion that power is shifting and relational—not a commodity or a thing that one person has and another lacks—could help to more adequately analyze systems of domination such as domestic abuse.[53] Domination, in this sense, is not unitary but indicative of power dynamics that systematically make groups unequal, exploited, or subject to abuse. Even if these power mechanisms are fragmentary and often self-sustaining, democratic agency can be undermined. In the context of domestic abuse, these theories could helpfully challenge many of the static and dangerous assumptions about abuse and abusers. For example, against the current trend of arguing that only certain groups are truly abused, researchers would have to recognize the commonalities *and* differences among all women who are abused. Nevertheless, any differences between groups of women who are abused would not thereby trump the commonalities. Rather, a truly intersectional approach would be applied that allowed for both sorts of observations without seeking a neat and unified resolution (of commonalities and differences), not to mention accounting for intragroup heterogeneity, changes over time, and even different subject positions of any one individual, depending on the context. It would also challenge the too easy linkage between "marginal" groups and violence, thus showing that violence and abuse are pervasive across different identities and classes.

Furthermore, the sorts of universalizing narratives that lump together lesbian intimate violence with heterosexual violence (including figuring out who represents the "man") would also be subject to critical interrogation.[54] Additionally, and most important, the abusers themselves should also be investigated rather than constantly having their actions assimilated, whitewashed, or ignored. The openings in society that allow abusers to act with impunity, to share joint custody of a child, and to even be celebrated as the antithesis of the "deadbeat dad" must also be challenged. Finally, but these are not the only questions that could be raised, we could also interrogate the definition of violence that requires targets to be absolute victims with (for example) an impeccable history of morality. At their best, poststructuralism and intersectionality would lead to more innovative perspectives on what has become a rather static and problematic set of assumptions regarding domestic abuse.

WHY DON'T YOU JUST TALK TO HIM?

As I have explored, a key issue connects abstract philosophy to practical reality in the coexistence and imbrication of two different systems: one that upholds Enlightenment ideals and contractual notions of intimacy and the other that is a manifestation of the death drive or Thanatos. I have suggested that abuse is not love gone wrong or an unhealthy manifestation of Eros, but instead is often more wholly destructive. In making these connections, I do not mean to equate Enlightenment or liberal notions with Eros (a binding force that draws us together). In fact, many of these "enlightened" understandings of and solutions to violence illegitimately *coerce* the libidinal bond where there is none. In this way, using the "family" as a unit or seeing the target as the provocateur preserves and assimilates Thanatos rather than providing truly constructive bonds between people. In this context, I have suggested that the abuser is a "monster," defying Enlightenment norms in every possible way and yet often being ignored or even rewarded in these power structures. An intersectional approach allows us to see that the same person who can be a monster to his partner can also be charming, have a wide circle of friends, and be successful in other areas of his life.

Today the problematic approach to targets of violence does not merely force targets to be intimate with their abusers—through mediation, counseling and co-parenting classes—but often also punishes them harshly. Despite the patterns of abuse that can be identified, which again, I would call a spiral and not a cycle, the issue has been individualized and the target has been pathologized. At the same time, the "group" (family) approach in counseling and law undermines any legal recognition of individual harms and obfuscates deep asymmetries within the family unit.[55] In relation to these problems, I had devised the title of this book as "Why Don't You Just Talk to Him?" to interrogate the use of communication-based, depoliticized strategies to "solve" the issue of abuse. In one sense, this commonly uttered sentence[56] indicates that if a target simply communicated the right way, the harms she is suffering will come to the surface or she will cease to be harmed. Language itself is then taken as neutral and the position of the target-speaker is not recognized as being in a subordinate position. Drawing on Patricia Evans's work, I have argued that one interlocutor is using the power mechanisms and speech of the Enlightenment, thus trying to communicate as an equal, while the other is using language to establish hierarchy and domination. But this is not to assume, in the case of the Enlightenment speaker, that communication, knowledge, and rationality are "pure" or without hierarchy. In this particular respect, the literature on the subaltern—particularly the now-famous question "Can the subaltern speak?"—indicates a radical alterity to the Enlightenment that disavows both positive and negative alternatives to modernist discourse.[57] These debates demonstrate how language and communication are part of colonial and even postcolonial (subintern) projects. In this way, attempts to pose a radical alternative while upholding the main categories of the Enlightenment and modernity then simply pluralize these dominant forms rather than truly challenging them. While this comparison can only go so far, the power relationships constructing intimacy, what counts as domestic abuse, and solutions are relevant to these broader debates.

Another presupposition indicated in the question "Why don't you just talk to him?" is the idea that the abuser will be enlightened and corrected through the proper means of communication, as if language can displace or trump narcissistic subject positions and aggressive behaviors. The desire to see the issue of intimate abuse as a working-class one or something that occurs only in certain ethnic or racial communities is related to the notion that the less well-educated a group is, the more violent it will be (and vice versa). The result is to make the poor and racial minorities the target of abuse intervention through coercive communication and what is essentially punishment, while often altogether ignoring those who are middle-class or wealthy. Alternatively, domestic abuse often economically marginalizes people within relationships, even if they are ostensibly middle-class or wealthy—accordingly, the power mechanisms of control and abuse explode fixed notions of class and privilege, as I have argued throughout this book.

Communication, education, and therapy also signal a radical depoliticization of these issues. They are not developmental steps to the political or micro-instances of a macro approach—rather, they serve to hierarchize, individualize, and effectively neutralize (as Foucault would put it). For all these reasons, the significance of the commonly uttered question, "Why don't you just talk to him?" is to paradoxically *communicate* defeat and facilitate inequality. The target must negotiate, beg, and develop secret alternatives and practices of micro-resistance precisely because of the failures of formal and informal political structures. "Why don't you just talk to him?" can essentially mean "You're on your own." To extend these arguments, even if domestic abuse only affected a small number of people,[58] the tolerance for and even societal cruelty toward targets have much broader meanings and consequences that demonstrate how uprooting and alienating Enlightenment notions can be.

Quite a lot of the dynamics I have analyzed in this book are evidence of fears of a male crisis in power as well as a conservative backlash against single mothers, racial minorities, the LGBQT community, and the poor. These broad trends of domination indicate a disdain for targets of abuse, including punishment of the abused, which is also indicative of a series of more general backlashes against feminism and women's rights, not to mention biases emerging from debates about LGBQT unions and parenthood. Narratives of male loss and fatherhood movements, combined with academic works that also see a male crisis, provide at least part of the explanation for the complex processes that seem to abandon targets of abuse and yet use them as the vehicle of family unity.[59] Other changes—including neoliberal policies that have entailed welfare austerity—have led to a perhaps cynical return to the family, affecting family law and the dominant therapeutic and medical interventions in abuse situations, as Kristin Bumiller has argued and which I discussed in Chapter 2.

SOCIAL CHANGE: A "SHARED SCRIPT"

Envisioning social change entails a different approach to political theorizing itself, which has turned to "high theory" without a political meaning and/or reverted to depoliticized ethical discussions that are often blindly undemocratic and universalizing.[60] The relatively recent interest in reviving realism is pertinent to the investigations in this book. Various political theory interventions in this revival have criticized how analytic philosophy and political theory have pursued ethical questions over political ones.[61] This ethical turn has been manifest in justice-oriented texts, care theory, and some Habermasian works focusing on philosophical ends but not the means. Means, in this sense, can be interpreted both as status quo analytic frameworks and normative solutions based on these unquestioned, often depoliticized frameworks. Part of this depoliticization is based on an abstract adherence to universal norms that evades the who, how, and what of political action. Although I have argued throughout this text that domestic abuse is much more systematic, politically based, and societally fostered than conventional wisdom holds, a crucial failure of this loose, fragmented system is ignoring the perpetrator almost entirely and making the target the simultaneous cause of abuse and yet intermediary for enlightened intervention. Bringing subjectivity into this equation allows for a more focused set of responses, including reauthorizing both perpetrator and target to speak, to be held accountable (in the case of the abuser) and to define her needs (in the case of the target).

Another part of this depoliticization entails putting violence in a separate sphere deemed as exceptional but paradoxically drawing on violent means, if they suit the ethical ends. To the degree that neoliberalism has influenced contemporary power dynamics, a broad point can be made that democratic power and constructive work (in Gandhi's sense of construction)[62] are entirely bypassed to achieve a quick, temporally neat end. In conjunction with neoliberal orientations, the consequences of ethics-, care- or justice-oriented analyses expose the limits of American liberalism: premising intimate relations and solutions to abuse on egalitarianism, communication, consent, and mutuality not only preserves the status quo but makes abuse possible and actively fosters it. In this sense, realism is not accounting only for violence but also radical inequality as a regular feature of daily life. This last point is important in deducing solutions that are not egalitarian at any level but which are not undemocratic either, in that they entail a constructive and restorative link between the individual and society. This radical asymmetry and accounting for violence should be the basis of new strategies to change formal political institutional responses and informal, street-level abuse strategies. Recognizing power asymmetries then helps to define the "who" and "what" of any strategic actions. Accordingly, it is the mechanisms of resistance themselves that matter rather than finding a perfect notion of justice. That is, the instruments of justice should matter less than local and strategic mechanisms specifically addressed to the unique imbalance that allowed for abuse to happen and which seeks to rectify the multiple manifestations of abuse. While these imbalances require the presence and agency of both or all parties to the abuse, there should also be a politics of distance and respect, rather than coerced familiarity. Targets should not be made to convince, cajole, or attempt to change abusers; children should not be forced into traumatic situations and then given the "choice" of which parent to live with[63]; and perpetrators should never be allowed direct access to the target of their abuse, unless she chooses this. For all of these reasons, notions of political agency must go beyond a narrowly legal framework and a rights-based notion of citizenship.

Perhaps a crucial part of rethinking power relations is conceiving of a new (or renewed) political psychology based on a hybrid: Enlightenment ideals mixed with Freud's notion of a death drive. Debate, conflict, and tension would not be anomalous to political dynamics and strategies but neither would silence, isolation, and alienation. Women's passions would not be pathologized and male abusers' passions would not be interpreted as logical but misguided, as interest rather than as destruction. Giving up on the Enlightenment as the singular framework of democratic politics does not mean a turn to romanticism or law-and-order politics; rather it means coming to grips with the challenges that an individualized, therapeutically and medicalized response to abuse has posed. More simply, if abuse attacks the core of the target's identity, it must be viewed as absolutely destructive and not "love gone wrong." Political realism must account for how reason can be paired with destructive passions, while on the part of the targets and their advocates "dramatic displays of commitment—through acts of conscious and willed suffering—would effectively weaken entrenched positions."[64] The key to political change in this area is not to educate the violence out of people but rather to create new conditions under which domestic abuse is no longer socially accepted and even rewarded, and the multiple inequalities that are wielded through abuse can be understood in a broader context. This would provide a time and place in which targets would be allowed self-determination.

In the 1970s, Evan Stark recounts how shelters were often improvised, and because they were short-staffed, the targets of abuse were also the staff and key decision-makers. They aimed to heal themselves and provide help and support to others. As he argues, they came together and often discovered a "shared script,"[65] which allowed them to contextualize what appeared to be individual experiences as common power mechanisms and behaviors. Patricia Evans and Lundy Bancroft have often articulated this shared script, allowing readers to see how what they conceived of as personal and unique was in fact quite characteristic of abusers in general. These shared scripts of the 1970s provided a basis for targets of abuse to treat one another as their own best judges and witnesses—no second party or clinical expert was needed to interpret their experiences for them or paternalistically make decisions for them.[66] Given this history and Stark's notion of targets as Foucaultian actors, I have suggested throughout this book that the abused have not been duped so much as they have had to develop "hidden transcripts" of resistance, given that there is very little constructive help.[67] These transcripts and power mechanisms will remain largely hidden or in underground institutions as long as perpetrators can act with impunity, and as long as shelters and legislators geographically isolate and hide the abused. In contrast, the notion of a shared script (to me) does not indicate consensus or homogeneity but a possibility of communicating in a context of trust and with an egalitarian spirit. A shared script, constituted by targets of abuse in the open and without need of corroboration, would be an achievement.

As I have argued, targets of abuse are not victims—at least, given what this classification signifies. But they are also not often survivors, as popular discourse would have it.[68] The notion of a domestic abuse survivor indicates that there is some sort of justice that would actually prevent or punish abuse—but a "survivor" has often just barely survived or managed to flee. If targets of abuse can cleanly remove themselves from the abuser, that is great, but it still implies a politics of bare life and survival rather than democratic agency broadly conceived. It deploys "incomplete mourning," by asking the party who has been dominated to leave everything behind and assimilate to new circumstances. But again, most texts and studies on abuse find that abusers often find ways to "hook" their targets, ensuring that fleeing will have severe costs (not to mention that this is when targets are most likely to be assaulted or murdered).[69] This exacerbates the trauma of incomplete mourning: the abuser can retain property or partial custody of the children, while the target must leave. In the best circumstances, if a mother leaves with her children and negotiates their way to safety, this does not diminish her losses but does make them relatively less traumatic.

Lacinda Hummel, a friend of mine who has been a community advocate and public policy scholar, has suggested in private conversations that abuse targets should be put in to Witness Protection. If nothing were to change at all, this solution would be the safest method of ensuring that a target is not constantly forced to deal with her abuser or to allow her children to have visitation with the abuser. I have also often thought that if radical lawyers, legal advocates, and anonymous shelters worked together, an Underground Railroad could be formed that allowed for truly constructive help and a politics of solidarity. If nothing else changes, these two reforms would foster solidarity and help to establish a parallel polis.[70]

However, abusers would remain untouched. The more difficult but politically necessary task is to attack, challenge, and alter the contours of the "war" between Thanatos and our impoverished version of Eros, the Enlightenment. This will only occur when two other things happen first. First, abuse must be delegitimized, and abusers must face stronger power mechanisms than talking, particularly to their targets. Second, targets must truly have political agency to tell their truth, define their problems, and devise the solutions they need. Given other structural inequalities in the job market, standards of parenting, and continued political inequalities, significant change will be difficult. As I have suggested in this book and many authors have also done, human rights organizations and institutions may be the vanguard of change, even if these policies and discourses are still problematic and uneven.[71]

Today, the most interesting instantiations of targets' resistance to abuse and to the shelter and policy systems cannot be considered as ideal speech situations that transcend the myriad of practices and long-term effects of abuse.[72] Rather, acts of democratic spontaneity and even solidarity in underground groups have occurred within these radically unstable and uprooting circumstances that Foucault and Agamben would theorize as bio-political and thanato-political.[73] If we want change, it must be revolutionary, and it requires acting in concert.[74] As Linda Zerilli suggests, these changes may only occur with the free play of imagination, unbound from fixed rules and predetermined judgment.[75]

P.S.

In this book I have proposed a realist conception of politics that entails recognizing asymmetries and acknowledging violence as a key part of political inclusion. As someone who has been a target of violence, threats, and coercion, these chapters are not merely theoretical to me. There is something perverse in hearing from one family member that if my ex has threatened to take our daughter away that I must have similarly threatened him. Likewise, there is something perverse in belonging to a family foundation that purports to help women and children but also holds that domestic abuse is a personal matter arising in conflict, and that it can be solved if the parties to the conflict follow the correct protocol. The situation becomes even more perverse when one's family members and colleagues are committed to democracy on paper but think a protective order or the legal system is equipped to deal with such a problem. Or, they believe that shelters somehow provide help that is an alternative to the legal system. There are long-term effects when an ex sets up an economically unviable situation (I know: I am thousands of dollars in debt) and some colleagues at my previous position were surprised to learn that I was at risk of losing my job, even though my ex called my office twenty times a day and did other things to ensure that I was a nervous wreck when arriving to my classes or to the office. I have not recognized my story in descriptions by major researchers, but I did when I read Bancroft, Evans, and Stark because what I was experiencing was intermittent and yet ongoing—and quite honestly, the law can just as easily be turned against me as it can an abuser.[76] While I admire and agree with the arguments made by authors like Leigh Goodmark and others who recommend that lawyers and judges should change, I know that most of the time we targets do not even get that far—the conversations do not even happen, or we have only so much money for lawyers. "Why don't you just talk to him?" is a refrain I have heard from family, colleagues, and some professionals, but it's after I explain the impossibility of my own and my daughter's situation that they urge me to just talk to him. It is a phrase of last resort and a phrase that reflects diminished economic circumstances. It is also the sort of advice that holds a great deal of faith in the power of speech and communication. I am also grateful for all that my daughter and I have—we are truly privileged in many ways, but it's because I have had the help of numerous people off the books and who unofficially helped us. From many sources—from some San Antonio police officers; from lawyers who have consulted with me free of charge; from a truly great organization in Chicago—we have found tactics to not just be "safe" (the shelter mantra) but to enjoy life and flourish. Unfortunately, I cannot reveal these tactics or name the people or groups because although we got away, the threats, stalking, and harassment continue—we are still in it. I wrote this book to understand why.

ACKNOWLEDGMENTS

This book is a very different project for me and I want to thank my editor, Angela Chnapko, for supporting it. I am very grateful for the rich and constructive advice of the anonymous reviewers, and I believe the project is better because of their suggestions. Any errors are my own. I have presented most of this material at conferences, including the American Political Science Association meeting of 2013, the Midwest Political Science Association Meeting of 2013, and the Northeast Political Science Meeting of 2012. I am grateful to the panel participants and the incredibly helpful insights of the discussants at APSA and MPSA, Lori Marso and N. Susan Gaines, respectively. Since arriving at DePaul, I have also taught some of the material in a class on women and politics as well as in my class on immigration law. In the women and politics class, I ran a domestic abuse workshop thanks to the help and support of students such as Anna Kinderman, Gabrielle Goldstein, and Quinn Stifler (and the initial interest of Hayley DiPerna). So many students in that class helped to make it unique and our conversations went far beyond the classroom—I am grateful to all those students. Students in my immigration classes have written about the asylum cases I discuss in Chapter 3, and it has been rewarding to discuss and read their papers while I was also writing about these cases. I would also like to express general gratitude to those in Chicago who have provided me access to asylum adjudication processes and cases that most academics would not have. Access to these sources allowed me to understand the *Matter of RA* and the *Matter of LR* from an (I hope) unique perspective. Beyond the academic setting, I appreciate the friends and support my daughter Hannah and I have had in San Antonio and now in Chicago. This includes Cindy Hummel, Sara Wohlleb, Shaker and Molly Colhmia, Ruben Koolman, and many others who have been there (I apologize if I am forgetting someone). I would also like to thank friends outside of Chicago who have stood by us and been there for us: Nicholas Xenos, Joshua Miller, Karen Zivi, Chris Sturr, Eugene

Sheppard, Joshua Dienstag, Rudy Rosales, Jonathan Bernstein, Amy Jasperson, Richard Gambitta, Ashley Diaz, and so many others to whom I am grateful and yet cannot name. One individual, Lee Riggs, helped me at a crucial time in 2010, and Melissa Murphy, who I cite in this text, was also an amazing support—they are both superb advocates who combine knowledge of gender subordination, bureaucratic inefficiency (or inequity), and a model of advocacy that understands targets as strategic agents and not victims. When I write about grassroots advocates who understand intimate abuse as political and who effectively navigate formal and informal power mechanisms, it is these two people (and their respective organizations) I have in mind.

This project is not different because I focus on gender—I have always focused on gender as one aspect of a complex reality in my research on homelessness, low-tier labor, and immigration. What is different is that I began this research in order to understand how someone I dated only briefly and who repeatedly assaulted me, including while I was pregnant, could have joint custody of our child with me. While I did try to get help from numerous places, the advice I received was split: one set of people encouraged me to flee San Antonio, because the laws could confine me there until Hannah was 18. Maybe I should have done that, but it seemed risky at best. The other side had bought into the emerging father's-rights discourse and the importance of the biological father in the child's life at any cost. They kept asserting that he had rights, that there was no proof of danger (but if there were, I would be the liable party, not him), and that I just needed to relax. In fact, they thought if I just talked to him, he would understand the (minor) harm he was causing. The subtext of this discourse was not merely that fathers have rights but that we cannot expect that much of them—each of my stories was often matched by a friend's or professional's story about her neglectful husband. There were also people in the middle—many who thought I just needed to get the courage to use the legal system more than I had. Given the extremes of the binary advice I usually received, the middle was and still is more appealing to me. However, I wrote this book to understand how this middle course could not work and to explain to these friends how I could not take this course. While I did solve part of my problem through moving out of state with my daughter, there are lingering issues that put my daughter in a continuously stressful situation, although thankfully for only brief periods of time. And I could only solve my problem by jeopardizing my career—leaving a tenure track job before my tenure case was considered to accept a more precarious but saner job in a city where I have extended family and more academic acquaintances.

But again, we have not fully resolved our issues, and that is why unfortunately I cannot share more—I cannot include the names of organizations that have helped me or tactics that help me to avoid or neutralize the monthly onslaught of accusations from my ex. One of the most helpful texts I read during the time I was still living in San Antonio was Anna Marie Smith's book on welfare. All the phrases that lawyers were uttering to me—"we will force him to be a father" or citing how the mere presence of the biological father is allegedly salutary for a child—now made sense. But if her book explained my situation I also realized that the changed discourses and norms of welfare that she analyzes had parallel if not related changes in family law and broader policy discourses. A second book that explained my situation better than any book was Lundy Bancroft's *Why Does He Do That?* I had felt ashamed that my boyfriend yelled at me and tried to choke me, that he often didn't show up at times he said he would, and that he left me with a newborn. But I had also thought it was personal and that my ex's behavior was so odd—so often unprovoked and with him accusing me of things that could not possibly be true—that he must be mentally ill. Bancroft's book describes a pattern with its own abusive logic—a logic that ends when a third party is present—that made me realize that I must stop writing him letters; stop trying to communicate with him to change; stop going to therapy sessions where we often perversely explored *his* feelings after an egregious action but not mine. One session in particular made me realize that therapy itself could retraumatize a target—for an hour we had to explore why he stood outside my apartment for about 24 hours screaming "fuck you" and trying to break my door down. What had triggered this orgy of feeling (a phrase borrowed from Nietzsche)? I had said something on the phone rather quickly: "Oh I wish I had known you were running late." Once I read Bancroft I could see the power dynamics for what they were—even if very few others could. During that time, friends such as Verity Smith and Karuna Mantena were invaluable supports, but we have now gone our separate ways, in part because of the long-term strain of this situation.

This book was not easy for me to write and it was not therapeutic—if anything, I have felt nauseated, developed severe headaches when writing Chapter 3, and even recently have had a difficult time going through information about dual arrests and mothers being charged with "exposing" their children to abuse. It is horrifying to know that abusers often win joint or full custody. But this book is me—it derives from my experiences with the police, therapists, and lawyers—and this is how I process difficult events. The book is at least a marker of a changed and improved setting for us, even if we still need things to change more.

Even if I risked my career to move, I have enjoyed being at DePaul and getting to know students in a healthier environment. I got to know one of these students, Arthur Devaun Martin, very well in the past few years. He could be quiet in class, but when he spoke and in his writing, his analysis of complex theory was a unique blend of intellectual and emotional insight. He was one of the smartest students I have had and one of the most empathetic. He was one of the few people I have met recently with whom I could converse easily for hours, perhaps because he doesn't see a split between the theories we studied and his own life. He was also funny, interested, and never judgmental. He excelled in classes, often showing up in a suit and spectacles and speaking with restraint and humility but not timidity or lack of confidence (reminding me of a former Harvard colleague and friend, Tommie Shelby). But he was willing to get in the mud to help people—he began working with University of Chicago friends in a network to help victims of sexual trafficking, participated in other groups that helped those in need, and was so proud and happy to be working with a Chicago alderman. He never shied away from difficult conversations or topics, in my experience. Once in a while Arthur would be absent from class and explain that he had nightmares that kept him up and made him weak in the morning. At another university he had been attacked by a group of white men and the police deemed it a racial attack (Arthur was African American)—he continued to suffer from PTSD until he fell off a balcony in March 2014. In this book, I do not feel like I have adequately captured what it is like to be a highly functional person who is also triggered into fight or flight by past events. The best I could do was to reappropriate Bonnie Honig's notion of "incomplete mourning" to describe what it was like (for me at least) to ditch everything, to risk everything (including coming close to foreclosure), and start again. But never with complete resolution—always with the possibility of triggering the out-of-control heartbeat and shaking hands of the past. Arthur's incomplete mourning was not resolved when he passed away—it was a part of him and it made me admire him even more when he told me about the attack and his struggles with PTSD. He died far too young but he was not someone with unfulfilled potential—he had already done so much, acted on behalf of just causes, and was not afraid to vocalize his experiences. I dedicate this book in part to him and in part to my daughter—two people I feel such solidarity with and who are/were both wise beyond their years.

NOTES

INTRODUCTION

1. I use the term *target* rather than *victim* to call attention to the power dynamics at work and particularly to require the grammatical subject—the abuser—to be implicated in the verbal description. This usage goes against Carisa Showden's recent work in which she argues that the term *victim* is not harmful when discussing this subject. Despite this difference, her emphasis on agency as independent from autonomy is similar to the arguments I pursue. See Carisa R. Showden, *Choices Women Make: Agency in Domestic Violence, Assisted Reproduction, and Sex Work* (Minneapolis: University of Minnesota Press, 2011), 3 and the first chapter more generally.

2. Edward Said develops the same line of argumentation in *Orientalism*, but with regard to colonized areas of the Middle East, India, and Africa. Although his focus is different from mine, his analysis of the Western masking of violence through power-knowledge is highly relevant to my analysis. Edward Said, *Orientalism* (New York: Vintage, 1979).

3. For example, domestic abuse court advocates that work for community councils in Chicago, Mujeres Unidas in Pilsen, as well as more anonymous groups that service the community.

4. See, for example, Margaret F. Brown, "Domestic Violence Advocates' Exposure to Liability for Engaging in the Unauthorized Practice of Law," *Columbia Journal of Law and Social Problems* 34, no. 4 (Summer 2001): 279–300.

5. Something Carisa Showden also advocates in *Choices Women Make*.

6. In earlier work, Michael P. Johnson has identified this issue as the confusion between "situational" couple violence and "intimate terror" in Michael P. Johnson, *A Typology of Domestic Violence: Intimate Terrorism, Violent Resistance, and Situational Couple Violence* (Lebanon, NH: Northeastern University Press, 2008). Through decades of research, Johnson shows that most data (the most comprehensive) are rooted in situational conflicts that give the appearance of gender symmetry. Johnson convincingly argues that once a typology of violence is identified, researchers will be able to identify the very different characteristics of intimate terror (asymmetrical abuse). Taking his insights into account, I do not want to challenge them but want to take a different approach for at least two reasons: (1) because of the deterrent effect of public policy, domestic abuse may have changed over time. Evan Stark argues that this is the case and that most abuse is right under the line that would constitute

physical harm. On the other hand, some studies suggest that almost no policy solutions have had deterrent effects. (2) Johnson himself emphasizes how emotional abuse and control are what define abuse for women (i.e., in women's interpretation of the circumstances), with violent assault merely being one part of abuse. From another perspective, I am simply drawing on a more Foucaultian account of "control" as a sort of base and violent assault as epiphenomenal.

7. For a lengthy exploration of this notion of "disaggregated" power, see Akhil Gupta, *Red Tape: Bureaucracy, Structural Violence, and Poverty in India* (Durham, NC: Duke University Press, 2012).

8. Among others, the work of Kristin Bumiller. Lisa Brush, Celeste Montoya, Carisa Showden, Evan Stark, and Jacqui True.

9. Legal theory is more complex in this regard but still often presupposes a "privileged group" that can somehow get the police to take reports, doctors to correctly diagnose and document abuse, and judges to act more sympathetically. Kimberlé Crenshaw's now canonical article on domestic abuse hints at these difficulties and opens a broader interpretive terrain to question the degree to which anyone can be privileged. Kimberlé Crenshaw, "Mapping the Margins: Intersectionality, Identity, Politics, and Violence against Women of Color," *Stanford Law Review* 43, no. 6 (1991): 1242–1265. See also a very nice synthesis of more complex and contemporary literature on domestic abuse by Lisa D. Brush, "In an Abusive State," *Gender and Society* 23, no. 2 (April 2009): 273–281. The authors draw from criminology, social work, sociology, and legal theory.

10. Evan Stark, *Coercive Control* (New York: Oxford, 2009), 8. To reduce the scope of his claim, I would argue that there are many distinct articles that make important points about abuse, but that these different points could be brought together and recast as distinctively political. But perhaps one could argue that a violence-centered definition of abuse is inherently depoliticizing, and thus his perspective is also sounder methodologically.

11. Stark, *Coercive Control*, 366.

12. See the special edition of *Violence against Women* dedicated to Stark's book (*Coercive Control*), including Lisa Brush, Guest Editor's Introduction, *Violence against Women* 15 (2009): 1423–1431. See also the work of Lisa D. Brush, Kristin Bumiller, Michael Johnson, and Carisa Showden.

13. A different way to put it is that compared to earlier writings on domestic abuse (from the 1700s through the 1970s), which recognized the asymmetrical nature of domestic abuse, the increasing popularity of symmetrical models and approaches has changed research and policy prescriptions.

14. Although Linda Mills's recent work is perhaps the more prominent example of symmetry assumptions, Lisa D. Brush's excellent review of the literature discusses how Suzanne Steinmetz's 1978 article on the subject was foundational to these arguments. See Suzanne Steinmetz, "The Battered Husband Syndrome," *Victimology* 2 (1978): 499–509; Lisa D. Brush, "In an Abusive State," *Gender and Society*. See a critique of symmetry arguments and data in Jack C. Straton, "The Myth of the 'Battered Husband Syndrome,'" NOMAS (National Organization for Men against Sexism) website, n.d., http://www.nomas.org/node/107 (accessed December 16, 2013).

15. See Linda G. Mills, *Violent Partners: A Breakthrough Plan for Ending the Cycle of Abuse* (New York: Basic Books, 2008). For an alternative perspective, see the

brief but excellent analysis of symmetry claims and the alleged "gender-bias" in domestic abuse research in Philip Rossiter, "A Thorn in the Flesh That Cannot Fester: Habermas, the Duluth Model, Domestic Violence Programmes," *Waikato Law Review* 19, no. 2 (2011): 196–206. See pages 200–202 in particular.

16. Based on notions of restorative justice. See Johnson on restorative justice, which he believes is appropriate for situational violence (e.g., the sort of violence that may occur one time during a conflict) and inappropriate for asymmetrical domestic abuse (what he calls "intimate terror"). Johnson, *A Typology of Domestic Violence*, 77–78.

17. Jack Straton critiques specific projects on domestic violence that claims that symmetry is the most prevalent type of domestic conflict. With regard to Murray Straus's work (as an example of symmetry arguments) he points out that first, Straus' work "equates a woman pushing a man in self-defense to a man pushing a woman down the stairs"; "It labels a mother as violent if she defends her daughter from the father's sexual molestation"; "It combines categories such as 'hitting' and 'trying to hit' despite the important difference between them"; "Because it looks at only one year, this study equates a single slap by a woman to a man's 15-year history of domestic terrorism." Straton, "The Myth of the 'Battered Husband Syndrome,'" NOMAS (National Organization for Men against Sexism).

18. Kristin Bumiller also recounts the remarks of a counselor who believed she would respond to violence better than her client and could thus model a more appropriate reaction to a violent attack. Kristin Bumiller, *In an Abusive State: How Neoliberalism Appropriated the Feminist Movement against Sexual Violence* (Durham, NC: Duke University Press, 2008), 89. As someone who is physically fit and teaches group exercise, I can attest that no amount of physical training (except perhaps in martial arts) can make women overpower someone who is roughly eight inches taller, more muscular, and whose moral compass is not oriented toward talking but destruction. It is easy to *hypothesize* that one could simply run away from a bigger, stronger, more violent individual, but the "reality principle" diminishes this will-to-equality. In my experience, fighting back only leads to more injuries and a more prolonged attack. This is not to dismiss arguments supporting fighting back or scholarly findings that fighting back works—my point is that when people want women to fight back, they don't realize what they are asking, because they have not been in that situation and are not taking it seriously. As someone who has been in that situation, I personally have tried to defend myself and essentially "lost." Regarding differences in physical strength (particularly between men and women), see Richard B. Felson, "Big People Hit Little People: Sex Differences in Physical Power and Interpersonal Violence," *Criminology* (August 1996): 433–452. Although Felson's work is viewed as conservative and antifeminist, this particular article could be used to support my contentions about attempting to resist violent attacks. However, the broad thrust of his work does not: he is arguing that gender does not matter when analyzing interpersonal violence. In essence, he is making biologically essentialist claims about size and instinct that are held to trump more socially constructed patterns and behaviors, particularly in intimate relations.

19. Leigh Goodmark draws on a similar model (truth commissions) to very different ends. I am not sure I agree with her conclusions, which are sophisticated in

terms of feminist analysis but end in calling for mediation, which entails ne-gotiating with the abuser. At the very least, her work is an interesting variant of Mills's work. See Leigh Goodmark, *A Troubled Marriage: Domestic Violence and the Legal System* (New York: NYU Press, 2013).

20. On this complex issue, see Radha Iyengar, "Does the Certainty of Arrest Reduce Domestic Violence? Evidence from Mandatory and Recommended Arrest Laws," *Journal of Public Economics* 93 (2009): 85–98. Iyengar finds that reporting is significantly a problem in states that have mandatory arrest laws, particularly if they carry the threat of dual arrest.

21. See Johnson, *A Typology of Domestic Violence*, who does not question empiri-cism per se but why there have been dichotomous results in surveys regarding what definitions of abuse and how prevalent it is among couples.

22. I should note that others disagree with this comment, including one of the anonymous reviewers for Oxford. She or he states that symmetry data "comes from broadly epidemiological community surveys, not from narrow clinical, shelter, or batterer intervention program studies." My comment is merely a suggestion and not a blanket statement; it reflects my long-standing suspicion of any empirical data based on self-reporting in a context of profound inequal-ity. I do apologize if this suggestion is offensive; it is not my intent.

23. See David S. Riggs, Marie B. Caulfield, and Amy E. Street, "Risk for Domestic Violence: Factors Associated with Perpetration and Victimization," *Journal of Clinical Psychology* 56, no. 10 (2000): 1289–1316, particularly the section "Re-search on Domestic Violence" (1291–1292), which questions the accuracy of empirical data on domestic violence, given these limitations. For a critique of symmetry, see Straton, "The Myth of the 'Battered Husband Syndrome.'"

24. See Olson, 73 on "deformalization" in family law; see Bumiller, *In an Abusive State*, 84–90, on "conjoint" models of therapy in abuse situations. Frances Olson, "The Family and the Market" in Patricia Smith, *Feminist Jurisprudence* (New York: Oxford University Press, 1993), 65–89.

25. Johnson, *A Typology of Domestic Violence: Intimate Terrorism, Violent Resistance, and Situational Couple Violence*. As I have noted above, I choose to analyze abuse as control first and violence second. My approach, following Stark, is analyzing asymmetrical abuse situations as part of control and power first rather than following a typology of violence as the foundational premise of abuse. This may seem like splitting hairs, in that Johnson's and Stark's work is not opposite but often complementary, but Stark more explicitly begins with control.

26. See Steinmetz; Mills; Stark; and in particular, Lisa D Brush, "Philosophical and Political Issues in Research on Women's Violence and Aggression," *Sex Roles* 52 (June 2005): 867–872.

27. See Kristin Bumiller's interesting review of Michelle L. Meloy, Susan L. Miller *The Victimization of Women: Law, Politics, and Politics* regarding attention to targets' stated needs: Kristin Bumiller, "The Victimization of Women: Law, Policies, and Politics," By Michelle L. Meloy and Susan L. Miller (New York: Oxford University Press, 2011) in *Law & Society Review* 46, no. 1 (March 2012): 203–205.

28. Regarding the last point, the work of Catharine MacKinnon and Kimberlé Crenshaw is particularly important as they have (separately) pointed out how quite a lot of gender analyses are undercut by the failure to see how various institutions and the media try to separate sex (as gender and as intimacy) and

violence when in fact these two exist unalloyed in a myriad of relations and cultural forms.

29. In this way, my analysis differs from Bumiller's, who conceives of a more unified system that regularly screens any woman than I do. Perhaps the difference in our approaches can be explained by the fact that she treats sexual assault and rape together with domestic violence. Bumiller, *In an Abusive State*. On police indifference, see Stark, *Coercive Control*, 36–37. With regard to dual arrests, Stark finds that it is (surprisingly) white, young, unmarried, single women who suffer the most; Stark, *Coercive Control*, 58.

30. Stark calls this a "calculus of injuries"; Stark, *Coercive Control*, 57.

31. A difficulty that both Linda Mills and (from a much different perspective) Carisa Showden have recently recognized.

32. A simple Internet search on this bias yields hundreds of websites dedicated to the alleged preference for women and mothers over men and fathers in courts.

33. See, for example, Jeanne A. Fugate, "Who's Failing Whom? A Critical Look at Failure-To-Protect Laws," *New York University Law Review* 76 (April 2001): 272–308, http://www.thelizlibrary.org/liz/fugate.pdf.

34. For example, if a father hides his income or assets when the state is determining child support, a motion must later be filed that is independent of seeking a protective order.

35. Unfortunately, most of these professionals do not understand how different domestic abuse is from more mutual forms of family conflict, and thus they proceed as if they can handle the situation.

36. A couple of examples include disclosing a target's full address to the abuser without her permission or without devising an alternative (such as a post office box) or blindly compartmentalizing abuse such that visitations are allowed with children, even when abuse was committed in their presence (or children were used to manipulate the target). A broader problem may be that lawyers need an Elizabeth Kübler-Ross figure to teach them how to be more humane to potential clients—targets of abuse do not need to be shamed or scared into retaining legal counsel. Leigh Goodmark has addressed these issues in great depth in "Clinical Cognitive Dissonance: the Values and Goals of Domestic Violence Clinics, the Legal System and the Students Caught in the Middle," *Journal of Law and Policy* 20 (2012): 301–323 and "When Is a Battered Woman Not a Battered Woman? When She Fights Back," *Yale Journal of Law and Feminism* (2008): 76–129. Having dealt with two or three lawyers who have studied in a family conflict program, I do not share her optimism about learning to listen better and so on. Throughout this book, I argue that educational programs will not help abusers to become less violent; perhaps something similar could be said about lawyers being educated to learn to listen better or to think outside the box.

37. I will discuss this at length in the book. Basically, the target of abuse is caught in a double bind. She must somehow know whom to call or inform of different events, and that person must also be receptive to the problem and document what is happening in the appropriate manner. However, the following problems present themselves: a completely uneven response by the police; doctors who misconstrue situations or who blame the target of abuse for "failure to protect" a minor against the abuser; child welfare systems who investigate both parents but always begin with the mother even when it is the father who is suspected of abuse; and more broadly, the fact that most of these

interlocutors (such as lawyers and psychologists) don't listen, refuse to read documentation, and make snap judgments despite their formal training or despite their ignorance of how abuse is different from neglect.

38. In fact, Stark notes that law professor Ruth Jones "urges courts to assume guardianship over the woman's affairs, much as they now do with children or the frail elderly, a paternalistic approach that shifts the source of a woman's dependence but does nothing to free her." Stark, *Coercive Control*, 366.

39. On failure to protect, see Kim Ahearn, et al. (also known as "Failure to Protect" Working Group of Child Welfare Committee of New York City Inter-Agency Task Force against Domestic Violence), "Charging Battered Mothers with 'Failure to Protect,' Still Blaming the Victim," *Fordham Urban Law Journal* 27, no. 3 (1999): 849–873. Available at: http://ir.lawnet.fordham.edu/cgi/viewcontent.cgi?article=2011&context=ulj; Michelle S. Jacobs, "Requiring Battered Women Die: Murder Liability for Mothers Under Failure to Protect Statutes," *Journal of Criminal Law and Criminology* 88 (1998): 88, no. 2 (1998): 579–660.

40. See Lundy Bancroft, *Why Does He Do That?* (New York: Berkley Books, 2002), 263–266.

41. See the work of Lisa D. Brush regarding how domestic abusers undermine their targets' ability to keep jobs or to perform well while being harassed, threatened, and abused. Lisa D. Brush, "Battering and the Poverty Trap," *Journal of Poverty* 8, no. 3 (2004): 23–43.

42. See Chantal Mouffe regarding maternal or care theory and why she argues that it is inherently undemocratic. Chantal Mouffe, "Feminism, Citizenship, and Radical Democratic Politics," in *Feminist Social Thought: A Reader*, ed. Diana Tietjens Meyers, (New York: Routledge, 1997), 532–544.

43. A dynamic that Berns notes is reflected in popular treatments of the subject; see Nancy Berns, "'My Problem and How I Solved It'": Domestic Violence in Women's Magazines," *The Sociological Quarterly* 40, no. 1 (Winter 1999): 85–108.

44. See Mark Poster, Review: "Domestic Tyranny: The Making of American Social Policy against Family Violence from Colonial Times to the Present" by Elizabeth H. Pleck, *Signs* 14, no. 1 (Autumn 1988): 216–219; see also Guillaumin, 161, where she argues that "rules and material facilities" for bearing and raising children are "socially manipulated" and yet naturalized. Colette Guillaumin, *Racism, Sexism, Power and Ideology* (New York: Routledge, 1995).

45. See Hobbes, ch. xx (138–145); Locke, ch. vii (§78–85). While Locke famously reverts to might equals right thinking, arguing that men should settle disputes because they are the "abler and stronger" (§82), his analysis preceding this statement is interesting in that he suggests that women are denied natural rights to life, liberty, and property when they are married. Thomas Hobbes, *Leviathan*, ed. Richard Tuck (Cambridge: Cambridge University Press, 1999); John Locke, *Second Treatise of Government*, ed. C. B. Macpherson (Cambridge: Hackett Publishing, Classic Series, 1980).

46. Even if this suspension was uneven at times, allowing for power and agency at different times. See Tracy A. Thomas, Tracey Boisseau, *Feminist Legal History: Essays on Women and Law* (New York: NYU Press, 2011), Introduction.

47. See Berns, "'My Problem and How I Solved It.'"

48. As I note in the body of this text, I use this term loosely to capture a range of understandings based on rationality, consent and contract, communication, and the absence of violence.

49. On the subject of self-defense, which is often called "violence" or "violent re-taliation" in the literature, see Johnson, *A Typology of Domestic Violence*; see also Goodmark, "When Is a Battered Woman Not a Battered Woman? When She Fights Back."

50. For the purposes of this book, I treat domestic abuse as if it were completely *unequal* and thus am not considering lower-level, more mutual uses of violence during conflict as "domestic abuse." Assumptions about symmetry may be true to an extent but overall, these arguments take attention away from or are even held to negate abuse that is highly unequal and terroristic.

51. See also Johnson, *A Typology of Domestic Violence*, although my usage of the term *terrorism* is founded in the notion of control as a conceptual base while his is rooted in violence.

52. As Bumiller notes, women are viewed as more responsive to therapy, whereas male abusers have been found to be largely unresponsive. Bumiller, *In an Abusive State*, 83. Lundy Bancroft's work with abusers in batterer intervention programs has led to similar conclusions but with an interesting caveat: abusers are "rational" when they submit to psychological tests and lie-detector tests, but are largely unresponsive to therapy and batter intervention programs (which I should note, are only "interventions" after the man has abused a woman). Lundy Bancroft, *Why Does He Do That?* (New York: Berkley Books, 2002).

53. As I argue in Chapter 2, this divide is legally constructed—I am not arguing that motherhood is a burden per se. On discourses of motherhood, see Karen Zivi, "Contesting Motherhood in the Age of AIDS: Maternal Ideology in the Debate over Mandatory HIV Testing," *Feminist Studies* 31, no. 2 (Summer 2005): 347–374.

54. See Bancroft, *Why Does He Do That?*, 266; see also 266–272.

55. This is true even if the abuser claims to love his target and that is the point of this book—an abuser's love is profoundly inegalitarian and destructive. In turn, this has its parallels in Freud's notion of Thanatos, the destructive elements of modern society. Sigmund Freud, *Civilization and Its Discontents*, ed. and trans. James Strachey, standard edition (New York: Norton, 1961).

56. Bancroft has worked extensively with abusers and has concluded that most batterers manipulate counseling sessions and anger management programs, not to mention BIPs (batterer intervention programs) but judges, lawyers, and counselors often believe them when they denigrate their target, allege that the abuse is imaginary, and so on. See *Why Does He Do That?*; see also Lundy Bancroft and Jay G. Silverman, *The Batterer as Parent: Addressing the Impact of Domestic Violence on Family Dynamics*, SAGE Series on Violence (Thousand Oaks, CA: SAGE Publications, 2002). See also Jackson Katz, *The Macho Paradox: Why Some Men Hurt Women and How All Men Can Help* (Sourcebooks, 2006).

57. See, for example, Phyllis B. Frank, Gail K. Golden, "When 50-50 Isn't Fair: The Case against Couple Counseling in Domestic Abuse," Op-Ed in *Social Work* 39 no. 6 (November 1994), 636–637; significantly, they contend that "Arresting batterers is actually the most effective 'therapeutic' intervention yet discovered. . . . Conversely, family systems therapy, which isolates the problem in the relationship, endangers battered women. . . . So does mediation, which assumes that the two parties have equal standing in a dispute and the ability to negotiate fairly. In fact, 'mediation of an assault' is a conflict in terms. . . . The power imbalance and the violence preclude equitable negotiations between the two parties." (637)

58. This claim is very important in Bancroft's work and Patricia Evans's work. Bancroft, *Why Does He Do That?* and Patricia Evans, *The Verbally Abusive Relationship*, 2nd ed. (Avon, MA: Adams Media Corporation, 1996). Related to these arguments, Rossiter argues that research demonstrates that anger and violence are not linked. See Philip Rossiter, "A Thorn in the Flesh That Cannot Fester: Habermas, the Duluth Model, Domestic Violence Programmes," *Waikato Law Review* 19, no. 2 (2011): 196–206. For example, he contends that "there is research that indicates that, consistent with the Duluth Model, violence against women is not anger based. Prisoners incarcerated for violent crimes showed no difference between their propensity for violence and anger. Anger management programmes do not appear, of themselves, to be effective in curbing violent behavior in prisoners convicted of violent crimes. Another study concluded that the majority of partner abusive men do not present with anger-related disturbances." Rossiter, 201.
59. I am reframing his ideas in terms of the Enlightenment.
60. Regarding abusers' lack of guilt, see David S. Riggs, Marie B. Caulfield, and Amy E. Street, "Risk for Domestic Violence: Factors Associated with Perpetration and Victimization," *Journal of Clinical Psychology* 56, no. 10 (2000): 1289–1316; see also Stark and Bancroft. Regarding the benefits of bullying, see Jeremy Hobson, "Does Bullying Serve a Purpose?" interview with Elizabeth Englander, author of *Bullying and Cyberbullying: What Every Educator Needs to Know* on *Here and Now*, NPR, November 18, 2013, http://www. capradio.org/news/npr/story?storyid=246021593.
61. See Kimberlé Crenshaw, "Beyond Racism and Misogyny: Black Feminism and 2 Live Crew," in *Feminist Social Thought: A Reader*, ed. Diana Tietjens Meyers (New York: Routledge, 1997), 245–263; Walter DeKeseredy, Martin Schwartz, Joseph Donnermeyer, *Dangerous Exits: Escaping Abusive Relationships in Rural America* (Rutgers University Press, 2009).
62. Evans, *The Verbally Abusive Relationship*, 29–31.
63. Evans, *The Verbally Abusive Relationship*, 31.
64. Evans, *The Verbally Abusive Relationship*, 56.
65. Although abusers often claim to love their targets and even justify their abuse as misguided passion, experts report that the same abusers often feel that the woman provoked the abuse and that the abuse was justified; experts also hypothesize that statements of love and remorse serve to keep the relationship intact and are made because a third party discovered the abuse. Lundy Bancroft, *Why Does He Do That?* 69–73; see also the expert testimony in *The Matter of RA* that finds that abusers feel justified in treating their women as unequal because of societal norms, gendered expectations, and the belief that their partners or wives violated these norms in some way. See Karen Musalo, "A Short History of Gender Asylum," University of California at Hastings Center for Gender and Refugee Studies, http://cgrs.uchastings.edu/sites/default/files/short_history_of_gender_asylum_Musalo_2010_0.pdf.
66. See, for example, Bethany J. Price, Alan Rosenbaum, "Batterer Intervention Programs: A Report from the Field," *Violence and Victims* 24, no. 6 (2009): 757–770. At the time this article was written, the authors provide useful information about the two dominant types of BIPs and how and why they are increasingly prevalent. They note that "at present, most states [45] have enacted legislation empowering and encouraging the courts to utilize BIPs in sentencing and in some cases as a diversionary program," 757.

67. Ahearn et al.: "There are still strong prejudices against women who do not leave their batterers, and the players in the child welfare system routinely blame the victims of domestic violence for the harm to the children," 854.

68. Bancroft, *Why Does He Do That?*; see also Riggs et al., "Risk for Domestic Violence: Factors Associated with Perpetration and Victimization."

69. This finding—that abuse affects targets far more than it does abusers—is also important in Evan Stark's research.

70. In an otherwise excellent chapter, Kathleen Waits's article on abuse relies on this older, heteronormative, marriage-oriented cycle of abuse. Today, this cycle is used against targets, effectively allowing the state to give up on actually preventing the problem, because it is held that "they always go back." See Kathleen Waits, "The Criminal Justice System's Response to Battering" in Patricia Smith, *Feminist Jurisprudence* (New York: Oxford University Press, 1993), 188–206. Bumiller investigates this subject in *In an Abusive State*.

71. This particular line of argumentation is based on personal experience and research. I develop this analysis in Chapter 4. Michael Johnson notes that therapists often mistakenly believe that violence is largely event-specific, mutually provoked, and limited. He argues that this is because their clients are mostly likely involved in "situational" conflict and that targets of "intimate terror" are then treated as if they are part of this first group. Johnson, 83.

72. See Evans, *The Verbally Abusive Relationship*, 64–67.

73. There are very interesting parallels in the immigration literature on "strategic invisibility"—see Hector Perla and Susan Bibler Coutin, "Legacies and Origins of the 1980s US–Central American Sanctuary Movement," *Refuge* 26, no. 1 (Spring 2009): 7–19, as well as Roberta Villalón's work on what could be called strategic assimilation in Roberta Villalón, "Passage to Citizenship and the Nuances of Agency: Latina Battered Immigrants," *Women's Studies International Forum* 33 (October 12, 2010): 552–560.

74. Evan Stark, "Symposium on Reconceptualizing Violence against Women by Intimate Partners: Critical Issues: Re-Presenting Woman Battering: From Battered Woman Syndrome to Coercive Control" *Albany Law Review* 58 (Spring 1995): 973–1026.

75. See Brush review and essays dedicated to Stark in VAWA: Lisa Brush, Guest Editor's Introduction, *Violence against Women* 15 (2009): 1423–1431.

76. Even if this recognition is in its nascent stages. See Eleanor Acer, Tara Magner, "Restoring America's Commitment to Refugees and Humanitarian Commitment," *Georgetown Immigration Law Journal* 27 (Spring 2013): 445–484; Karen Musalo, "A Short History of Gender Asylum" http://cgrs.uchastings.edu/sites/default/files/short_history_of_gender_asylum_Musalo_2010_0.pdf.

77. For a detailed account of how international governmental organizations are accounting for violence against women (or not), see Jacqui True, *The Political Economy of Violence against Women* (New York: Oxford University Press, 2012). I have also written about deficiencies in current human rights policies and nongovernmental work while also advocating transnational civil society as the most · important sphere to foster democratic solutions to neoliberal policies in the conclusion to Kathleen R. Arnold, *American Immigration After 1996: The Shifting Ground of Political Inclusion* (College Station: Penn State University Press, 2011).

78. Bonnie Honig's term in *Democracy and the Foreigner* (Princeton, NJ: Princeton University Press, 2001), 67–72. Second, I should note that the Board of Immigration Appeals has just reversed on these decisions. See Ashley Huebner

and Lisa Koop, "New BIA Decisions Undermine U.S. Obligations to Protect Asylum Seekers," National Immigrant Justice Center (A Heartland Alliance Program), February 18, 2014, https://www.immigrantjustice.org/litigation/blog/new-bia-decisions-undermine-us-obligations-protect-asylum-seekers#.UyWUqs6a-Ck (accessed March 16, 2014). Immigration and refugee advocates are waiting for a more final determination on setting five rules for these sorts of cases (secondary actors) from the Obama administration.

79. I should note that where I use the term *refugee*, it is in the colloquial sense and to provide variety; technically, both RA and LR sought relief after they arrived in the United States and therefore, applied for asylum.

80. Honig, *Democracy and the Foreigner*, 67–72.

81. See Olson, "The Family and the Market."

82. My own approach to intersectionality takes into account the following articles: Ange-Marie Hancock, "When Multiplication Doesn't Equal Quick Addition: Examining Intersectionality as a Research Paradigm," *Perspectives on Politics* 5, no. 1 (March 2007): 63–79; Deborah K. King, "Multiple Jeopardy, Multiple Consciousness: The Context of a Black Feminist Ideology," in *Feminist Social Thought: A Reader*, ed. Diana Tietjens Meyers (New York: Routledge, 1997), 219–242; and Crenshaw, "Mapping the Margins." In particular, I note how even the most seemingly victimized person may also have sites and relations of power and how identity is shifting and contested. While Crenshaw's article may be the most famous of the three, authors often focus on her empirical examples and lose sight of the broader implications of her theory, although Hancock's and King's work are true to her ideas.

83. See Roberta Villalón's work.

84. Catharine MacKinnon, *Toward a Feminist Theory of the State* (Cambridge, MA: Harvard University Press, 1991), 172.

85. Violence in LGBQT relationships has important similarities to violence in heterosexual relationships but also deserves to have unique and well-written research that does not merely extrapolate from heteronormativity. See Cheshire Calhoun on why and how an entirely different analysis is warranted in discussing, for example, lesbian theory. Cheshire Calhoun, "Separating Lesbian Theory from Feminist Theory," in *Feminist Social Thought: A Reader*, ed. Diana Tietjens Meyers (New York: Routledge, 1997), 199–218.

86. As I note elsewhere in this book, I was encouraged to flee San Antonio by a therapist who was seeing my ex-boyfriend and me. I was also encouraged to flee by a lawyer who specializes in domestic violence—partly because she said it's too difficult to prove in Texas. And a high-ranking military officer also warned me to move from Texas because the laws are "pro-mother" (the mother is usually designated as the primary caretaker) but also "pro-father" (the mother can be confined to the county—if she is being threatened with violence, stalked, and harassed—this is absolutely untenable).

87. A friend, Lacinda Hummel, has suggested the use of federal witness protection for abused women fleeing abusers. If nothing else changes, this is an excellent idea.

88. And children should have rights and protections that reflect their actual situations, including who is actually caring for them—not privileging the "payer" over everyone else in the family unit. Regarding the creation of this category—payer—see Anna Marie Smith, *Welfare Reform and Sexual Regulation* (New York: Cambridge University Press, 2007).

CHAPTER 1

1. The Family Violence Prevention and Services Act was established in 1984 (reauthorized by Obama in 2010), and funding for victims was allotted through the 1984 Victims of Crime Act. See Radha Iyengar, "Does the Certainty of Arrest Reduce Domestic Violence? Evidence from Mandatory and Recommended Arrest Laws," *Journal of Public Economics* 93 (2009): 87 n1. See also Leigh Goodmark, "Autonomy Feminism: An Anti-Essentialist Critique of Mandatory Interventions in Domestic Violence Cases," *Florida State Law Review* (2009), http://ssrn.com/abstract=1354047.

2. See Iyengar 87, 87 n2, and 87 n3. See also Goodmark, "Autonomy Feminism," for a more detailed account of the Thurman case.

3. See Iyengar, "Does the Certainty of Arrest Reduce Domestic Violence?"; see also Radha Iyengar, "The Protection Battered Spouses Don't Need," *New York Times*, August 7, 2007, http://www.nytimes.com/2007/08/07/opinion/07iyengar.html?_r=0.

4. Mandatory arrests are policies in twenty-two states and the District of Columbia. Many other states have policies that allow some police discretion but do also permit a warrantless arrest. Research tends to support this latter policy because homicide rates have actually increased in the former states (Iyengar, "Does the Certainty?") and because with mandatory arrests often come the threat of dual arrest or even "erroneous" arrest of targets of abuse, not to mention a whole host of problems if the target is arrested. See National Institute of Justice, "Dual Arrest," http://www.nij.gov/publications/dv-dual-arrest-222679/exhibits/Pages/table1.aspx; UK (University of Kentucky) Center for Research on Violence against Women, "Top Ten things Advocates Need to Know," 2010, http://www.uky.edu/CRVAW/files/TopTen/05_Mandatory_Arrest.pdf; Wider Opportunities for Women, "Arrest Policy and Survivors," Justice System Policy Series, October 2012, http://www.wowonline.org/wp-content/uploads/2013/05/Economic-Security-for-Survivors-Arrest-Policy-Policy-Brief-2012.pdf.

5. See Evan Stark's discussion of this policy in his introduction—it begins by arguing that a revolution began, but ends with a discussion of why the revolution has stalled. The act was weakened considerably by the Supreme Court in 2000, but renewed (in its weakened state) that year and again in 2005. Evan Stark, *Coercive Control* (New York: Oxford, 2009). More recently, the reauthorization of VAWA was in question because the bill's proponents wanted it extended to undocumented immigrants (expanding the availability of U Visas); Native Americans (including the right to sue non–Native American men who abuse women on tribal land); and LGBQT relationships. Regarding these issues, see Jennifer Bendery, "VAWA Vote: Senate Rejects GOP Alternative That Omits LGBT, Native American Protections," *Huffington Post*, February 7, 2013, http://www.huffingtonpost.com/2013/02/07/vawa-vote_n_2639168.html?utm_hp_ref=gay-voices (accessed February 8, 2013). More generally, see the Department of Justice's website: http://www.ovw.usdoj.gov/. It was finally passed by Congress in February 2013, based on a revised Senate version of the bill, which was closer to the 2012 version. See "Violence against Women Act," *New York Times*, March 10, 2103, http://topics.nytimes.com/top/reference/timestopics/subjects/d/domestic_violence/index.html (accessed March 20, 2013). See Mary Hawkesworth's brief but insightful comments about the delays in reauthorization in 2013: Mary Hawkesworth, "Combating Violence

against Women: A Discussion of Celeste Montoya's *From Global to Grassroots: The European Union, Transnational Advocacy, and Combating Violence against Women,*" *Perspectives on Politics* 12, no. 1 (March 2014): 181–183.

6. In Stark's account, a key part of domestic violence policy and solutions has been developed outside of feminist theory. In contrast, Johnson's account of feminist research is that it has held relatively steady but has tended to focus on gender asymmetry only while symmetry researchers have studied "situational couple violence." In a certain respect, Johnson's argument may be similar to Stark's in that the degree to which domestic abuse still isn't taken seriously is because feminists are being marginalized or ignored. But Johnson in 2008 is also far more optimistic than Stark is in 2009. Evan Stark, *Coercive Control* (New York: Oxford, 2009); Michael P. Johnson, *A Typology of Domestic Violence: Intimate Terrorism, Violent Resistance, and Situational Couple Violence* (Lebanon, NH: Northeastern University Press, 2008). On this history, see also Leigh Goodmark, "When Is a Battered Woman Not a Battered Woman? When She Fights Back," *Yale Journal of Law and Feminism* (2008): 76–129.

7. On the emergence of this literature, see Kathleen J. Ferraro and Michael P. Johnson, "Research on Domestic Violence in the 1990s: Making Distinctions," *Journal of Marriage and Family* 62, no. 4 (November 2000): 948–963.

8. See Stark, *Coercive Control*, Introduction—this is the heart of his work.

9. Conversely, this sort of focus can lead to another attitude: ignoring and mocking a victim of domestic assault. In the USA network's new program *Rush*, the main character is a doctor who proclaims that he will treat anyone who pays, including jerks because he himself is a jerk. In the next scene, he is called to treat a woman beaten up by her boyfriend who is a star baseball player. The woman is absolutely immobile while the doctor and baseball player joke about why he beat her up. First, they discuss how the boyfriend needs to take off his rings the next time so he does less damage to her face. Then the boyfriend tells the doctor that this time the assault was because she drank his juice. The only time the doctor speaks to her, he looks at her and says in a mocking tone, "Next time, don't drink his juice."

10. See Nancy Berns, "'My Problem and How I Solved It': Domestic Violence in Women's Magazines," *The Sociological Quarterly* 40, no. 1 (Winter 1999): 85–108.

11. See Ferraro and Johnson, "Research on Domestic Violence in the 1990s"; Berns, "'My Problem and How I Solved It.'"

12. See Walter DeKeseredy, Martin Schwartz, and Joseph Donnermeyer, *Dangerous Exits: Escaping Abusive Relationships in Rural America (Critical Issues in Crime and Society)* (New Brunswick, NJ: Rutgers University Press, 2009) regarding this argument in rural areas.

13. These assumptions have unfortunately been dominant in a family foundation of which I am a member; put forth by two people who are influential not only in this foundation but also in the domestic violence shelter system in the city where the foundation is located.

14. See Wider Opportunities for Women, "Arrest Policy and Survivors," Justice System Policy Series, October 2012, http://www.wowonline.org/wp-content/uploads/2013/05/Economic-Security-for-Survivors-Arrest-Policy-Policy-Brief-2012.pdf. See also Lisa Brush's excellent analysis of the surveillance of the welfare state combined with the surveillance of controlling partners and a hostile ("undomestic") work environment. Lisa Brush, *Poverty, Battered Women,*

and Work in US Public Policy (Oxford, 2011). In particular, Brush notes how abuse and control spill over into the workplace and public sphere, while "welfare surveillance reproduces the coercive, controlling dynamics of abuse." (13)

15. Jacqueline Rose, "Deadly Embrace," *London Review of Books* 26, no. 21 (November 2004): 21–24.

16. See a discussion of this in Karuna Mantena's recent work. She examines how recently, critics like Bonnie Honig have argued that political science—and theory, in particular—has become increasingly oriented toward normative political theory and ethical questions. That is, it has increasingly been concerned with political ideals (the "ought") rather than practical contexts of political dynamics today (the "is"). In this way, one of the dominant frameworks in contemporary US political science is essentially apolitical. Karuna Mantena, "Another Realism: the Politics of Gandhian Nonviolence," *American Political Science Review* 106, no. 2 (May 2012): 455–470. See also Bonnie Honig, untitled book reviews, *Perspectives on Politics*, 8, no. 2 (June 2010): 657–660.

17. Ferraro and Johnson, "Research on Domestic Violence in the 1990s," 956.

18. Iyengar and other authors, including Stark, have found that there are some differentials based on race and income. For example, high-income Anglo women may not seek help, whereas wealthier African American women do. Michael Johnson has also found evidence that the marriage contract doesn't necessarily lead to abuse, and that other forms of intimate partnership are more often characterized by abuse. Michael P. Johnson, *A Typology of Domestic Violence: Intimate Terrorism, Violent Resistance, and Situational Couple Violence* (Lebanon, NH: Northeastern University Press, 2008).

19. While many of the criminology articles on the effects of mandatory arrest treat the problem as an empirical one, what is recognized is that when targets call, they can also be arrested or suffer from secondary effects of a perpetrator's arrest. See Iyengar, "Does the Certainty of Arrest Reduce Domestic Violence?"

20. Stark, *Coercive Control*, 3.

21. Stark, *Coercive Control*, 3. On the Simpson case, see also Lisa McLaughlin, "Gender, Privacy and Publicity in 'Media Event Space,'" in *News, Gender, and Power*, ed. Cynthia Carter, Gill Branston, and Stuart Allan (London: Routledge, 1998), ch. 4, 71–90.

22. Which Evan Stark claims is evident in Alan Dershowitz's work; Alan Dershowitz, cited in Stark, *Coercive Control*, 9. See Stark's discussion of this in *Coercive Control*, 9. Alan Dershowitz, *The Abuse Excuse and Other Cop-Outs, Sob Stories, and Evasions of Responsibility* (Boston: Back Bay Books, 1994). Although I am not a fan of Dershowitz, I am not sure he is using the abuse excuse as a way to dismiss all abuse cases.

23. As Stark argues, this becomes a "calculus of injuries" (*Coercive Control*, 57) about which abusers are aware. According to Stark, most abusers now employ lower-level tactics that are more pervasive (both in terms of the number of women affected and the pervasiveness of control in their lives) but which do not count as abuse.

24. My definition is largely derived from Evan Stark's work but also heavily influenced by Patricia Evans and Lundy Bancroft. Lundy Bancroft, *Why Does He Do That?* (New York: Berkley Books, 2002); Patricia Evans, *The Verbally Abusive Relationship*, 2nd ed. (Avon, MA: Adams Media Corporation, 1996). The section on psychology below is derived from my personal experiences first and research second.

25. The psychological typologies introduced in Michael Johnson's *A Typology of Domestic Violence* are an example of these attitudes.

26. Interestingly, certain states have acted on the idea that abuse is a rational and controlled behavior and thus, bar anger management classes as a component of batterer intervention programs. Bethany J. Price, Alan Rosenbaum, "Batterer Intervention Programs: A Report from the Field," *Violence and Victims* 24, no. 6 (2009): 763. "Several states cautioned that anger and stress management were only appropriate with the caveat that abuse is a controlled behavior, not an anger response." Some states, including West Virginia, "prohibit anger management" because it is viewed as an excuse for abuse and these programs cannot substitute for BIPs.

27. See Stark, *Coercive Control*.

28. Ferraro and Johnson, "Research on Domestic Violence in the 1990s," 959.

29. Ferraro and Johnson, "Research on Domestic Violence in the 1990s," 957.

30. See Jack C. Straton, "The Myth of the 'Battered Husband Syndrome,'" NOMAS (National Organization for Men against Sexism) website, n.d., http://www.nomas.org/node/107 (accessed December 16, 2013).

31. See conservative criminologist Richard B. Felson, "Big People Hit Little People: Sex Differences in Physical Power and Interpersonal Violence," *Criminology* (August 1996): 433–452. His aim is to reduce gender to physical size, thus arguing that gender inequality is not a root cause of abuse per se.

32. With regard to these debates, see Lisa D. Brush, "Philosophical and Political Issues in Research on Women's Violence and Aggression," *Sex Roles* 52, nos. 11/12 (June 2005): 867–872; Suzanne Steinmetz, "The Battered Husband Syndrome," *Victimology* 2 (1978): 499–509; Straton, "The Myth of the 'Battered Husband Syndrome.'"

33. On the effects of being hit just one time, see bell hooks, "Violence in Intimate Relationship: A Feminist Perspective," *Talking Back: Thinking Feminist, Thinking Black* (Boston: South End Press, 1989), 84–91; see also Lundy Bancroft, *When Dad Hurts Mom: Helping Your Children Heal the Wounds of Witnessing Abuse* (New York: Berkley Books, 2004).

34. Ferraro and Johnson, "Research on Domestic Violence in the 1990s," 959.

35. Lundy Bancroft's research on the effects of partner abuse on children suggests the opposite; in contrast to Ferraro, who mixes empirical evidence with pure speculation, Bancroft is careful to use primary research, draw on secondary sources, and refer to actual evidence. Lundy Bancroft, *When Dad Hurts Mom*.

36. Which is why children's rights have been promoted over and above mother's rights in courts. This is evident in the overall punishment of women for being abused and in claims that women must be punished for "exposing" their children to abuse. Evan Stark discusses this "competitive victimization" that pits children's rights against their mothers (ignoring abusers altogether) and there is quite a lot of literature on exposure claims. See Stark, 44; regarding exposure to abuse prosecution, see Jeanne A. Fugate, "Who's Failing Whom? A Critical Look at Failure-To-Protect Laws," *New York University Law Review* 76 (April 2001): 272–308, http://www.thelizlibrary.org/liz/fugate.pdf. Anecdotally, if one were to recount a pattern of violent assaults to fellow professors, it is always surprising to hear "But is he a good father?" from academics who otherwise can discern broad structures of coercion and more insidious forms of normative power.

37. In this way, I am arguing that Bancroft's work, together with Patricia Evans's and Stark's, are more historically grounded and politically logical than

research that simply calculates physical acts of violence through surveys and analyzes these acts without any context. See Stark, *Coercive Control*, Chapter 2.

38. See Stark's constructive analysis of Johnson's categories, which rightly praise Johnson's contributions to domestic abuse research. As Stark argues, Johnson "challenges us to map the tactical combinations of coercion and control used in relationships, reformulate a theory of harms accordingly, and link the dynamic and outcomes in these situations to social factors. Facing this challenge could awaken the field from the stupor in which it has languished since it adapted the reductionist equation of abuse with violence." Evan Stark, "Commentary on Johnson's 'Conflict and Control: Gender Symmetry and Asymmetry in Domestic violence,'" *Violence against Women* 12 (2006): 1019. The article's full page range is 1019–1025. Although Stark argues that coercive control and Johnson's notion of intimate terror are "identical" (1021), he also notes key methodological differences that still separate their work. In particular, "Johnson finesses the political differences between a feminist and mainstream paradigm by resorting to behaviorism. Instead of conceptualizing *control* as a political structure and consequence infused with social power and meaning, he pictures it as an 'act' that can be catalogued alongside violence" (1023). As Foucault might argue, Stark introduces an analytics of abuse as power while Johnson's work rests on more static assumptions analyzing abusive acts rather than power relations. Given these differences, Johnson's work is still excellent and a distinct contribution to understanding popular and academic assumptions about abuse. Another excellent critique of Johnson's typology is Philip Rossiter, "A Thorn in the Flesh That Cannot Fester: Habermas, the Duluth Model, Domestic Violence Programmes," *Waikato Law Review* 19, no. 2 (2011): 196–206.

39. This is Stark's argument throughout *Coercive Control*, but see 57 in particular.

40. Various reactions to Jackson Katz's *The Macho Paradox* and his training sessions on Amazon and in the following article also suggest these changes (the changing nature of abuse coupled with its continuing ubiquity). See Nina Burleigh, "Hear Him Roar," *Elle*, July 23, 2014, http://www.elle.com/life-love/society-career/jackson-katz-the-macho-paradox-4.

41. Stark, *Coercive Control*, 57.

42. Andrea C. Westlund, "Pre-Modern and Modern Power: Foucault and the Case of Domestic Violence," *Signs* 24, no. 4, Institutions, Regulation and Social Control (Summer 1999): 1045–1066.

43. See Westlund, "Pre-Modern and Modern Power: Foucault and the Case of Domestic Violence." Westlund argues that domestic abuse constitutes a separate, premodern sphere of violence that Foucault did not account for. Only when the woman steps out of the house and into the public sphere does she encounter disciplinary (i.e., modern) power. Westlund further argues that this disciplinary power can actually "empower" women. I challenge this neat separation of spheres; particularly, her nearly exclusive focus on targets of abuse, including advocating disciplinary mechanisms to help victims who don't seem to know how to conduct their own lives.

44. While there are a number of good clinical articles on alienation and obsessive alienation (often of children's affections), Stark analyzes it in terms of a tool of abuse when there is nothing left for the father to do: Evan Stark, "Symposium on Reconceptualizing Violence against Women by Intimate Partners: Critical Issues: Re-Presenting Woman Battering: From Battered Woman Syndrome to Coercive Control" in *Albany Law Review* 58 (Spring 1995):

973–1026. Tangential spouse abuse can be a sudden interest in filing for sole custody when an abuser has no other methods of manipulation.

45. See Evans, for example—against most assumptions about the targets of abuse, they have not fully internalized abusers' messages. Evans, *The Verbally Abusive Relationship.*

46. While "dual-arrest" policies are increasingly normal in some cities, this attempt at "gender neutrality" obfuscates a major and life-threatening power dynamic that permits regular violence and abuse against women but is now prosecuting (or attempting to) women's self-defense or violent resistance. Because the definition of DV is centered on violent, isolated, concrete events and in the context of these efforts at gender-neutral arrests, quite a lot is missed. Stark has found that young, white, unmarried, single women suffer most from these policies (Stark, *Coercive Control*, 58). This can include being subject to detention and removal (deportation) if the woman is a legal or undocumented resident immigrant—thus, the stakes are very high. See Amy Goodman et al., "A Look inside U.S. Immigration Prisons," *Democracy Now!* May 4, 2006, http://www.democracynow.org/2006/5/4/a_look_inside_u_s_immigration.a (accessed March 17, 2013).

47. See Amy Goodman et al., "A Look inside U.S. Immigration Prisons." See also Roberta Villalón, "Passage to Citizenship and the Nuances of Agency: Latina Battered Immigrants," *Women's Studies International Forum* 33 (October 12, 2010): 552–560.

48. See Wider Opportunities for Women, "Arrest Policy and Survivors," Justice System Policy Series, October 2012, http://www.wowonline.org/wp-content/uploads/2013/05/Economic-Security-for-Survivors-Arrest-Policy-Policy-Brief-2012.pdf.

49. "Michelle Warner Body Found: Mark Castellano Leads Texas Police to Former Lover's Body," *Huffington Post*, October 1, 2012, http://www.huffingtonpost.com/2012/10/01/michelle-warner-body-found_n_1928829.html.

50. Warner's ex-boyfriend blamed her for the murder, arguing that she tried to hit him first. He was subsequently convicted of murder. See Brian Rogers, "Jurors Deliberate in Murder Trial of Man Who Talked to Dr. Phil," *Houston Chronicle*, June 4, 2014, http://www.chron.com/news/houston-texas/houston/article/Jurors-deliberate-in-murder-trial-of-man-who-5529060.php.

51. While Stark has argued this in *Coercive Control*, I have also worked in and studied shelters and have witnessed the disciplinary tactics of shelter workers and rules. Surprisingly, Andrea Westlund does not deny these dynamics but argues that they are a form of "good" discipline that targets need. Westlund, "Pre-Modern and Modern Power: Foucault and the Case of Domestic Violence," 1046, 1056. "The central disciplinary practices of well-run shelters play a key role in authorizing survivors to speak (and be heard) in otherwise inaccessible arenas and are thus integral to the formulation and implementation of intelligible and effective strategies of resistance." Westlund, 1057.

52. Thus including, for example, a transgendered individual who identifies as feminine.

53. See Ferraro and Johnson, "Research on Domestic Violence in the 1990s" on these limitations. See also Lundy Bancroft's introduction to *Why Does He Do That?*, where he provides an excellent analysis of gender and how the LGBQT communities can gain insight from these observations as well as the limitations of understandings of heteronormative gender divisions.

54. To put it differently, following Cheshire Calhoun, because I do not believe that I can simply take this analysis and easily apply it to nonheterosexual relationships, I am narrowing the analysis to heterosexual intimate abuse to avoid false universals and easy binaries that misunderstand the specific dynamics of LGBT intimate partnerships (among other things). Cheshire Calhoun, "Separating Lesbian Theory from Feminist Theory," in *Feminist Social Thought: A Reader*, ed. Diana Tietjens Meyers (New York: Routledge, 1997), 199–218.

55. I am not trying to assert that the United States is more violent than countries with similar levels of political and economic attainment. For some examples of statistics about American violence, some of which do find that our country is more violent than many others, see American Bar Association, "The U.S. Compared to Other Nations," n.d., http://www.americanbar.org/groups/committees/gun_violence/resources/the_u_s_compared_to_other_nations.html (accessed May 20, 2013); U.S. Department of Health and Human Services, Health Resources and Services Administration, "U.S. Teens in Our World Rockville," (Maryland: U.S. Department of Health and Human Services, 2003), http://www.mchb.hrsa.gov/mchirc/_pubs/us_teens/index.htm (accessed May 20, 2013); Julia Sommer, "Crime Is Not the Problem, Lethal Violence Is, Say UC Berkeley Researchers," UC Berkeley Public Affairs Website, September 16, 1997, http://www.berkeley.edu/news/media/releases/97legacy/zimring.html (accessed May 20, 2013).

56. On these debates, see Lawrence Douglas, "The Force of Words: Fish, Matsuda, MacKinnon, and the Theory of Discursive Violence," *Law and Society Review* 29, no. 1 (1995): 169–190.

57. See Douglas, "The Force of Words: Fish, Matsuda, MacKinnon . . ." This is an excellent discussion of the First Amendment and injurious speech and images. This stands in stark contrast to a history of ideological intolerance since at least the first Red Scare of the early twentieth century. See Daniel Kanstroom, *Deportation Nation* (Cambridge, MA: Harvard University Press, 2007) on this history. For a critique of MacKinnon as harming First Amendment freedoms, see Wendy Brown, *States of Injury: Power and Freedom in Late Modernity* (Princeton, NJ: Princeton University Press, 1995). Mocking MacKinnon, Brown states, "not freedom but censorship, not First Amendment guarantees but more rights to sue for damages, not risky experiments with resignification and emancipation but more police, more regulation, better deadbolt locks on the doors," Brown, 94.

58. Catharine MacKinnon, *Toward a Feminist Theory of the State* (Cambridge, MA: Harvard University Press, 1991); see her chapter on "Rape: On Coercion and Consent," particularly 172.

59. On these criticisms—which may have some kernel of truth but which are also wildly exaggerated in terms of distorting her claims and dismissing her work as a whole—see, Judith Butler, "Review: "Disorderly Woman," *Transition* 53 (1991): 86–95; Drucilla Cornell, "Sexual Difference, the Feminine, and Equivalency: A Critique of MacKinnon's *Toward a Feminist Theory of the State*," *Yale Law Journal* 100, no. 7 (May 1991): 2247–2275.

60. Not to mention the work of Kristin Bumiller with specific regard to media portrayals of gendered violence. See Kristin Bumiller, *In an Abusive State: How Neoliberalism Appropriated the Feminist Movement against Sexual Violence* (Durham, NC: Duke University Press, 2008).

61. Kimberlé Crenshaw, "Beyond Racism and Misogyny Black Feminism and 2 Live Crew," in *Feminist Social Thought: A Reader*, ed. Diana Tietjens Meyers (New York: Routledge, 1997), 257.

62. Crenshaw, "Beyond Racism and Misogyny," 257.

63. Crenshaw, "Beyond Racism and Misogyny," 254.

64. Crenshaw, "Beyond Racism and Misogyny," 250.

65. Crenshaw, "Beyond Racism and Misogyny," 255.

66. Kimberlé Crenshaw, "Mapping the Margins: Intersectionality, Identity, Politics, and Violence against Women of Color," *Stanford Law Review* 43, no. 6 (1991): 1255. See also Bancroft, *When Dad Hurts Mom: Helping Your Children Heal the Wounds of Witnessing Abuse*; Stark, "Symposium on Reconceptualizing Violence against Women by Intimate Partners." Linda Mills also accounts for an intergenerational cycle of violence. Linda G. Mills, *Violent Partners: A Breakthrough Plan for Ending the Cycle of Abuse* (New York: Basic Books, 2008).

67. Mary P. Koss, "Review: [untitled]," *Signs* 24, no. 2 (Winter 1999): 534.

68. A term I appropriated from David Garland: David Garland, *Culture of Control* (Chicago: University of Chicago, 2001) from 2004 on and only recently learned that Kristin Bumiller did the same in her text on domestic abuse, *In an Abusive State*. I thank Lori Marso for recommending Bumiller's book in September of 2013.

69. Although, as Evan Stark suggests, there are now movies and TV programs that also show sympathy for abused women. These programs do not displace violent images in comedy, cartoons (like "the Family Guy"), music, and mainstream shows and movies but do "share" programming time. Stark, *Coercive Control*, 45–46. As noted above, the new USA program *Rush* arguably promotes a hipster image in one episode (July 2014) by ignoring a woman who was violently assaulted by her boyfriend and whose immobility indicates absolute terror.

70. As Wendy Brown indicates, "Or do the commitments of postfoundationalist feminist analysis condemn it to a certain political marginalization, to permanent gadfly status, to a philosopher's self-consolation that she is on the side of 'truth' rather than power?" Brown, *States of Injury*, 79. See also Leigh Goodmark's discussion of radical feminism in Leigh Goodmark, *A Troubled Marriage: Domestic Violence and the Legal System* (New York: NYU Press, 2013), Chapter 1.

71. Although I believe they are most forceful when her analysis extrapolates too easily from the law to culture or private experiences.

72. See Butler, "Review: 'Disorderly Woman'"; Brown, *States of Injury*; Cornell, "Sexual Difference, the Feminine, and Equivalency"; Douglas, "The Force of Words: Fish, Matsuda, MacKinnon . . ."

73. As Michael Johnson (in *A Typology*) has pointed out, feminist authors have been leaders in identifying key facets of "intimate terrorism" (i.e., asymmetrical abuse) and so the state of feminist theory is not the problem per se but rather broader academic articles that draw on a mix of conventional assumptions and/or empirical work from "situational" couple violence.

74. Granted that both authors identify (–ied) themselves as Marxists and this is a Foucaultian term.

75. MacKinnon, *Towards a Feminist Theory*, 172.

76. Today, in the United States, *Gonzales v. Carhart* 550 U.S. 124 (2007) has not simply dismantled the trimester structure of *Roe* but has potentially undermined women's informed consent in medical issues.

77. Exploited workers are the group that she uses to negatively define sexage. In this comparison, sexage is more like servitude than capitalist exploitation.
78. Colette Guillaumin, *Racism, Sexism, Power and Ideology* (New York: Routledge, 1995), 162. For a more contemporary analysis of similar dynamics in the United States, see Jackson Katz, *The Macho Paradox: Why Some Men Hurt Women and How All Men Can Help* (Naperville, IL: Sourcebooks, 2006).
79. Guillaumin, *Racism, Sexism, Power and Ideology*, 162.
80. Guillaumin, *Racism, Sexism, Power and Ideology*, 190: "Unlike other dominated groups with labor power, we women are in relations between sexes, non-sellers of our labor power and our appropriation evinces itself precisely in this fact; we are distinct from those oppressed people who can bargain beginning with disposition of their labor power—that is to exchange it or sell it."
81. *Chicago Parent*'s consistent assumption that women are the primary caretakers, that work should come second, and that men are reliably the breadwinners is evident in various headlines and bylines. For a compelling account of "maternal ideology," see Karen Zivi, "Contesting Motherhood in the Age of AIDS: Maternal Ideology in the Debate over Mandatory HIV Testing," *Feminist Studies* 31, no. 2 (Summer 2005): 347–374.
82. I should point out that I am not construing motherhood as a burden and fatherhood as a cakewalk, but discussing relations of legal and normative positions (much as Marx and Foucault discuss how power constructs certain naturalized subjectivities).
83. I use this term with Evan Stark's notion of "coercive control" in mind as well as Mark Poster's argument that domestic violence should be classified as domination. As noted in the preface, Kristin Bumiller has used this term in a similar context, for slightly different but related reasons (she is referring to David Garland's work on control). Bumiller, *In an Abusive State*.
84. Guillaumin, 187–188.
85. Guillaumin, 187–190. This normative power can be identified even if the law itself and what is taken to be the "state" are in fact fragmented, contested, and shifting.
86. Which is why Butler calls gender norms "regulatory fictions." Judith Butler, "Excerpt from Gender Trouble," in *Feminist Social Thought: A Reader*, ed. Diana Tietjens Meyers (New York: Routledge, 1997), 118.
87. As both Carole Pateman and (separately) MacKinnon have noted, the crucial distinction in determining "illegitimate violence"—that is whether a crime occurred—is not public or private space per se but rather the relationship a target had with the perpetrator. And despite the fact that it's recognized that most violent crimes, kidnapping, and sexual crimes are attempted by social intimates, policy takes the opposite view—that these crimes occur only if a stranger committed them. See Carole Pateman, *The Disorder of Women* (Palo Alto, CA: Stanford University Press, 1992), Chapter 4; Catharine MacKinnon, *Toward a Feminist Theory of the State* (Cambridge, MA: Harvard University Press, 1991); and see Susan Estrich, "Real Rape," in Patricia Smith, *Feminist Jurisprudence* (New York: Oxford University Press, 1993), 158–182.
88. It is important to note that these norms don't actually prevent rape, which is most often perpetrated on the elderly, sick, or isolated.
89. For example, a man who killed wife for the way she cooked eggs: http://www.cbsnews.com/8301-504083_162-20016224-504083.html; see also this site

devoted to domestic abuse homicides: http://intimateviolencedeathnews. blogspot.com/2010/05/mountain-view-ca-two-people-found-shot.html.

90. This particular case is fascinating in terms of ascribing a horrific murder to burned pasta: "Husband Suspected of Mutilating Wife," *New York Times* archive, August 31, 1995, http://www.nytimes.com/1995/08/31/us/husband-suspected-of-mutilating-wife.html.

91. Susan Bordo, *Unbearable Weight: Feminism, Western Culture, and the Body* (Berkeley, CA: University of California Press, 2004).

92. MacKinnon, *Toward a Feminist Theory of the State*, 179.

93. See MacKinnon, *Toward a Feminist Theory*, 176; Bancroft, *Why Does He Do That?* Introduction; Patricia Evans, *The Verbally Abusive Relationship*, Introduction; and Michael Johnson's work on intimate partner violence, which finds some "symmetry" in situational partner conflict but an almost exclusive gender imbalance in heterosexual partnerships with intimate terror.

94. MacKinnon, *Toward a Feminist Theory*, 176.

95. Although it should be noted that even the term *epistemology* may be too wedded to static, Enlightenment norms of rationality. See Linda Zerilli's critique of feminist standpoint epistemology (which may be complementary to but is not equivalent to MacKinnon's radical feminism) in Linda M. G. Zerilli, *Feminism and the Abyss of Freedom* (Chicago: University of Chicago Press, 2005).

96. MacKinnon, *Toward a Feminist Theory*, 180; Estrich disagrees, arguing that the United States would benefit from relying on mens rea. Estrich, "Real Rape," 158–182.

97. See Pateman's strikingly similar work on this in *The Disorder of Women*, Chapter 4.

98. In Michel Foucault, *The History of Sexuality, Volume I: An Introduction*, trans. Robert Hurley (New York: Vintage Books, 1980). On the difference between these two authors' explanatory power, see Honig's discussion, Bonnie Honig, untitled book reviews, *Perspectives on Politics* 8, no. 2 (June 2010): 657–660.

99. See Michel Foucault, *The Foucault Reader*, ed. Paul Rabinow (New York: Pantheon, 1984), "Truth and Power."

100. Nancy Fraser and Linda J. Nicholson, "Social Criticism without Philosophy: An Encounter between Feminism and Postmodernism," in *Feminist Social Thought: A Reader*, ed. Diana Tietjens Meyers (New York: Routledge, 1997), 132–146.

101. John Stuart Mill, *On Liberty*, ed. Elizabeth Rapaport (Indianapolis: Hackett, 1978), 206–210.

102. Mill, *On Liberty*, 206–210.

103. MacKinnon, *Toward a Feminist Theory*, 172.

104. Bumiller rightly discusses this cultivation of fear, and her analysis is especially interesting regarding media treatment of rape and rape culture, for example. However, adding domestic abuse to this argument does not work: domestic abuse is almost impossible to prosecute, and therefore jails are not filled with offenders nor are abusers stigmatized in the future (as Bumiller suggests). Further, against some of Bumiller's arguments, I hold that our culture is arguably indifferent to or even tolerant of domestic abuse. See Bumiller, *In an Abusive State*.

105. As Katie Roiphe has argued in *The Morning After: Sex, Fear, and Feminism On Campus* (Boston: Little Brown, 1993).

106. MacKinnon, *Toward a Feminist Theory*, 179.

107. Roiphe, *The Morning After*; Alan Dershowitz, *The Abuse Excuse and Other Cop-Outs, Sob Stories, and Evasions of Responsibility* (Boston: Back Bay Books, 1994).

108. See Mary P. Koss, "Review: [untitled]," *Signs* 24, no. 2 (Winter 1999): 532–535.

109. See Stark, *Coercive Control*, Introduction. More broadly, see Linda G. Mills, *Violent Partners: A Breakthrough Plan for Ending the Cycle of Abuse* (Basic Books, 2008) for an account of domestic violence as mutual (i.e., symmetrical).

110. Minority theory is composed of texts that disrupted the assumptions and categories of canonical philosophy. This is Collette Guillaumin's term; see *Racism, Sexism, Power and Ideology*.

111. Andrea Westlund's claim that domestic violence is "premodern" simply because it has existed throughout history is one example of this universalizing tendency. Andrea C. Westlund, "Pre-Modern and Modern Power: Foucault and the Case of Domestic Violence," *Signs* 24, no. 4, Institutions, Regulation, and Social Control (Summer 1999): 1045–1066. Related to this critique, I also disagree with her analysis of Foucault's work. He argues that history is not progressive and so, for example, a city like Philadelphia can have both ancient forms of imprisonment alongside new models of prisons; and to give a similar comparison, one could argue that immigration has always occurred but we still think that researchers and analysts must distinguish between immigration in ancient Greece versus immigration to the United States in the year 2014; there are often more differences than similarities, when power dynamics—and not simply immigration itself—are examined. Michel Foucault, *Discipline and Punish*, trans. Alan Sheridan (New York: Vintage, 1979).

112. DSM: Diagnostic and Statistical Manual of Mental Disorders.

113. See Westlund, "Pre-modern Power," 1057–1059.

114. Julietta Hua, "Feminism, Asylum, and the Limits of Law," *Law, Culture, and Humanities* (July 7, 2010): 375–393. See also Kathryn Libal and Serena Parekh, "Reframing Violence against Women as a Human Rights Violation: Evan Stark's *Coercive Control*," *Violence against Women* 15 n12 (October 15, 2007): 1477–1489.

115. Malcolm X, "On Black People and War," http://www.hartford-hwp.com/archives/45a/646.html (accessed April 25, 2014).

116. I should note that I disagree with Michael Johnson's choice to characterize targets' self-defense as "violent retaliation." His explanation for this is that women's resistance to physical assaults doesn't fit the legal definition of self-defense, but one could argue that is also true for his definitions of domestic abuse, so this choice seems arbitrary. Second, the term *self-defense* automatically connotes a context, whereas labeling targets "violent" or as acting in "violent retaliation" suggests a less reactive and more autonomous meaning that I don't think fits. See Johnson, *A Typology of Domestic Violence*.

117. On the definition of domination, see Iris Marion Young, "Is Male Gender Identity the Cause of Male Domination?" in *Feminist Social Thought*, ed. Diana Tietjens Meyers (New York: Routledge, 1997).

118. Westlund recognizes that abuse is political and gendered: "Much work has been done within the battered women's movement (and within the feminist movement more broadly) to unmask the systematic and political nature of that violence, emphasizing repeatedly that men who batter do so not because they are stressed or sick or crazy but because they want to assert and maintain absolute power over their partners." Westlund, "Pre-Modern Power," 1047.

119. See Patricia Evans on these dual realities.

120. On the number of batterer intervention programs (BIPs) and an analysis of the two dominant approaches (generally either "the coordinated community approach and the focus on power and control as the primary etiological factor in IPV" or psychoeducational treatment) (758), see Bethany J. Price, Alan Rosenbaum, "Batterer Intervention Programs: A Report from the Field," *Violence and Victims* 24, no. 6 (2009): 757–770. BIPs are now one of the major solutions to domestic violence issues and are heavily used as an alternative to jail in the majority of states.
121. Mantena, "Another Realism: the Politics of Gandhian Nonviolence," 459.
122. Mantena, "Another Realism," 459.
123. Niccolo Machiavelli, *The Prince*, second edition, trans. and ed. Harvey Mansfield (Chicago: University of Chicago Press, 1998).
124. Niccoló Machiavelli, *Discourses on Livy*, Book 1, Chapter 2, Chapter 4, http://www.constitution.org/mac/disclivy1.htm.
125. *Discourses*, Book 1, Chapter 4
126. *Discourses*, Book 1, Chapter 4. Giorgio Agamben has a much different view of tumults and the right of *iustitium* in *State of Exception*. See Chapter 3, 41–46.
127. *Discourses*, Book 1, Chapter 11, Chapter 12.
128. *Discourses*, Book 2, Chapter 2.
129. *Discourses*, Book 2, Chapter 2.
130. Again, see *Discourses*, Book 2, Chapter 2.
131. Machiavelli, *The Prince*, 88. Niccolo Machiavelli, *The Prince*, second edition, trans. and ed. Harvey Mansfield (Chicago: University of Chicago Press, 1998).
132. To me, a truly helpful form of political realism would be based on texts such as Machiavelli's *Discourses* (not the *Prince* per se), Nietzsche's *On the Genealogy of Morals*, and Max Weber's varied writings on religion and modern power, particularly his discussion in "Politics as a Vocation" about the comparison between a politics of absolute ends versus consideration of the means. The impulses in these various texts are captured in more contemporary authors' writings, including the work of Arendt, Foucault, Sheldon Wolin, and Chantal Mouffe. Hannah Arendt, *The Origins of Totalitarianism* (New York: Harcourt Brace Jovanovich, 1979); Chantal Mouffe, "Feminism, Citizenship, and Radical Democratic Politics," in *Feminist Social Thought: A Reader*, ed. Diana Tietjens Meyers (New York: Routledge, 1997), 532–544; Sheldon Wolin, *Politics and Vision* (Princeton: Princeton University Press, 2006).
133. See Mary Dietz, "Trapping the Prince: Machiavelli and the Politics of Deception," *American Political Science Review* 80, no. 3 (September 1986): see 777–787 in particular; Wolin, *Politics and Vision*, Chapter 7 (175–213).
134. Martin Luther King, "Letter from a Birmingham Jail," April 16, 1963, https://kinginstitute.stanford.edu/king-papers/documents/letter-birmingham-jail.
135. William Galston, "Realism in Political Theory," *European Journal of Political Theory* 9, no. 4 (2010): 385–411.
136. Galston, "Realism in Political Theory," 393, 396.
137. As if international and regional groups have not emerged in the past few decades—that is, a whole new civil society beyond and below the nation-state.
138. Authors like Geuss hold similar assumptions. Raymond Geuss, *Philosophy and Real Politics* (Princeton, NJ: Princeton University Press, 2008). See Bonnie Honig, untitled book reviews, *Perspectives on Politics*, 8, no. 2 (June 2010): 657–660.

139. That is, I am tempering the interpretation of violent acts as political agency with Freud's notion of Thanatos or the death drive (which I examine in more depth in Chapter 4). Rather than viewing violence as uniting the animal in us to whitewashed or hypocritical Enlightenment ideals, the issue of domestic abuse unmasks its purely destructive aims when exercise against a weaker party or group. At the very least, a distinction should be made between aggressive and bullying abuse and the violence of self-defense.

140. Karuna Mantena, "Another Realism: the Politics of Gandhian Nonviolence," *American Political Science Review* 106, no. 2 (May 2012): 455–470.

141. Mike Davis, *City of Quartz* (New York: Vintage, 1992).

142. Advocated in Linda Mills's work: see Linda G. Mills, *Violent Partners: A Breakthrough Plan for Ending the Cycle of Abuse* (New York: Basic Books, 2008).

143. Foucault, *History of Sexuality* vol. 1, 137.

144. Catharine MacKinnon, "Symposium on Unfinished Business: Points against Postmodernism," *Chicago-Kent Law Review* 75 (2000): 687–695.

145. See Malcolm X; Simone de Beauvoir, *The Second Sex*, trans. and ed. H. M. Parshley (New York: Vintage Books, 1989); Franz Fanon, *The Wretched of the Earth*, intro by Jean-Paul Sartre, foreword by Homi K. Bhabha (Grove Press).

146. In discussing domestic abuse in one of my classes, one of my students asserted that trying to stop it from happening is "attempting to legislate morality." Morality in this case stands in for the private sphere.

CHAPTER 2

1. Emily Collins, "Reminiscences of Emily Collins," in *The Feminist Papers: From Adams to de Beauvoir*, ed. Alice S. Rossi (Boston: Northeastern University Press, 1988), 421–426; John Stuart Mill, "On the Subjection of Women," in *The Feminist Papers*, ed. Alice S. Rossi (Boston: Northeastern University Press, 1988), 201–202, 207; John Stuart Mill, *On Liberty*, ed. Elizabeth Rapaport (Indianapolis: Hackett, 1978), 102–105; Florence Kelley, in *The Feminist Papers*, ed. Alice S. Rossi (Boston: Northeastern University Press, 1988), 474–475. As Laurie Naranch points out, the "Declaration of Sentiments" also calls for an end to husbands' rights to physically chastise wives. See Laurie Naranch, "Naming and Framing the Issues: Demanding Full Citizenship for Women," in *Feminists Negotiate the State: the Politics of Domestic Violence*, ed. Cynthia R. Daniels (Lanham, MD: University Press of America, 1997), Chapter 2.

2. For an overview of this history, see Anna Clark, "Domestic Violence, Past and Present," *Journal of Women's History* 23, no. 3 (Fall 2011): 193–202; Elizabeth Felter, "A History of the State's Response to Domestic Violence," in *Feminists Negotiate the State: the Politics of Domestic Violence*, ed. Cynthia R. Daniels (Lanham, MD: University Press of America, 1997), Chapter 1; Mark Poster, Review: "Domestic Tyranny: The Making of American Social Policy against Family Violence from Colonial Times to the Present" by Elizabeth H. Pleck, *Signs* 14, no. 1 (Autumn 1988): 216–219; and Kathleen Waits, "The Criminal Justice System's Response to Battering," in *Feminist Jurisprudence*, ed. Patricia Smith (New York: Oxford University Press, 1993), 188–206.

3. See Felter, "A History of the State's Response to Domestic Violence."

4. See Olson's excellent article on this history, "The Family and the Market," in *Feminist Jurisprudence*, ed. Patricia Smith (New York: Oxford University Press, 1993), 65–89.

5. Olson, "The Family and the Market," 69–72.

6. The writings of Frances Fukuyama and Harvey Mansfield attest to this continued anxiety.

7. Olson, 73.

8. They also involve changes in the economy, as I have written about more broadly in Kathleen R. Arnold, *America's New Working Class* (College Station, PA: Penn State Press, 2007) and which Lisa Brush discusses in great depth, bridging work on neoliberalism to work on welfare as well as abuse. See Lisa D. Brush, *Poverty, Battered Women, and Work in U.S. Welfare Policy* (New York: Oxford University Press, 2011).

9. Patricia Evans, *The Verbally Abusive Relationship*, 2nd ed. (Avon, MA: Adams Media Corporation, 1996). See my discussion of her work in the introduction.

10. This is not to whitewash the past. On the one hand, there were early attempts to criminalize domestic abuse (in the 1880s) and on the other, in the period that I am identifying as the best for shelters, domestic abuse was often still accepted as a normal facet of intimacy.

11. Kristin Bumiller, *In an Abusive State: How Neoliberalism Appropriated the Feminist Movement against Sexual Violence* (Durham, NC: Duke University Press, 2008), 64. I do not agree that these changes are neoliberal altogether. For example, they also signal a backlash against feminism that cannot be reduced to economic reasoning. Nor do I believe that a neo-Protestant ethic that blames victims is purely neoliberal. Regardless of these disagreements, her arguments are still compelling in analyzing broad tendencies to politicize an issue while also blaming and entrapping targets.

12. As I discuss in terms of welfare and ascetic discourses in Kathleen R. Arnold, *America's New Working Class* (College Station, PA: Penn State Press, 2007).

13. See Wendy Brown, *States of Injury: Power and Freedom in Late Modernity* (Princeton, NJ: Princeton University Press, 1995), Chapter 6; Karen Zivi, "Who or What are We? The Identity Crisis in Feminist Politics," *Polity* 36, no. 2 (January 2004): 323–340.

14. For these critiques see Deborah K. King, "Multiple Jeopardy, Multiple Consciousness: The context of a Black Feminist Ideology," in *Feminist Social Thought: A Reader*, ed. Diana Tietjens Meyers (New York: Routledge, 1997), 219–242; Kimberlé Crenshaw, "Mapping the Margins: Intersectionality, Identity, Politics, and Violence against Women of Color," *Stanford Law Review* 43, no. 6 (1991): 1242–1299; Ange-Marie Hancock, "When Multiplication Doesn't Equal Quick Addition: Examining Intersectionality as a Research Paradigm," *Perspectives on Politics* 5, no. 1 (March 2007): 63–79.

15. Olson, "The Family and the Market" in Smith, 65–89.

16. She is discussing notions of family in the "modern" (roughly 1850s through 1950s) period.

17. See Olson on Blackstone and early notions of the family, 69.

18. Olson, 70–71. There were also some attempts to criminalize domestic abuse in the late 1800s. See Evan Stark, *Coercive Control* (New York: Oxford, 2009), 25–26.

19. Olson, 70.

20. Olson, 70.

21. Olson, 70.

22. Olson, 70.

23. Olson, 70. For example, there is quite a lot of contemporary research (both academic and informal) on the discourse against single mothers, particularly

since the 1990s: Greg Kaufmann, "This Week in Poverty: US Single Mothers—' The Worst Off,'" *The Nation*, December 21, 2012, http://www.thenation.com/ blog/171886/week-poverty-us-single-mothers-worst#; Tonya Janiece Redman, "Negotiating Matriarchy: The Discourse of Single Mothers Taking Care of their Families on Small Incomes," unpublished thesis prepared for the graduate school of the University of Texas at Arlington, December, 2007, http://dspace.uta.edu/bitstream/handle/10106/727/umi-uta-1914. pdf?sequence=1; Cheryl Seelhoff, "The Motherhood Penalty—On Discrimination against Mothers as Mothers," Women's Space website, April 16, 2012, http://womensspace.wordpress.com/2012/04/16/the-motherhood-penalty-on-discrimination-against-mothers-as-mothers/; Karen Zivi, "Contesting Motherhood in the Age of AIDS: Maternal Ideology in the Debate over Mandatory HIV Testing," *Feminist Studies* 31, no. 2 (Summer 2005): 347–374.

24. Tort: civil wrongdoing; not a breach of contract; wrongful or negligent act that results in injury, loss, and so on.
25. Olson, 71.
26. Olson, 71.
27. Olson, 72.
28. Olson, 72. Today, some state and local authorities will accept an affidavit attesting to abuse rather than police reports or medical documentation. However, according to lawyers I have consulted, judges will not consider past history and most do not consider an affidavit sufficient proof of harm even if it is enough documentation to issue a no-contact order. Another difficulty that lawyers have conveyed is that judges in paternity court act far more arbitrarily than they do in divorce court. Anecdotally, lawyers have reported to me that in Chicago, for example, paternity court is racist, biased against single mothers, and class-biased, not to mention heteronormative. The same lawyers have also expressed concern about the "intelligence" of various officers of the court dealing with family cases in paternity court, in contrast to a more adequate system for those who have state-sanctioned heterosexual partnerships. Regarding the refusal of judges to consider any past history of abuse, see Kim Ahearn et al. (also known as "Failure to Protect" Working Group of Child Welfare Committee of New York City Inter-Agency Task Force against Domestic Violence), "Charging Battered Mothers with 'Failure to Protect,' Still Blaming the Victim," *Fordham Urban Law Journal* 27, no. 3 (1999): 849–873. Available at http://ir.lawnet.fordham.edu/cgi/viewcontent.cgi?article=2011& context=ulj; Jennifer Jack, "Note: Child Custody and Domestic Violence Allegations: New York's Approach to Custody Proceedings Involving Intimate Partner Abuse," *Albany Government Law Review* 5 (2012): 885–913. Available at http://www.albanygovernmentlawreview.org/Articles/Vol05_3/5.3.885-Jack.pdf.
29. Olson, 72–73.
30. As she discusses, delegalization views the family in a sort of state of nature and therefore in an arena of "anarchy." Olson, 73.
31. Olson, 73.
32. Olson, 73.
33. Olson, 73.
34. Olson, 73.
35. Olson, 73.
36. Olson, 73.

37. As Stark has put it, these extralegal authorities have not been an extension of the political sphere but instead have replaced it. Stark, *Coercive Control*, 45.
38. See Bumiller for a similar argument. Bumiller, *In an Abusive State: How Neoliberalism Appropriated the Feminist Movement against Sexual Violence*. See my analyses of these changes in Arnold, *America's New Working Class*.
39. As Villalón argues, this coverture is reinforced in immigration law and particularly in the case of immigrant women who are the targets of abuse; see Roberta Villalón, "Passage to Citizenship and the Nuances of Agency: Latina Battered Immigrants," *Women's Studies International Forum* 33 (October 12, 2010): 552–560.
40. See Lundy Bancroft, *When Dad Hurts Mom: Helping Your Children Heal the Wounds of Witnessing Abuse* (New York: Berkley Books, 2004), 240.
41. They are firmly linked de facto: a payer will always have visitation rights unless visits prove not to be in the best interests of the child. Conversely, a relationship with a child does not necessarily establish the right to visitation.
42. Indeed, in my experience in San Antonio, I was repeatedly told things like "We will force him to be a father" and informed that if there was any conflict in a custodial situation, both parties would have to attend co-parenting classes, even when one parent was filling parenthood duties and the other was not. This seemed puzzling to me until I read Anna Marie Smith's work and understood the broader move to the dichotomous notion of fatherhood—he is either a deadbeat or a payer (and therefore a good parent). Anna Marie Smith, *Welfare Reform and Sexual Regulation* (New York: Cambridge University Press, 2007).
43. Bancroft, *When Dad Hurts Mom*, 240.
44. Bancroft, *When Dad Hurts Mom*, 240. See also Kim Ahearn et al., "Charging Battered Mothers with 'Failure to Protect,' Still Blaming the Victim," 862. Unfortunately, in a context in which showing mere interest as a father is being a good father (a development related to the 1996 welfare changes), seeking sole custody appears to be interpreted as being motivated by extreme (positive) interest in a child rather than by revenge or control. Being a good mother or seeking sole custody can be framed as overmothering or simply fraudulent, in contrast. Jennifer Jack quotes Elayne Greenberg, a New York state mediator: "Batterers are statistically more successful than survivors at securing custody of their children"; Jack, "Note: Child Custody and Domestic Violence Allegations: New York's Approach to Custody Proceedings Involving Intimate Partner Abuse," 892.
45. See Smith, *Welfare Reform and Sexual Regulation*; on the father's rights movement, see Susan Bordo, *Unbearable Weight: Feminism, Western Culture, and the Body* (Berkeley: University of California Press, 2004), 88–93.
46. I know this from personal research over the past years, consulting lawyers in Texas and Illinois. Again, while child support and visitation are not supposed to be linked, once a payment history has been established along with regular visitations, considerable harm must be shown to request supervised visitation or to alter the visitation in any way. San Antonio attorney Mark Ilan Unger has been invaluable in explaining these dynamics, but any errors are my own.
47. See Evan Stark, *Coercive Control* (New York: Oxford, 2009), Introduction.
48. Bancroft, *When Dad Hurts Mom*; Bancroft, *Why Does He Do That?*
49. Bancroft, *When Dad Hurts Mom*, 243.

50. See *US v. Morrison* 529 U.S. 598, 120 S. Ct. 1740, 146 L. Ed. 2d 658 (2000), http://www.casebriefs.com/blog/law/constitutional-law/constitutional-law-keyed-to-chemerinsky/the-federal-legislative-power/united-states-v-morrison/ (accessed March 9, 2014).
51. See Stark's introduction on how enforcement is weak to nonexistent, as well as his excellent (but disturbing) conclusion. Stark, *Coercive Control*.
52. Keith Guzik, "The Forces of Conviction: the Power and Practice of Mandatory Prosecution upon Misdemeanor Domestic Battery Suspects," *Law and Social Inquiry* 32, no. 1 (Winter 2007): 41–74.
53. On dual arrest, see Radha Iyengar, "Does the Certainty of Arrest Reduce Domestic Violence? Evidence from Mandatory and Recommended Arrest Laws," *Journal of Public Economics* 93 (2009): 85–98; National Institute of Justice, "Dual Arrest," http://www.nij.gov/publications/dv-dual-arrest-222679/exhibits/Pages/table1.aspx.
54. Guzik, "Forces of Conviction," 43. On the difficulty of getting help for abuse in rural areas—and particularly, calling the police or pressing charges—see Walter DeKeseredy, Martin Schwartz, and Joseph Donnermeyer, *Dangerous Exits: Escaping Abusive Relationships in Rural America* (New Brunswick, NJ: Rutgers University Press, 2009).
55. See Guzik, 49; but in countless texts of feminist jurisprudence, the many-headed hydra argument has been invoked by courts all the way up to the Supreme Court to dismiss gender-bias claims; this is also used in refugee cases—see Sara L. McKinnon, "Positioned In/By the State: Incorporation, Exclusion, and Appropriation of Women's Gender-Based Claims," *Quarterly Journal of Speech* 97, no. 2 (2011): 178–200 regarding one instance of this argument.
56. See Guzik, 49–50.
57. See Guzik's use of this term, 42, 45, 46, 48, 49.
58. Or encouraged, as DeKeseredy et al. find in *Dangerous Exits*.
59. Guzik, 43.
60. See Estrich's analyses of key cases reframing what could be called rape and domestic abuse as "seduction"—particularly in the case of a father and his daughters: *State v. Lester* (a 1984, North Carolina case). Susan Estrich, "Real Rape," in Patricia Smith, *Feminist Jurisprudence* (New York: Oxford University Press, 1993), 169.
61. Regarding the perception by police officers and judges that a no-contact order will inevitably be violated, see Guzik. In fact, the system depends on the abuser violating the order. While this may lead to a minimum of justice, it endangers the target once again.
62. See Jeanne A. Fugate, "Who's Failing Whom? A Critical Look at Failure-To-Protect Laws," *New York University Law Review* 76 (April 2001): 272–308, http://www.thelizlibrary.org/liz/fugate.pdf. On 274, Fugate notes, "In the gender-neutral terms of failure-to-protect statutes, the laws seem to be logical responses to an epidemic of child abuse. But the application of failure-to-protect laws is anything but gender-neutral: Defendants charged and convicted with failure to protect are almost exclusively female." This is because "the overwhelming prevalence of female defendants can be explained best by the higher expectations that women face in the realm of parenting and child care." See also Susan Bordo, "Are Mothers Persons? Reproductive Rights and the Politics of Subject-ivity," *Unbearable Weight*, 71–97.

63. Regarding the US approach to intimate violence—particularly rape—see Estrich, "Real Rape," 163–167. Estrich notes the difficulties in turning to mens rea in the UK, but even given these deficiencies, she advocates its use in the United States. On the other hand, Catharine MacKinnon and Carole Pateman have separately investigated the dangers of using mens rea in rape cases.

64. In contrast to Bumiller, I do not think these two issues always do overlap.

65. Stark, *Coercive Control*, 7.

66. See Mary P. Koss, "Review: [untitled]," *Signs* 24, no. 2 (Winter,1999): 532–535. See 534, in particular.

67. And if a woman is also poor and part of a racial minority or an immigrant, she may be suspicious of police aid or live in a neighborhood in which the police response is not there.

68. I owe this knowledge to discussions with San Antonio family attorney Becky Galván, but any errors are my own. I should also add that it is not easy to gain access to these cases (i.e., to obtain any written record) even when there is a case number. See Stark, *Coercive Control*, 36–37.

69. I have discussed the police response in Chicago extensively with one (former) domestic abuse court advocate from Rogers Park (in the Chicago metropolitan area). When I related to her my general failure to get help from the San Antonio police but argued that perhaps it was because they were not specifically trained in domestic violence, she related that in her years working as an advocate, Chicago police were often no better, and each precinct has an officer specially trained in domestic abuse issues. According to this advocate, unless there is a protective order of some sort, having a trained officer does not make much difference. To point out the obvious, one normally cannot get a protective order without a police report or other documentation and thus a vicious circle is created.

70. See Lundy Bancroft, *Why Does He Do That?* (New York: Berkley Books, 2002).

71. This is against the typical assertion that wealthy or at least insured women can get the sort of counseling that poorer women cannot. The presumption is that therapists know what they are doing and that they understand that this particular issue defies nearly every presupposition of therapy—this is not the case.

72. Interestingly, Boston's Northeastern University Law School has one of the only domestic abuse programs for lawyers in the country but no database of practicing lawyers or information about how to hire any of their graduates.

73. See Kathleen J. Ferraro and Michael P. Johnson, "Research on Domestic Violence in the 1990s: Making Distinctions," *Journal of Marriage and Family* 62, no. 4 (Nov. 2000): 948–963.

74. See, for example, Emily Collins, "Reminiscences of Emily Collins," 421–426.

75. For different historical accounts of abuse in Western/northern literature see two excellent reviews of historical research: Poster, Review: "Domestic Tyranny . . ." 216–219; Clark, "Domestic Violence, Past and Present," 193–202; and more generally, Waits, "The Criminal Justice System's Response to Battering," 188–206.

76. Even Lisa Brush—whose work is some of the best contemporary scholarship on domestic abuse—has argued that targets are "traditional" and thus failed feminists: "Women are endorsing their own subordination when they conform to normative femininity, especially when they affirm normative femininity by suffering men's conformity to hegemonic masculinity. Men are enforcing their

own dominance when they conform to hegemonic masculinity, especially when they reinforce hegemonic masculinity by policing women's conformity to normative femininity." Lisa D. Brush, "Philosophical and Political Issues in Research on Women's Violence and Aggression," *Sex Roles* 52, nos. 11/12 (June 2005): 870.

77. Thus, I do not agree with either Linda Mills or Kristin Bumiller—granted that their work is very different—for their blame on feminists for the issues targets of abuse face today, including inadequate shelters and weak enforcement. Linda G. Mills, *Violent Partners: A Breakthrough Plan for Ending the Cycle of Abuse* (New York: Basic Books, 2008); Bumiller, *In an Abusive State*. See Stark's account of these historical changes, *Coercive Control*, 24–25.

78. See Stark, *Coercive Control*, Introduction. As I state elsewhere in this text, I do not want to whitewash this account: while this may have been an ideal moment in shelter history, there was little to no policy protecting targets from abusers and there were very few shelters. See also Felter, "A History of the State's Response to Domestic Violence."

79. "Something Andrea Westlund argues is a "good" form of disciplinary power because abused women need empowerment, protection, and guidance. "In spite of the problems with modern legal and medical institutions, the importance of establishing physical safety and security, as a first measure, cannot be overemphasized." By resorting to subsistence-level reasoning—physical security, mere life—she accepts the status quo rather than challenging it and proceeds to argue that the usual solutions—shelters, protective orders, and jail sentences for batterers—will liberate women. Andrea C. Westlund, "Pre-Modern and Modern Power: Foucault and the Case of Domestic Violence," *Signs* 24, no. 4, Institutions, Regulation and Social Control (Summer 1999), 1054, 1055.

80. Stark, *Coercive Control*, Introduction regarding this history and his arguments about the conservative appropriation of this issue.

81. See Kathleen R. Arnold, "Homelessness and Drag," in *Professional Lives, Personal Struggles: Ethics and Advocacy in Research on Homelessness*, eds. Martha Trenna Valado and Randall Amster (Lanham, MD: Lexington Books, 2012).

82. Kathleen R. Arnold, *Homelessness, Citizenship, and Identity* (Albany, NY: SUNY Press, 2004).

83. As Westlund herself implies; see Westlund, "Pre-Modern Power," 1056.

84. Granted, I am generalizing; when I was a shelter advocate in Boston, I also heard condescending remarks by staff dealing with the homeless and there are certain institutions that rely on an individual responsibility model. But the broad point is that this system primarily rewarded knowledge and treated the homeless as if they were citizens.

85. Of course there are exemplary shelters; the homeless protest on their own behalf and run their own newspapers; they are not absolute victims.

86. For example, Evan Stark's excellent (Foucaultian) work on these connections has been frequently dismissed as "political." See Koss, "Review: [untitled]," *Signs* 24, 532–535. See also Lisa D. Brush, "Battering and the Poverty Trap," *Journal of Poverty* 8, no. 3 (2004): 23–43.

87. Smith, *Welfare Reform and Sexual Regulation*.

88. See Monica Varsanyi on how these changes affected immigrants at the state and local levels. Monica Varsanyi, "Rescaling the 'Alien,' Rescaling Personhood: Neoliberalism, Immigration, and the State," *Annals of the Association of American Geographers* 98, no. 4 (2008): 877–896.

89. Smith, *Welfare Reform and Sexual Regulation*.
90. Or her rights are subsumed under the father's and even the child's rights. See Susan Bordo, "Are Mothers Persons? Reproductive Rights and the Politics of Subject-ivity," *Unbearable Weight*, 71–97.
91. Smith, 2–5, 17.
92. What this means varies by state. In Texas, it means automatic "joint custody" even though women have far more de facto responsibilities toward children than men do. The observations in this paragraph are deduced from Smith's book as well as my research and experience.
93. To be clear, I am not arguing that motherhood is a burden but that custodial agreements require primary caretakers to not only perform all of the necessary duties of parenting but also, for example, to disseminate the information to the other party. The other party is the recipient of this information (and can endlessly and arbitrarily demand more) and can interfere in the parenting duties (or add to them), but is not required by law to perform the same duties (aside from making payments).
94. Smith, *Welfare Reform and Sexual Regulation*, 130–136.
95. "Unfortunately, the heightened awareness of the harm domestic violence causes children has also resulted in a punitive policy toward battered women in the child welfare system. Increasingly in New York City, abuse and neglect proceedings are brought against battered mothers. Their children are removed from them, and the only allegation is based upon their children's exposure to domestic violence." Ahearn et al., "Charging Battered Mothers with 'Failure to Protect,' Still Blaming the Victim."
96. Lisa Brush's analyses of the connection between the surveillance of abusers, low-tier work under neoliberalism, and punitive welfare measures is broader than Smith's, demonstrating how these three spheres do not merely interact but mutually constitute one another. Brush, *Poverty, Battered Women, and Work in U.S. Welfare Policy*.
97. All of these examples are deduced from my on-the-ground experience with abuse and regular consultation with a wide range of lawyers, counselors, and some therapists, not to mention frequent discussions with the police.
98. See Greg Kaufmann, "This Week in Poverty: US Single Mothers—'The Worst Off,'" *The Nation*, December 21, 2012, http://www.thenation.com/blog/171886/week-poverty-us-single-mothers-worst#; Katie Wright, "5 Things to Know About Single Mothers in Poverty," Center for American Progress, May 11, 2012, http://www.americanprogress.org/issues/poverty/news/2012/05/11/11634/5-things-to-know-about-single-mothers-in-poverty/.
99. Of course, there is also pressure to name the father—at least in my experience, an agent of the state enters the hospital room after the woman gives birth and gives her the paternity forms. No explanation is provided as to the ramifications of signing the paternity papers and of course, having just given birth, the woman is often in a vulnerable state.
100. A fact that Smith denies; see Smith, *Welfare Reform and Sexual Regulation* 5; 81–84; 130–131.
101. Additionally, Lisa Brush has done important empirical work regarding how abusers have attempted to undermine poor women's employment. Brush, "Battering and the Poverty Trap," *Journal of Poverty*. The issues these low-tier workers face are not exclusive to low-tier workers but could affect any single

mother with a full-time job and an abusive partner or former partner. Some issues are failure to show up to pick up children, making the mother late for work or making her miss work, and harassing her while she is at work.

102. See Crenshaw on the unintended consequences of paying too much attention to poorer populations; see Poster also; another way to put the problem is that her intersectional approach is really not intersectional—it privileges class and race; see Crenshaw, "Mapping the Margins"; Poster, Review: "Domestic Tyranny."

103. As I have discussed, Evan Stark combines sophisticated political theory with policy analysis and grassroots experience—and does so in a highly accessible way—but is often dismissed for talking about politics at all. That is, the very fact that he puts domestic violence in a political context has been assailed. For example, see Koss, "Review: [untitled]," *Signs*, 535. Koss argues that a political interpretation of abuse then obfuscates individual psychological factors that helped to create the context for and perpetuate abuse. But one could argue this about nearly any social issue—worker exploitation, homelessness, and immigration, for example—and yet this does not preclude the significance of a political context in which individual factors are disciplined, normalized or assimilated, for example. It is also disturbing that Stark's work, which is so powerful in its adept use of interdisciplinary material, then becomes a site of struggle when he is one of the only authors trying to put this issue in political context.

104. In New York these changes began in 1996, and a key case that began the wave of criminalizing the target of abuse (including the immediate loss of her children with no investigation of circumstances) is a May 1998 case: *In re Lonell J.*; Ahearn et al., "Charging Battered Mothers with 'Failure to Protect,' Still Blaming the Victim."

105. I have written extensively about the feminization of labor and changes in low-tier work under neoliberalism in Kathleen R. Arnold, *America's New Working Class* (College Station, PA: Penn State Press, 2007).

106. In contrast to the pretense of neoconservatism in the past few decades and particularly to family values, it is interesting that state authorities are willing to break apart families in cases of poverty or domestic abuse, or in their treatment of undocumented immigrants or refugees.

107. Another way to put this is through Stark's observation that if there are two victim groups in abuse situations—women and children—child welfare advocates have decided that the best interests of the child can and should be asserted against the mother. Stark, *Coercive Control*, 44. Given this dynamic, I would add that if the abuser is ignored and father's rights are also being promoted, he inadvertently "wins." In *Unbearable Weight*, Susan Bordo also notes that given the backlash against women and the promotion of rights, not to mention continuing material inequalities for women, the stronger party—the father—will be rewarded.

108. On this importance, see Linda Mills, Kristin Bumiller, Patricia Evans, Evan Stark, and Lundy Bancroft; Mills, however, is the only one who advocates the dominant model while also denying that it is dominant. Mills, *Violent Partners*; Bumiller, *In An Abusive State*; Evans, *The Verbally Abusive Relationship*; Stark, *Coercive Control* (particularly 45—his account differs slightly from mine); Bancroft, *Why Does He Do That?*.

109. See Bancroft and how and why this is dominant and why it is damaging to targets of abuse. Bancroft, *Why Does He Do That?*

110. See Anna Marie Smith, *Welfare Reform and Sexual Regulation*. Psychological statistics were then released, arguing for the role of the biological father. News reports that summarized these studies did not contextualize the policy changes that publicized these sorts of claims and suppressed other findings.

111. For an older account of this cycle, see Kathleen Waits, "The Criminal Justice System's Response to Battering" in Patricia Smith, *Feminist Jurisprudence* (New York: Oxford University Press, 1993), 188–206; see also Bumiller, *In An Abusive State*, 68, 70, 84–85.

112. See Bumiller, 84–90; see also Evan Stark on the failure of batterer intervention programs and Lundy Bancroft, who has counseled abusers, in *Why Does He Do That?* xix–xxi, 11–19; Stark, *Coercive Control*, 7, 26. Stark notes on page 7, "Batterer intervention programs (BIPs) are widely offered as an alternative to incarceration. But these programs are little more effective than doing nothing at all. Regardless of intervention, the vast majority of perpetrators continue their abuse."

113. Linda Mills is a key proponent of this developmental claim. Mills, *Violent Partners*.

114. See Bumiller on these assumptions: 84–90.

115. See Pateman on the appearance of contract and consent; Engels; and Olson on these dual truths: asymmetry in the family that is made equal through legal discourse. Carole Pateman, *The Disorder of Women* (Palo Alto, CA: Stanford University Press, 1992); Carole Pateman, *Sexual Contract* (Palo Alto, CA: Stanford University Press, 1988); Friedrich Engels, from *The Origin of the Family*, in *Feminist Papers*, ed. Alice S. Rossi (Boston: Northeastern University Press, 1988), 480–495; Olson, "The Family and the Market."

116. This last point is developed by Bumiller, but I am not sure it is particularly neoliberal in that therapy has its own logic and set of problems that have developed apart from any neoliberal agenda. Bumiller, *In an Abusive State*.

117. Linda Mills holds that this approach is dominant and is splitting families and communities apart. Mills, *Violent Partners*.

118. To provide an example in Chicago: if a target of abuse wants to work with a group like Between Friends or Mujeres Unidas, these groups are low-cost, nonprofit, and combine legal advocacy and counseling in a more Foucaultian manner. In a search for more conventional counseling in Chicago, only two therapists in the city claim to have domestic abuse credentials and both have admitted over the phone that they rarely draw on this expertise. They also warn that if prospective clients have a child and there is any hint of abuse, that they will have to report these fears to child protective services. Aside from these caveats, both therapists also admit that they do not feel comfortable practicing counseling in this area. In contrast to these two, the average therapist suffers more from the Socratic problem—thinking they know what they don't actually know—and will take on a case, thinking that the issue is really low-level conflict and not abuse. Because they are not trained in the sorts of observations that Evans and Bancroft warn about, they do not realize that viewing abuse as symmetrical can (1) lead to the denial that abuse is occurring at all; (2) lead to the advice not to seek legal action because it will only cause conflict (and repeat this message in front of a child, which tells the child that seeking help is the problem and not the abuser; or, if the child is intelligent, the message is that no one gets it and no one is "on our side"); (3) hold that staging an intervention with the abuser is the answer to this

intrafamilial conflict. I derive all of these possibilities from personal experience. In effect, there is no "system"–it is entirely disaggregated, but through its Elmer Fudd–like approach, it can end up retraumatizing targets of asymmetrical relations.

119. Akhil Gupta, *Red Tape: Bureaucracy, Structural Violence, and Poverty in India* (Durham, NC: Duke University Press, 2012). Discussions about unintentional racism are also relevant to these claims; authors like Robert Miles and Tommie Shelby have investigated whether racism from ignorance is still racism. At the very least, the actions, jokes, and assumptions are racist if not the ignorant person.

120. Although not directly related to this discussion, Nancy Luxon's new work on psychoanalysis provides a new lens regarding the therapeutic process: one that is asymmetrical in certain respects but is more dynamic and less wedded to Enlightenment norms. See Nancy Luxon, *Crisis of Authority: Politics, Trust, and Truth-Telling in Freud and Foucault* (New York: Cambridge University Press, 2013).

121. Mills, *Violent Partners*. As some reviewers note, while her claims are interesting, she does not often back them up with statistical evidence.

122. See Bumiller, 85. Bumiller does not account for the individual model of therapy that Mills discusses.

123. David S. Riggs, Marie B. Caulfield, and Amy E. Street, "Risk for Domestic Violence: Factors Associated with Perpetration and Victimization," *Journal of Clinical Psychology* 56, no. 10 (2000): 1289–1316.

124. Bumiller, 82: "The shift toward greater awareness of women battering, with concomitant heightened responsibility of physicians, is unsupported [by the medical field] precisely because it promotes a reinforcement of careful methods of diagnosis and treatment, and implicitly because professionals may actually increase the risk of women's exposure to violence if they fail to contain the rampant spread of this disease." See Bumiller, 80–82. Jacqui True calls it a "pandemic of violence." Jacqui True, *The Political Economy of Violence against Women* (New York: Oxford University Press, 2012).

125. Granted that she conceives of abuse mostly in terms of violence. Westlund, "Pre-modern Power," 1050.

126. Westlund, "Pre-modern Power," 1050.

127. For example, Westlund notes how DSM categories judged "from universalized male norms of independence and self-interest." Westlund, "Pre-modern Power," 1051.

128. Westlund, "Pre-modern Power," 1050.

129. Westlund, "Pre-modern Power," 1051.

130. Westlund, "Pre-modern Power," 1051.

131. See Westlund, "Pre-modern Power," 1057–1059.

132. Westlund, "Pre-modern Power,"1053. "Moreover, the penalties imposed on women who murder or otherwise strike out at their batterers tend to be significantly harsher than those imposed on men who batter and/or kill their partners (Browne 1987, 11), which suggests that it is the women's behavior that is considered to deviate most radically from an enforceable norm." To Westlund, this is a problem of empowerment; Westlund, 1053.

133. Westlund, "Pre-modern Power," 1049. She notes on this page that many women do seek help; that the focus turns to the target, evaluating and diagnosing her weaknesses in order to cure her; and that the police are largely ineffective in aiding in any way.

134. Westlund, "Pre-modern Power," 1052.
135. Evan Stark, "Symposium on Reconceptualizing Violence against Women by Intimate Partners: Critical Issues: Re-Presenting Woman Battering: From Battered Woman Syndrome to Coercive Control" in *Albany Law Review* 58.
136. A term Keith Guzik uses repeatedly, without any explanation or critical reflection, despite his seeming sympathy for targets of abuse. Keith Guzik, "The Forces of Conviction: the Power and Practice of Mandatory Prosecution upon Misdemeanor Domestic Battery Suspects," *Law and Social Inquiry* 32, no. 1 (Winter 2007): 41–74.
137. The latter two issues are critically discussed in Stark's "Symposium on Reconceptualizing Violence against Women by Intimate Partners."
138. Unfortunately evident in three separate incidents in 2014, where urban police have killed two African American men and one boy. The Los Angeles police have been accused of excessive force when dealing with African American suspects and some members of the Chicago police are currently accused of torturing suspects as of this writing (December 2014).
139. The psychoaffective matrix of relations is often acknowledged in the media to some degree—popular terms like PTSD (post-traumatic stress disorder), battered woman syndrome, and Stockholm syndrome are among the labels that are used to describe a situation in which a target comes to feel that the abuser is all-powerful. Hence, according to this logic, even when there is no overt threat of violence in a given moment, these targets would not take a chance to escape the situation in some way. This sort of logic focuses on the pathology of the target and assumes a sort of clear distinction between the act of violence and more "peaceful" time periods.
140. A second, very important issue: in this instance, the "best interests of the child" phraseology really seems like asserting the whims of the father, who is practicing what Evan Stark has called "tangential spouse abuse." Tangential spouse abuse occurs after a breakup, as a means of continuing to control the target, because the abuser has lost other tools of domination. Although there may have been lack of interest in or neglect of the child before the breakup, the abuser suddenly changes tactics and begins threatening to take the child away; using the legal system to gain rights to alienate or remove the child; and using visitation as a time to terrorize the child and the target. Stark, "Symposium on Reconceptualizing Violence against Women by Intimate Partners." See also Ahearn et al.: "Batterers may file custody proceedings against mothers or false reports to [child support services] as methods of continuing to harass and control their partners," 862.
141. See Fugate, "Who's Failing Whom? A Critical Look at Failure-To-Protect Laws": "Although couched in gender-neutral terms, defendants charged with failure to protect are almost exclusively female," 272.
142. Again, see Stark, "Symposium on Reconceptualizing Violence against Women by Intimate Partners."
143. In contrast, see Bumiller, 91, on this issue. She argues that the increasing use of BWS as a defense misses an opportunity to create a "special category of insanity for battered women. In fact, the indicators of battered women's syndrome on the prevailing tool, the DSM (*Diagnostic and Statistical Manual of Mental Disorders*) diagnostic criteria for post-traumatic stress disorders, are the same as the symptoms of schizophrenia and borderline personality disorders." I do not agree with this blanket pathologization and find it to be

pernicious—abusers are the ones we should be focusing on, not the alleged failings of the target.

144. Stark "Symposium on Reconceptualizing Violence against Women by Intimate Partners," 18.
145. See Waits, "The Criminal Justice System's Response to Battering," 195.
146. See Waits, "The Criminal Justice System's Response to Battering" 195.
147. A phrase that is repeated in every conventional account of domestic abuse from the 1980s on.
148. Stark, "Symposium on Reconceptualizing Violence against Women by Intimate Partners."
149. But as it has been pointed out by a discussant at the Midwest Political Science Association (March 2014)—N. Susan Gaines of the University of Leeds—this may be because the woman had to adopt masculine behavior. On this subject, see Joan W. Scott, "Deconstructing Equality-Versus-Difference: Or, the Uses of Poststructuralist Theory for Feminism," in *Feminist Social Thought*, ed. Diana Tietjens Meyers (New York: Routledge, 1997), 758–770.
150. Leigh Goodmark's work on African American women targets of abuse, who can be perceived differently by judges—particularly if they act in self-defense—may challenge Stark's assertions a bit, but his clientele and empirical work have also often tilted toward women who face multiple disadvantages. See Leigh Goodmark, "When Is a Battered Woman Not a Battered Woman? When She Fights Back," *Yale Journal of Law and Feminism* (2008): 76–129.
151. The fact that bullies and abusers attack the weak, the sick, or the socially vulnerable isn't often taken into account when analyzing intimate abuse, even though the dynamics are similar (or the same). The remedy to this triangulation is not to go back to a family model, but obviously an egalitarian model does not work either. Intimate relations cannot be extricated, such that there is some sort of bookkeeping of causal behaviors and harms. What is needed is to recognize that both areas require a model of radical and deep inequality and recognition that bullies and abusers gain quite a lot from their behavior, including social status and inclusion and economic gains. See a discussion of the advantages to bullying in this NPR interview: Jeremy Hobson, "Does Bullying Serve a Purpose?," interview with Elizabeth Englander, author of *Bullying and Cyberbullying: What Every Educator Needs to Know* on *Here and Now*, NPR, November 18, 2013, http://www.capradio.org/news/npr/story?storyid= 246021593.
152. See Wendy Brown, *States of Injury: Power and Freedom in Late Modernity* (Princeton, NJ: Princeton University Press, 1995), in particular, see 102–121.
153. Paul Apostolidis, *Breaks in the Chain: What Immigrants Can Teach America about Democracy* (Minneapolis, MN: University of Minnesota Press, 2010).
154. Brown, *States of Injury*, 66–67.
155. Brown, *States of Injury*, 191.
156. See also Michaele Ferguson's discussion of presidential candidates' appeals to women in the 2012 elections. Michaele Ferguson, "Women Are Not an Interest Group," *Theory & Event* vol. 16, issue 1, 2013, http://muse.jhu.edu/journals/ theory_and_event/v016/16.1.ferguson.html (accessed March 9, 2014).
157. Brown, *States of Injury*, 194.
158. And both are arguably rooted in essentializing identity.
159. See Ferguson on this appropriation. Ferguson, "Women Are Not an Interest Group,"

160. See Michaele Ferguson, "Feminism and Security Rhetoric in the Post–September 11 Bush Administration," in *W Stands for Women: How the George Bush Presidency Shaped a New Politics of Gender*, eds. Michaele L. Ferguson and Lori Jo Marso (Durham, NC: Duke University Press, 2007), 191–220.

161. John Stewart's exposure of the contractual agreement of Halliburton employees not to sue the company when they are gang-raped in the Middle East is a brilliant illustration of these private and yet contractual (legally based) dynamics of gender appropriation. See John Stewart "Rape Nuts," Daily Show website, http://www.thedailyshow.com/watch/wed-october-14-2009/rape-nuts (accessed March 9, 2014).

162. Bonnie Honig, *Democracy and the Foreigner* (Princeton, NJ: Princeton University Press, 2001), 68–71.

163. Interestingly, Andrea Westlund recognizes these issues and accepts them by claiming that they involve a form of "good" discipline: "Consider, for example, the fact that the typical domestic violence shelter is itself an environment of high surveillance and discipline: when a woman moves into a shelter, any disallowed habits (drugs, alcohol) are curtailed, and she is expected to follow timetables and respect curfews, to leave her medications under staff supervision, to carry out a regimen of assigned chores, and to abide by a list of fairly strict rules of conduct. Striking or threatening one's children, other residents, or shelter workers is strictly forbidden, and one may not leave one's children unattended at any time. Each resident is typically expected to attend daily house meetings and to meet regularly with an advocate who will track her progress and subject her plans to surveillance." Westlund, "Pre-modern Power," 1056.

164. This empathy was not shown for Janay Rice, wife of Baltimore Ravens football player Ray Rice. Instead, she has been viewed as having Stockholm syndrome—completely duped in the face of outright violence. Kay Nolan, "NFL Domestic Violence Policy Matters to More Than Just Football Wives," *Christian Science Monitor*, December 11, 2014, http://www.csmonitor.com/USA/Society/2014/1211/NFL-domestic-violence-policy-matters-to-more-than-just-football-wives-video.

165. I use gendered pronouns for two reasons: first, this project aims at exploring women's political status today, and second, nearly all empirical studies show that domestic abuse and assault overwhelmingly happens along gendered lines in heterosexual relationships, even if it also occurs in nonheterosexual partnerships. This is not to deny the importance of these intimate configurations but to limit the subject matter to the broader goal of understanding the gendered nature of citizenship in the contemporary United States.

166. A legal term frequently used in child custody cases, even when abuse has been demonstrated.

167. The crisis in male power has been declared since the 1990s—often self-evidently (i.e., without empirical proof of actual losses in wages, political office and so on) by authors ranging from Harvey Mansfield and Frances Fukuyama to authors on the left, such as Wendy Brown, *States of Injury*, 87–88, 92. See Drucilla Cornell's discussion of this criticism and her own argument that MacKinnon needs to positively affirm femininity: "Sexual Difference, the Feminine, and Equivalency," 2273. To Stark, quite a lot of the reason that the domestic violence revolution has faltered was because of the rise of (neo)conservatism, men's groups, conservative religious groups, and conservative

"feminists." To the degree that the latter group has criticized "mainstream feminists" but particularly radical feminists like MacKinnon "for exaggerating the extent and severity of male violence, portraying women primarily as victims, and relying on state interventions, which are as likely to hurt as help women," they may be correct. Stark, 9. Susan Bordo's analysis of this crisis and the consequent backlash against feminism is perhaps the best in terms of its accuracy. See Bordo, *Unbearable Weight*, 163; 166–167; 177–178; 241–242.

168. See Kathleen J. Ferraro and Michael P. Johnson, "Research on Domestic Violence in the 1990s: Making Distinctions," *Journal of Marriage and Family* 62, no. 4 (Nov. 2000): 948–963; Nancy Berns, "'My Problem and How I Solved It': Domestic Violence in Women's Magazines," *The Sociological Quarterly* 40, no. 1 (Winter 1999): 85–108.

169. A term Mark Poster rightly advocates for in analyzing intimate abuse. Poster, Review: "Domestic Tyranny: The Making of American Social . . ." 216–219.

170. As Melissa Murphy, a former legal advocate for abused women with Rogers Park Community Council in Chicago indicated (e.g., regarding certain police precincts in Chicago as well as a particular judge, who was trained in domestic abuse but has had several complaints filed against her. The judge has now been removed to the northern suburbs and lawyers avoid her court when possible). Personal interview, 2012.

171. Micro-practices: keeping logs, photographing texts, taping conversations (where legal), and so on; never meeting the abuser in a private place; and continuing to search for help and legal advice that are truly constructive. Like other legal problems in which the law itself constitutes the basis of inequality, micropractices and resistance will be long-term.

CHAPTER 3

1. I will use the technically correct term *asylum* when discussing these cases specifically and use the term *refugees* in more generalized statements, noting that anyone applying for humanitarian relief in the United States is in fact an asylum-seeker.

2. Or the "many-headed hydra" argument that seems ubiquitous in race and gender cases in the United States, as if there were infinite variations on these identities in the US context. This fear is raised in *US v. Morrison* 529 U.S. 598, 120 S. Ct. 1740, 146 L. Ed. 2d 658 (2000), http://www.casebriefs.com/blog/law/constitutional-law/constitutional-law-keyed-to-chemerinsky/the-federal-legislative-power/united-states-v-morrison/ (accessed March 9, 2014).

3. See "A Haven for Abused Women," *The New York Times*, April 29, 2004, A26.

4. Sara McKinnon argues that the United States accepts refugee claims from countries that are viewed as entirely foreign or distant (traditional, primitive) but rejects claims from Guatemala because it is a country whose history and culture are bound up with the United States. Sara L. McKinnon, "Positioned In/By the State: Incorporation, Exclusion, and Appropriation of Women's Gender-Based Claims," *Quarterly Journal of Speech* 97, no. 2 (2011): 178–200. See also Eleanor Acer, Tara Magner, "Restoring America's Commitment to Refugees and Humanitarian Commitment," *Georgetown Immigration Law Journal* 27 (Spring 2013): 445–484.

5. Granted in a limited and spectacular way.

6. Habermas's theories are relatively blind to gender inequality while Foucault's theories are more open to critiquing and analyzing gender hierarchies,

discerning underlying inequalities in facially neutral discourses, and accounting for violence even in the most rational power arrangements, as Nancy Fraser and Seyla Benhabib have discussed in numerous works for over a decade.

7. As Wendy Brown discusses in "Where Is the Sex in Political Theory?" *Women & Politics* 7 (Spring 1987): 3–24.

8. See Lundy Bancroft, *Why Does He Do That?* (New York: Berkley Books, 2002); Evan Stark, *Coercive Control* (New York: Oxford, 2009).

9. See a discussion of this in Kathleen J. Ferraro and Michael P. Johnson, "Research on Domestic Violence in the 1990s: Making Distinctions," *Journal of Marriage and Family* 62, no. 4 (November 2000), 956.

10. I am not critiquing the survivor literature specific to domestic abuse—particularly in legal theory—but rather the more conventional understanding of becoming a survivor when discussing this issue. See Leigh Goodmark, "When Is a Battered Woman Not a Battered Woman? When She Fights Back," *Yale Journal of Law and Feminism* (2008): 76–129 regarding survivor theory.

11. Kim Ahearn, et al., "Charging Battered Mothers with 'Failure to Protect,' Still Blaming the Victim," *Fordham Urban Law Journal* 27 (February 2000): 849–873, available at http://ir.lawnet.fordham.edu/cgi/viewcontent. cgi?article=2011&context=ulj; Nancy Berns, "'My Problem and How I Solved It': Domestic Violence in Women's Magazines," *The Sociological Quarterly* 40, no. 1 (Winter,1999): 85–108; Luisa Bigornia, "Alternatives to Traditional Criminal Prosecution of Spousal Abuse," *Journal of Contemporary Legal Issues* 11 (2000); Camille Carey, "Correcting Myopia in Domestic Violence Advocacy: Moving Forward in Lawyering and Law School Clinics," *Columbia Journal of Gender and Law* 21 (2011): 220–282. Available at http://papers.ssrn.com/sol3/ papers.cfm?abstract_id=1,809,979; Therese A. Clarke, "Why Won't Someone Help Me? The Unspeakable Epidemic of Domestic Violence: An Annotated Bibliography," *Northern Illinois Law Review* 23 (Summer 2003): 529–580; Kimberlé Crenshaw, "Mapping the Margins: Intersectionality, Identity, Politics, and Violence against Women of Color," *Stanford Law Review* 43, no. 6 (1991): 1242–1265; Phyllis B. Frank, Gail K. Golden, "When 50-50 Isn't Fair: The Case against Couple Counseling in Domestic Abuse," Op-Ed in *Social Work* 39 no. 6 (November 1994), 636–637; Amy Goodman et al., "A Look Inside US Immigration Prisons," *Democracy Now!* May 4, 2006, http://www.democracynow. org/2006/5/4/a_look_inside_u_s_immigration; Jennifer Jack, "Note: Child Custody and Domestic Violence Allegations: New York's Approach to Custody Proceedings Involving Intimate Partner Abuse," *Albany Government Law Review* 5 (2012): 885–913. Available at http://www.albanygovernmentlawreview.org/Articles/Vol05_3/5.3.885-Jack.pdf; Susan Lloyd, "The Effect of Domestic Violence on Women's Employment," *Law & Policy* 19, no. 2 (April 1997): 139–167; Mark Poster, Review: "Domestic Tyranny: The Making of American Social Policy against Family Violence from Colonial Times to the Present" by Elizabeth H. Pleck, *Signs* 14, no. 1 (Autumn 1988): 216–219.

12. To be clear, not all of these policies are to solve the problem of domestic abuse but are often mandated in the case of separation and child custody issues—even when one partner alleges that the other is an abuser. Other programs—such as couples counseling, anger management, parenting classes (which are often ordered by judges when one party alleges neglect or alienation and which must be attended by both parents), and abusers programs—are purportedly for couples with a history of abuse. Most studies find that these

programs do not merely ignore the reality of abuse but make circumstances worse for the target, even if she has left the abuser. See Lundy Bancroft's popular and academic work as well as Evan Stark's work on this subject.

13. Habermas does discuss domestic abuse as an example of feminist discourse, but his analysis is not particularly complex. See Jürgen Habermas, *Between Facts and Norms* (Polity Press/Oxford, 1996), 312–314; 420. For a more in-depth Habermasian account of current power dynamics regarding the issue of domestic abuse, see Philip Rossiter, "A Thorn in the Flesh That Cannot Fester: Habermas, the Duluth Model, Domestic Violence Programmes," *Waikato Law Review* 19, no. 2 (2011): 196–206 as well as the Habermasian account of domestic violence in the conclusion to the excellent book: Nancy Meyer Emerick, *The Violence Against Women Act of 1994: An Analysis of Intent and Perception* (Westport, CT: Praeger Publishers, 2001).

14. See Jürgen Habermas, *Theory of Communicative Action* vol. 1, ed. Thomas McCarthy (Boston: Beacon Press, 1985), 44.

15. See, for example, Bancroft, *Why Does He Do That?*; Bigornia, "Alternatives to Traditional Criminal Prosecution of Spousal Abuse"; Frank and Golden, "When 50-50 Isn't Fair: The Case against Couple Counseling . . ."; Jennifer Jack, "Note: Child Custody and Domestic Violence Allegations: New York's Approach to Custody Proceedings Involving Intimate Partner Abuse"; Andrea C. Westlund, "Pre-Modern and Modern Power: Foucault and the Case of Domestic Violence," *Signs* 24, no. 4, Institutions, Regulation and Social Control (Summer 1999): 1045–1066 (although I cite Westlund with some reservations).

16. On the undertheorization of violence in Foucault's notion of biopower, see Akhil Gupta, *Red Tape: Bureaucracy, Structural Violence, and Poverty in India* (Durham, NC: Duke University Press, 2012), particularly 16–17.

17. See Eric Bugyis, "Towards a Rational Critique of Violence: Beyond Habermas's Semantic Genealogy and Girard's Mimetic Anthropology," conference paper presented at 2010 Colloquium on Violence and Religion, Girard and Post-Structural Thought panel, http://transformingviolence.nd.edu/assets/26475/bugyis_paper.pdf.

18. Something Foucault suggests in *The Birth of BioPolitics; Lectures at the Collège de France, 1978–1979*, ed. Michel Senellart, trans. Graham Burchell (New York: Picador/Palgrave MacMillan 2004).

19. Paul Apostolidis, *Breaks in the Chain: What Immigrants Can Teach America about Democracy* (University of Minnesota Press, 2010); Zygmunt Bauman, *Globalization* (New York: Columbia University Press, 1998); Anna Marie Smith, *Welfare Reform and Sexual Regulation* (New York: Cambridge University Press, 2007).

20. Which, unfortunately, Westlund does and in a way that ends up pathologizing and infantilizing domestic abuse targets. Westlund, "Pre-Modern and Modern Power."

21. I am referring, in particular, to Hannah Arendt *The Origins of Totalitarianism* (New York: Harcourt Brace Jovanovich, 1979), Chapter 9 ("The Decline of the Nation-State and the End of the Rights of Man").

22. Westlund, "Pre-Modern Power."

23. Stark, *Coercive Control*; see Westlund on DSM categories that classify victims of abuse but not abusers.

24. For example, see Linda Foley, "Teacher Loses Job after Reporting Being a Domestic Violence Victim," examiner.com, June 12, 2013, http://www.examiner.com/article/teacher-loses-job-after-reporting-being-a-domestic-violence-victim.

Some states are considering legislation to protect individuals who have been classified as victims from job loss.

25. See Smith, *Welfare Reform*; Jennifer Jack, "Note: Child Custody and Domestic Violence Allegations"; Ahearn et al., "Charging Battered Mothers with 'Failure to Protect.'"

26. I have realized this when I have called the police myself. While the police could make some sort of classist-racist judgment based on one's neighborhood, other factors are undetermined. To put it differently, when I called the police in one particularly dire circumstance—my ex-boyfriend had broken into my condo and held my daughter and I there against our will for roughly half an hour—the police appeared at my door, refused to take a report at first and kept saying they could not "solve my personal problems." I was calm during this conversation; my ex-boyfriend had already left after I called 911 but the police officers saw me as an inherently hysterical caller and not a well-educated rational citizen. They finally did give me a case number, but only upon my insistence.

27. See Gupta, *Red Tape: Bureaucracy, Structural Violence, and Poverty in India*. Gupta's problematization of, for example, the record taking and government statistics of Indian bureaucrats is an interesting twist to Foucault's notions of disciplinary and bio-power.

28. It is important to note that most judges will not consider prior activity when judging a particular instance of domestic violence and particularly when considering a woman's self-defense or even murder of her abuser. See Stark, *Coercive Control*, 10: "*Courts treat each abuse incident they see as a first offense.* Because well over 95% of these incidents are minor, no one goes to jail." (my emphasis) See also Angela Campbell, "The Admissibility of Evidence of Animal Abuse in Criminal Trials for Children and Domestic Abuse," *Boston College Law Review* 43, no. 2, issue 2 (March 2002): 463–486. Available at http://lawdigitalcommons.bc.edu/cgi/viewcontent.cgi?article=2202&context=bclr, which also discusses the dangers of not allowing prior evidence of cruelty and abuse in current cases.

29. Similarly, see Linda Zerilli: "Whether we judge any particular feminist community or idea of 'women' to be legitimate in democratic terms will turn on its availability for questioning. But there is no neutral place from which we could so judge. The idea that a formal procedure could provide the guarantee of equal access to any debate about who is included in the feminist community, as advocates of Habermas's discourse ethics suggest, does not adequately address the question of what such access can mean if a certain version of the community is more or less invulnerable to question, or if the kind of questioning that can occur must remain within the parameters of what constitutes a certain definition of 'women.'" Linda M. G. Zerilli, *Feminism and the Abyss of Freedom* (Chicago: University of Chicago Press, 2005), 176–177.

30. On modifying Habermas's work to fit analyses of sexism and women's groups, see Nancy Fraser, "What's Critical about Critical Theory? The Case of Habermas and Gender," *New German Critique* 35 Special Issue on Jürgen Habermas (Spring–Summer 1985): 119. On a Habermasian interpretation of changes that need to be made to the domestic abuse system (granted that the subject is New Zealand and not the United States), see Rossiter, "A Thorn in the Flesh That Cannot Fester: Habermas, the Duluth Model, Domestic Violence Programmes."

31. Giorgio Agamben, *Homo Sacer: Sovereign Power and Bare Life*, trans. Daniel Heller-Roazen (Palo Alto, CA: Stanford University Press, 1998), 148.

32. The two cases that are considered precedents to the decisions issued in the *Matter of RA* are (1) *Matter of Acosta* (1985), which establishes that sex is an immutable characteristic and (2) *Matter of Kasinga* (1996), which, among other factors in this case, helped to establish sex as immutable. As Karen Musalo, the lead counsel in these cases, notes, the United Nations has issued commentary on gender as compatible with asylum claims based on persecution and so the United States' continuing hesitancy to grant asylum in these cases is not due to ambiguous language or because of a lack of precedents. Karen Musalo, "A Short History of Gender Asylum in the United States: Resistance and Ambivalence May Very Slowly Be Inching Towards Recognition of Women's Claims," *Refugee Survey Quarterly* 29, no. 2 (2010, UNHCR), http://cgrs.uchastings.edu/sites/default/files/short_history_of_gender_asylum_Musalo_2010_0.pdf.

33. Something that domestic abuse expert Lundy Bancroft has noted is rare—at least in the United States—where abusers lead more of a double life; regardless, the transition from private to public abuse is a significant escalation according to Bancroft. Lundy Bancroft, *Why Does He Do That?* (New York: Berkley Books, 2002). Nevertheless, according to Musalo and other experts she cites, Guatemalan society is more open in its support of wife abuse; see Karen Musalo, "Brief on Behalf of Rodi Alvarado Peña to the Attorney General of the United States (to: United States Department of Justice Attorney General John Ashcroft)," Hastings College of Law, University of California, 2004, http://cgrs.uchastings.edu/documents/legal/ra_brief_final.pdf, p 20.

34. Musalo, "Brief on Behalf of Rodi Alvarado Peña," 18.

35. Musalo, "Brief on Behalf of Rodi Alvarado Peña," 6.

36. Musalo, "Brief on Behalf of Rodi Alvarado Peña," 1.

37. On this difficulty, see Kathryn Libal and Serena Parekh, "Reframing Violence against Women as a Human Rights Violation: Evan Stark's *Coercive Control*" *Violence against Women* 15 n12 (October 15, 2007): 1477–1489. As the authors note regarding government inaction, "The legal precedent often cited for this view of responsibility is the Inter-American Court of Human Rights' 1989 decision on *Velasquez Rodriguez v. Honduras*." The decision held that the Honduran government was responsible for politically motivated disappearances that were not overtly carried out by government officials, 1482.

38. Carole Pateman, *The Disorder of Women* (Palo Alto, CA: Stanford University Press, 1992); Carole Pateman, *The Sexual Contract* (Palo Alto, CA: Stanford University Press, 1988).

39. Musalo, "Brief on Behalf of Rodi Alvarado Peña," 4–8, 6 in particular; see also 14–16. Wendy Brown adds to this discussion, noting that even with nontraditional partnerships, the "contract" is still invoked at these moments. Wendy Brown, *States of Injury: Power and Freedom in Late Modernity* (Princeton, NJ: Princeton University Press, 1995). As Roberta Villalón argues, there are elements of coverture in our immigration system when dealing with immigrant women who have suffered partner abuse. See Roberta Villalón, "Passage to Citizenship and the Nuances of Agency: Latina Battered Immigrants," *Women's Studies International Forum* 33 (October 12, 2010): 552–560.

40. Musalo, "Brief on Behalf of Rodi Alvarado Peña," 7.

41. UN Commission on HR, 52nd Session, Item 9 (a) of Provisional Agenda, *1996 Report of the Special Rapporteur on Violence against Women, Its Causes and*

Consequences, Resolution 1995/85, E/CN.4/1996/53 (1996)–14, section 50—regarding domestic violence as a form of torture, cited in Musalo, 10 n11. See Jacqui True's discussion of the United Nations' efforts regarding domestic abuse, as well as her criticisms and suggestions for what they need to do in the future: Jacqui True, *The Political Economy of Violence against Women* (New York: Oxford University Press, 2012).

42. Musalo, "Brief on Behalf of Rodi Alvarado Peña," 9.

43. Musalo, "Brief on Behalf of Rodi Alvarado Peña," 1.

44. On changes in the asylum system, particularly as they relate to gender-based claims, see the excellent article by Eleanor Acer and Tara Magner, "Restoring America's Commitment to Refugees and Humanitarian Commitment," *Georgetown Immigration Law Journal* 27 (Spring 2013): 445–484.

45. See Emily Rene Smith, "Putting Down Roots: A Case Study of the Participation of Somali Bantu Refugees in the Global Gardens Refugee Farming Project in Boise, Idaho," unpublished thesis submitted to the department of international studies and the graduate school of the University of Oregon, 2011. Unfortunately, as of this writing, the Board of Immigration Appeals (BIA) has just reversed its position on these criteria, although this reversal is not absolute. See also Ashley Huebner and Lisa Koop, "New BIA Decisions Undermine US Obligations to Protect Asylum Seekers," National Immigrant Justice Center (A Heartland Alliance Program), February 18, 2014, https://www.immigrantjustice.org/litigation/blog/new-bia-decisions-undermine-us-obligations-protect-asylum-seekers#.UyWUqs6a-Ck (accessed March 16, 2014). This article also explains the history of these claims in far more detail than I am doing here. The Obama Administration must still issue rules that will guide future decisions in gender-based claims.

46. On the legal basis of these cases, see Karen Musalo, "A Short History of Gender Asylum in the United States: Resistance and Ambivalence May Very Slowly be Inching Towards Recognition of Women's Claims," *Refugee Survey Quarterly* 29, no. 2 (2010, UNHCR), http://cgrs.uchastings.edu/sites/default/files/short_history_of_gender_asylum_Musalo_2010_0.pdf.

47. The immutability requirement was first established by the Board of Immigration Appeals, *In the Matter of Acosta*, in 1985. See Blaine Bookey "Gender-Based Asylum: Considering Protection in the Form of Asylum for Immigrant Survivors of Domestic Violence," presentation for Pathways to Justice Conference: Immigration and Family Law Issues for Domestic Violence Victims, n.d., www.calegaladvocates.org/library/attachment.216999.

48. Musalo, "Brief on Behalf of Rodi Alvarado Peña," 12: "In its seminal *Acosta* decision, the BIA ruled that for the particular social group ground to be interpreted consistently with the other statutory grounds, the defining characteristics of the group must be either immutable or fundamental"; see also Musalo brief, 13.

49. Musalo, "Brief on Behalf of Rodi Alvarado Peña," 16–17.

50. Musalo, "Brief on Behalf of Rodi Alvarado Peña," 17.

51. I am using the passive voice because RA's brief is the product of multiple collaborators.

52. From Rhonda Copelon, "Recognizing the Egregious in the Everyday: Domestic Violence as Torture," *Columbia Human Rights Law Review* 25 (1994), Musalo's emphasis; cited in Musalo, "Brief on Behalf of Rodi Alvarado Peña," 18.

53. Copelon, 304, cited in Musalo, "Brief on Behalf of Rodi Alvarado Peña," 18.

54. Copelon, 303 n 29, cited in Musalo, "Brief on Behalf of Rodi Alvarado Peña," 18.
55. From Dorothy Q. Thomas and Michele E. Beasley, "Domestic Violence as a Human Rights Issue," *Albany Law Review* 58 (1995), Musalo's emphasis, cited in Musalo, "Brief on Behalf of Rodi Alvarado Peña,"18.
56. Musalo, "Brief on Behalf of Rodi Alvarado Peña," 19, n33.
57. Catharine MacKinnon, "Feminism, Marxism, Method, and the State: An Agenda for Theory," in *Feminist Social Thought: A Reader*, ed. Diana Tietjens Meyers (New York: Routledge, 1997), 74. I interpret this quote as being oriented in praxis rather than privileging epistemology. On the difficulty of epistemology-based feminism, see Zerilli, *Feminism and the Abyss of Freedom*.
58. Musalo, "Brief on Behalf of Rodi Alvarado Peña," 22.
59. Musalo, "Brief on Behalf of Rodi Alvarado Peña," 23.
60. Musalo, "Brief on Behalf of Rodi Alvarado Peña," 28; that is, the time immediately after leaving the abuser. See also Walter DeKeseredy, Martin Schwartz, and Joseph Donnermeyer, *Dangerous Exits: Escaping Abusive Relationships in Rural America* (New Brunswick, NJ: Rutgers University Press, 2009).
61. Musalo, "Brief on Behalf of Rodi Alvarado Peña," 21.
62. Musalo, "Brief on Behalf of Rodi Alvarado Peña," 21.
63. See Loren G. Stewart, "Pointing Towards Clarity Or Missing the Point? A Critique of the Proposed 'Social Group' rule and Its Impact on Gender-Based Political Asylum," *Journal of Law and Social Change* 8 (2005): 37–62, https://www.law.upenn.edu/journals/jlasc/articles/volume8/issue1/Stewart8U.Pa.J.L.&Soc.Change37(2005).pdf. See also Jessica Marsden, "Domestic Violence Asylum After *Matter of L-R-*" *Yale Law Journal* 123, no. 7 (May 2014), http://www.yalelawjournal.org/article/domestic-violence-asylum-after-matter-of-l-r.
64. These cases are not based on precedent, even if there have been some arguments that even "discretion" must abide by some guidelines. On the issues of deciding cases on "mercy" or "grace," see Daniel Kanstroom, *Deportation Nation* (Cambridge, MA: Harvard University Press, 2007), 236–240.
65. See Department of Homeland Security, "In the Matter of ___," United States Department of Justice Executive Office for Immigration Review, Board of Immigration Appeals, Falls Church, Virginia, April 13, 2009, http://graphics8.nytimes.com/packages/pdf/us/20090716-asylum-brief.pdf; Center for Gender and Refugee Studies c, "Matter of L.R.," University of California Hastings Center for Gender and Refugee Studies website, n.d., http://cgrs.uchastings.edu/campaigns/Matter%20of%20LR.php.
66. Center for Gender and Refugee Studies c, "Matter of L.R."
67. Center for Gender and Refugee Studies c, "Matter of L.R."
68. Note: today, there are proposals to make the asylum deadline five years or to eradicate the deadline because one year is considered unrealistic. The current comprehensive immigration reform bill has contained language that would eliminate the deadline altogether. For a very important analysis of the effects of the deadline—which was established in 1996—see Philip G. Schrag, Andrew Schoenholtz, Jaya Ramji-Nogales, and James P. Dombach, "Rejecting Refugees: Homeland Security's Administration of the One-Year Bar to Asylum," *William and Mary Law Review* 52, no. 3 (2010): 651–804.
69. See Department of Homeland Security, "In the Matter of ___," although references about this concern refer to the previous administration (i.e. pre-Obama).

70. Center for Gender and Refugee Studies c.
71. Center for Gender and Refugee Studies c.
72. Center for Gender and Refugee Studies c.
73. Center for Gender and Refugee Studies c. My emphasis.
74. Granted that Jessica Marsden convincingly argues that there is a difference between violence on account of gender versus gendered violence. In LR's case, both conditions were satisfied (so to speak). See Marsden, "Domestic Violence Asylum after *Matter of L-R-*."
75. See Evan Stark on "tangential spouse abuse," which involves a man's use of children to retaliate against his partner/target, particularly when she is trying to leave the relationship: Evan Stark, "Symposium on Reconceptualizing Violence against Women by Intimate Partners: Critical Issues: Re-Presenting Woman Battering: From Battered Woman Syndrome to Coercive Control," *Albany Law Review* 58 (Spring 1995): 973–1026; See also Lundy Bancroft on traumatic bonding and on how male abusers often try to alienate children's affections from the mother or emotionally and physically abuse children to indirectly harm the mother: Lundy Bancroft, *When Dad Hurts Mom: Helping Your Children Heal the Wounds of Witnessing Abuse* (New York: Berkley Books, 2004).
76. Again: Department of Homeland Security, "In the Matter of ___," United States Department of Justice Executive Office for Immigration Review, Board of Immigration Appeals, Falls Church, Virginia, April 13, 2009.
77. Center for Gender and Refugee Studies c.
78. Center for Gender and Refugee Studies c.
79. The San Francisco office is known to be one of the best in the country, in part because of the strength of the area's bar association, civil society groups, and immigration judges. See Philip G. Schrag, Andrew Schoenholtz, Jaya Ramji-Nogales, and James P. Dombach, "Rejecting Refugees: Homeland Security's Administration of the One-Year Bar to Asylum," *William and Mary Law Review* 52, no. 3 (2010): 651–804.
80. For details on the asylum and U visa processes, see Roberta Villalón, "Passage to Citizenship and the Nuances of Agency: Latina Battered Immigrants," *Women's Studies International Forum* 33 (October 12, 2010): 552–560.
81. On recent changes at the BIA (i.e., after September 11, 2001), see Andrew I. Schoenholtz, "Refugee Protection in the United States Post–September 11," *Columbia Human Rights Law Review* 36, no. 2 (2005): 323–364.
82. See Schrag et al., "Rejecting Refugees."
83. Until 2014, again see Huebner and Koop, "New BIA Decisions Undermine US Obligations to Protect Asylum Seekers."
84. "A Haven for Abused Women," *The New York Times*, April 29, 2004, A26.
85. Bancroft, *Why Does He Do That?*; Stark, *Coercive Control*; Patricia Evans, *The Verbally Abusive Relationship*, 2nd ed. (Avon, MA: Adams Media Corporation, 1996); see Catharine MacKinnon's work on gender violence more generally. These gender inequities broadly structure women's continued inequality in a number of different spheres but also reflect vast differences in who commits domestic abuse. Despite some assertions of gender parity or symmetry in intimate violence—mostly based on the work of Linda Steinmetz and now Linda Mills—most scholars and advocates have found these claims to be empirically weak and politically motivated. Suzanne Steinmetz, "The Battered Husband Syndrome," *Victimology* 2 (1978): 499–509; Linda G. Mills, *Violent Partners:*

A Breakthrough Plan for Ending the Cycle of Abuse (New York: Basic Books, 2008); and a critique of these approaches in Jack C. Straton, "The Myth of the 'Battered Husband Syndrome,'" NOMAS (National Organization for Men against Sexism) website, n.d., http://www.nomas.org/node/107 (accessed December 16, 2013).

86. See McKinnon's analysis of the United States' views of Guatemala in determining Alvarado's asylum application. McKinnon, "Positioned In/By the State."

87. See Julietta Hua's interesting analysis of this dynamic in her exploration of 1990–2000 Iranian women's failed applications for asylum in the United States, "Feminism, Asylum, and the Limits of Law," *Law, Culture, and Humanities* 6, no. 3 (October 2010): 375–393. More broadly, see Karen Musalo, "A Short History of Gender Asylum in the United States: Resistance and Ambivalence May Very Slowly Be Inching Towards Recognition of Women's Claims."

88. An insight I picked up from McKinnon, granted she was applying it to Kassindja's case and in contrast to Alvarado's. I should point out that the court misspelled Kassindja's name and her case is *Matter of Kasinga*. McKinnon, "Positioned In/By the State."

89. A term I am borrowing from Hua but using differently. In particular, Hua continues to use the rubric "race" and racialization to understand gender, while I am using her term to indicate something about women and gender as deserving of specificity and attention. Hua, "Feminism, Asylum, and the Limits of Law."

90. See Hua's analysis of this in relation to Iranian women's asylum applications; again, I have borrowed her term. Hua, "Feminism, Asylum and the Limits of Law."

91. Including some scholars' work; alternative shelters; and numerous grassroots advocacy groups.

92. As noted above, elements of coverture are also evident in family-based immigration policies and policies for abused immigrant women when filing for a Violence against Women Act petition or a U visa. Again, see Villalón, "Passage to Citizenship and the Nuances of Agency: Latina Battered Immigrants."

93. What is more, a diagnosis such as this for a US resident can be dangerous, potentially leading to state intervention in a woman's life but not her abuser's. See Stark, *Coercive Control*, and Westlund, "Pre-modern Power," on these diagnoses and regarding the fact that there are no clinical diagnoses for abusive men.

94. The headline regarding Rodi Alvarado's case in 2004: "A Haven for Abused Women," *The New York Times*, April 29, 2004, A26.

95. See Eyal Press, "Family-Leave Values," *New York Times Magazine*, July 29, 2007, http://www.nytimes.com/2007/07/29/magazine/29discrimination-t.html?ref=magazine&_r=0.

96. On the plenary power doctrine, see Monica Varsanyi, "Rescaling the 'Alien,' Rescaling Personhood: Neoliberalism, Immigration, and the State," *Annals of the Association of American Geographers* 98, no. 4 (2008): 877–896; Kanstroom, *Deportation Nation*.

97. And criticized.

98. While documentation about RA does not stress PTSD, she now has permanent medical issues from the abuse (i.e., from being kicked repeatedly in major organs).

99. I am stating this from personal experience as a target but (perhaps obviously) not as an immigrant or refugee. On demands for docile targets, see Villalón.

100. See Stark, *Coercive Control*. As most people know, Alexander was permitted to try her case again in 2013. She is currently on an electronic anklet until her trial in March 2014 (this trial was postponed and a new one is pending). A longer sentence (60 years) is now being suggested.

101. Arendt, *Origins of Totalitarianism*, 269.

102. Bonnie Honig's term (incomplete mourning) *Democracy and the Foreigner* (Princeton, NJ: Princeton University Press, 2001), 67–72.

103. Arendt, *Origins of Totalitarianism*, 293.

104. Arendt, *Origins of Totalitarianism*, 294.

105. Arendt, *Origins of Totalitarianism*, 294.

106. That is, bio-power as a modality of power that increasingly led to the treatment of the population as a species. Massacres were then impersonal and pertained to the hygiene of the population, for example. Michel Foucault, *The History of Sexuality, Volume I: An Introduction*, trans. Robert Hurley (New York: Vintage Books, 1980), conclusion.

107. Arendt, *Origins of Totalitarianism*, 295.

108. Arendt, *Origins of Totalitarianism*, 295–296.

109. Arendt, *Origins of Totalitarianism*, 296.

110. On some of these questions see Zerilli, *Feminism and the Abyss of Freedom*. In particular, see 2–4, 23.

111. Arendt, *Origins of Totalitarianism*, 439.

112. Giorgio Agamben, *Remnants of Auschwitz*, trans. Daniel Heller-Rozen (New York: Zone Books, 1999), 63.

113. Agamben, *Remnants of Auschwitz*, 63.

114. Agamben, *Remnants of Auschwitz*, 64.

115. I am guessing this—neither Appel or Habermas are cited in the bibliography and there are no citations; the only clue is that Agamben refers to "Professor Appel."

116. Agamben, *Remnants of Auschwitz*, 64.

117. Agamben, *Remnants of Auschwitz*, 65.

118. As Zerilli argues, "Whether we judge any particular feminist community or idea of 'women' to be legitimate in democratic terms will turn on its availability for questioning. But there is no neutral place from which we could so judge. The idea that a formal procedure could provide the guarantee of equal access to any debate about who is included in the feminist community, as advocates of Habermas's discourse ethics suggest, does not adequately address the question of what such access can mean if a certain version of the community is more or less invulnerable to question, or if the kind of questioning that can occur must remain within the parameters of what constitutes a certain definition of 'women.'" *Abyss of Freedom*, 176–177.

119. Hannah Arendt, *On Violence* (New York: Harvest Book, Harcourt, Inc., 1969), 12.

120. See Arendt, *On Violence*, 14 n19 regarding Fanon, arguing that he is not an advocate of violence.

121. See Mantena for an interesting discussion of realism in Gandhi's nonviolence. Although she is not addressing the same questions directly, her analysis is certainly complementary to my assertions in this paragraph. Karuna Mantena, "Another Realism: the Politics of Gandhian Nonviolence," *American Political Science Review* 106, no. 2 (May 2012): 455–470.

122. Arendt, *On Violence*, 29–31.

123. Arendt, *On Violence*, 43.

124. Arendt, *On Violence*, 44.

125. Arendt, *On Violence*, 51.

126. Fanon adheres to a stage theory influenced by Marx but also radically revising many of Marx's preconceptions. Violence progresses through stages and eventually is displaced by political consciousness and a postracial power structure. But crude, misguided violence often occurs at first.

127. See Fraser, "What's Critical about Critical Theory? The Case of Habermas and Gender."

128. See Stark, *Coercive Control*, Introduction, but also Nancy Fraser's mental gymnastics in her attempt to reconceive of Habermas's theories in a feminist framework.

129. See my exchange with Paul Apostolidis on this in *Theory and Event*.

130. See Habermas, *Theory of Communicative Action* I, 319–324; Fraser on roles in "What's Critical about Critical Theory?"

131. Fraser, "What's Critical About Critical Theory?" For a slightly different Habermasian interpretations of feminist efforts to make domestic violence a public issue see: Nancy Meyer Emerick, *The Violence Against Women Act of 1994: An Analysis of Intent and Perception* (Westport, CT: Praeger Publishers, 2001), conclusion (pp 101–108); Rossiter, "A Thorn in the Flesh That Cannot Fester: Habermas, the Duluth Model, Domestic Violence Programmes," 198–200; and Emma Mackinnon, "Beyond Recognition: Habermas's 'Constitutional Patriotism' as a Response to Exclusion from the Public Sphere," paper presented at the University of Chicago Political Theory Workshop, November 18, 2013, http://ptw.uchicago.edu/Mackinnon13.pdf.

132. Michael Hardt and Antonio Negri, *Empire* (Cambridge, MA: Harvard University Press, 2000).

133. Although interestingly Zerilli suggests that Butler and her adherents simultaneously reaffirm the importance of identity as a key analytic lens by challenging essentialized notions of "woman" or femininity and reject the feminist project altogether because of this. See Zerilli conclusion,178 specifically. Although I interpret Foucault's work slightly differently than Zerilli, I believe that his focus on power as a relationship and investigation of identities as products of these relations help to draw on Butler's work and yet maintain a focus on power and gender rather than dismissing feminism.

134. But, as Roberta Villalón argues (and I agree), agency does not have to mean resistance. Agency can be compliance and a number of other agentic positions and behaviors.

135. Zerilli concludes something similar: "Whether we judge any particular feminist community or idea of 'women' to be legitimate in democratic terms will turn on its availability for questioning. But there is no neutral place from which we could so judge. The idea that a formal procedure could provide the guarantee of equal access to any debate about who is included in the feminist community, as advocates of Habermas's discourse ethics suggest, does not adequately address the question of what such access can mean if a certain version of the community is more or less invulnerable to question, or if the kind of questioning that can occur must remain within the parameters of what constitutes a certain definition of 'women.'" *Abyss of Freedom*, 176–177.

136. I am referring to Apostolodis's use of Wendy Brown's notion of ressentiment in analyzing immigrant workers who are not merely exploited but often sworn at and violently assaulted. The group that wants state help falls under this rubric, while the grassroots organizers who work outside of the state are not. His analysis shows a preference for the latter group, but I think it is understandable why people who are abused on every level might want help, even if their efforts are met with failure. Paul Apostolidis, *Breaks in the Chain: What Immigrants Can Teach America about Democracy* (University of Minnesota Press, 2010).

137. James C. Scott, "The Analysis of Corruption in Developing Nations," *Comparative Studies in Society and History* 11, no. 3 (June 1969): 315–341.

138. Samuel Huntington, "The Hispanic Challenge," *Foreign Policy*, March/April 2004, http://cyber.law.harvard.edu/blogs/gems/culturalagency1/SamuelHuntingtonTheHispanicC.pdf.

139. See Chavez on these two terms. Leo R. Chavez, *The Latino Threat: Constructing Immigrants, Citizens, and the Nation* (Palo Alto, CA: Stanford University Press, 2008); Leo R. Chavez, "A Glass Half Empty: Latina Reproduction and Public Discourse," *Human Organization* (Summer 2004) 63, no. 2. See also Melissa Wright's analyses in *Disposable Women and Other Myths of Global Capitalism* (New York and London: Routledge, 2006).

140. See Ange-Marie Hancock, "When Multiplication Doesn't Equal Quick Addition: Examining Intersectionality as a Research Paradigm," *Perspectives on Politics* 5, no. 1 (March 2007): 63–79.

141. Something Kimberlé Crenshaw's now famous "Mapping the Margins" effectively does.

142. The first organization that I am basing my analysis on (I cannot reveal the name) continues to work in the Chicago community and receives a mix of federal funds and private grants. The second excellent resource I have based many of my insights on—the domestic violence court advocacy program in Rogers Park Community Council—just lost its funding and was terminated in December, 2014.

143. This is only possible, however, if speech is truly dialogical and not the speech of the supplicant hoping to enter into the community.

CHAPTER 4

1. Following the analysis of Nancy Fraser and Linda J. Nicholson in "Social Criticism without Philosophy: An Encounter between Feminism and Postmodernism," in *Feminist Social Thought: A Reader*, ed. Diana Tietjens Meyers (New York: Routledge, 1997), 132–146.

2. Although some researchers have accepted abusers' arguments that their intense emotions—love—led them to hit their partners, researchers like Patricia Evans, Evan Stark, and Lundy Bancroft, as well as the expert testimony and references in the refugee cases all find the following commonalities of abusers: dehumanization of their targets, which increases over time; a belief that the target is unequal and inferior, including believing the target is "property"; and a belief that the gendered division of labor justifies a mother doing most of the daily work in raising children or managing a household, while the male partner's role (or the masculinized role) is to manage and ultimately decide from a distance.

3. Patricia Evans, *The Verbally Abusive Relationship*, 2nd ed. (Avon, MA: Adams Media Corporation, 1996).

4. For example, reactions to Janay Palmer, then fiancée of NFL player Ray Rice, were rather judgmental when her words and actions did not conform to societal expectations in the summer of 2014. From ignoring the fact that the police arrested her after she was punched and knocked unconscious to disregarding her feelings for Rice, comments posted on popular news sites tended to see her as a duped victim who could leave if she wanted and who could get the protection of the law if she were only strong enough to do so. This is not to say that reactions were unsympathetic but rather that they were not politically astute or democratically supportive—the focus went to Palmer as the mediatrix of abuse. See, for example, Jill Martin and Steve Almasy, "Ray Rice Terminated by Team, Suspended by NFL after New Violent Video," CNN.com, September 16, 2014, http://www.cnn.com/2014/09/08/us/ray-rice-new-video/index.html.

5. Evans, *The Verbally Abusive Relationship*. See, in particular, 29–31.

6. In a domestic abuse workshop I gave at DePaul during the academic year 2013–2014, I asked a student friend to come in and speak to the class about her work as a court advocate. Students were surprised to learn that turning a target's family against her is one of the most common tactics abusers use. They were also surprised to learn that because judges do not consider past incidents of abuse, judges were often swayed by tactics such as these. Another tactic is filing false charges against the target; see Kim Ahearn et al., "Charging Battered Mothers with 'Failure to Protect,' Still Blaming the Victim," *Fordham Urban Law Journal* 27, no. 3 (1999): 849–873, particularly 861–862. Available at http://ir.lawnet.fordham.edu/cgi/viewcontent.cgi?article=2011&context=ulj.

7. See Lundy Bancroft, *Why Does He Do That?* (New York: Berkley Books, 2002), although this is a tactic nearly any domestic abuse target is familiar with.

8. See Jill Elain Hasday, "The Military, Sex, and Extrajudicial Constitutional Change," in *Feminist Legal History: Essays on Women and Law*, eds. Tracy A. Thomas and Tracey Boisseau (New York: NYU Press, 2011), 100–117.

9. This is most grossly exemplified in the Magen Tzedek label, which is a sign that workers—like cage-free chickens—were treated humanely in kosher meat processing. These workers' rights are then contingent on consumer preference rather than truly being rights in any stable or political sense.

10. This is evident in recent Supreme Court decisions that are related to issues in this book—abortion availability and the recent Hobby Lobby decision—even if they do not directly pertain to abuse. These decisions (*Gonzales v. Carhart* 550 US 124 [2007] and *Burwell v. Hobby Lobby* 573 US __ [2014]) are notable for the refusal to recognize empirical and scientific evidence; these cases were instead decided on various iterations of societal feelings (which are not proved either).

11. Alexis de Tocqueville, *Democracy in America*, ed. J. P. Mayer, trans. George Lawrence (New York: Perennial Classics, 2000), 565.

12. I have written about these trends extensively in Kathleen R. Arnold, *America's New Working Class* (College Station, PA: Penn State Press, 2007), exploring the increasingly punitive and individualized discourses regarding sexism, racism, and class bias concurrent with the feminization of labor and the feminization of poverty. Notably, women become key workers under neoliberalism but configured as welfare parasites, affirmative action beneficiaries, and job-stealers.

13. As in Habermas's theory of communicative action. See Jürgen Habermas, *Theory of Communicative Action* vol. 1, ed. Thomas McCarthy (Boston: Beacon Press, 1985); Jürgen Habermas, *Theory of Communicative Action* vol. 2, ed. Thomas McCarthy (Boston: Beacon Press, 1985).
14. As in Ferguson, Missouri, summer 2014.
15. Which the Chicago police have recently been charged with, summer 2014.
16. My analysis owes a deep debt to Patricia Evans's conception of reality I and reality II. Again, reality I is "power over" (31, 34), while reality II is based on mutuality. Patricia Evans, *The Verbally Abusive Relationship*, 2nd ed. (Avon, MA: Adams Media Corporation, 1996).
17. But also owing a debt to the insights of Patricia Evans and Lundy Bancroft that I explore at the beginning of this book.
18. Sigmund Freud, *Civilization and Its Discontents* (New York: Norton, 1961), 79.
19. Freud, *Civilization and Its Discontents*, 78.
20. Freud, *Civilization and Its Discontents*, 81.
21. Freud, *Civilization and Its Discontents*, 81.
22. Including viewing the other partner as equal; ensuring that there is a mutual power dynamic with mutual decisions. Evans is particularly insightful on this point. Evans, *The Verbally Abusive Relationship*.
23. See Lundy Bancroft, *Why Does He Do That?* (New York: Berkley Books, 2002); Evans, *The Verbally Abusive Relationship*.
24. I am putting this together, based on analyses by Evans, Bancroft, and Stark, as well as on personal experience.
25. I am indebted to the work of Evans, Bancroft, and Stark in formulating this idea.
26. See Lisa D. Brush, "Battering and the Poverty Trap," *Journal of Poverty* 8, no. 3 (2004): 23–43.
27. As Lundy Bancroft notes, even when an abuser cries, says he is sorry, or acts dramatic, these behaviors often end when the police show up or when a third party appears. Bancroft's point is that while abusers often play up their out-of-control passions, they can control them. Lundy Bancroft, *Why Does He Do That?* (New York: Berkley Books, 2002). On this subject, see also Philip Rossiter, "A Thorn in the Flesh That Cannot Fester: Habermas, the Duluth Model, Domestic Violence Programmes," *Waikato Law Review* 19, no. 2 (2011): 196–206.
28. Which is why abuse is more like a spiral than a cycle.
29. See Evan Stark, *Coercive Control* (New York: Oxford, 2009); Bancroft, *Why Does He Do That?*; see Bumiller on the consequences of this failure. Kristin Bumiller, *In an Abusive State: How Neoliberalism Appropriated the Feminist Movement against Sexual Violence* (Durham, NC: Duke University Press, 2008). Bancroft has had direct experience with batterers in batterer intervention programs and thus he is perhaps the best positioned of these three researchers to assert this failure.
30. Regarding batterer intervention programs, Stark notes that "batterer intervention programs (BIPs) are widely offered as an alternative to incarceration. But these programs are little more effective than doing nothing at all. *Regardless of intervention, the vast majority of perpetrators continue their abuse.*" (Stark, 7, my emphasis); see also Bancroft on the effectiveness of abuser programs. Stark, *Coercive Control*; Bancroft, *Why Does He Do That?*
31. Indeed, an abuser can use family and friends to stalk and harass a woman; see Stark regarding O. J. Simpson, *Coercive Control*, 3.

32. See Patricia Evans on this split, which she calls reality I versus reality II. Evans, *The Verbally Abusive Relationship*, 32–47. See also my discussion of authentic love in de Beauvoir's work in Arnold, *America's New Working Class*.

33. Patricia Evans argues that most abusers "minimize abuse" and are "insensitive" to the harm they cause. Evans, 40.

34. Miami resident Derek Medina was so convinced his wife deserved what she got (he murdered her after alleging that she was going to attack him) that he posted pictures of her body on Facebook afterwards. See Michael Walsh and Daniel Beekman, "Miami Man Derek Medina Posts Sick Facebook Photo of Dead Wife Jennifer Alfonso with Apparent Murder Confession: 'I'm Going to Prison or Death Sentence for Killing my Wife,'" *New York Daily News* website, August 8, 2013, http://www.nydailynews.com/news/crime/south-miami-man-allegedly-kills-wife-posts-pic-dead-body-article-1.1421670.

35. See Bancroft, *Why Does He Do That?*; Evans, *The Verbally Abusive Relationship*. Most experts on this subject recognize that abusers often eventually attempt to murder their targets.

36. As Lundy Bancroft points out in *Why Does He Do That?*, Stark also analyzes the rational aspects of abuse (including adaptation to the law: committing minor injuries to avoid arrest), and DeKeseredy et al. also suggest the rational aspects of abuse. Walter DeKeseredy, Martin Schwartz, and Joseph Donnermeyer, *Dangerous Exits: Escaping Abusive Relationships in Rural America* (New Brunswick, NJ: Rutgers University Press, 2009).

37. These arguments were made in the days before the Oscars, when Woody Allen's adopted daughter exposed his abuse. The reaction on his behalf was basically, "If he was so abusive, why did he only abuse her?" This is not to say there have not been expressions of sympathy for his daughter, but to illustrate how conventional thinking does not see how triangulation is often a key mechanism of abuse.

38. See David S. Riggs, Marie B. Caulfield, and Amy E. Street, "Risk for Domestic Violence: Factors Associated with Perpetration and Victimization," *Journal of Clinical Psychology* 56, no. 10 (2000): 1289–1316. Again, against the notion that abuse is predictable and systematic (thus, a cycle), the abuser often acts to disrupt happy periods or to surprise and destabilize his partner. As Patricia Evans notes, "The partner of a verbal abuser usually feels startled or shocked when her mate is suddenly irritated or angry, puts her down, or is sarcastic. Since verbal abuse is, in essence, unexpected and unpredictable, the partner is often relaxed, serene, happy, or enthusiastic about something when she is suddenly thrown off balance, or shocked by her mate." Evans, 66.

39. Targets are still the best assessors and predictors of abuse—not the police, therapists, or other "experts." David S. Riggs, Marie B. Caulfield, and Amy E. Street, "Risk for Domestic Violence: Factors Associated with Perpetration and Victimization," *Journal of Clinical Psychology* 56, no. 10 (2000): 1289–1316.

40. Freud, *Civilization and Its Discontents*, 112.

41. I should note that my discussion does not lead to the same conclusions that the state (broadly conceived) has arrived at regarding abusers—that because they are incurable, the focus should be on targets of abuse. Rather, I am exposing the roots of the problem as both societal (not merely qualities of the abuser) and as defying Enlightenment norms, such that new solutions are needed. On the state's overfocus on women as both cause of abuse and target of therapeutic intervention, see Kristin Bumiller, *In an Abusive State: How*

Neoliberalism Appropriated the Feminist Movement against Sexual Violence (Durham, NC: Duke University Press, 2008), 23. In my experience, I have been told by our therapist that when my ex-boyfriend tried to break down my door, screamed "fuck you" for hours outside my apartment, or tried to choke me on repeated occasions, that he clearly loved me but didn't know how to express that love. When he was seen with our daughter in San Antonio, people would say he was really "stepping up." And when he threatened to take our daughter away from me in front of a San Antonio lawyer (who knew he had repeatedly assaulted us), she remarked that she had never seen a father express such love for his child.

42. Kathleen R. Arnold, "Domestic War: Locke's Concept of Prerogative and Implications for US 'Wars' Today," January 2007, *Polity* 39.1.

43. See Sheldon Wolin, "Democracy and the Welfare State: the Political and Theoretical Connections between Staatsräson and Wohlfahrsstaatsräson," *The Presence of the Past: Essays on the State and the Constitution* (Baltimore, MD: Johns Hopkins Press, 1989).

44. See Honig's critique of Rogers Smith's "multiple traditions" thesis in Bonnie Honig *Democracy and the Foreigner* (Princeton, NJ: Princeton University Press, 2001).

45. Like Lisa D. Brush, *Poverty, Battered Women, and Work in US Welfare Policy* (New York: Oxford University Press, 2011). I have explored the punitive and disciplinary aspects of welfare with regard to the homeless (Kathleen R. Arnold, *Homelessness, Citizenship, and Identity* [Albany, NY: SUNY Press, 2004]) and with regard to poor women (Kathleen R. Arnold, *America's New Working Class* [College Station, PA: Penn State Press, 2007]).

46. This was true even of treatment of the working class, which Mill criticizes at the end of *On Liberty* and in greater depth in *Principles of Political Economy*. John Stuart Mill, *On Liberty*, ed. Elizabeth Rapaport (Indianapolis: Hackett, 1978); John Stuart Mill, *Principles of Political Economy* (New York: Oxford, 2008). See Mantena on Mill's distinctions between civilization and barbarity in Karuna Mantena, *Alibis of Empire* (Princeton, NJ: Princeton University Press, 2010).

47. See Mill's critical remarks on the family and protective policies toward the poor (e.g., controlling drinking/pubs) in the "Applications" section of *On Liberty*, and Mill, *Principles of Political Economy*.

48. Mill, *On Liberty*; see Arendt on these methods of colonization and Karuna Mantena's far more complex and sophisticated analysis of the same relationships in *Alibis of Empire*. Hannah Arendt *The Origins of Totalitarianism* (New York: Harcourt Brace Jovanovich, 1979).

49. See Wendy Brown, *States of Injury: Power and Freedom in Late Modernity* (Princeton, NJ: Princeton University Press, 1995); Sheldon Wolin, "Democracy and the Welfare State: The Political and Theoretical Connections between Staatsräson and Wohlfahrsstaatsräson," *The Presence of the Past: Essays on the State and the Constitution* (Baltimore, MD: Johns Hopkins Press, 1989); Kathleen R. Arnold, "Domestic War: Locke's Concept of Prerogative and Implications for US 'Wars' Today," January 2007, *Polity* 39.1.

50. Carole Pateman, *Sexual Contract* (Palo Alto, CA: Stanford University Press, 1988).

51. See Pateman, *Sexual Contract*; Friedrich Engels, excerpt from *The Origin of the Family, Private Property, and the State* in *Feminist Papers: From Adams to de*

Beauvoir, ed. Alice S. Rossi (Boston: Northeastern University Press, 1988), 485–487.

52. Simone de Beauvoir, *The Second Sex*, trans. and ed. H. M. Parshley (New York: Vintage Books, 1989), 124.
53. John Locke, *Second Treatise of Government*, ed. C. B. Macpherson (Cambridge, CA: Hackett Publishing, 1980), sections 83–86.
54. As T. H. Marshall has analyzed. See for example, T. H. Marshall and Tom Bottomore, *Citizenship and Social Class*, Pluto Perspectives (London: Pluto Press, 1987).
55. See Locke, *Second Treatise*, sections 78–80. Of course, only when one enters a polity can his or her inalienable rights truly be defended.
56. And this is suggested in Locke's "Letter on Toleration" in that he includes women in his defense of religious tolerance (which Professor Richard Ashcraft used to point out in his undergraduate lectures in the Introduction to Political Theory class at the University of California, Los Angeles). John Locke, *A Letter Concerning Toleration*, ed. James Tully (Cambridge, CA: Hackett Publishing, 1983).
57. Carole Pateman, *The Disorder of Women* (Palo Alto, CA: Stanford University Press, 1992), 26, 27; in the same book, see also Pateman's "Wollstonecraft Dilemma," 196–204.
58. Mary Wollstonecraft, "Vindication of the Rights of Women," in *Feminist Papers: From Adams to de Beauvoir*, ed. Alice S. Rossi (Boston: Northeastern University Press, 1988), 58.
59. Wollstonecraft, "Vindication of the Rights of Women," 55.
60. Wollstonecraft, "Vindication of the Rights of Women," 58.
61. Wollstonecraft, "Vindication of the Rights of Women," 68.
62. Mill, *On Liberty*, 73.
63. See John Stuart Mill, "On the Subjection of Women," in *Feminist Papers: From Adams to de Beauvoir*, ed. Alice S. Rossi (Boston: Northeastern University Press, 1988), 200–201.
64. Mill, "On the Subjection of Women," 198.
65. Mill, "On the Subjection of Women," 198–202; 207–209. See Emily Collins, "Reminiscences of Emily Collins," in *The Feminist Papers*, ed. Alice S. Rossi (Boston: Northeastern University Press, 1988), 421–426; Mill, *On Liberty*, 102–105; Florence Kelley, in *The Feminist Papers*, ed. Alice S. Rossi (Boston: Northeastern University Press, 1988), 474–475.
66. See Mill, "On the Subjection of Women," 200–201.
67. Which is why de Beauvoir's statement that she is not interested in happiness but liberty is so important. *Second Sex*, xxxv.
68. Which is why authors like Pateman and Mackinnon each argue that consent cannot be the litmus test of democracy or citizenship, nor more broadly drawn upon as a measure of democratic legitimacy.
69. Locke, *Second Treatise*, section 82.
70. On this relationship, see Elizabeth Frazer and Kimberly Hutchings, "On Politics and Violence: Arendt Contra Fanon," *Contemporary Political Theory* 7 (2008): 90–108.
71. De Beauvoir, *Second Sex*, 60.
72. Engels, *Origin of the Family*, 485.
73. Engels, *Origin of the Family*, 486.
74. Engels, *Origin of the Family*, 486.

75. Engels, *Origin of the Family*, 491–492.

76. De Beauvoir, *Second Sex*, Chapter VIII (109–138).

77. Wendy Brown, *States of Injury: Power and Freedom in Late Modernity* (Princeton, NJ: Princeton University Press, 1995).

78. In that except for foreigners, no one really consents to citizenship. See Bonnie Honig, *Democracy and the Foreigner* (Princeton, NJ: Princeton University Press, 2001).

79. See Carole Pateman, *Disorder*; Wendy Brown on Pateman's work and the relevance of the social contract today, *States of Injury*, 136–140; Bonnie Honig on immigrant performance of the contract in *Democracy and the Foreigner*; and finally Rogers Smith's advocacy of some sort of social contract for all, in Rogers Smith and Peter Schuck, *Citizenship without Consent: Illegal Aliens in the American Policy* (New Haven, CT: Yale University Press, 1985). With regard to the marriage contract itself, Guillaumin argues, "The marriage contract is only the individualized expression of a general class relationship," 193. This statement could be interpreted to mean that the marriage contract is merely one individualized instantiation of a more general gender hierarchy. Colette Guillaumin, *Racism, Sexism, Power, and Ideology* (New York: Routledge, 1995), 193.

80. See Frances Fukuyama, "Immigrants and Family Values," in *Arguing Immigration*, ed. Nicolaus Mills (New York: Simon and Schuster, Touchstone Book, 1994), for example.

81. More accurately, legal and extralegal agents in the domestic abuse system who create and maintain these norms.

82. See Patricia Evans, who calls this "malevolent mores," in *The Verbally Abusive Relationship*, 114–116.

83. Such as economic abuse, harming one's pets, or harming children.

84. This is from personal research conducted in Texas and Illinois through consulting family and criminal lawyers as well as domestic abuse advocates. Patterns of abuse must be well-documented and recent.

85. Bancroft, *Why Does He Do That?*, xix–xxi.

86. See Lundy Bancroft, *When Dad Hurts Mom: Helping Your Children Heal the Wounds of Witnessing Abuse* (New York: Berkley Books, 2004).

87. Ahearn et al., "Charging Battered Mothers with 'Failure to Protect,' Still Blaming the Victim," 849–850.

88. See Bordo on this distinction, although she believes it exists only while the woman is pregnant. I challenge this second assumption. Susan Bordo, *Unbearable Weight: Feminism, Western Culture, and the Body* (Berkeley, CA: University of California Press, 2004), 71–97. More specifically, see Evan Stark's notion of "competitive victimization," which I discuss in the conclusion. This term means that the rights of the child and the mother are pitted against one another and that the best interests of the child prevail over those of the mother. Stark, *Coercive Control*, 44.

89. For a discussion and critique of economic solutions to abuse, see Brush, *Poverty, Battered Women, and Work in US Welfare Policy*.

90. As authors like Kathleen Ferraro, Michael Johnson and Evan Stark argue, targets do seek help. See, for example, Evan Stark, *Coercive Control* (New York: Oxford, 2009), 7. The societal perception that they do not seek help is rooted in targets' lack of success to change their circumstances quickly or cleanly and; it is also based on the perception that policy, institutions, and nonprofits actually help targets.

91. Ahearn et al., "Charging Battered Mothers with 'Failure to Protect,' Still Blaming the Victim," 853.

92. See Ahearn et al., "Charging Battered Mothers with 'Failure to Protect,' Still Blaming the Victim," 861–862. See also Jennifer Jack, "Note: Child Custody and Domestic Violence Allegations: New York's Approach to Custody Proceedings Involving Intimate Partner Abuse," *Albany Government Law Review* 5 (2012): 885–913. Available at: http://www.albanygovernmentlawreview.org/Articles/Vol05_3/5.3.885-Jack.pdf. With regard to a North Dakota statute on weighing domestic abuse in determining custody, Jack notes that the "North Dakota statute will not trigger a presumption even where a batterer is a known danger to his or her partner and child: abusers therefore can, and likely will, be granted some form of sole or joint custody of their child." 910.

93. Giorgio Agamben, *Remnants of Auschwitz*, trans. Daniel Heller-Rozen (New York: Zone Books, 1999).

94. Or not in the way demanded by courts and legal personnel. Joan Scott exposes the black and white thinking of courts in her discussion of the *Sears* case (*Equal Employment Opportunity Commission v Sears Roebuck*) in Joan W. Scott, "Deconstructing Equality-Versus-Difference: Or, the Uses of Poststructuralist Theory for Feminism," in *Feminist Social Thought*, ed. Diana Tietjens Meyers (New York: Routledge, 1997), 758–770.

95. See Stark, *Coercive Control*.

96. See Nancy Berns, "'My Problem and How I Solved It': Domestic Violence in Women's Magazines," *The Sociological Quarterly* 40, no. 1 (Winter 1999): 85–108.

97. Stark argues something similar in *Coercive Control*, 57.

98. For example, it is assumed that targets know whom to speak to immediately after an issue arises or incident occurs; that she knows the correct language to use and can tell her story repeatedly (perhaps) and consistently despite feeling abused or threatened; and that different agents, ranging from the police to domestic abuse counselors to therapists to judges, will all listen and help in a mutual, egalitarian, and constructive manner.

99. For example, Evan Stark's otherwise innovative and sophisticated analysis of domestic abuse in the United States also dismisses the positive contributions of radical feminist thought. See Stark, *Coercive Control*, 29–30.

100. Catharine MacKinnon, *Toward a Feminist Theory of the State* (Cambridge, MA: Harvard University Press, 1991), see "Rape: On Coercion and Consent" (171–183); Colette Guillaumin, *Racism, Sexism, Power, and Ideology* (New York: Routledge, 1995).

101. MacKinnon, "Rape: On Coercion and Consent," *Toward a Feminist Theory of the State*.

102. For example, as I discuss in the notes in the next chapter, Evan Stark wrote one reaction to a class action lawsuit that resulted in mothers who were assaulted losing their children for "exposure" to violence (even in one case when the assault happened once), exploring how "good people" (domestic violence advocates, social workers and others) could participate in this travesty of justice. See Evan Stark, "*Nicholson v. Williams* Revisited: When Good People Do Bad Things," *Denver University Law Review* 82 (2004–2005): 691–722.

103. Stark, *Coercive Control*, 10: "Viewing woman abuse through the prism of the incident-specific and injury-based definition of violence has concealed its major components, dynamics, and effects, including the fact that it is neither

'domestic' nor primarily about 'violence.' Failure to appreciate the multidimensionality of oppression in personal life has been disastrous for abuse victims."

104. And all the same dilemmas present themselves with rape.

105. See Ferraro and Johnson's review of 1990s literature in Kathleen J. Ferraro and Michael P. Johnson, "Research on Domestic Violence in the 1990s: Making Distinctions," *Journal of Marriage and Family* 62, no. 4 (November 2000): 948–963; see Mala Htun and S. Laurel Weldon, "The Civic Origins of Progressive Policy Change: Combating Violence against Women in Global Perspective, 1975–2005," *American Political Science Review* 106, no. 3 (August 2012): 548–569.

106. See for example, Fiona Robinson, *Globalizing Care: Ethics, Feminist Theory, and International Relations* (Boulder, CO: Westview Press, 1999); for background information about this academic subfield, see "Care Ethics" *Internet Encyclopedia of Philosophy*, http://www.iep.utm.edu/care-eth/#H7.

107. Adam Smith, *Theory of Moral Sentiments (Glasgow Edition of the Works and Correspondence of Adam Smith)*, vol. 1 (Indianapolis, IN: Liberty Fund, 2009).

108. Moyn discusses Hunt's analysis of Rousseau in Samuel Moyn, "On the Genealogy of Morals," *The Nation*, March 29, 2007, http://www.thenation.com/article/genealogy-morals#.

109. Moyn, "On the Genealogy."

110. Moyn, "On the Genealogy." See also Hannah Arendt *The Origins of Totalitarianism* (New York: Harcourt Brace Jovanovich, 1979), 451, on the public suspicion of survivors' accounts.

111. On this sort of philosophical process (the attempt to universalize philosophical claims and aim at a telos), see Samuel Weber, "The Politics of Protection and Projection," in *Religion beyond a Concept*, ed. Hent de Vries (New York: Fordham University Press, 2008), 626–646.

112. Moyn, "On the Genealogy."

113. One recent example is the argument that because Guantánamo Bay is shutting down, Judith Butler's work on this detention center is now irrelevant. Paul Smith, "Review: Precarious Politics," *symplokē* 12, no.½, Fiction's Present (2004): 254–260. This sort of perspective denies, for example, what goes on in detention centers throughout the United States or how most likely other versions of Guantánamo will most likely resurface in Eastern Europe or other places.

114. Stark, *Coercive Control*, 5: "But the primary harm abuse men inflict is *political*, not physical, and reflects the deprivation of rights and resources that are critical to personhood and citizenship." See Stark, *Coercive Control*, 3, regarding major abuse cases that were not settled because the physical assault in each case wasn't considered severe enough. He is referring to two cases—Nicole Simpson Brown and Terrie Traficonda: "Ironically, focusing on incidents of severe violence trivialized the strategies used to entrap Terry, Nicole, and millions of women in similar situations, leaving them unprotected," 3. Bumiller argues something very similar about rape in Kristin Bumiller, *In an Abusive State: How Neoliberalism Appropriated the Feminist Movement against Sexual Violence* (Durham, NC: Duke University Press, 2008).

115. Evan Stark argues that most abuse is predominantly emotional and controlling with regular, minor assaults the norm: "Viewing woman abuse through the prism of the incident-specific and injury-based definition of violence has

concealed its major components, dynamics, and effects, including the fact that it is neither 'domestic' nor primarily about 'violence.' Failure to appreciate the multidimensionality of oppression in personal life has been disastrous for abuse victims. Regardless of its chronic nature, *courts treat each abuse incident they see as a first offense.* Because well over 95% of these incidents are minor, no one goes to jail." Stark, *Coercive Control*, 10.

116. I have chosen to phrase it this way in lieu of stating the problem as "attempts to help victims of human rights abuse."

117. For the classic rehearsal of the value of care theory, see the section entitled "Care and Its Critics," which includes work by Carol Gilligan, Sara Ruddick, Annette Baier, Virginia Held, and Claudia Card; and for older but still relevant critiques of care theory, see (in the same book) Marilyn Friedman and Chantal Mouffe. All essays are in *Feminist Social Thought*, ed. Diana Tietjens Meyers (New York: Routledge, 1997).

118. See Pateman's discussion of the Wollstonecraft dilemma in which she analyzes the paradoxes (and ultimately, uselessness) of celebrating difference. Carole Pateman, *Disorder of Women* (Palo Alto, CA: Stanford University Press, 1992), Chapter 8.

119. On the *Unheimliche*, see Sigmund Freud, *The Uncanny*, 1919, available for example in a 2003 Penguin edition; see also my own work on this in relation to the home and homelessness in Kathleen R. Arnold, *Homelessness, Citizenship, and Identity* (Albany, NY: SUNY Press, 2004), Chapter 3; and Chantal Mouffe's careful critique of these notions. For a broader but highly relevant discussion, see Wendy Brown, *States of Injury: Power and Freedom in Late Modernity* (Princeton, NJ: Princeton University Press, 1995), Chapter 7.

120. MacKinnon, "Rape: On Coercion and Consent" in *Toward a Feminist Theory of the State*, 171–183. Nietzsche similarly develops this argument at the philosophical level in *On the Genealogy of Morals*.

121. See Linda Zerilli's arguments about the role of feminist theory and attempts to regulate or order, via theory, what is in fact an "abyss of freedom," in *Feminism and the Abyss of Freedom* (Chicago: University of Chicago Press, 2005).

122. See Sen for the best of what I think is still a problematic literature. Amartya Sen, "More Than 100 Million Women Are Missing," *New York Review of Books* 37, no. 20, December 20, 1990, http://www.nybooks.com/articles/archives/1990/dec/20/more-than-100-million-women-are-missing/.

123. Stephen K. White, "Fullness and Death: Depth Experience and Democratic Life," *American Political Science Review* 104, no. 4 (November 2010): 800–816.

124. Stephen K. White, "Fullness and Death: Depth Experience and Democratic Life," political theory colloquium, Northwestern University, November 22, 2010, noon talk.

125. I am referring to White's talk at Northwestern; he also discusses this example briefly in "Fullness and Death: Depth Experience and Democratic Life," *American Political Science Review* 104, no. 4 (November 2010): 811.

126. See Kimberlé Crenshaw on the effects of music and other media on children (her exploration of representational intersectionality): Kimberlé Crenshaw, "Mapping the Margins: Intersectionality, Identity, Politics, and Violence against Women of Color," *Stanford Law Review* 43, no. 6 (1991): 1242–1265; see also Colette Guillaumin's arguments regarding how rape and domestic violence discipline all women, whether they are direct targets of abuse or not—Colette Guillaumin, *Racism, Sexism, Power, and Ideology* (New York:

Routledge, 1995); and similarly, see MacKinnon's arguments that rape (for example) is not prohibited but controlled. MacKinnon, "Rape: On Coercion and Consent" in *Toward a Feminist Theory of the State*, 171–183.

127. Not to mention victim blaming, as is evidenced in Holocaust denial. Again, see Arendt on this, for example, *Origins*, 451.

128. For example, Benhabib's recent work on cosmopolitanism. Seyla Benhabib, *Another Cosmopolitanism* ed. Robert Post (London and New York: Oxford University Press, 2006).

129. Sen, "More Than 100 Million Women Are Missing." Theorists of human rights seem to miss the irony of wanting to convince people to grant rights to others; as Jacqueline Jones has stated in her work on minority workers, rights should not be negotiable. Jacqueline Jones, *American Work* (New York: Norton, 1998), "Epilogue," 338–342.

130. Fanon has recognized this in the colonial context: "Let us leave this Europe which never stops talking of man yet massacres him at every one of its street corners, at every corner of the world." Frantz Fanon, *The Wretched of the Earth* (New York: Grove Press, 2005), 235.

131. This statement needs to be unpacked more fully: a certain set of binaries since the Enlightenment can be discerned, in which racial, ethnic, and gendered others are made to be subordinate and "primitive." I want to suggest a more complicated relationship in which these are binary modes of operation that are inextricably tied, even as they are posed as opposite. For a typical (and excellent) analysis of these norms in feminist literature, see Susan Bordo, *Unbearable Weight*, and in comparative literature, see Edward Said's classic *Orientalism* (New York: Vintage, 1979).

132. Brown, *States of Injury*, 67–73.

133. I prefer the word *target*, as I have explained at the beginning of this book.

134. See Slavoj Zizek, "Are we in a war? Do we have an enemy?" *London Review of Books* 24, no. 10, May 23, 2002 www.lrb.co.uk/; Slavoj Žižek, "Against Human Rights," *New Left Review* 34 (July–August, 2005). www.newleftreview.org/?page=article&view=2573 (accessed 5/14/09).

135. Emotions instead can cause a rupture; they can be unpredictable, contradictory, and outside of prescribed social norms. As R. Clifton Spargo notes, mourning in the Freudian model, for example, may involve a sort of closed system ("a redundant site of played-out obligations"), but it also "elicits a break in the normative possibilities of politics, reconceiving it if only by an act of futile dissent the rigorously economic logic by which the sovereign will declare certain losses to be permissibly familiar and, since included in the bounded relationships legitimated by the state, also culturally significant." R. Clifton Spargo, *The Ethics of Mourning* (Baltimore, MD: Johns Hopkins University Press, 2004), 35; Judith Butler also investigates the connection between emotions and political action, granted in a more conventional manner; see Judith Butler, "Photography, War, Outrage," *PMLA* 120, no. 3 (May 2005): 822–827.

136. See Jacques Rancière, "Who is the Subject of the Rights of Man?" *South Atlantic Quarterly* 103 no. 23 (Spring/Summer 2004): 297–310.

137. A better word than *victimized*.

138. One example is that when a doctor or nurse calls child protective services, the mother's name is on the file; she is interviewed as someone who is potentially "exposing" her child to abuse or also abusing her child; and the father often

plays a secondary role. Another example is a "loving and caring order" in a child custody case which may have been aimed at a parent who tries to alienate the child's affections, but which can then be used against the primary caretaker or nonabusive parent even if the primary aim is allegedly to rectify the behavior of the abuser. Furthermore, these sorts of directives can ironically be used as threats by the abuser against the target.

139. As Bordo has argued, women's bodies "speak," even when the women are not allowed to speak themselves; to put it differently, societal interpretations of women's body language trump her inner reality; this is not a departure from disciplinary power so much as a more refined application of it to go beyond normalization. Bordo, *Unbearable Weight*.

140. See Lundy Bancroft, *When Dad Hurts Mom: Helping Your Children Heal the Wounds of Witnessing Abuse* (New York: Berkley Books, 2004) and Lundy Bancroft and Jay G. Silverman, *The Batterer as Parent: Addressing the Impact of Domestic Violence on Family Dynamics*, SAGE Series on Violence (Thousand Oaks, CA: SAGE Publications, 2002).

141. At least in the context of the subject matter of this book.

142. Even if, in reality, policy and societal norms contradictorily expect both: a target should talk and try to change the abuser but the target should also leave because all of the liability is with her.

CHAPTER 5

1. Thus, Stark argues, control is a "freedom of movement" issue. Evan Stark, "Entrapment," *Assemblage* 20, Violence Space (April 1993): 76–77.

2. In psychology, this is called "alienation" and, if the abuser continues to do this to the child when there is little to no contact between the abuser and his target, "obsessive alienation." See "Parental Alienation" on the Divorce Source website, n.d., http://www.divorcesource.com/info/alienation/alienation.shtml.

3. I have not explored economic aspects of abuse in any detail but plan to do so in the future. Money constitutes a method of control that cannot be easily escaped if there is child support involved, even if a target manages to move away. First, if many separation arrangements are never heard by a judge or welfare authorities, there will not be state discovery regarding the abuser's income or assets. He can provide information in mediation or less formal negotiations that is not subject to scrutiny. Second, if he is a private contractor or owns his own business (particularly a cash business, such as a construction business), it can be relatively easy for him to minimize his income, even if there is scrutiny. This has happened to me and to numerous friends, and I have heard of partners asking their employers to pay them as a private contractor. Once this is set in motion, it can be very difficult to revisit child support. For example, I know from personal research that if someone has moved out of state, most lawyers do not know which state determines child support. Even if the target could go back to court, it can cost thousands of dollars in legal fees to rectify the situation or she can represent herself, but the time involved can undermine her parenting and work schedule. Finally and again anecdotally (from speaking to lawyers), most of us have "willingly" given up most child support because the party was threatening numerous other things (including geographical restriction) and was acting violently. It seems like a small price to pay to get away—the result in my case is that my income has

diminished, I must work a second job, and I am thousands of dollars in debt due to the custody agreement. In exchange, we were allowed to move and get away from regular home intrusions, stalking, harassment, and daily sabotage of my tenure track job in Texas. An award-winning book on economic aspects of abuse is Jacqui True, *The Political Economy of Violence against Women* (New York: Oxford University Press, 2012).

4. See Walter DeKeseredy, Martin Schwartz, and Joseph Donnermeyer, *Dangerous Exits: Escaping Abusive Relationships in Rural America* (New Brunswick, NJ: Rutgers University Press, 2009), 3–4 (this discussion is broader, discussing abused women as a whole and how they are not psychologically different from "average" women).

5. Just as analyses of facially neutral policies expose inherent biases in the laws or policies or selective impact at the enforcement level.

6. To understand why and how this attention does not amount to much, see Michaele Ferguson, "Women Are Not an Interest Group," *Theory & Event* 16, issue 1, 2013, http://muse.jhu.edu/journals/theory_and_event/v016/16.1.ferguson.html. There is also a whole literature on how and why women should receive heightened judicial scrutiny.

7. On these expectations by nonprofit workers and advocates, see Roberta Villalón, "Passage to Citizenship and the Nuances of Agency: Latina Battered Immigrants," *Women's Studies International Forum* 33 (October 12, 2010): 552–560. On perceptions of who counts as a victim and who does not (African American women who resist their abusers often fall under this latter category), see Leigh Goodmark, "When Is a Battered Woman Not a Battered Woman? When She Fights Back," *Yale Journal of Law and Feminism* (2008): 76–129. More broadly, see the sophisticated analyses of Lisa Brush in *Poverty, Battered Women, and Work in U.S. Welfare Policy* (New York: Oxford University Press, 2011) regarding the difficulties in keeping a job—particularly low-tier positions and workfare employment—while being controlled and harassed, not to mention trying to care for children.

8. As most of the authors cited in this book would argue—particularly Bancroft, Stark, and Goodmark. All of these dynamics are exacerbated when helping agents also operate from racist, class-biased, or other prejudiced assumptions.

9. For this reason, I also challenge empirical studies that are not framed as being preliminary and selective, given the nature of abuse and the multiple obstacles to getting documentable aid that actually helps a target.

10. In fact, as noted throughout the book, this is the most dangerous time for the target. See DeKeseredy, Schwartz, and Donnermeyer, *Dangerous Exits*, which explores the prevalence of rape and other assaults when women try to leave (granted that the authors argue that this is exacerbated in rural areas for at least two reasons: a culture that actually *encourages* intimate abuse and lack of enforcement or help); Donna Coker, "Shifting Power for Battered Women: Law Material Resources and Poor Women of Color," *University of California Davis Law Review* 33 (2000): 1009–1055. Available at http://papers.ssrn.com/sol3/papers.cfm?abstract_id=2,011,468. See also Lundy Bancroft, *Why Does He Do That?* (New York: Berkley Books, 2002) regarding an abuser's tactics to entrap a target. As someone who has been subjected to a myriad of tactics that Bancroft identifies, I was surprised to go through his lists of abusive mechanisms. I had thought that quite a lot of the rather bizarre behavior my ex-boyfriend had exhibited was absolutely anomalous—from sexual violence to

"accidentally" impregnating me and then abandoning us and yet stalking us. After reading this book, it becomes clear how one cannot solve this problem, because it has now turned into numerous problems requiring different remedies.

11. See Lundy Bancroft, *Why Does He Do That?* (New York: Berkley Books, 2002), 266–272; Lundy Bancroft, *When Dad Hurts Mom: Helping Your Children Heal the Wounds of Witnessing Abuse* (New York: Berkley Books, 2004), 166–170, all of Chapter 10, 248–253. More broadly, see Chris Fusco and Tony Arnold, "Child-Abuse, Neglect Deaths in Illinois Remain High in DCFS-involved Cases," WBEZ91.5 website (NPR), January 20, 2014, http://www.wbez.org/news/child-abuse-neglect-deaths-illinois-remain-high-dcfs-involved-cases-109,545 (accessed April 26, 2014).

12. And as stated in Guzick's study, most court personnel expect the no-contact order to be violated. Keith Guzik, "The Forces of Conviction: the Power and Practice of Mandatory Prosecution upon Misdemeanor Domestic Battery Suspects," *Law and Social Inquiry* 32, no. 1 (Winter 2007): 41–74.

13. Again, see Bancroft, *When Dad Hurts Mom*. In fact, if a target attempts to allege that her children are being sexually abused, she faces the greatest risks in losing them. Bancroft, *When Dad Hurts Mom*, 248–253. See also Fusco and Arnold, "Child-Abuse, Neglect Deaths in Illinois Remain High." The *Chicago Sun-Times* has also done quite a lot of investigative journalism to expose the neglect and death rates in the Midwest in 2014.

14. See Jeanne A. Fugate, "Who's Failing Whom? A Critical Look at Failure-to-Protect Laws," *New York University Law Review* 76 (April 2001): 272–308, http://www.thelizlibrary.org/liz/fugate.pdf.

15. Anecdotally, several lawyers (including one lawyer who went through North-eastern University's domestic abuse program) have suggested to me that flight—including changing one's name and hiding one's identity—is the only option. The fact that the Northeastern-trained lawyer suggested flight to me reveals that even Leigh Goodmark's work on programs such as this can certainly improve the legal profession but not the system as it is currently configured.

16. On this discourse, see Linda Martín Alcoff and Laura Gray, "Survivor Discourse: Transgression or Recuperation?" Linda Martín Alcoff's website, n.d., http://www.alcoff.com/content/survdis.html; see also Linda Alcoff and Laura Gray, "Survivor Discourse: Transgression or Recuperation?" *Signs: Journal of Women in Culture and Society* 27, no. 3 (Spring 2002): 743–775.

17. Clearly the case at this moment with the recent popularity of Thomas Piketty's work: Thomas Piketty, *Capital in the Twenty-First Century* (Cambridge, MA: Harvard University Press, 2014).

18. Although admittedly, this sympathy may be temporary and trendy. I have written at least two books—one on the relatively undemocratic treatment of homelessness, and the other on the devalorization of the working class—that would challenge my statements about this sympathy.

19. If only because the target is hypothetically never off the clock, and sexual assault and rape are therefore more possible and more prevalent.

20. As Stark argues, because there is a "calculus of injuries," most abusers maintain an even more thorough set of controls and physical assaults, but they try to keep the latter under the legal threshold. Evan Stark, *Coercive Control* (New York: Oxford, 2009), 57.

21. That is, the sort of exploitation that occurs on a job site but involves the generation of surplus-value and other mechanisms of control that are largely impersonal. In this ideal situation (i.e., a Weberian ideal type), the worker is not directly harmed or attacked by managers and furthermore can retreat to the public sphere and home after work. Fanon has argued that this is a form of bourgeois exploitation that differs from the colonial situation in which the body itself is implicated in colonial and postcolonial racial exploitation. Frantz Fanon, *The Wretched of the Earth* (New York: Grove Press, 2005).

22. What Guillaumin calls sexage and Stark has argued constitutes a hostage situation. Colette Guillaumin, *Racism, Sexism, Power, and Ideology* (New York: Routledge, 1995). I should also note that I have analyzed this more thoroughgoing bodily appropriation in the case of free-trade zones and guest-worker schemes in Kathleen R. Arnold, *American Immigration after 1996: The Shifting Ground of Political Inclusion* (College Station, PA: Penn State University Press, 2011). The point is distinguishing between "bourgeois" forms of exploitation (as Fanon would put it) where the worker can retreat to the home and more thorough relations of exploitation that allow no such relief and involve systematic compromising of bodily integrity.

23. See, for example, Jacqui True, *The Political Economy of Violence against Women* (New York: Oxford University Press, 2012) and see (again) Brush on the interactive dynamics between abuse, exploitative work conditions, and welfare surveillance. Brush, *Poverty, Battered Women, and Work in U.S. Welfare Policy*.

24. Regarding maquila workers' micro-resistance, see Leslie Salzinger, "From High Heels to Swathed Bodies: Gendered Meanings under Production in Mexico's Export-Processing Industry," *Feminist Studies* 23, no. 3 (Autumn 1997).

25. For example, Charles Lee's work. See Charles Lee, "Bare Life, Interstices, and the Third Space of Citizenship," paper prepared for the 2010 Western Political Science Association, SSRN, http://papers.ssrn.com/sol3/papers.cfm?abstract_id=1,580,843, and see his forthcoming work on "abject" or "ingenious" citizenship.

26. See Roberta Villalón's interrogation of the term *resistance*. As she argues, a domestic abuse target's assimilation into a nonprofit may entail a great deal of agency, without resistance (in the combative sense). Roberta Villalón, "Passage to Citizenship and the Nuances of Agency: Latina Battered Immigrants," *Women's Studies International Forum* 33 (October 12, 2010): 552–560.

27. Sheldon Wolin, "What Revolutionary Action Means Today," in *Dimensions of Radical Democracy*, ed. Chantal Mouffe (New York and London: Verso, 1992).

28. Stark, *Coercive Control*, 44.

29. See Susan Bordo, *Unbearable Weight: Feminism, Western Culture, and the Body* (Berkeley: University of California Press, 2004), 88–93; especially 89.

30. Alexis de Tocqueville, *Democracy in America*, ed. J. P. Mayer, trans. George Lawrence (New York: Perennial Classics, 2000), 503–506.

31. Roberta Villalón describes an important instance of this when she asserts that nonprofit agencies conceive of ideal clients as docile and not assertive in any way. Villalón, "Passage to Citizenship and the Nuances of Agency."

32. Which I think is a very interesting argument and which Simone de Beauvoir often advances in discussing a certain "imperialism of the human consciousness" when investigating the origins of gender inequality. Simone de Beauvoir, *The Second Sex*, trans. and ed. H. M. Parshley (New York: Vintage Books, 1989), 58.

33. Catharine MacKinnon, "Rape: On Coercion and Consent," *Toward a Feminist Theory of the State* (Cambridge, MA: Harvard University Press, 1991), 174.

34. Like Judith Butler. On third-wave thinkers' rejection of the feminist project, see Linda M. G. Zerilli, *Feminism and the Abyss of Freedom* (Chicago: University of Chicago Press, 2005), particularly the conclusion.

35. See Goodmark, "When Is a Battered Woman Not a Battered Woman?"

36. See Crenshaw's discussion of racist and ethnically biased assumptions about domestic abuse. Kimberlé Crenshaw, "Mapping the Margins: Intersectionality, Identity, Politics, and Violence against Women of Color," *Stanford Law Review* 43, no. 6 (1991): 1242–1299.

37. See Crenshaw, "Mapping the Margins"; Stark, *Coercive Control*.

38. To be clear, I am not arguing that the reduced circumstances of a highly privileged woman are equivalent to that of other targets who are treated in class-biased, racist or other prejudiced ways. Rather, the point is that abuse itself creates a set of problems that defy fixed rubrics of identity.

39. See Linda G. Mills, *Violent Partners: A Breakthrough Plan for Ending the Cycle of Abuse* (New York: Basic Books, 2008); Kristin Bumiller, *In an Abusive State: How Neoliberalism Appropriated the Feminist Movement against Sexual Violence* (Durham, NC: Duke University Press, 2008).

40. This is perhaps a problem even in Zerilli's excellent work on feminism—identifying waves still homogenizes a very diverse set of arguments, efforts, and texts. Zerilli, *Abyss of Freedom*.

41. From Foucault, *History of Sexuality*.

42. See Stark, *Coercive Control*, on radical feminists, 29–30; Bumiller on feminists in *In an Abusive State: How Neoliberalism Appropriated the Feminist Movement against Sexual Violence*; Mills, *Violent Partners: A Breakthrough Plan for Ending the Cycle of Abuse*, who also critiques feminism, but it is unclear exactly whom Mills has in mind. With Bordo (*Unbearable Weight*), I believe this does not mean dismissing all other feminist literature but reading these older and more conventional texts through a poststructural lens.

43. Deborah K. King, "Multiple Jeopardy, Multiple Consciousness: The Context of a Black Feminist Ideology," in *Feminist Social Thought: A Reader*, ed. Diana Tietjens Meyers (New York: Routledge, 1997), 219–242.

44. As Foucault argues in *History of Sexuality, Volume I: An Introduction*, trans. Robert Hurley (New York: Vintage Books, 1980).

45. As de Beauvoir would argue. See *The Second Sex*, trans. and ed. H. M. Parshley (New York: Vintage Books, 1989).

46. Something suggested by Zerilli, even if she finds that Butler, Derrida (or Derrideans), and Brown (in another way) often reaffirm what they are challenging. Zerilli, *Abyss of freedom*.

47. Joan W. Scott, "Deconstructing Equality-Versus-Difference: Or, the Uses of Poststructuralist Theory for Feminism," in *Feminist Social Thought*, ed. Diana Tietjens Meyers (New York: Routledge, 1997), 760–761, 768.

48. Again, for an updated analysis of this issue, see Zerilli, *Aybss of Freedom*.

49. Chantal Mouffe, "Feminism, Citizenship, and Radical Democratic Politics," in *Feminist Social Thought: A Reader*, ed. Diana Tietjens Meyers (New York: Routledge, 1997), 532–544.

50. On the specifics of this disturbing case, see "*Nicholson v. Williams* (Defending Parental Rights of Mothers Who Are Domestic Violence Victims)," New York

Civil Liberties Union website, n.d., http://www.nyclu.org/case/nicholson-v-williams-defending-parental-rights-of-mothers-who-are-domestic-violence-victims. The case was modified upon appeal in 2004, and it was ruled that being the victim of domestic abuse cannot be the only determining factor in removing custody. Thus, the burden is still on the target and not the abuser, but the standards are now weakened.

51. On the incredibly disproportionate treatment of mothers who lack access to key institutions or who are otherwise disadvantaged, see Donna Coker, "Shifting Power for Battered Women: Law Material Resources and Poor Women of Color," *University of California Davis Law Review* 33 (2000): 1009–1055. Available at http://papers.ssrn.com/sol3/papers.cfm?abstract_id=2,011,468.

52. Ange-Marie Hancock, "When Multiplication Doesn't Equal Quick Addition: Examining Intersectionality as a Research Paradigm," *Perspectives on Politics* 5, no. 1 (March 2007): 63–79.

53. Foucault, *History of Sexuality*, volume 1.

54. On this subject, see Drucilla Cornell on MacKinnon's account of lesbianism; see also Joan Cocks's examination of lesbian S&M, as a challenge to MacKinnon. Drucilla Cornell, "Sexual Difference, the Feminine, and Equivalency: A Critique of MacKinnon's *Toward a Feminist Theory of the State*," *Yale Law Journal* 100, no. 7 (May 1991): 2247–2275; Joan Cocks, *The Oppositional Imagination: Feminism, Critique, and Political Theory* (Abingdon, Oxon, and New York: Routledge, Kegan and Paul, 1989).

55. Which is why training lawyers to be better listeners or to train judges in domestic abuse are weak reforms and not revolutionary in any respect.

56. Which I only know from personal experience, volunteering in shelters, working more formally with shelters, and having a wide range of friends and neighbors who have been abused.

57. See Jakeet Singh's work, for example, "Violence, Religion, and the Politics of Post-secularism," presented at the conference Towards "the Dignity of Difference": Neither "The Clash of Civilizations" nor "The End of History," University of Alberta, Edmonton, AB, Canada, October 3, 2009, http://dofdifference.org/Dignity_of_Difference/Jakeet_Singh.html.

58. Evan Stark argues that the commonly asserted "one in four women will be attacked before age 40" is a bit exaggerated. He claims that the truth is that since laws on violent assault have become stricter, most abuse involves constant but more minor injuries combined with mechanisms of control. He surmises that given these caveats, abuse is actually more prevalent than in the past but with characteristics different from dominant legal definitions. Stark, *Coercive Control*, 57.

59. See Susan Bordo, *Unbearable Weight*, 88–93.

60. See Sheldon Wolin, *Politics and Vision*, expanded edition (Princeton, NJ: Princeton University Press, 2004).

61. Karuna Mantena, "Another Realism: the Politics of Gandhian Nonviolence," *American Political Science Review* 106, no. 2 (May 2012): 455–470. For a broader discussion of this, see Marjorie Garber, Beatrice Hanssen, and Rebecca L. Walkowitz, eds., *Ethics* (New York: Routledge, 2000).

62. See Karuna Mantena, "Another Realism: the Politics of Gandhian Nonviolence," *American Political Science Review* 106, no. 2 (May 2012): 455–470.

63. A situation that Bancroft analyzes in *Why Does He Do That?*

64. Mantena, "Another Realism: the Politics of Gandhian Nonviolence," 463. I am obviously applying her quote to my own analysis.

65. Stark, *Coercive Control*, 29.

66. I am indebted to Foucault's critique of therapy in *The History of Sexuality, Volume I: An Introduction*, trans. Robert Hurley (New York: Vintage Books, 1980); see also Murray Edelman, "The Political Language of the Helping Professions," *Politics & Society* 4 (1974): 295–310.

67. James Scott, *Domination and the Arts of Resistance: Hidden Transcripts* (New Haven, CT: Yale University Press, 1992). A correlated point is that if women are traumatized from abuse, this may not mean a wholesale internalization of abuse so much as the realization that there is little consistent help or recourse. That is, the trauma is caused for very real reasons.

68. I should note that I am not addressing or critiquing "survivor" tactics. See Leigh Goodmark, "Clinical Cognitive Dissonance: The Values and Goals of Domestic Violence Clinics, the Legal System, and the Students Caught in the Middle," *Journal of Law and Policy* 20 (2012): 301–323. Available at http://digitalcommons.law.umaryland.edu/cgi/viewcontent.cgi?article=2463&context=fac_pubs; Goodmark, "When is a Battered Woman Not a Battered Woman?"

69. See DeKeseredy et al., *Dangerous Exits*.

70. As Vaclav Havel has theorized in *The Power of the Powerless* (New York: M. E. Sharpe, 1985).

71. On human rights approaches to intimate abuse, uneven implementation and responses, and the value of transnational actors, see Kathryn Libal and Serena Parekh, "Reframing Violence against Women as a Human Rights Violation: Evan Stark's *Coercive Control*," *Violence against Women* 15, no. 12 (October 15, 2007): 1477–1489; Celeste Montoya *From Global to Grassroots: The European Union, Transnational Advocacy, and Combating Violence against Women* (New York: Oxford, 2013); True, *The Political Economy of Violence against Women*.

72. These groups do not somehow uncouple the colonization of politics by capital (to bastardize Habermas's terms).

73. More simply, there is no "outside" to power.

74. As Sheldon Wolin would perhaps urge, if he were interested in this subject.

75. Zerilli, *Feminism and the Abyss of Freedom*.

76. I am also currently reading Bill Eddy and Randi Kreger, *Splitting: Protecting Yourself while Divorcing Someone with Borderline or Narcissistic Personality Disorder* (New Harbinger Publications, Inc. 2011) which my now former attorney recommended. While it is a popular book without the depth of other similar books I have cited (Evans and Bancroft in particular), it is critical of courts and investigates how the court system actually *triggers* abusive situations and produces unjust outcomes. This is not the best self-help book out there, but it is incredibly interesting for those of us who need to keep fighting (or going) on a daily basis.

SELECTED BIBLIOGRAPHY

Eleanor Acer and Tara Magner, "Restoring America's Commitment to Refugees and Humanitarian Commitment," *Georgetown Immigration Law Journal* 27 (Spring 2013): 445–484.

Giorgio Agamben, *Homo Sacer: Sovereign Power and Bare Life*, trans. Daniel Heller-Roazen (Stanford: Stanford University Press, 1998).

Giorgio Agamben, *Remnants of Auschwitz*, trans. Daniel Heller-Rozen (New York: Zone Books, 1999).

Giorgio Agamben, *State of Exception*, trans. Kevin Attell (Chicago: University of Chicago Press, 2005).

Kim Ahearn, et al. (also known as "Failure to Protect" Working Group of Child Welfare Committee of New York City Inter-Agency Task Force against Domestic Violence), "Charging Battered Mothers with 'Failure to Protect,' Still Blaming the Victim," *Fordham Urban Law Journal* 27, no. 3 (1999): 849–873. Available at http://ir.lawnet.fordham.edu/cgi/viewcontent.cgi?article=2011&context=ulj.

American Bar Association, "The U.S. Compared to Other Nations," n.d. http://www.americanbar.org/groups/committees/gun_violence/resources/the_u_s_compared_to_other_nations.html (accessed May 20, 2013).

Paul Apostolidis, *Breaks in the Chain: What Immigrants Can Teach America about Democracy* (University of Minnesota Press, 2010).

Hannah Arendt, *On Violence* (New York: Harvest/HBJ, 1969).

Hannah Arendt, *The Origins of Totalitarianism* (New York: Harcourt Brace Jovanovich, 1979).

Kathleen R. Arnold, *American Immigration after 1996: The Shifting Ground of Political Inclusion* (College Station, PA: Penn State University Press, 2011).

Kathleen R. Arnold, *America's New Working Class* (College Station, PA: Penn State Press, 2007).

Kathleen R. Arnold, "Homelessness and Drag," in *Professional Lives, Personal Struggles: Ethics and Advocacy in Research on Homelessness*, eds. Martha Trenna Valado and Randall Amster (Eds.) (Lanham, MD: Lexington Books, 2012).

Kathleen R. Arnold, *Homelessness, Citizenship, and Identity* (Albany, NY: SUNY Press, 2004).

Kathleen R. Arnold, "Locke on "Domestic War: Locke's Concept of Prerogative and Implications for U.S. 'Wars' Today," January 2007, *Polity*, 39.1.

Lundy Bancroft, *When Dad Hurts Mom: Helping Your Children Heal the Wounds of Witnessing Abuse* (New York: Berkley Books, 2004).

Lundy Bancroft, *Why Does He Do That?* (New York: Berkley Books, 2002).

Lundy Bancroft and Jay G. Silverman, *The Batterer as Parent: Addressing the Impact of Domestic Violence on Family Dynamics*, SAGE Series on Violence (Thousand Oaks, CA: SAGE Publications, 2002).

Zygmunt Bauman, *Globalization* (New York: Columbia University Press, 1998).

Simone de Beauvoir, *The Second Sex*, trans. and ed. H. M. Parshley (New York: Vintage Books, 1989).

Erica Beecher-Monas, "Domestic Violence: Competing Conceptions of Equality in the Law of Evidence," *Loyola Law Review* 47, part 1 (2001): 81–136.

Jennifer Bendery, "VAWA Vote: Senate Rejects GOP Alternative That Omits LGBT, Native American Protections," *Huffington Post*, February 7, 2013, http://www.huffingtonpost.com/2013/02/07/vawa-vote_n_2639168.html?utm_hp_ref=gay-voices (accessed February 8, 2013).

Raquel Kennedy Bergen and Elizabeth Barnhill, "Marital Rape: New Research and Directions," Applied Research Forum: National Online Resource Center on Violence against Women, February 2006, http://new.vawnet.org/Assoc_Files_VAWnet/AR_MaritalRapeRevised.pdf.

Nancy Berns, "'My Problem and How I Solved It'": Domestic Violence in Women's Magazines," *The Sociological Quarterly* 40, no. 1 (Winter 1999): 85–108.

Susan Bordo, *Unbearable Weight: Feminism, Western Culture, and the Body* (Berkeley, CA: University of California Press, 2004).

John Brocklesby and Stephen Cummings, "Foucault Plays Habermas: an Alternative Philosophical Underpinning for Critical Systems Thinking," *Journal of the Operational Research Society* 47, no. 6 (June 1996): 741–754.

Margaret F. Brown, "Domestic Violence Advocates' Exposure to Liability for Engaging in the Unauthorized practice of Law," *Columbia Journal of Law and Social Problems* 34, no. 4 (Summer 2001): 279–300.

Wendy Brown, *States of Injury: Power and Freedom in Late Modernity* (Princeton: Princeton University Press, 1995).

Wendy Brown, "Where Is the Sex in Political Theory?" *Women & Politics* 7 (Spring 1987): 3–24.

Lisa D. Brush, "Battering and the Poverty Trap," *Journal of Poverty* 8, no. 3 (2004): 23–43.

Lisa Brush, "Guest Editor's Introduction," *Violence against Women* 15(2009): 1423–1431.

Lisa D. Brush, "In an Abusive State," *Gender and Society* 23, no. 2 (April 2009): 273–281.

Lisa D. Brush, "Philosophical and Political Issues in Research on Women's Violence and Aggression," *Sex Roles* 52, nos. 11/12 (June 2005): 867–872.

Lisa D. Brush, *Poverty, Battered Women, and Work in U.S. Welfare Policy* (New York: Oxford University Press, 2011).

Eric Bugyis, "Towards a Rational Critique of Violence: Beyond Habermas's Semantic Genealogy and Girard's Mimetic Anthropology," conference paper presented at 2010 Colloquium on Violence and Religion, Girard and Post-Structural Thought panel, http://transformingviolence.nd.edu/assets/26475/bugyis_paper.pdf.

Elsa M. Bullard, "Insufficient Government Protection: The Inescapable Element in Domestic Violence Asylum Cases," *Minnesota Law Review* 95 (2011): 1867–1898, http://www.minnesotalawreview.org/wp-content/uploads/2011/05/Bullard_PDF.pdf.

Kristin Bumiller, *In an Abusive State: How Neoliberalism Appropriated the Feminist Movement against Sexual Violence* (Durham, NC: Duke University Press, 2008).

Judith Butler, "Review: "Disorderly Woman," *Transition* 53(1991): 86–95.

Judith Butler, "Excerpt from Gender Trouble," in *Feminist Social Thought: A Reader*, ed. Diana Tietjens Meyers (New York: Routledge, 1997).

Angela Campbell, "The Admissibility of Evidence of Animal Abuse in Criminal Trials for Children and Domestic Abuse," *Boston College Law Review* 43, no. 2, issue 2 (March 2002): 463–486. Available at http://lawdigitalcommons.bc.edu/cgi/viewcontent.cgi?article=2202&context=bclr.

Camille Carey, "Correcting Myopia in Domestic Violence Advocacy: Moving Forward in Lawyering and Law School Clinics," *Columbia Journal of Gender and Law* 21, no. 1 (2011): 220–282. Available at: http://papers.ssrn.com/sol3/papers.cfm?abstract_id=1809979.

CBS News, "Fla. Mom Gets 20 Years For Firing Warning Shots," CBS News website, May 12, 2012, http://www.cbsnews.com/8301-8201_162-57433184/fla-mom-gets-20-years-for-firing-warning-shots/.

Anna Clark, "Domestic Violence, Past and Present," *Journal of Women's History* 23, no. 3 (Fall 2011): 193–202.

Therese A. Clarke, "Why Won't Someone Help Me? The Unspeakable Epidemic of Domestic Violence: An Annotated Bibliography," *Northern Illinois Law Review* 23, Part 3 (Summer 2003): 529–580.

Joan Cocks, *The Oppositional Imagination: Feminism, Critique, and Political Theory* (New York: Routledge, Kegan and Paul, 1989).

Donna Coker, "Shifting Power for Battered Women: Law Material Resources and Poor Women of Color," *University of California Davis Law Review* 33 (2000): 1009–1055. Available at http://papers.ssrn.com/sol3/papers.cfm?abstract_id=2011468.

Emily Collins, "Reminiscences of Emily Collins," in *The Feminist Papers*, ed. Alice S. Rossi (Boston: Northeastern University Press, 1988), 421–426.

Drucilla Cornell, "Sexual Difference, the Feminine, and Equivalency: A Critique of MacKinnon's *Toward a Feminist Theory of the State*," *Yale Law Journal* 100, no. 7 (May 1991): 2247–2275.

Bethany Coston, "Intimate Partner Violence by Angela J. Hattery" (Review), *Gender and Society* 23, no. 4, Heteronormativity and Sexualities (August 2009): 581–583.

Kimberlé Crenshaw, "Beyond Racism and Misogyny: Black Feminism and 2 Live Crew," in *Feminist Social Thought: A Reader*, ed. Diana Tietjens Meyers (New York: Routledge, 1997), 245–263.

Kimberlé Crenshaw, "Mapping the Margins: Intersectionality, Identity, Politics, and Violence against Women of Color," *Stanford Law Review* 43, no. 6 (1991): 1242–1299.

Cynthia R. Daniels, ed., *Feminists Negotiate the State: the Politics of Domestic Violence* (Lanham, MD: University Press of America, 1997).

Walter DeKeseredy, Martin Schwartz, and Joseph Donnermeyer, *Dangerous Exits: Escaping Abusive Relationships in Rural America* (Rutgers University Press, 2009).

Alan Dershowitz, *The Abuse Excuse and Other Cop-Outs, Sob Stories, and Evasions of Responsibility* (Boston: Back Bay Books, 1994).

Lawrence Douglas, "The Force of Words: Fish, Matsuda, MacKinnon, and the Theory of Discursive Violence," *Law and Society Review* 29, no. 1 (1995): 169–190.

Murray Edelman, "The Political Language of the Helping Professions," *Political & Society* 4(1974): 295–310.

Friedrich Engels, excerpt from *The Origin of the Family*, in *Feminist Papers*, ed. Alice S. Rossi (Boston: Northeastern University Press, 1988), 480–495.

Susan Estrich, "Real Rape," in *Feminist Jurisprudence*, ed. Patricia Smith (New York: Oxford University Press, 1993), 158–187.

Patricia Evans, *The Verbally Abusive Relationship*, 2nd ed. (Avon, MA: Adams Media Corporation, 1996).

Frantz Fanon, *The Wretched of the Earth* (New York: Grove Press, 2005).

Richard B. Felson, "Big People Hit Little People: Sex Differences in Physical Power and Interpersonal Violence," *Criminology* (August 1996): 433–452.

Elizabeth Felter, "A History of the State's Response to Domestic Violence," in *Feminists Negotiate the State: the Politics of Domestic Violence* ed. Cynthia R. Daniels (Lanham, MD: University Press of America, 1997), chapter 1.

Michaele Ferguson, "Feminism and Security Rhetoric in the Post–September 11 Bush Administration," in *W Stands For Women: How the George Bush Presidency Shaped a New Politics of Gender*, eds. Michaele L. Ferguson and Lori Jo Marso (Duke University Press, 2007), 191–220.

Michaele Ferguson, "Women Are Not An Interest Group," *Theory & Event* 16, no. 1 (2013), http://muse.jhu.edu/journals/theory_and_event/v016/16.1.ferguson.html.

Kathleen J. Ferraro and Michael P. Johnson, "Research on Domestic Violence in the 1990s: Making Distinctions," *Journal of Marriage and Family* 62, no. 4 (November 2000): 948–963.

Linda Foley, "Teacher Loses Job After Reporting Being a Domestic Violence Victim," examiner.com, June 12, 2013, http://www.examiner.com/article/teacher-loses-job-after-reporting-being-a-domestic-violence-victim.

Michel Foucault, *The Birth of BioPolitics; Lectures at the Collège de France, 1978–1979*, ed. Michel Senellart, trans. Graham Burchell (New York: Picador/Palgrave MacMillan 2004).

Michel Foucault, *Discipline and Punish*, trans. Alan Sheridan (New York: Vintage, 1979).

Michel Foucault *The Foucault Reader*, ed. Paul Rabinow (New York: Pantheon, 1984).

Michel Foucault, *The History of Sexuality, Volume I: An Introduction*, trans. Robert Hurley (New York: Vintage Books, 1980).

Michel Foucault, *Security, Territory, Population: Lectures at the Collège de France 1977–1978*, ed. Michel Senellart et al. (New York: Picador, 2009).

Michel Foucault, *Society Must be Defended: Lectures at the Collège de France 1975–1976*, trans. David Macey (New York: Picador, 2003).

Phyllis B. Frank and Gail K. Golden, "When 50-50 Isn't Fair: The Case against Couple Counseling in Domestic Abuse," Op-Ed in *Social Work* 39, no. 6 (November 1994), 636–637.

Nancy Fraser, "What's Critical about Critical Theory? The Case of Habermas and Gender," *New German Critique* 35, Special Issue on Jürgen Habermas (Spring–Summer, 1985): 97–131.

Nancy Fraser and Linda J. Nicholson, "Social Criticism without Philosophy: An Encounter between Feminism and Postmodernism," in *Feminist Social Thought: A Reader*, ed. Diana Tietjens Meyers (New York: Routledge, 1997), 132–146.

Elizabeth Frazer and Kimberly Hutchings, "On Politics and Violence: Arendt Contra Fanon," *Contemporary Political Theory* 7 (2008): 90–108.

Sigmund Freud, *Civilization and Its Discontents*, ed. and trans. James Strachey, standard edition (New York: Norton, 1961).

Lisa Frydman and Kim Thuy Seelinger, "*Kasinga's* Protection Undermined? Recent Developments in Female Genital Cutting Jurisprudence," *Bender's Immigration Bulletin*, September 1, 2008, 1073–1105, http://cgrs.uchastings.edu/sites/default/files/Kasinga%27s_Protection_Undermined_Frydman_Seelinger_2008.pdf.

Jeanne A. Fugate, "Who's Failing Whom? A Critical Look at Failure-To-Protect Laws," *New York University Law Review* 76 (April 2001): 272–308, http://www.thelizlibrary.org/liz/fugate.pdf.

Chris Fusco and Tony Arnold, "Child-Abuse, Neglect Deaths in Illinois Remain High in DCFS-involved Cases," WBEZ91.5 website (NPR), January 20, 2014, http://www.wbez.org/news/child-abuse-neglect-deaths-illinois-remain-high-dcfs-involved-cases-109545 (accessed April 26, 2014).

William Galston, "Realism in Political Theory," *European Journal of Political Theory* 9, no. 4 (2010): 385–411.

Alison E. Gerenscer, "Family Mediation: Screening for Domestic Abuse," *Florida State University Law Review* 23 (1995), http://www.law.fsu.edu/journals/lawreview/issues/231/gerencse.html (accessed November 20, 2013).

Amy Goodman et al., "A Look inside U.S. Immigration Prisons," *Democracy Now!*, May 4, 2006, http://www.democracynow.org/2006/5/4/a_look_inside_u_s_immigration.

Leigh Goodmark, "Clinical Cognitive Dissonance: the Values and Goals of Domestic Violence Clinics, the Legal System, and the Students Caught in the Middle," *Journal of Law and Policy* 20 (2012): 301–323. Available at http://digitalcommons.law.umaryland.edu/cgi/viewcontent.cgi?article=2463&context=fac_pubs.

Leigh Goodmark, "When Is a Battered Woman Not a Battered Woman? When She Fights Back," *Yale Journal of Law and Feminism* 20 (2008): 75–129. Available at http://digitalcommons.law.umaryland.edu/cgi/viewcontent.cgi?article=2460&context=fac_pubs.

Colette Guillaumin, *Racism, Sexism, Power, and Ideology* (New York: Routledge, 1995).

Akhil Gupta, *Red Tape: Bureaucracy, Structural Violence, and Poverty in India* (Durham, NC: Duke University Press, 2012).

Keith Guzik, "The Forces of Conviction: the Power and Practice of Mandatory Prosecution upon Misdemeanor Domestic Battery Suspects," *Law and Social Inquiry* 32, no. 1 (Winter 2007): 41–74.

Jürgen Habermas, *Theory of Communicative Action* vol. 1, ed. Thomas McCarthy (Boston: Beacon Press, 1985).

Jürgen Habermas, *Theory of Communicative Action* vol. 2, ed. Thomas McCarthy (Boston: Beacon Press, 1985).

Ange-Marie Hancock, "When Multiplication Doesn't Equal Quick Addition: Examining Intersectionality as a Research Paradigm," *Perspectives on Politics* 5, no. 1 (March 2007): 63–79.

Donna Haraway, "A Manifesto for Cyborgs: Science, Technology, and Socialist Feminism in the 1980s," in *Feminist Social Thought: A Reader*, ed. Diana Tietjens Meyers (New York: Routledge, 1997), 501–531.

Mary Hawkesworth, "Combating Violence against Women: A Discussion of Celeste Montoya's *From Global to Grassroots: The European Union, Transnational*

Advocacy, and Combating Violence against Women," *Perspectives on Politics* 12, no. 1 (March 2014): 181–183.

Bonnie Honig, *Democracy and the Foreigner* (Princeton: Princeton University Press, 2001)

Bonnie Honig, untitled book reviews, *Perspectives on Politics* 8, no. 2 (June 2010): 657–660.

bell hooks, "Violence in Intimate Relationship: A Feminist Perspective," *Talking Back: Thinking Feminist, Thinking Black* (Boston: South End Press, 1989), 84–91.

Mala Htun and S. Laurel Weldon, "The Civic Origins of Progressive Policy Change: Combating Violence against Women in Global Perspective, 1975–2005," *American Political Science Review* 106, no. 3 (August 2012): 548–569.

Julietta Hua, "Feminism, Asylum, and the Limits of Law," *Law, Culture, and Humanities* 6, no. 3 (October, 2010): 375–393.

Ashley Huebner and Lisa Koop, "New BIA Decisions Undermine U.S. Obligations to Protect Asylum Seekers," National Immigrant Justice Center (A Heartland Alliance Program), February 18, 2014, https://www.immigrantjustice.org/litigation/blog/new-bia-decisions-undermine-us-obligations-protect-asylum-seekers#.UyWUqs6a-Ck (accessed March 16, 2014).

"Husband Suspected of Mutilating Wife," *New York Times* archive, August 31, 1995, http://www.nytimes.com/1995/08/31/us/husband-suspected-of-mutilating-wife.html.

In the Matter of LR, Department of Homeland Security, "In the Matter of ___," United States Department of Justice Executive Office for Immigration Review, Board of Immigration Appeals, Falls Church, Virginia, April 13, 2009, http://graphics8.nytimes.com/packages/pdf/us/20090716-asylum-brief.pdf.

Radha Iyengar, "Does the Certainty of Arrest Reduce Domestic Violence? Evidence from Mandatory and Recommended Arrest Laws," *Journal of Public Economics* 93(2009): 85–98.

Radha Iyengar, "The Protection Battered Spouses Don't Need," *New York Times*, August 7, 2007, http://www.nytimes.com/2007/08/07/opinion/07iyengar.html?_r=0.

Jennifer Jack, "Note: Child Custody and Domestic Violence Allegations: New York's Approach to Custody Proceedings Involving Intimate Partner Abuse," *Albany Government Law Review* 5 (2012): 885–913. Available at http://www.albanygovernmentlawreview.org/Articles/Vol05_3/5.3.885-Jack.pdf.

Michelle S. Jacobs, "Requiring Battered Women Die: Murder Liability for Mothers under Failure to Protect Statutes," *Journal of Criminal Law and Criminology* 88, no. 2 (1998): 579–660.

Michael P. Johnson, *A Typology of Domestic Violence: Intimate Terrorism, Violent Resistance, and Situational Couple Violence* (Lebanon, NH: Northeastern University Press, 2008).

Jacqueline Jones, *American Work* (New York: Norton, 1998).

Daniel Kanstroom, *Deportation Nation* (Cambridge, MA: Harvard University Press, 2007).

Jackson Katz, *The Macho Paradox: Why Some Men Hurt Women and How All Men Can Help* (Naperville, IL: Sourcebooks, 2006).

Greg Kaufmann, "This Week in Poverty: US Single Mothers—'the Worst Off,'" *The Nation*, December 21, 2012, http://www.thenation.com/blog/171886/week-poverty-us-single-mothers-worst#.

Deborah K. King, "Multiple Jeopardy, Multiple Consciousness: The Context of a Black Feminist Ideology," in *Feminist Social Thought: A Reader*, ed. Diana Tietjens Meyers (New York: Routledge, 1997), 219–242.

Mary P. Koss, "Review: [untitled]," *Signs* 24, no. 2 (Winter 1999): 532–535.

John Randolph LeBlanc, *Edward Said and the Prospects of Peace in Palestine and Israel* (New York: Palgrave MacMillan, 2013).

Kathryn Libal and Serena Parekh, "Reframing Violence against Women as a Human Rights Violation: Evan Stark's *Coercive Control*" *Violence against Women* 15, no. 12 (October 15 2007): 1477–1489.

Dana Liebelson, "Many Women Are Shot by Their Abusers. Kentucky's Response? Arm Them," *Mother Jones*, July 18, 2014, http://www.motherjones.com/politics/2014/07/kentuckys-answer-domestic-violence-offenders-shooting-victims-more-guns.

Christine Littleton, "Reconstructing Sexual Equality," in *Feminist Social Thought: A Reader*, ed. Diana Tietjens Meyers (New York: Routledge, 1997), 715–734.

John Locke, *A Letter Concerning Toleration*, ed. James Tully (Indianapolis and Cambridge, MA: Hackett Publishing, 1983).

John Locke, *Second Treatise of Government*, ed. C. B. Macpherson (Indianapolis and Cambridge, MA: Hackett Publishing, 1980).

Heather Love, "Dwelling in Ambivalence," *The Women's Review of Books* 22, no. 2 (November 2004): 18–19.

Niccolo Machiavelli, *The Prince and The Discourses* (Boston: McGraw-Hill, 1950).

Catharine MacKinnon, "Feminism, Marxism, Method, and the State: An Agenda for Theory," in *Feminist Social Thought: A Reader*, ed. Diana Tietjens Meyers (New York: Routledge, 1997), 64–91.

Catharine MacKinnon, "Symposium on Unfinished Business: Points against Postmodernism," *Chicago-Kent Law Review* 75(2000): 687–695.

Catharine MacKinnon, *Toward a Feminist Theory of the State* (Cambridge, MA: Harvard University Press, 1991).

Karuna Mantena, *Alibis of Empire* (Princeton, NJ: Princeton University Press, 2010).

Karuna Mantena, "Another Realism: The Politics of Gandhian Nonviolence," *American Political Science Review* 106, no. 2 (May 2012): 455–470.

Jessica Marsden, "Domestic Violence Asylum after *Matter of L-R-*" *Yale Law Journal* 123, no. 7 (May 2014), http://www.yalelawjournal.org/article/domestic-violence-asylum-after-matter-of-l-r.

Sara L. McKinnon, "Positioned in/by the State: Incorporation, Exclusion, and Appropriation of Women's Gender-Based Claims," *Quarterly Journal of Speech* 97, no. 2 (2011): 178–200.

John Stuart Mill, *On Liberty*, ed. Elizabeth Rapaport (Indianapolis: Hackett, 1978).

John Stuart Mill, "On the Subjection of Women," in *Feminist Papers: From Adams to de Beauvoir*, ed. Alice S. Rossi (Boston: Northeastern University Press, 1988).

Linda G. Mills, *Violent Partners: A Breakthrough Plan for Ending the Cycle of Abuse* (Basic Books, 2008).

Minnesota Advocates for Human Rights, "Improving Judicial Response to Domestic Violence in the Courtroom," 2003, http://www1.umn.edu/humanrts/svaw/domestic/training/materials/Judicialresponse.PDF (accessed November 20, 2013).

Chantal Mouffe, "Feminism, Citizenship, and Radical Democratic Politics," in *Feminist Social Thought: A Reader*, ed. Diana Tietjens Meyers (New York: Routledge, 1997), 532–544.

Samuel Moyn, *The Last Utopia: Human Rights in History* (Cambridge: Harvard University Press, 2010).

Samuel Moyn, "On the Genealogy of Morals," *The Nation*, March 29, 2007, http://www.thenation.com/article/genealogy-morals.

Suellen Murray and Anastasia Powell, "What's the Problem? Australian Public Policy Constructions of Domestic and Family Violence," *Violence against Women* 15(2009): 532–552.

Karen Musalo, "Brief on Behalf of Rodi Alvarado Peña to the Attorney General of the United States (to: United States Department of Justice Attorney General John Ashcroft)," Hastings College of Law, University of California, 2004, http://cgrs.uchastings.edu/documents/legal/ra_brief_final.pdf.

Karen Musalo, "A Short History of Gender Asylum in the United States: Resistance and Ambivalence May Very Slowly Be Inching Towards Recognition of Women's Claims," *Refugee Survey Quarterly* 29, no. 2 (2010), http://cgrs. uchastings.edu/sites/default/files/short_history_of_gender_asylum_ Musalo_2010_0.pdf.

Laurie Naranch, "Naming and Framing the Issues: Demanding Full Citizenship for Women," in *Feminists Negotiate the State: the Politics of Domestic Violence*, ed. Cynthia R. Daniels (Lanham, MD: University Press of America, 1997), Chapter 2.

National Institute of Justice, "Dual Arrest," http://www.nij.gov/publications/dv-dual-arrest-222679/exhibits/Pages/table1.aspx.

National Organization for Women, "Violence against Women in the United States: Statistics," n.d. http://www.now.org/issues/violence/stats.html (accessed May 20, 2013).

Frances Olson, "The Family and the Market," in *Feminist Jurisprudence*, ed. Patricia Smith (New York: Oxford University Press, 1993), 65–93.

Carole Pateman, *The Disorder of Women* (Palo Alto, CA: Stanford University Press, 1992).

Carole Pateman, *Sexual Contract* (Palo Alto, CA: Stanford University Press, 1988).

Hector Perla and Susan Bibler Coutin, "Legacies and Origins of the 1980s US–Central American Sanctuary Movement," *Refuge* 26, no. 1 (Spring 2009): 7–19.

Alejandro Portes and Rubén Rumbaut, *Immigrant America*, 3rd ed. (Los Angeles: University of California Press, 2006).

Mark Poster, Review: "Domestic Tyranny: The Making of American Social Policy against Family Violence from Colonial Times to the Present" by Elizabeth H. Pleck, *Signs* 14, no. 1 (Autumn 1988): 216–219.

Eyal Press, "Family-Leave Values," *New York Times Magazine*, July 29, 2007, http://www.nytimes.com/2007/07/29/magazine/29discrimination-t.html?ref=magazine&_r=0.

Julia Preston, "New Policy Permits Asylum for Battered Women," *New York Times*, July 15, 2009, http://www.nytimes.com/2009/07/16/us/16asylum.html?ref=domesticviolence&_r=0 (accessed March 10, 2013).

Bethany J. Price and Alan Rosenbaum, "Batterer Intervention Programs: A Report from the Field," *Violence and Victims* 24, no. 6 (2009): 757–770.

Tonya Janiece Redman, "Negotiating Matriarchy: The Discourse of Single Mothers Taking Care of Their Families on Small Incomes," unpublished thesis, University of Texas at Arlington, December, 2007, http://dspace.uta.edu/bitstream/handle/10106/727/umi-uta-1914.pdf?sequence=1.

David S. Riggs, Marie B. Caulfield, and Amy E. Street, "Risk for Domestic Violence: Factors Associated with Perpetration and Victimization," *Journal of Clinical Psychology* 56, no. 10 (2000): 1289–1316.

Katie Roiphe, *The Morning After: Sex, Fear, and Feminism On Campus* (Boston: Little, Brown, 1993).

Jacqueline Rose, "Deadly Embrace" *London Review of Books* 26, no. 21, November 4, 2004, http://www.lrb.co.uk/v26/n21/jacqueline-rose/deadly-embrace.

Andrew I. Schoenholtz, "Refugee Protection in the United States Post–September 11," *Columbia Human Rights Law Review* 36, no. 2 (2005): 323–364.

Philip G. Schrag, Andrew Schoenholtz, Jaya Ramji-Nogales, and James P. Dombach, "Rejecting Refugees: Homeland Security's Administration of the One-Year Bar to Asylum," *William and Mary Law Review* 52, no.3 (2010): 651–804.

Joan W. Scott, "Deconstructing Equality-Versus-Difference: Or, the Uses of Post-structuralist Theory for Feminism," in *Feminist Social Thought*, ed. Diana Tietjens Meyers (New York: Routledge, 1997), 758–770.

Cheryl Seelhoff, "The Motherhood Penalty—On Discrimination against Mothers as Mothers," April 16, 2012, Women's Space website, http://womensspace. wordpress.com/2012/04/16/the-motherhood-penalty-on-discrimination-against-mothers-as-mothers/.

Amartya Sen, "More Than 100 Million Women Are Missing," *New York Review of Books* 37, no. 20, December 20, 1990, http://www.nybooks.com/articles/archives/1990/dec/20/more-than-100-million-women-are-missing/.

Carisa R. Showden, *Choices Women Make: Agency in Domestic Violence, Assisted Reproduction, and Sex Work* (Minneapolis, MN: University of Minnesota Press, 2011).

Anna Marie Smith, *Welfare Reform and Sexual Regulation* (New York: Cambridge University Press, 2007).

Rogers Smith and Peter Schuck, *Citizenship Without Consent: Illegal Aliens in the American Policy* (New Haven, CT: Yale University Press, 1985).

Julia Sommer, "Crime Is Not the Problem, Lethal Violence Is, Say UC Berkeley Researchers," UC Berkeley Public Affairs Website, September 16, 1997, http://www.berkeley.edu/news/media/releases/97legacy/zimring.html (accessed May 20, 2013).

R. Clifton Spargo, *The Ethics of Mourning* (Baltimore: Johns Hopkins University Press, 2004).

Evan Stark, *Coercive Control* (New York: Oxford, 2009).

Evan Stark, "Commentary on Johnson's 'Conflict and Control: Gender Symmetry and Asymmetry in Domestic Violence,'" *Violence against Women* 12 (2006): 1019–1025.

Evan Stark, "Entrapment," *Assemblage* 20 (April 1993): 76–77.

Evan Stark, "Symposium on Reconceptualizing Violence against Women by Intimate Partners: Critical Issues: Re-Presenting Woman Battering: From Battered Woman Syndrome to Coercive Control," *Albany Law Review* 58 (Spring 1995): 973–1026.

Suzanne Steinmetz, "The Battered Husband Syndrome," *Victimology* 2(1978): 499–509.

Loren G. Stewart, "Pointing Towards Clarity or Missing the Point? A Critique of the Proposed 'Social Group' Rule and Its Impact on Gender-Based Political Asylum," *Journal of Law and Social Change* 8 (2005): 37–62, https://www.law.upenn.edu/journals/jlasc/articles/volume8/issue1/Stewart8U.Pa.J.L.&Soc.Change37(2005).pdf.

Jack C. Straton, "The Myth of the 'Battered Husband Syndrome,'" NOMAS (National Organization for Men against Sexism) website, n.d., http://www. nomas.org/node/107 (accessed December 16, 2013).

Tracy A. Thomas and Tracey Boisseau, eds. *Feminist Legal History: Essays on Women and Law* (New York: New York University Press, 2011).

Jacqui True, *The Political Economy of Violence against Women* (New York: Oxford University Press, 2012).

UK (University of Kentucky) Center for Research on Violence against Women, "Top Ten Things Advocates Need to Know," 2010, http://www.uky.edu/CRVAW/files/TopTen/05_Mandatory_Arrest.pdf.

UN Commission on HR, 52nd Session, Item 9 (a) of Provisional Agenda, 1996 *Report of the Special Rapporteur on Violence against Women, Its Causes and Consequences*, Resolution 1995/85, E/CN.4/1996/53 (1996).

US Department of Health and Human Services, Health Resources and Services Administration, "US Teens in Our World" (Rockville, Maryland: U.S. Department of Health and Human Services, 2003), http://www.mchb.hrsa.gov/mchirc/_pubs/us_teens/index.htm (accessed May 20, 2013).

US v Morrison 529 U.S. 598, 120 S. Ct. 1740, 146 L. Ed. 2d 658 (2000), http://www.casebriefs.com/blog/law/constitutional-law/constitutional-law-keyed-to-chemerinsky/the-federal-legislative-power/united-states-v-morrison/ (accessed March 9, 2014).

Monica Varsanyi, "Rescaling the 'Alien,' Rescaling Personhood: Neoliberalism, Immigration and the State," *Annals of the Association of American Geographers* 98, no. 4 (2008): 877–896.

Roberta Villalón, "Passage to Citizenship and the Nuances of Agency: Latina Battered Immigrants," *Women's Studies International Forum* 33 (October 12, 2010): 552–560.

"Violence against Women Act," *New York Times*, March 10, 2013, http://topics.nytimes.com/top/reference/timestopics/subjects/d/domestic_violence/index.html (accessed March 20, 2013).

Kathleen Waits, "The Criminal Justice System's Response to Battering," in *Feminist Jurisprudence*, ed.Patricia Smith (New York: Oxford University Press, 1993), 188–209.

Andrea C. Westlund, "Pre-Modern and Modern Power: Foucault and the Case of Domestic Violence," *Signs* 24, no. 4, Institutions, Regulation and Social Control (Summer 1999): 1045–1066.

Stephen K. White, "Fullness and Death: Depth Experience and Democratic Life," *American Political Science Review* 104, no. 4 (November 2010): 800–816.

Wider Opportunities for Women, "Arrest Policy and Survivors," Justice System Policy Series, October 2012, http://www.wowonline.org/wp-content/uploads/2013/05/Economic-Security-for-Survivors-Arrest-Policy-Policy-Brief-2012.pdf.

Kirk R. Williams, "Arrest and Intimate Partner Violence: Toward a More Complete Application of Deterrence Theory," *Aggression and Violent Behavior* 10(2005): 660–679.

Wendy Williams, "The Equality Crisis: Some Reflections on Culture, Courts, and Feminism," in *Feminist Jurisprudence*, ed. Diana Tietjens Meyers (New York: Routledge, 1997), 695–713.

Sheldon Wolin, "Democracy and the Welfare State: The Political and Theoretical Connections Between Staatsräson and Wohlfahrsstaatsräson," *The Presence*

of the Past: Essays on the State and the Constitution (Baltimore, MD: Johns
    Hopkins Press, 1989).
Sheldon Wolin, *Politics and Vision*, expanded edition (Princeton, NJ: Princeton
    University Press, 2004).
Sheldon Wolin, "What Revolutionary Action Means Today," in *Dimensions of Radical
    Democracy*, ed. Chantal Mouffe (New York and London: Verso, 1992).
Mary Wollstonecraft, "Vindication of the Rights of Women," in *Feminist Papers:
    From Adams to de Beauvoir*, ed. Alice S. Rossi (Boston: Northeastern University
    Press, 1988).
Katie Wright, "5 Things to Know about Single Mothers in Poverty," Center for
    American Progress website, May 11, 2012, http://www.americanprogress.
    org/issues/poverty/news/2012/05/11/11634/5-things-to-know-about-
    single-mothers-in-poverty/.
Iris Marion Young, "Is Male Gender Identity the Cause of Male Domination?" in
    Feminist Social Thought, ed. Diana Tietjens Meyers (New York: Routledge,
    1997), 22–37.
Linda M. G. Zerilli, "Doing Without Knowing: Feminism's Politics of the Ordinary,"
    Political Theory 26, no. 4 (August 1998): 435–458.
Linda M. G. Zerilli, *Feminism and the Abyss of Freedom* (Chicago: University of
    Chicago Press, 2005).
Karen Zivi, "Contesting Motherhood in the Age of AIDS: Maternal Ideology in the
    Debate over Mandatory HIV Testing," *Feminist Studies* 31, no. 2 (Summer
    2005): 347–374.
Karen Zivi, "Who or What Are We? The Identity Crisis in Feminist Politics" *Polity*
    36, no. 2 (January 2004): 323–340.

INDEX

Note: Locators followed by the letter 'n' refer to notes